Basic Statistics

Basic Statistics

An Introduction with R

TENKO RAYKOV
Michigan State University

and

GEORGE A. MARCOULIDES
University of California at Riverside

ROWMAN & LITTLEFIELD PUBLISHERS, INC.
Lanham • Boulder • New York • Toronto • Plymouth, UK

Published by Rowman & Littlefield Publishers, Inc.
A wholly owned subsidiary of The Rowman & Littlefield Publishing Group, Inc.
4501 Forbes Boulevard, Suite 200, Lanham, Maryland 20706
www.rowman.com

10 Thornbury Road, Plymouth PL6 7PP, United Kingdom

British Library Cataloguing in Publication Information Available

Library of Congress Cataloging-in-Publication Data

Raykov, Tenko, author.
  Basic statistics : an introduction with R / Tenko Raykov and George A. Marcoulides.
    p. cm.
  Includes bibliographical references and index.
    ISBN 978-1-4422-1846-8 (cloth : alk. paper)—ISBN 978-1-4422-1847-5 (pbk. : alk. paper)
  1. Mathematical statistics—Data processing. 2. R (Computer program language) I. Marcoulides, George A., author. II. Title.
  QA276.45.R3R39 2012
  519.5—dc23

                                                                    2012020638

Printed in the United States of America

Contents

Preface

About a quarter of a century ago, an influential revolution in the field of statistics began to unfold. A state-of-the-art, highly comprehensive, and freely available software package called R was conceptualized and developed. This software changed the landscape of statistical analysis and computer programming implementations in a number of ways, some perhaps more profoundly than anticipated by its original creators.

Over the past two decades, R has become increasingly popular and is frequently used for a variety of statistical applications. A considerable number of books on using R have also appeared, particularly during the last few years, which clearly document its exceptionally wide utility. Despite this plethora of treatments on how to use R for various analyses and modeling purposes, it appeared to us that a text on basic statistics implementing R would still be desirable to a large portion of undergraduate or graduate students and researchers in the behavioral, biological, educational, medical, management, and social sciences, who have had no or only marginal exposure to statistics, and even that perhaps some years ago.

Our pragmatic goal with this book is to provide a coherent introduction to statistics from the viewpoint of its applications with R, and an introduction to R from the viewpoint of basic statistical applications. This text offers a nontechnical treatment of many statistical concepts and their relationships and uses mathematical formulas mainly in their definitional meaning. The audience for which the book is most suitable consists primarily of undergraduate students, graduate students, and researchers in the behavioral, biological, educational, medical, management, and social science disciplines, who need an introduction to the basic principles of statistics and its applications and wish to accomplish it using the free, comprehensive, and state-of-the-art software R. We aim with this text to offer a first course in statistics and in the use of R for basic statistical analyses.

There are three features that set apart our book from others in this broad field, especially those covering applications of R for statistical analyses. For the purposes of this text, we use R commands with as few subcommands as possible. In our view, students and researchers with limited or no exposure to statistics and applications of R tend to be "turned off" by alternative discussions demonstrating the use of a multitude of possible command and subcommand options, which accomplish what may be seen from their perspective as potentially very specialized analyses and graphical presentations that often go well beyond what may be the initial goals of those users. It is our view that they can pursue quite well on their own the study of such subcommands and options at a later time. We find that once students are introduced to the basic commands accomplishing a particular type of analysis with R, they can much more easily deepen their knowledge of how to use available subcommands for more specialized analyses and graphing activities if needed.

Further, in our opinion many books dealing with applications of R in statistics do not provide sufficient discussions at an introductory level of basic concepts in statistics and their relationships. Instead, those books are predominantly concerned with the use of R to accomplish statistical analyses, including basic analyses. The present book was developed around the premise that a more thorough introduction to basic statistical notions and their interrelationships is first needed before effective applications of statistical analysis software can be discussed. This principle is followed throughout the book.

As a third feature worth mentioning here, we use primarily examples stemming from the educational, behavioral, and social sciences. We aim to demonstrate with them the ease of obtaining highly informative analyses in these disciplines, employing relatively limited input commands submitted to R. We hope that in this way the popularity of this software among students and researchers in these sciences will be enhanced, an audience where in our experience R has not yet received the attention that it deserves.

This book has been substantially influenced by our interactions with a number of colleagues over the past several years. We would like to express our gratitude in particular to S. Dass, A. Galecki, V. Melfi, S. Penev, U. Pötter, and W. Revelle for valuable discussions on statistical and related applications of R. A number of our students provided very useful feedback on the lecture notes we first developed for our courses in basic statistics, from which this book emerged. We are also very grateful to several anonymous referees for their critical comments on an earlier draft of the manuscript, which contributed substantially to its improvement. Thanks are also due to our production editor, who was instrumentally helpful in advanced stages of preparation of the book. Last but not least, we are more than indebted to our families for their continued support in lots of ways. The first author is indebted to Albena and Anna; the second author is indebted to Laura and Katerina.

1

Statistics and Data

1.1. STATISTICS AS A SCIENCE

The past few decades have witnessed a tremendous increase in the amount of data being collected in our modern society. For example, data about individual spending habits and patterns, school and college achievement, aptitude or intelligence are collected frequently by various persons and organizations—e.g., banks, teachers, schools, instructors, colleges, clinicians, administrators. Accompanying this data buildup is also a great deal of interest in analyzing these data to address specific questions of interest using statistics.

Statistics can be defined as a science that helps design empirical studies to collect data, as well as to organize, classify, analyze, and interpret these data, in order to make decisions in situations that are often characterized by uncertainty. This uncertainty generally results from the at times very limited information contained in the data obtained through these empirical studies. Additionally, this information can be potentially highly variable across the examined individuals, cases, subjects, or units of analysis considered. Based upon these features, statistics can be regarded as a scientific discipline used in almost all aspects of modern society to greatly facilitate the process of learning from data.

In this book, we will be mainly interested in the application of basic statistics to a variety of empirical studies in the behavioral, biological, educational, medical, management, and social sciences. One can distinguish thereby between the following four stages of using statistics to conduct research in these sciences (e.g., Ott & Longnecker, 2010):

(i) defining the problem to be studied,
(ii) collecting the data that contains the necessary information about the problem,
(iii) summarizing the data, and
(iv) analyzing and modeling the data, interpreting and communicating results.

Each of these stages is essential for the process of applying statistics to address questions within the above-mentioned sciences. If any of these stages is bypassed or carried out in an inappropriate way, the outcome of the subsequent stage(s) may well be significantly affected if not totally compromised. Additionally, the ultimate results and interpretation of the study in question may be seriously misleading. As it turns out, this four-stage process closely resembles the scientific method that underlies scientific inquiry (e.g., Graziano & Raulin, 2009). The scientific method is essentially a set of principles and procedures used to advance any empirical science. It consists of the following phases:

(a) the formulation of a research goal,
(b) the design of an experiment or an observational study,
(c) the collection of data (observations), and
(d) the analysis and modeling of the data, and testing of research hypotheses.

We note that the phases (a) through (d) listed above closely resemble the statistical application stages (i) through (iv).

As an example, let us consider the following study, which we will return to frequently in this book. In this investigation, our main interest lies with examining the presence of possible gender differences in depression in older adults in the United States. To begin with, the detailed description of the study's goals accomplishes much of the above stage (i) of using statistics in the process of empirical research. We need to note also that since we cannot realistically examine each and every elderly person in the entire country, due to resource- and time-related limitations, we will have to rely on information obtained from just a subset of the population. This is a generally relevant issue that we will often make reference to as we advance through this book. Then in accordance with stage (ii), we collect data by using a well-established instrument (e.g., a scale) for measuring depression on a randomly selected group of say $n = 500$ elderly adults that represents well the population of aged persons in the United States. Section 1.2 of this chapter deals with general issues pertaining to this stage and with the selection of the group to be studied, which is called a *sample*. In stage (iii), we obtain summary indexes signifying for instance average depression score and degree of variability within each of the two genders from the sample studied (as well as conduct further activities, in general, which depend on the specific research questions being asked). Chapter 2 discusses matters pertaining to this stage in a more general context. Finally, in stage (iv), we may examine for instance the gender differences on these summary indexes (and/or possibly carry further activities, again depending on the research questions pursued). In addition, we may draw conclusions about those differences and communicate our results in writing or verbally to an intended audience. Much of the remainder of this book will deal with the various statistical methods that could be appropriately used during this fourth stage.

This depression study example illustrates that when using statistics one is usually interested in *drawing conclusions about large groups of subjects*, typically referred to as populations, while *data are available from only portions of these groups*, referred to as samples. (We will provide further discussion on these two concepts of population and sample in a later section of this chapter.) In this sense, statistics deals with a *major inferential problem*—how to achieve trustworthy conclusions about a given large group (a population), based on limited data obtained from only a subgroup selected from it (a sample), which data in addition is most likely going to be varied. This variability is a particular feature for variables or subject characteristics in studies where statistics is applicable. Specifically, different subjects will usually give rise to (*quite*) *different scores* on considered measures or variables (e.g., depression in the above example). This is essentially what we meant when we stated above that the data will be varied. Hence, given this likely diversity of resulting scores, the task of statistics is to permit one to reach credible conclusions about the large group of subjects (population) that are of actual concern, based on a *multiplicity* of different scores on given variable(s) measured only on a small group of subjects (sample).

The above discussion leads us to the following stricter definition of major relevance to statistics and to the application of statistics in empirical research.

Definition: *Population* is the set of all possible measurements on a given variable of concern that are of interest in a specific research question.

We note that the precise definition of a population in a particular empirical setting may well depend on the research question and/or on the variable or subject characteristics of interest to be studied. In this book, a population will most often consist of scores on particular variable(s) that could be measured on subjects from a potentially very large group of persons, which is of substantive interest. At times, these may be scores for aggregates of subjects, such as schools or classes, hospitals or districts, companies or corporations. When no confusion arises, we will just refer to the large group of subjects themselves as a population, as is usually done in the behavioral and social science literature. (Part of the reason for the possible confusion is that in an empirical study one usually collects data on more than a single variable or subject characteristic. Rather than conceiving of multiple populations of relevance to the same study—one per variable of possible interest—one considers only one population, viz., the collection of all subjects to which inference is to be made.)

A closely related concept that we will also routinely use in this book is that of the part or subset of a population under consideration that is exhaustively studied. This is the notion of a *sample*. We define a sample as a selected (drawn) subset of the population, in which every unit of analysis is examined or measured on the variable(s) of concern to a given empirical investigation. Similarly to a population, a sample may consist of subject aggregates, e.g., schools or classes, hospitals, neighborhoods, companies, cities, nursing homes.

To return for a moment to the aging example given above, we observe that depression is the variable of main concern in it. The scores on this measure of all elderly adults in the United States constitute the population of interest in the posed research question. In addition, the actually studied group of depression scores based on the $n = 500$ persons is the sample drawn from that population. We reiterate that often for convenience the set of all subjects that one wishes to make conclusions about is referred to as population, while the set of subjects drawn from it who actually participate in the study are referred to as sample. Alternatively, depending on the research question one can think of a population as consisting of aggregates of subjects (hospitals, companies, schools, etc.), and a sample as an appropriate subset of such aggregates. Similarly, as we will elaborate on in a later section of the book, most of the time in empirical research one is interested in studying not just one but multiple variables on a given sample of subjects and sometimes examining their interrelationships. To simplify subsequent discussions and terminology, when we make reference to a population in this book we will typically mean a set of subjects (or more specifically subject scores on variables of interest); then samples will be appropriately selected subsets of populations under investigation (or specifically of individual scores). We will return to this issue again in Chapter 2, where we will elaborate on it further.

1.2. COLLECTING DATA

As indicated above, obtaining data in a study represents the second stage in the outlined four-step process of using statistics in empirical research. Data are typically collected in a well-thought-out and planned process, leading to either conducting an experiment or nonexperimental study (also more generally referred to as an observational study), including the development of a survey, a questionnaire, or some other particular measurement device or instrument. This process itself also evolves through the following several steps (e.g., King & Minium, 2003):

(a) specifying the objective of the study, survey, or experiment,
(b) identifying the variable(s) of interest,
(c) choosing an appropriate design (for an experiment, or sample for an observational study), and
(d) obtaining the data.

To illustrate further this process, let us revisit again the earlier depression example in which the objective is the examination of gender differences in depression of older adults (defined as elderly persons aged 65 or older). This observation represents step (a) mentioned above. In step (b), we identify the score on a depression scale (measure) as the variable of interest. We then choose a measuring device or instrument(s), such as the Beck Depression Inventory (Beck et al., 1977), to collect subsequently these scores from the subjects (the units of analysis) in the drawn sample. In step (c), we decide how to select the subjects to be included into the actual study. Let us suppose for now that we were able to obtain a random sample of 250 men and 250 women from the population of elderly in the United States. In step (d), we administer the measure(s) (scale, test, instrument), and then score the results we obtain on it from each person in the sample.

Frequently, step (b) of the discussed process requires a detailed consideration of measures that can be of interest in the context of the study to be conducted. Experts in the substantive (subject-matter) field of application may be asked for their opinion on this issue during this step. Similarly, step (c) may involve time- and effort-consuming activities to come up with samples that are representative of the studied population(s). Due to the complexities involved in this activity, a special branch of statistics referred to as *sampling theory* has actually been developed to meet the demands of obtaining a representative sample (as well as carrying out subsequently appropriate related data analyses). We will touch upon some of these complexities and activities in a later chapter of the book. Finally, in step (d), one needs to ensure that specific and detailed instructions are precisely followed when administering the measure(s) of concern, as well as that their objective and accurate scoring is accomplished at the end of the data collection process. We note that if the study is indeed experimental, then further activities are also involved in steps (b) through (d). Although elaborating on these activities is beyond the scope of this introductory book, they are discussed in greater detail in more specialized experimental design sources and books (e.g., Kirk, 1989).

1.3. WHY STUDY STATISTICS?

There are a number of reasons that the study of statistics is very beneficial to advancing knowledge in the empirical sciences. For one, statistics can be used to summarize and interpret correctly published numerical data (e.g., data from surveys or various other forms of reports). Further, statistics can be used to help develop a critical and informed way of interpreting data and evaluating possible conclusions drawn from examined data sets. For instance, the media continually expose us to large bodies of information through news and advertising agencies. Reports on economic conditions, political issues, surveys about opinions on diverse matters, and many other communications frequently have one feature in common—they all contain certain statistics to support related arguments. Statistics as a science is necessary to help us make sense of this vast amount of data and thereby better understand the world we live in.

Thus, statistics is indispensable in the empirical sciences where data on samples from studied populations are routinely made available. For instance, the application of statistics is essential for answering questions like "Are observed group (treatment, program, intervention) differences in responding to a studied drug 'real' or are they only the result of random variation resulting from the fact that only subjects in a randomly drawn, relatively limited sample from the population under investigation were examined?"

The remainder of this book is concerned with discussing a number of basic statistical methods that can help scientists make progress in their empirical research. In addition to describing some of the technical details that underlie each method, we also will employ for analysis the popular statistical software package R. We will specifically use it in order to carry out data analysis and modeling on illustrative data sets as we proceed through each chapter in the book. This popular software is highly comprehensive, state-of-the-art, and obtainable free of charge. Indeed, the software package R can be located and downloaded via any available search engine by simply using the letter "R" or "R-project" as a keyword (and following the prompts; see also Venables, Smith, & The R Development Core Team, 2012). We believe that the package R is in many ways a software for the next decade and beyond.

2

An Introduction to Descriptive Statistics: Data Description and Graphical Representation

2.1. DESCRIPTIVE STATISTICS

In the previous chapter we defined statistics as a science to help us collect, organize, analyze, and interpret empirical data. We also introduced a four-stage process for applying statistics in empirical research, and we discussed the first two phases of problem definition and data collection. In this chapter, we deal with the third stage of this process, which is concerned with the summarization of data. The summarization of data comprises an important part of statistics that can be further divided into two main branches—descriptive and inferential statistics. This and the next chapter attend to some essential features of descriptive statistics. Later chapters of the book will be concerned with aspects related to inferential statistics.

Descriptive statistics represents a set of methods and activities that permit the description of a given body of data, without making inferences about another set of possible observations (from a larger group, e.g., a population). Descriptive statistics is also used when a whole population of subjects (or aggregates of such) is observed, such as in a population census. For example, if census data are available on income levels of adults living in the United States, we can obtain various descriptors of income, e.g., broken down by gender, race, ethnicity, geographical location, etc. Descriptive statistics enables us to represent potentially vast amounts of data in ways that permit the reader, consumer, or user of the results to obtain relatively quickly an informative summary and even provide a graphical presentation of the data. When an entire population cannot be studied exhaustively, a sample is drawn from it, and descriptive statistics helps summarize and present the sample data collected.

Descriptive statistics includes methods that accomplish (a) various graphical displays providing valuable insights to the scientist or user, and (b) numerical data descriptions via summary indexes that can contain important information about research questions of interest. In this chapter we discuss methods that fall under category (a), and we will be concerned with methods in category (b) in the next chapter. Because graphical displays differ depending on the number of variables involved, we cover first the case of just a single variable. Situations involving several variables will be attended to in later sections of the book. As far as numerical indexes are concerned, we note that we will familiarize ourselves with several of them in Chapter 3, where we will also see in detail how they summarize important features of sets of scores in given samples (or populations).

2.2 GRAPHICAL MEANS OF DATA DESCRIPTION FOR A SINGLE VARIABLE

A *main principle* to follow when graphically presenting collected data from studied samples (populations) is that data should be arranged in any display in such a way that *any single measurement falls within only one possible category*. Thereby, we need in particular to make sure that the boundaries of adjacent categories do not overlap and are not identical in any possibly misleading way. We demonstrate this potential problem on examples used later in this section.

We begin by considering the following example study:

Example 2.1.   Suppose we have obtained data on the number of faculty that are employed in a college of education at a particular state university. Let us also assume that the observations given in Table 2.1 represent the obtained faculty data. As indicated earlier, we need to make sure that each single measurement falls within only one possible category. In other words, we need to ensure either that there are no faculty members with a joint appointment in another department, or that any faculty member with such an appointment is only counted in one of the departments he or she is affiliated with. If we ignore

Table 2.1   Number of faculty from five departments in a College of Education at a state university (Example 2.1).

Department	Number of Faculty
Educational Psychology	12 faculty
Teacher Education	13 faculty
School Psychology	9 faculty
Measurement, Evaluation, and Statistics	4 faculty
Educational Administration	15 faculty

such a situation (joint appointment), then the actual total number of faculty counted will be incorrect.

Since statistics is a science that deals by definition with potentially sizable amounts of data, it is usually easier to achieve the goals of statistics via the use of a statistical package such as R rather than doing things manually. However, in order to be able to use R for conducting descriptive or other statistical types of analyses, it is necessary that we first communicate to R the data set we wish to use. Once this communication has occurred, R will be in a position to analyze the data set on our behalf accordingly. We attend next to these initial issues.

2.2.1. Reading data into R

The process of communicating a given data set to R typically represents the first activity that a researcher becomes involved with in the process of applying descriptive statistics. This process is often simply referred to as the "reading" of the data set into R. This is a routine activity that is in fact the first step of preparing the data in a form amenable to any kind of analysis using statistical software such as R.

In order to read data into R, it is convenient to enter the data set initially into a universal file format, such as a "plain text" or "text only" file, often referred to as an "ASCII file."* This can be achieved if one enters the data into a window opened when starting a standard text editor like Notepad (or WordPad, either of which is available on a Windows-based PC under "Accessories" after clicking the "Start" button on the computer screen, followed by selecting "All Programs"). Once we are in that window, the data must be typed in such a way that *each unit of analysis represents a single row* (department in this example—although in many cases within social and behavioral studies it will be individual subject data that comprise the unit of analysis). Therefore, it will be very beneficial if we ensure that within each row the consecutive scores on the measured (collected or recorded) variables are *separated by at least one blank* space. This format of data entry is often referred to as "free format" and usually is the most convenient format to work with subsequently. It is also typical to give names to each column of the resulting data file, in its top row, which names are those of the variables they represent. This practice is highly recommended in order to keep track of what the considered data set represents.

With this in mind, for our above Example 2.1 we first create an ASCII file

---

* ASCII stands for "American Standard Code for Information Interchange" and is a character-encoding scheme for representing text to computers and digital devices that use text.

that is similar to the one presented in the main body of Table 2.2, using also for simplicity the abbreviation "dept" for "department" (cf. Table 2.1). We note that the first column of Table 2.2 contains the abbreviation of the name of the department (initials), and the second column is the number of faculty in each department. We also notice that the first row of this file contains the names of the two variables—'department' and 'faculty'. We save this data file using an easy-to-remember file name, such as CH2_EX21.dat.

Now in order to read this small data set into R, we need to use a particular command. Before we give it, however, we note that for ease of presentation we adopt the convention of using the Courier font to represent both the command submitted to the R software and the output sections produced by the statistical analysis of the program itself. This same convention for commands and output will be followed throughout the book. We also begin the representation of each used command with the conventional R prompt, which is the sign ">" (we emphasize that when one is actually using a computer to type a command, there is no need to precede any R command with the prompt, as it is generated automatically). With this in mind, the command to read the data from Example 2.1 into R (as provided in Table 2.2) is 'read.table', which we use here as follows:

```
> d = read.table("C://data/CH2_EX21.dat", header = T)
```

We note that one needs to provide with this command the path leading to the specific subdirectory where the ASCII/plain text file resides on the computer used, placed in inverted commas. (In this case, the file is located in the computer subdirectory "data" in drive C; see the Note at the end of this chapter.) The subcommand 'header = T' instructs R to read the first line not as numbers but as variable names (i.e., as "character strings"—sequences of characters or letters; see Note to this chapter).

When the R command 'read.table' is executed by the software, it creates an *object* with the name 'd'. The object named 'd' represents the data that have

Table 2.2   Contents of data file for number of faculty per department (Example 2.1).

dept	faculty
ep	12
te	13
sp	9
ms	4
ea	15

been read in by the program. We observe at this point that R is a case-sensitive software package, and we note in passing a simple rule to keep in mind: in a sense everything in R is an object. (For example, an output from an R command is also an object.) To be in a position to analyze data on any of the variables in the data set under consideration, we need next to make it accessible to R. This is accomplished with the command 'attach' as is illustrated in the command line below (for the data set CH2_EX21.dat that was made available in the created object 'd'):

```
> attach(d)
```

For the remainder of the book, whenever an example is considered for analysis, we will assume that the data from the study under consideration have already been read into R and made accessible to R in the aforementioned specific way.

2.2.2. Graphical representation of data

There are numerous ways available within R to represent graphically data on a variable of interest. There are also a multitude of sources available that provide detailed descriptions of each of the different graphical ways. It is beyond the scope of this chapter and book to discuss all of them. In this chapter we only present detailed descriptions of a few important graphical ways for two main types of variables—qualitative and quantitative. Qualitative variables, also frequently referred to as categorical variables, have "scores" (or values that they take) that differ from one another in kind rather than in quantity. That is, the data values on a qualitative variable are in fact just classifications or categories, which is the reason that data stemming from such variables are at times referred to as categorical data. The categories of a qualitative variable are also often referred to as levels (or even labels) of the variable. Example 2.1 illustrates such a variable—the variable 'department' is a qualitative (categorical) variable.

In contrast to qualitative variables, a quantitative variable has scores (or values) that differ from one another in quantity. That is, their scores—the actual data—are "legitimate" numbers, i.e., as close as possible to real numbers in meaning. For example, the following mathematics test–taking anxiety (MTA) study illustrates the inclusion of such a quantitative variable, the anxiety score.

Example 2.2 (**MTA study**): A mathematics test–taking anxiety study was carried out with $n = 36$ elementary school students, using an established measuring instrument referred to as the MTA scale. The resulting data are provided in Table 2.3 and saved under the name CH2_EX22.dat. In Table 2.3, 'id' denotes a

Table 2.3   Data from *n* = 36 students in a study of mathematics test–taking anxiety (the first row represents the names of the two variables involved: id = person identifier, y = anxiety score).

id	y
1	15
2	17
3	19
4	21
5	23
6	32
7	18
8	19
9	22
10	23
11	25
12	21
13	22
14	25
15	25
16	24
17	23
18	27
19	19
20	17
21	21
22	29
23	27
24	31
25	19
26	19
27	23
28	25
29	25
30	27
31	29
32	29
33	21
34	24
35	23
36	28

subject identifier, and 'y' the score for each student obtained using the mathematics test–taking anxiety measuring instrument (i.e., the student MTA score). For ease of presentation, we adopt here the convention that when representing subject data in this book, we will typically use the first column as the person (case) identifier.

Next we use the two previously discussed examples (see Tables 2.2 and 2.3) to pictorially represent the data on both the qualitative and quantitative variables involved. This is done in order to obtain a first idea of the relationships between the values (scores or categories) that the subjects (the units of analysis) take on them. Two very popular yet distinct methods for graphically representing data on studied variables are discussed next. First, some methods that can be used to graphically represent qualitative variables are presented. These are followed by an illustration of methods for graphically representing quantitative variables.

2.2.2.1. Pie charts and barplots

For a given qualitative variable of interest, the *pie chart* and *bar chart* (sometimes also referred to as *barplot* or bar graph) are two common methods that can be used to graphically represent the frequencies of its obtained values in a particular data set. The charts display graphically (correspondingly either in terms of pie slices or bars) the observed frequencies. Specifically, the size of the pie or the height of the bar represents the frequency of the pertinent data value. Usually, the pies are presented in relative frequency—in other words, their sizes can be interpreted as percentages. The heights of the bars often represent "raw" frequencies but have the same shape when considered for relative frequencies. The relative frequencies are defined as the ratios of observed or raw frequencies to the total number of units of analysis (i.e., usually subjects in this text) in the group studied.

To illustrate this discussion, suppose we wish to obtain the pie chart for the 'faculty' variable in Example 2.1 (see data in Table 2.2). A pie chart graphically represents the data in the form of slices of a circle, which are typically filled in with different colors, and their sizes reflect the relative frequencies with which the variable in question takes its values. To obtain a pie chart graph, we use the R command 'pie' that we state at the R prompt. We use thereby as an "argument"—i.e., an entity we place within parentheses following the actual command—the name of the variable that needs to be graphed, which is here the variable 'faculty':

```
> pie(faculty)
```

This command yields the pie chart displayed in Figure 2.1—this pie chart is shown by R in a separate graphics device window opened by the software after one completes the command (i.e., after one submits the command to R).

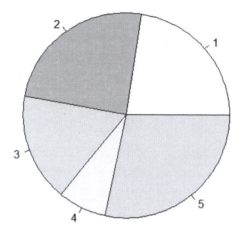

FIGURE 2.1.

Pie chart of the number of faculty per department.

While Figure 2.1 readily presents a rough idea about the relations between the number of faculty members in each department, the labeling of the displayed slices is not immediately informative. In particular, the specific numbers attached to the slices here by R are simply those of the consecutive rows of Table 2.1. Such a graphical display does not provide a clear enough picture of the data and would require one to refer back to the raw data in order to interpret the relative sizes of the slices presented. To deal with this limitation of the displayed figure, it would be best to add the names of the departments (in the abbreviation notation used in Table 2.2). This is possible in R by using the subcommand 'labels', and we attach a title to the figure using the subcommand 'main', leading to the following extended command:

```
> pie(faculty, labels = dept, main = "Piechart of Faculty by Department")
```

As can be seen from this command line, we set the subcommand 'labels' equal to the name of the variable containing those of the departments, and set the subcommand 'main' equal to the title we want to use, which we place in quotation marks. To simplify matters throughout the remainder of the book, we will always make a reference to any R commands and subcommands within the main body of the text by using quotation marks. Using the above pie-chart command produces the output displayed in Figure 2.2.

The pie chart as a graphical device is very useful when one is interested in displaying qualitative data in the form of slices in a circle. Another very popular alternative and equivalent data presentation method is the so-called bar chart (barplot). In its simplest form, in a barplot the levels of a variable under consideration are presented successively (following the order from top to bot-

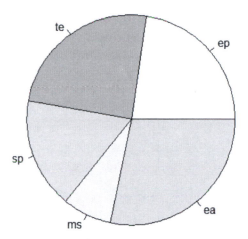

FIGURE 2.2.
Pie chart of faculty by department, using slice labeling and figure title.

tom in the data file), and the frequencies (relative frequencies) with which the variable takes its values are represented by the height of bars—vertical rectangles positioned above these levels. For our currently considered example, we can obtain the barplot of the 'faculty' variable in R with the command 'barplot' as follows:

```
> barplot(faculty)
```

This command yields the graph displayed in Figure 2.3. Along its horizontal axis, the departments are represented from left to right as they follow from top to bottom in the original data file. Above them are the bars, whose heights reflect the number of faculty members per department.

While we can easily obtain from Figure 2.3 an idea about the relations between the number of faculty across each department—which numbers are represented along the vertical axis—it is unclear from the figure alone which department is associated with which of the bars. To assign the names of the departments to the horizontal axis, we use the subcommand 'names.arg', and as above use the subcommand 'main' to attach a title to the figure. The resulting, somewhat extended command we need for these aims, is now as follows:

```
> barplot(faculty, names.arg = dept, main = "Relative Frequency of
Faculty by Department")
```

This extended command furnishes the bar chart displayed in Figure 2.4.

This bar chart is now far more informative than the one displayed earlier

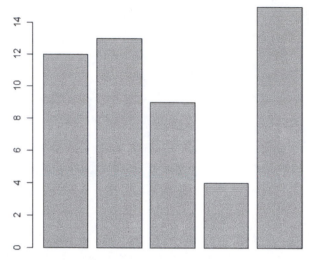

FIGURE 2.3.
Barplot of faculty by department.

in Figure 2.3, and in addition may be seen as more informative than the pie chart presented in Figure 2.2. The reason is in particular the fact that by referring to the vertical axis one can see the values that the 'faculty' variable takes across departments. These are the above-mentioned raw frequencies that equal the number of faculty per department. If we wish to obtain a bar chart

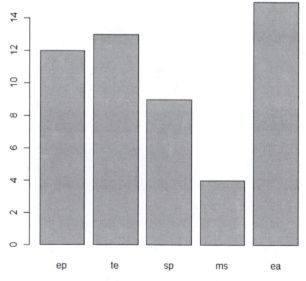

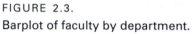

FIGURE 2.4.
Barplot of faculty by department.

not of the raw frequencies as in Figure 2.4, but of the relative frequencies, we can divide the raw frequencies by the total number of cases in the data set—here the total number of faculty at the college in question. In general, as mentioned before, the relative frequency for a given variable category ('department' in this example) is defined as the ratio of observed frequency, denoted for clarity as f, to the total number of cases studied—denoted n—which is the sample size in a study under consideration:

(2.1) $$r = f / n ,$$

where r is used to denote relative frequency. That is, to obtain the relative frequency of faculty per department in our example, for each department we need to divide their number by the total sample size. In most studies one would know the sample size already at the beginning of the analysis, but at times it may be necessary to obtain it alternatively (e.g., by having the R software do it for us). We can simply obtain sample size by summing the values of the variable 'faculty' across all departments, which is accomplished with the R command 'sum':

```
> sum(faculty)
```

This command yields the following result for our example:

```
[1] 53
```

In this output, the first number presented in brackets, [1], indicates that immediately following is the first element of the output produced by R. Since in this case all we need from R is a single number (i.e., the studied group size, or sample size), it is presented right after the symbol "[1]." Thus, 53 is the total number of faculty in the college under consideration. We will often encounter this simple pattern of output presentation in the remainder of the book.

Once we know the group size, we can request from R the barplot of relative frequencies per department using the above command 'barplot', where we now divide the variable in question by this size. We achieve this by using the division sign '/' as follows:

```
> barplot(faculty/53, names.arg = dept, main = "Barplot of Faculty by
Department")
```

We stress that the first argument in this command (the first entry in its parentheses, from left to right) is formally the ratio of the variable in question to studied group size (sample size). The last presented, extended 'barplot' command produces the relative frequencies bar chart displayed in Figure 2.5. From this barplot, it can now be readily observed that the largest percentage of faculty are employed in the Educational Administration Department, about a quarter of all faculty are in the Teacher Education Department, less than 10% are in the Measurement, Evaluation, and Statistics Department, and about 17% of all faculty are employed in the School Psychology Department.

2.2.2.2. Graphical representation of quantitative variables

The above section dealing with the pie charts and barplots demonstrated how one can graphically represent a variable that is qualitative. Specifically, we considered some ways to present the frequencies with which the variable 'department' takes its values (categories) or levels—as measured by the number of faculty affiliated with each department. That is, the variable 'department' had the values (levels) 'ep', 'te', 'sp', 'ms', and 'ea'—for the names of departments—which we might as well consider simply labels for the departments. The frequencies associated with these labels were formally presented in the variable named 'faculty'. (We note that we could just as well have also called the 'faculty' variable 'frequency', which it actually is with regard to the levels of the 'department' variable). Since the levels (categories) of the variable 'department'—being the different departments in the college in question—differ from one another only in kind rather than in quantity, 'department' is considered a qualitative variable. For such qualitative variables, the pie chart and barplot are very useful and informative methods to graphically represent

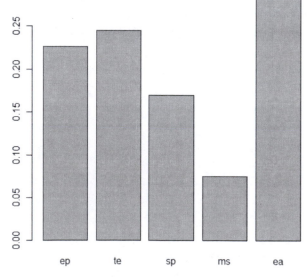

FIGURE 2.5.
Relative frequencies bar chart for faculty by department.

the frequencies or relative frequencies with which these variables take their values or levels.

Although qualitative variables are often encountered in empirical research, data arising from quantitative variables are just as common (or at least from variables that could be treated as quantitative). As mentioned earlier, the values of a quantitative variable differ from one another in quantity rather than in quality as is the case for a qualitative variable. For quantitative variables, it is equally necessary to have methods that can be used to graphically represent their values in a way that provides an informative summary of them.

A very popular method that can be used to graphically represent data from a quantitative variable is the so-called histogram. A *histogram* is basically a series of vertical rectangles that represent the frequency with which scores fall in the interval that is at the bottom of that rectangle. Fortunately, these intervals, including their length and position, are automatically chosen for us by the R software through some built-in, reasonable, and widely applicable defaults. In fact, with R the intervals are defined by default as including the number positioned at their right end, but not at their left end. With this feature, the histogram gives an impression of what the *distribution* of a variable under study actually looks like. We mention in passing that the distribution is the way in which scores on the variable relate to one another, and we will have more to say about this concept in a later section of the book.

To illustrate the construction of a histogram, let us return to Example 2.2 where we were interested in the mathematics test–taking anxiety (MTA) variable in a study with a sample of $n = 36$ students. Suppose we wish to construct the histogram of the variable 'anxiety score' (i.e., the MTA score obtained with an established measuring instrument used in that study); we recall that this variable was denoted as 'y' in Table 2.3. Now using this data file, R can readily produce a histogram for the variable with the command 'hist':

```
> hist(y, main = "Histogram of anxiety scores")
```

We note that in this command the name of the variable for which a histogram is to be obtained is given first (which here is denoted as 'y'). In addition, the subcommand 'main' is used to attach a title to the top of the generated histogram. Figure 2.6 provides the histogram for the MTA scores generated using this command statement.

As can be readily seen from this histogram, there are for example in total seven scores that are either 23 or 24, since the bar corresponding to the interval (22, 24] has a height of seven units—i.e., the frequency of scores in this interval is seven. (We note that the symbol "(.,.]" is used to denote an interval including the number at its right end but not the number at its left end.) Similarly, there are three scores in the interval (16, 18], as can also be verified by inspecting the data in Table 2.3. (Below we also illustrate an alternative

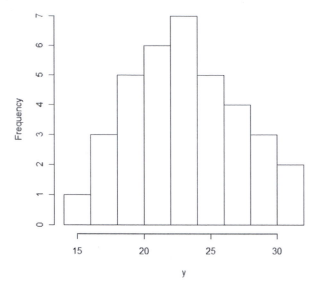

FIGURE 2.6.

Histogram of mathematics test–taking anxiety scores (Example 2.2).

way of achieving the same graphical representation aim using the so-called stem-and-leaf plot.)

When informally presenting a histogram, often one may wish to connect the middle points of the top sides of these rectangles. If one uses thereby corresponding segments of straight lines, the resulting curve is commonly referred to as a frequency polygon. If one connects these middle points by a smooth curve rather than segments, the resulting curve is informally also referred to as variable "distribution" curve (or just distribution). We will discuss this alternative notion for graphical presentation of data in more detail in a later section of the book.

Histograms are very useful devices to present data, but depending on how their class intervals are built, they can sometimes conceal some important information (e.g., Verzani, 2005). For example, such a situation may arise when grouping together fairly different scores (as may happen with variables that have wide ranges of scores). For this reason, it can be particularly informative to examine the actual frequency with which a particular score appears in a data set. This is readily accomplished with the *stem-and-leaf plot*. In it, the *stem* is composed of all numbers apart from their last digit, and the *leaves* are their last digits.

Using the same anxiety score data for Example 2.2 considered above, we can obtain their stem-and-leaf plot (graph) with R using the command 'stem'. Thereby, the subcommand 'scale' used requests that the last digit of the scores be presented as leaves, and all the preceding digits as stem:

```
> stem(y, scale = .5)
```

```
1 | 577899999
2 | 1111223333344
2 | 555557778999
3 | 12
```

FIGURE 2.7.
Stem-and-leaf plot of the anxiety scores (Example 2.2).

The generated stem-and-leaf plot is presented in Figure 2.7.

This plot reveals some additional detail about the considered data set. For example, looking at the first row of the plot, it can be readily determined that there is only one score of 15 in the data set under consideration, two 17's, one 18, and five scores of 19. Similarly, looking at the second row it can be determined that there are four 21's, two 22's, five 23's, and two 24's. Similar details can be revealed by examining the remaining aspects of the stem-and-leaf plot. Such details are readily seen by connecting each stem with each of the leaves on the right from the vertical bar within each row of the plot.

While graphical approaches can at times be excellent visual aids, they can also present data in ways that allow different and possibly even contradictory subjective interpretations. As a consequence, it is recommended that conclusions about populations of interest based only on sample data graphs not be hastily drawn. As it turns out, there are more advanced methods that should be used in order to reach such conclusions in an objective manner. A more detailed discussion concerning these fundamental approaches will be provided in a later section of the book. To begin this discussion, we consider in the next chapter some simple numerical indexes that can be initially used to objectively summarize data.

NOTE

In the remainder of the book, when explicitly including R commands for reading data, we will indicate the corresponding paths where the data sets employed reside on the computer used by the authors. (For most examples, these data sets reside in their subdirectory "C://data.") These paths obviously need to be modified correspondingly when the data sets are utilized by readers.

3

Data Description: Measures of Central Tendency and Variability

The previous chapter highlighted the subjective limitation of interpreting graphical presentations of data in general. In addition to this limitation, another important shortcoming stems from the fact that graphs are difficult to use for inferential purposes. In other words, they are not very helpful when one is interested in drawing conclusions about large sets of observations (populations) using data obtained from samples. Unlike these graphs, numerical descriptors in terms of indexes are very useful summaries of data. We primarily employ them with quantitative variables. Two commonly used types of measures in descriptive statistics are the so-called measures of central tendency or location and measures of variability or dispersion, which we discuss in turn throughout this chapter.

3.1. MEASURES OF CENTRAL TENDENCY

3.1.1. The mode

For any qualitative or quantitative variable, the *mode* is the score that occurs the most often in a given data set. We define the *mode* as the score(s) in a given data set (variable) that occurs with the highest frequency. For example, let us consider the following twelve intelligence (IQ) test scores:

$$95, 97, 100, 101, 103, 101, 102, 105, 101, 95, 97, 101.$$

The mode of this data set is 101—as can be easily ascertained—since it occurs four times in this set of scores. In this simple example, there is only one mode, but in general their number can be larger, as seen in the next examples.

The mode can be readily obtained with R by examining via the stem-and-leaf plot the frequencies with which scores in a given sample or group are taken (see Chapter 2 as to how to obtain the steam-and-leaf plot). The score(s) with the highest frequency(-ies) is then the mode of the examined variable in the studied group. To illustrate, let us take a look at the stem-and-leaf plot (Figure 2.7) of the mathematics test–taking anxiety (MTA) scores in Example 2.2 considered in the last chapter. For ease of presentation we repeat the stem-and-leaf plot below as Figure 3.1. As can be readily seen from the graph in Figure 3.1, there are three modes in the MTA example data set. These are the scores 19, 23, and 25. The reason is that each of them occurs five times among the 36 anxiety scores, and all remaining scores occur less frequently.

We note in passing that in a multiple-variable data set, each variable has its own mode that need not be the score of the same person across the variables, nor for that matter the same score(s). For example, suppose that in a study of mathematics ability three tests are administered to high school seniors: (i) an algebra test, (ii) a geometry test, and (iii) a trigonometry test. Then the mode on the algebra test could be 25, the mode on the geometry test 27, and the mode on the trigonometry test 22. The modes can also be scores obtained by different subjects across these three tests.

We emphasize that the mode need not be uniquely defined. This is because there may be more than just a single number that occurs with the highest observed frequency. In fact, it all depends on the data of the variable under consideration, and some data sets may have more than one mode. A way in which this can happen is when we consider several groups of subjects but disregard group membership (i.e., consider them as a single data set), e.g., males and females on a variable of interest. Data sets (variables) with two modes are often referred to as *bi-modal*, and similarly defined in terms of the number of modes are *tri-modal* or *multi-modal* data sets or variables in general. For instance, the MTA data set presented in Figure 3.1 (Example 2.2 from Chapter 2) is tri-modal as we saw above. Also, in a data set where each separate score appears the same number of times, either score can be viewed as a mode.

An especially useful feature of the mode is that it is in general not affected by extreme observations (e.g., even in the problematic cases when these are the results of entry errors). This feature is often referred to as "resistance" or "robustness" of the mode to extreme values. To illustrate, consider the following example. Suppose that when recording or entering the data in the first

```
1 | 577899999
2 | 1111223333344
2 | 555557778999
3 | 12
```

FIGURE 3.1.
Stem-and-leaf plot of the anxiety scores (Example 2.2).

considered example in this chapter with the IQ test scores, a researcher mistakenly entered 995 rather than 95. That is, in his/her version of the above data set, the following were the actually entered (recorded) scores

995, 97, 100, 101, 103, 101, 102, 105, 101, 95, 97, 101.

However, despite this flagrant error, the mode is still 101 as it occurs the most frequently. That is, in this case the mode is unaffected by the data entry/ data recording mistake.

At the same time, it is worthwhile noting that it is also possible that an entry or recording error might be made when entering the score that most frequently occurs in the data set, in which case the mode may well be affected. For example, when the second most frequent score appears only one less times than the actual mode in the original data set, then due to such a recording error both these scores may appear equally often. In such a case, two modes will be proclaimed for a data set that actually has only a single mode. Obviously a variety of other examples of similar errors can be easily constructed as well, where the actual mode of a data set is misrepresented due to a data entry or recording error.

A useful feature of the mode is that while it is easily defined for quantitative variables, it is the only measure of "central tendency" that is meaningful for a qualitative variable. (The concept of "central tendency" is not well defined for such variables, and we use it here in a loose sense, viz., in the sense of most "fashionable'" category—i.e., one with the highest observed frequency.) Finally, we note that the mode has the unique feature of being a score that is actually contained in the data set under consideration. That is, the mode is in fact a score taken by/measured on a studied subject (unit of analysis). This need not be the case with the two other measures of central tendency that we turn to next.

3.1.2. The median

The above-mentioned resistance or robustness feature of the mode is also shared by another measure of central tendency, called the median. The *median* can be defined as the middle value of a set of scores under consideration. When the data set has an uneven number of scores, it is the middle value when they are arranged from lowest to highest. In contrast, when the data set contains an even number of scores, then it is the average of the middle two values. We note in passing that this arrangement from lowest to highest is frequently referred to as "rank ordering" of the observed data. (We usually imply an increasing, or ascending, rank ordering when using this term in the remainder of the book, although a reverse ordering can also be meaningful in some cases.)

From the above-provided definition a simple, "manual" procedure to obtain the median—especially with small data sets—would consist of using the R command 'sort' to rank order a given set of scores, and then work out the median by counting from left or right half as many scores as there are in the data set (or averaging the middle two scores if there is an even number of scores in the data set). For instance, for the earlier mathematics test–taking anxiety example (Chapter 2; see Table 2.3), we can "manually" obtain the median of the MTA score—denoted 'y' there—as follows. First we sort the data:

```
> sort(y)
```

This command produces the following output, whereby the prefixes [1] and [23] signal that the first and 23rd consecutive MTA scores follow immediately after them (which prefixes we just ignore most of the time):

```
 [1] 15 17 17 18 19 19 19 19 19 21 21 21 21 22 22 23 23 23 23 23 24 24
[23] 25 25 25 25 25 27 27 27 28 29 29 29 31 32
```

To find the median of this variable, we need to take the middle score, if sample size is an uneven number, or the average of the middle two scores, if sample size is even. In this particular example, we happen to know that the sample size is 36, but at times the sample size may not be known beforehand. In such cases, in order to work out the sample size for a given study or variable, we can use the command 'length'. This command determines the length of the array (row, set) of scores that comprise the available observations on a variable in question. For our MTA example, the command produces the following result (given immediately beneath the command):

```
> length(y)
[1] 36
```

That is, the sample size is 36 here—something we knew beforehand for this MTA example but may not know in another data set of interest.

Since the number of scores on the variable 'y' of interest in this data set is even, in order to work out its median we take the average of the 18th and 19th scores from left (or from right) in their above-sorted sequence. As it happens, both these middle scores are 23, and thus they are each equal to their average, which is declared to be the median value of the MTA variable, viz., 23.

We would like to note here that all of these same computational activities can be accomplished alternatively in an automated fashion with the specific R command 'median':

```
> median(y)
```

This command yields for the mathematics test–taking anxiety (MTA) example the median value of

```
[1] 23
```

which as expected, is identical to the answer we manually obtained above.

Like the mode, the median is "resistant" or "robust" with regard to (a relatively limited number of) extreme values, such as abnormal values on a given variable. For example, if we have entered the value 117 in lieu of the second number 17 in the MTA data set, the median would still be 23. (As an aside, this can be readily checked out, by first manipulating the data in this way, saving it under a new name, reading it into R as usual, and then evaluating the median on the "new" variable 'y'.)

3.1.3. The mean

A measure of central tendency that is very popular, but does not share the above resistance or robustness property with regard to extreme values, is the mean. The mean is defined for a quantitative variable only, as the arithmetic average of the scores under consideration (see further below for a more formal definition). To obtain the mean with R, we use the command 'mean'. To illustrate with the data from the earlier MTA example, the command

```
> mean(y)
```

yields

```
[1] 23.25
```

Since the mean is so widely used, we will spend next some time on its more formal discussion (e.g., Raykov & Marcoulides, 2011, ch. 2). Let us first denote a given variable of interest by the letter y—a notation that will be used quite often in the rest of this book. The mean of y in a population of N subjects—N being typically large and finite, as is usually the case in current behavioral and social research and assumed throughout the rest of this book—is defined as:

$$(3.1) \qquad \mu_y = \frac{1}{N}(y_1 + y_2 + \ldots + y_N) = \frac{1}{N}\sum_{i=1}^{N} y_i,$$

where y_1 through y_N denote the values of the variable y for the members of the population, beginning with the first and up to the Nth member, and μ_y designates the mean of y in the population of interest. (We may eventually dispense with using the sub-index $(_y)$ attached to the symbol μ for population mean values in later discussions, when no confusion may arise.) We note also the presence of the summation symbol, Σ, in Equation (3.1). This symbol is utilized to denote the process of adding together all y scores with sub-indexes ranging from $i = 1$ to $i = N$, i.e., the sum $y_1 + y_2 + \ldots + y_N$. We will also frequently use this short summation index, Σ (with appropriate ranges of associated sub-indexes), in the rest of the book.

We rarely have access, however, to an entire population of interest. Rather, we typically only have available a sample from the population of interest. How can we then use this sample to extract information about the population mean, i.e., obtain a good "guess" of the population mean? To this end, we wish to combine in an appropriate way the studied variable values obtained from the sample, so as to render such a good "guess" of the population mean. This process of combining appropriately the sample values to furnish information about an unknown quantity, like the mean, is called in statistical terminology *estimation*. Unknown population quantities, like the mean (or median), which characterize a population distribution on a variable of interest, are called *parameters*. We wish to estimate these parameters using data obtained from the sample.

For any given parameter, we accomplish this estimation process utilizing an appropriate combination, or function, of the sample values or scores on the studied variable. This function is typically referred to as *statistic*. That is, we estimate unknown parameters using statistics. A major property of "good" statistics is that they appropriately combine sample values (observations) in order to extract as much as possible information about the values of unknown parameters in a population(s) under investigation. When using statistics to estimate parameters, the statistics are often referred to as *estimators* of these parameters. That is, in a sense an estimator is a statistic, or a formula, that is generally applicable for the purpose of estimating a given parameter. In a given sample, the value that the statistic takes represents the *estimate* of this specific parameter.

Returning to the mean considered earlier in this section, as we indicated before it is estimated by the arithmetic average of the scores on y obtained in the studied sample, i.e., by

$$(3.2) \qquad \hat{\mu}_y = \bar{y} = \frac{1}{n}(y_1 + y_2 + \ldots + y_n) = \frac{1}{n}\sum_{i=1}^{n} y_i,$$

where a caret ($\wedge$) symbolizes estimator of the parameter underneath—a practice that is also followed throughout the rest of this book. In Equation (3.2), y_1 through y_n now symbolize the scores in the available sample, and n denotes as usual its size (i.e., the number of subjects (units of analysis) in the sample). We stress that Equation (3.2) represents the mean estimator, often denoted $\bar{y}$. The value obtained when the sample scores on the variable y are entered into the right-hand of this equation, is the mean estimate for that sample, $\bar{y}$. That is, the value obtained in $\bar{y}$ is an estimate furnished using a statistic (estimator) to estimate an unknown population parameter in a given sample, the mean. It is these estimates of parameters that are of key interest and are usually reported in most empirical research.

An important limitation of the mean as indicated above is the fact that it is sensitive (i.e., not resistant or not robust) to abnormal values, such as excessively high or low values on a studied variable. In particular, even a single data entry error can change substantially the mean. For example, if we incorrectly entered the value 117 instead of the accurate value of 17 in the MTA data set in Table 2.2, the resulting mean of 25.85 would be quite different from the mean of the original data/variable that was found above to be 23.25.

For this reason, a variant of the mean has also been developed, the so-called trimmed mean. One may be interested in the 5%-trimmed mean, which is the mean of the "middle" 90% of the scores in a given data set. To obtain this trimmed mean, after rank ordering the scores, the top and bottom 5% of the scores are first deleted. The average of the remaining scores in the now reduced data set is then the so-called 5%-trimmed mean. (We note that a higher percentage could also be dropped from either end if needed, e.g. 10%, if there are reasons to consider it; this would lead to the so-called 10%-trimmed mean.) The 5%-trimmed mean is readily obtained with R using the subcommand 'trim' of the command 'mean' as follows (assuming the variable denoted 'y' is of interest):

```
> mean(y, trim=5)
```

Specifically for the data set in Example 2.2 (see the MTA example in Chapter 2), the 5%-trimmed mean is obtained with this R command as

```
[1] 23
```

which is quite similar to the untrimmed mean of 23.25 we found earlier in this subsection. This similarity would actually be expected, given that none of the 36 scores on MTA in this example appears "abnormal" (i.e., "sticks out" from the rest in terms of its magnitude—see, e.g., Raykov & Marcoulides, 2008, ch. 3, for a more detailed and nontechnical discussion of the concept of an "outlier," often used synonymously to represent an unusual, aberrant, abnormal, or extreme value, score, or observation that could be the result of either gross data entry errors or perhaps originating from a person or unit that is not a member of the population of interest).

While the measures of central tendency discussed in this section are very useful for providing summary information pertaining to the central location of a variable under study (e.g., the MTA score in the considered example), none of them contains information about any potential individual differences that might be present within the data. We address this issue next.

3.2. MEASURES OF VARIABILITY

Individual differences on studied variables are frequently of special interest in empirical research. In fact, in many areas scientists are particularly interested in explaining individual differences on certain variables—usually referred to as dependent variables, response variables, or outcome variables—in terms of differences on other variables, typically called independent variables, "predictors," explanatory variables, or covariates. For instance, do individual differences in parental motivational practices or upbringing style account for possible observed differences in mathematics achievement in elementary and secondary school? Similarly, do urban/suburban differences account for disparities in mathematics achievement? Or perhaps it is gender, SES, or school sector differences that can explain potential achievement differences?

In order to evaluate individual differences, however, some new measures called *measures of variability or dispersion* are needed. These are necessitated by the observation mentioned above that the measures of central tendency do not address the stated concerns. Rather, the needed new measures of variability should respond to the following main question: "To what extent is the mean on a variable informative, in the sense of being 'representative' of the scores that this variable takes in a group of studied individuals (or units of analysis)?" For distributions with a wide spread around the mean, the latter is obviously far less informative than in distributions for which the majority of scores are tightly clustered around the mean. We stress that none of the central tendency measures contain information that bears upon the answer to this question about individual differences, since all these measures are primarily concerned with the location of the scores rather than with their differences.

As it turns out, the last question is commonly answered using the important concepts of variance or standard deviation of a given variable. These two measures, like the mean, are typically defined for quantitative variables. To introduce them, we look first at individual scores and how close they are to the mean. Specifically, the degree to which the mean is representative of most scores in a population on a variable under consideration (i.e., the extent to which the values on this variable are dispersed around its mean there) is captured at the individual level by the *deviation scores*. For a given population of size N, let us denote the scores on the studied variable y as $y_1, y_2,..., y_N$. Then the deviation scores are defined as follows:

(3.3) $$u_i = y_i - \mu_y \ (i = 1, 2, \ldots, N).$$

In a given sample, these individual deviations are obtained by subtracting the average of the scores in the sample from each score (since the average is the estimate of the mean in the available sample). Denoting the n sample values as $y_1, y_2,... y_n$, the deviation scores in the sample are $u_i = y_i - \bar{y} \ (i = 1,... ,n)$; as mentioned before, usually n is much smaller than N). Hence, to furnish the individual deviation scores with R, after rendering the mean estimate we simply subtract it from each observed score. For our earlier utilized MTA example (Example 2.2 in Chapter 2), we obtain them as follows:

```
> u = y - mean(y)
```

To see the result of this action, we ask R to print to the screen the elements of the newly obtained vector u, by simply stating its symbol at the R prompt:

```
> u
```

This prints to the computer screen the individual deviation scores as follows (the prefixes "[13]" and "[25]" signal that the 13th and 25th individual deviation score follows immediately after them, in this listing, and are ignored as usual):

```
 [1] -8.25 -6.25 -4.25 -2.25 -0.25  8.75 -5.25 -4.25 -1.25 -0.25  1.75  -2.25
[13] -1.25  1.75  1.75  0.75 -0.25  3.75 -4.25 -6.25 -2.25  5.75  3.75   7.75
[25] -4.25 -4.25 -0.25  1.75  1.75  3.75  5.75  5.75 -2.25  0.75 -0.25   4.75
```

While the individual deviation scores represent the degree to which individuals (individual units of analysis) deviate from the mean, they have the property that they always sum up to zero, no matter how large any one of them is. In other words, the sum of the deviations of individual scores around the mean will always be equal to zero. Indeed, if we sum them up using R (for which we can use the command 'sum' as indicated in the preceding chapter), we readily observe that the result is zero:

```
> sum(u)
```

which returns as expected

```
[1] 0
```

Thus, any data set—no matter how many scores it consists of or how different the individual scores are from their mean—has the same overall sum of the individual deviation scores, viz., zero. Hence, it would seem that this information does not appear to help much in differentiating between different sets of scores. In addition, the individual mean deviations are scores that are characteristic for each person studied. Therefore, when one simply examines these deviations, no data reduction (summarization) is actually being achieved. Yet this type of reduction or summarization is what is frequently sought when using statistics in most empirical research.

For these reasons, we need a summary measure of individual differences, which measure does not share the limitations just mentioned. At the population level, such a measure is the *variance* of the studied variable, which is defined as follows (later in the book, for ease of presentation we may dispense with the subindex 'y' to σ^2, when no confusion may arise):

$$(3.4) \qquad \sigma_y^2 = \frac{1}{N} \sum_{i=1}^{N} u_i^2 = \frac{1}{N} \sum_{i=1}^{N} (y_i - \bar{y})^2.$$

Based on this equation, it should be evident that the variance is the average squared mean deviation. (We assume throughout the rest of the book that the variance, as well as the mean, of any variable considered is finite, which is a fairly mild if at all restrictive assumption in empirical research.) We also observe from this definition in Equation (3.4) that the variance has as units of measurement the *squared* units underlying the individual scores (measurements). Because of these squared units, the variance is somewhat difficult to directly interpret in an empirical setting. To avoid this problem of interpreting squared units, the standard deviation is also considered, which is defined as the square root of the variance:

$$(3.5) \qquad \sigma_y = \sqrt{\frac{1}{N} \sum_{i=1}^{N} u_i^2} = \sqrt{\frac{1}{N} \sum_{i=1}^{N} (y_i - \bar{y})^2},$$

where a positive square root is taken.

Equations (3.4) and (3.5) allow us to determine the variance and standard deviation of a studied random variable y, if an entire (finite) population of concern were available. As already mentioned, this will rarely be the case in empirical social and behavioral research that typically works, due to a number of reasons, with samples from populations of interest. As a consequence, the variance and standard deviation for a variable of concern are estimated in an available sample correspondingly by using the following equations:

$$(3.6) \qquad \hat{\sigma}_y^2 = s_y^2 = \frac{1}{n-1} \sum_{i=1}^{n} (y_i - \bar{y})^2$$

and

$$(3.7) \qquad \hat{\sigma}_y = s_y = \sqrt{\frac{1}{n-1} \sum_{i=1}^{n} (y_i - \bar{y})^2},$$

with a positive square root taken in the last equation. We emphasize that we divide in Equation (3.6) the sum of squared mean deviations by $(n - 1)$ rather than by n. We do this in order to obtain an "unbiased" estimate/ estimator of variance. This means that the resulting estimate on average equals the population variance, across possible samples taken from the population (all of them being with the same size, n). This unbiasedness feature is a desirable property for any estimator of any parameter. Alternatively, if we divide just by n in Equation (3.6), then on average—that is, across repeated sampling from the same population—the variance estimate will underestimate the true variance (i.e., will be associated with a negative bias).

The variance and standard deviation sample estimates are also readily obtained with R using the commands

```
> var(y)
```

and

```
> sd(y)
```

respectively. We note in passing that the variance and standard deviation of the original data in y are the same as those of the individual deviation scores u. (While this is a generally valid result (e.g., Agresti & Finlay, 2009), one can readily see it on the above example data using R, by applying instead the last two 'var' and 'sd' commands on the set of scores u representing these individual deviations.)

Although the variance and standard deviation of a given variable are quite useful indexes, as we will see later in this book, they have the limitation that they are not immediately interpretable in a substantive domain in terms of individual variation. For instance, what does it actually mean to say that an IQ score measured on second graders has a variance of nine or a standard deviation of three? We will see below that under some additional assumptions these numbers do actually attain important meaning. However, if the assumptions are not correct, these numbers tell us little about the degree to which individual scores are indeed scattered around the mean on a studied variable.

A measure of variability that can be immediately interpreted is the *range*. It is defined as the difference between the largest and smallest scores in a given data set (on a studied variable). Denoting by y this variable, the range r is defined as

(3.8) $r = \max(y) - \min(y),$

where max(.) and min(.) are the largest and smallest score on y, respectively.

With R, we obtain the range by simply using its definitional equation:

```
> r = max(y) - min(y)
```

The result of this activity is that the range of the variable y is stored or created as the object r. As before, in order to see its contents—e.g., to see what the range of the MTA score is—we need to state next the symbol of the range at the R prompt:

```
> r
```

which yields

```
[1] 17
```

That is, the distance between the highest and lowest mathematics test–taking anxiety score in the example studied sample of 36 students is equal to 17. Alternatively, we can also use the command 'range', to obtain the smallest and largest number in the data set:

```
> range(y)
```

In the above MTA example (Example 2.2 in Chapter 2), this command returns

```
[1] 15 32
```

From this result, the range is obviously determined to be $r = 32 - 15 = 17$, although we would need to manually obtain it in this case.

An interesting relation holds between the standard deviation s_y and the range on a given variable (y) (e.g., Ott & Longnecker, 2010). Accordingly, its range is generally expected to be about four times larger than its standard deviation:

(3.9) $r \approx 4s_y.$

We stress, however, that this is only an approximate relationship, and it is presented here merely to provide a rough connection between the two indexes involved.

An important limitation of the range is the fact that it is obviously affected by "outliers," i.e., unusually large/small observations—e.g., data entry errors (e.g., Raykov & Marcoulides, 2008, ch. 3). As such, the range may give misleading indications of what may be a very large dispersion of scores around their mean, which is however spurious due to the presence of extreme scores in a given data set.

A measure of variability that does not suffer from this drawback (at least not to the same degree in general) is the *inter-quartile range* (IQR). The IQR is defined as the interval that contains the middle 50% of the scores on a given variable. That is, the IQR represents the distance between the median of all scores that are positioned below the median of the variable being studied, on the one hand, and the median of all scores positioned above the median on that variable. With R, we obtain the IQR using the same-named command, 'IQR' (note the capitals). For our earlier MTA example, we thus obtain (with the result again given beneath the R command used):

```
> IQR(y)
[1] 5
```

That is, the middle half (in the rank ordering of) the scores of the $n = 36$ students examined in this anxiety study differ from each other by up to five points.

Unfortunately, any of the summary indexes discussed in this section has the limitation that sets of scores with very different mean values could still have the same variability measures. In order to relate variability to the position of the actual range within which scores vary from one another, the *coefficient of variation* (CV) can be used. The CV index provides by definition the variability per unit mean and is determined as

$$(3.10) \qquad\qquad c_y = \sigma_y / \mu_y$$

for a given variable y in a population of interest. In an available considered sample, the CV can obviously be estimated as

$$(3.11) \qquad\qquad \hat{c}_y = \hat{\sigma}_y / \hat{\mu}_y = s_y / \bar{y} \ .$$

For our earlier MTA example, this coefficient is obtained with R as follows:

```
> c = sd(y)/mean(y)
```

which yields

```
[1] 1.789
```

The CV becomes quite relevant when one considers different populations that may have similar variability but different mean values. Under such circumstances, their CV indexes will also differ, as a reflection of the population differences.

3.3. THE BOXPLOT

We have discussed so far in this chapter a number of measures for determining both central tendency and variability in studied data sets. With this multitude of indexes, a natural question that arises is whether there may be a way of integrating them into a single "picture" of data under consideration. As it turns out, this goal is readily accomplished with the so-called boxplot.

The *boxplot* is a very popular graphical device in applications of descriptive statistics, which integrates a number of measures of central tendency and variability. Indeed, with just a single glance at a boxplot, one can obtain a fairly large amount of information about the set of scores considered. To define the boxplot, we need first to attend to the concept of quartile.

3.3.1. Quartiles

The term *quartile* is commonly used to describe the division of observations into defined intervals based on the values of the data. (We note in passing that a quartile can also be thought of as a particular quantile; see below.) There are two main quartiles for a given variable, a lower and an upper quartile. The *lower quartile* cuts out at the left (i.e., the lowest) 25% of the scores on the distribution, i.e., the lowest quarter of the distribution. Conversely, the *upper quartile* cuts out at the right (i.e., the highest) 25% of the scores, i.e., the upper quarter of the distribution. That is, the upper quartile can be thought of as being the median of all scores that are positioned above the median of the original data set; similarly, the lower quartile would be the median of the scores below the median of the original data. In other words, the earlier discussed inter-quartile range (IQR) is just the difference between these two quartiles, which thus enclose the middle 50% of the scores on a given variable.

The lower and upper quartiles are readily obtained with R using the command 'quantile'. To obtain the lower quartile, we use

```
> quantile(y, 1/4)
```

while we can determine the upper quartile with

```
> quantile(y, 3/4).
```

We stress the use of the numbers 1/4 and 3/4 at the end of these commands (and after a comma separating them from the name of the variable in question), since $1/4$ and $3/4$ of all scores correspond to the left of the lower and to the left of the upper quartile, respectively.

To illustrate, for our earlier MTA example (Example 2.2 of Chapter 2), we obtain the following values of these quartiles (with the results again given beneath the command used):

```
> quantile(y, 1/4)
 25%
20.5
```

```
> quantile(y, 3/4)
 75%
25.5
```

That is, the smallest 25% of the anxiety scores in this example are no higher than 20 (since they are all whole numbers, as seen from Table 2.2 in Chapter 2), while the highest 25% of the anxiety scores are at least 26.

These two quartiles can be readily obtained for a quantitative variable in a given data set, along with its mean, median, maximal, and minimal value, using alternatively the command 'summary'. This R command produces the *six-point summary of the variable.* For instance, considering again the MTA example, we obtain the following results (given beneath the used R command):

```
> summary(y)
  Min. 1st Qu.  Median    Mean 3rd Qu.    Max.
15.00   20.50   23.00   23.25   25.50   32.00
```

As before, we observe from this output the minimum and maximum values being 15 and 32 respectively (see earlier discussion of the 'range' command in this chapter). We also notice the values of the mean and median being correspondingly 23.25 and 23, and finally the lower and upper quartiles as 20.5 and 25.5, respectively. With these features, the command 'summary' provides a quick and convenient summarization of the data on a quantitative variable.

3.3.2. Definition of the boxplot and its empirical construction

Returning to our discussion of the graphical device of a boxplot for a studied variable, the IQR is represented by a "box" in it. The two horizontal ends (lower and upper) of this box, also called *hinges*, represent the lower and upper quartiles. To these hinges, two *whiskers* are attached. The whiskers extend from the lower and upper hinges to the most extreme observation that is still within $1.5 \times$ IQR units away from the nearest hinge ('$\times$' denoting multiplication). The observations further away from the median are presented by separate points and can be viewed informally as extreme scores (possible outliers; cf. Raykov & Marcoulides, 2008, ch. 3).

We obtain the boxplot with R using the command 'boxplot':

```
> boxplot(y, main = "Boxplot of Anxiety Scores", ylab = "Anxiety  Score")
```

where we now add in the subcommand 'ylab' a title for the vertical axis—the one of anxiety scores. This command yields Figure 3.2 for the earlier MTA example.

In this displayed boxplot, the thick horizontal line in its middle represents the median of the anxiety scores of interest, which is equal to 23. As mentioned before, the two thinner lines (hinges) enclose the box at the upper and lower quartiles of 20.5 and 25.5, respectively. That is, the distance of the latter two statistics is the IQR, viz., 5 in this example. In other words, this box encloses the "middle" half of the scores, as one moves along the vertical axis

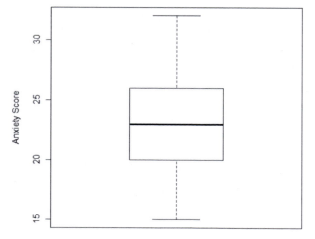

FIGURE 3.2.
Boxplot of anxiety scores.

representing the range of the MTA scores under consideration. In the boxplot, the whiskers are the dashed lines that stretch away from the hinges and until the smallest and largest value (15 and 32, respectively) in the sample, which fall within 1.5 IQR units from the closest box end. As mentioned before, when a data set contains possible "outliers" (i.e., extremely small or large values), they are visually located outside of the whiskers. We do not have such "outliers" in the present data set, since none of its scores extends further than 1.5 × IQR = 7.5 points from the lower and upper quartiles (20.5 and 25.5, respectively).

There are a number of important pieces of information that can be extracted by examining a boxplot for a variable under consideration. First, the median can be easily located by examining where the thick horizontal line is located within the box—the height of this line is the median. (See the vertical axis in Figure 3.2 and the score on it pertaining to the line; that score is the median, 23, in the presently considered example.) Second, the length of the box (i.e., the IQR) is a measure of variability, as discussed earlier in this chapter. This measure is visually represented by the distance between the lower and upper hinges of the box. In case the median is positioned in the center of the box and the two whiskers are of the same length, with no points further away from the lower and upper ends of the whiskers, the distribution of the variable is fairly symmetric. If the median is not positioned in the center of the box, however, there is evidence of some asymmetry in this distribution. In that case, the longer tail of the distribution is to be found in the direction of the longer whisker (and further extreme observations if any). This asymmetry usually is opposite to the direction in which one finds the hinge that is closer to the median. Points outside of the ends of the whiskers are also indicative of possible outliers as mentioned before.

When a distribution is not symmetric, it is called *skewed*. In a skewed distribution, the scores above (below) the median are spread more and further away from it, than the scores below (above) the median. More specifically, there are two types of skewed distributions—positively and negatively skewed distributions. A positively skewed distribution has the median usually positioned lower than the center of the box and closer to the lower whisker. In such a distribution, the scores above the median are spread more and further away from it, than the scores below the median. That is, the right tail of the distribution is longer. Conversely, a negatively skewed distribution has the median usually positioned closer to the upper hinge, and the lower whisker being longer than the upper whisker. In such a distribution, the scores below the median are spread more and further away from it, than the scores above the median; that is, the left tail of the distribution is longer. We will discuss further the notion of asymmetry and quantify it in a later chapter of the book.

3.3.3. Boxplots and comparison of groups of scores

Boxplots are also very useful when comparing informally several groups of scores. For instance, an educational researcher may be interested in comparing college aspiration scores for male and female applicants. We illustrate the details in the following example.

Example 3.1 (college aspiration in high school students): Let us consider a study in which 40 high school sophomores (boys and girls) were administered a scale evaluating their levels of college aspiration. Using a boxplot graphical device, we are interested in comparing the two sets of obtained scores for boys and for girls. The data set CH3_EX31.dat contains their data (whereby the following designations are used in the file: id = identifier, y = college aspiration score, g = gender—0 for boys, 1 for girls) and is presented in Table 3.1.

To examine simultaneously the boxplots of both genders, after reading in the entire data set (see Chapter 2), we use with R the following command:

```
> boxplot(y~g, main = "Boxplot of College Aspiration Scores by  Gender",
ylab = "College Aspiration Score", xlab = "Gender: Boys = 0, Girls  = 1")
```

We note the use of the symbol '~', which effectively requests comparison of the variable 'y' within the values of the variable 'g', i.e., for each of the genders here. Furthermore, we have also added the 'xlab' subcommand to provide a title for the horizontal axis. The last stated R command yields the graphical representation provided in Figure 3.3.

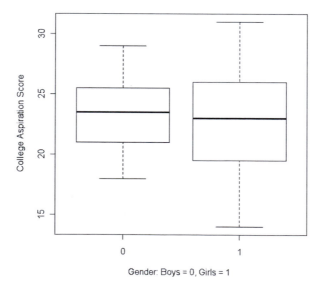

FIGURE 3.3.

Simultaneous boxplots for boys and girls on a college aspiration measure.

Table 3.1   Data from a college aspiration study
(*n* = 40).

id	y	g
1	14	1
2	18	1
3	17	1
4	22	0
5	23	1
6	31	1
7	18	0
8	19	0
9	22	1
10	23	1
11	25	0
12	21	0
13	22	0
14	25	0
15	25	0
16	24	0
17	23	1
18	26	0
19	19	1
20	17	1
21	21	1
22	29	0
23	27	0
24	31	1
25	20	1
26	19	0
27	23	0
28	25	1
29	25	0
30	27	1
31	28	0
32	29	1
33	21	0
34	24	1
35	23	1
36	28	0
37	21	0
38	24	1
39	23	0
40	28	1

As can be seen by examining Figure 3.3, boys have a slightly higher median than girls on the college aspiration scale; they also have less pronounced inter-individual differences. Additional group comparisons can also be readily made using this data set. For example, in this group comparison context, a question of actual interest could be whether these observed group differences are "real," i.e., if they exist also in the two examined populations (of boys and of girls) from which these two samples came. After all, the research question was concerned with population differences to begin with—whether such existed—rather than with differences in randomly drawn samples from them. Answering this important question will be the concern of later chapters of the book. Before we turn our attention to them, however, we need to discuss in the next chapter a concept of fundamental relevance for statistics and its applications, that of probability and its related notions.

4

Probability

4.1. THE IMPORTANCE OF PROBABILITY

As we indicated earlier in the book, most questions of interest in the behavioral and social sciences involve *populations* of subjects (or aggregates of subjects, such as schools, wards, hospitals, facilities, firms, cities). These populations are, however, very difficult to study in their entirety. For these reasons scientists generally resort to taking *samples* from the populations of concern, which they can study exhaustively. The samples are supposed to be representative of the populations. Yet no matter how much care is taken when drawing (selecting) such subsets from a population, a sample is never going to be identical to the studied population. We thus need to assess the extent to which certain quantities, or estimates, that we obtain from the samples (such as mean, variance, standard deviation, etc.) represent their counterparts or parameters in the population. This is of particular relevance when decisions must be made based only on the observation of samples, as is often done in social and behavioral research. In such cases, these decisions are made under conditions of *uncertainty*, i.e., when lacking complete knowledge about the populations or variables involved. As it turns out, these decisions can be substantially helped by appropriate uses of the concept of probability and its related notions. Thus, the concept of probability is of fundamental relevance for statistics and its applications. In fact, no mastery of statistics is really possible without a good understanding of the notion of probability. For this reason, the present chapter deals with the concept of probability and a number of closely related notions.

4.2. DEFINITION OF PROBABILITY

The concept of probability has been the subject of intense study for more than 400 years, dating back to some of the early writings by the mathematicians Pierre de Fermat and Blaise Pascal. This process has led to a variety of different probability definitions. We will mention here three such definitions.

4.2.1. Classical definition

In the context of the *classical definition* of probability, each possible *outcome* of an observation (e.g., an experiment) is called an outcome, and an *event* is a set of outcomes. Let us denote the number of all possible outcomes with the symbol N. (We note that this symbol N is not to be confused with population size; we will not discuss any populations in the rest of this chapter.) For example, when rolling a single dice, there are six possible outcomes of which of course only one occurs—these are the numbers one through six. That is, here $N = 6$. Let us consider as an example the event E: "The dice yields an odd number." Obviously, this event consists of three possible outcomes—the dice rolled up a one, three, or five. Hence, there are $N_E = 3$ favorable outcomes for the event E, and the remaining three are not favorable for it. To give the classical definition of probability, we assume that all outcomes are equally likely to occur (as in this example). Then this definition of probability, denoted Pr, is as follows:

$$(4.1) \qquad \Pr(E) = \Pr(\text{event } E) = \frac{N_E}{N} = \frac{\#\ favorable\ events}{\#\ outcomes},$$

for an event E under consideration.

This definition of probability can be used whenever a study (e.g., an experiment) is carried out in such a way that the number of favorable outcomes for an event(s) of interest out of the set of all possible outcomes can be worked out. We also note that if the assumption of all outcomes being equally likely to occur is not true, then the classical definition will yield incorrect and potentially misleading results. A definition that does not depend on this assumption is provided next.

4.2.2. Relative frequency definition

A definition of probability is also possible based on the relative frequency of occurrence of a particular event in a long series of independent repetitions of observations (experiments). This is also commonly called the *empirical approach* to defining probability. Accordingly, if the experiment (observation) is repeated n times, with n being large, and an event E of interest is observed thereby n_E times, then its probability is defined as

$$(4.2) \qquad \Pr(E) \approx \frac{n_E}{n}.$$

This is an "approximate" definition, as is seen from the use of the approximate equality sign '$\approx$' in Equation (4.2). The reason is that in order to exactly define probability we have to carry out an infinitely long series of observations, which we do not really do in an empirical setting.

As an example, suppose we are given a coin (with two sides, heads and tails), for which we do not know whether it is fair or not. The probability of getting a tail then would be approximated, in a long series of independent tosses of the coin, by the ratio of the number of tails occurring to the total number of tosses—according to Equation (4.2). Thereby, the larger the number of trials (assumed as mentioned above to be independent of one another), the better the resulting estimate of probability.

When the outcomes of an observation (experiment) are equally likely, the relative frequency definition of probability may be viewed informally as an empirical implementation of the classical interpretation (definition) of probability. This can be seen by considering the set of all conducted trial results as that of all possible outcomes, while those when the event in question has occurred are viewed as favorable for it.

4.2.3. Subjective definition

In many situations of theoretical and empirical relevance in the behavioral and social sciences, even a single repetition of an observation/experiment (let alone many repetitions) cannot be imagined as meaningful or possible. Nevertheless, repetitions are essential for the relative frequency definition of probability. Under such circumstances, one could use instead the *subjective definition of probability*. This definition relates probability to the subjective "belief" of likelihood for the occurrence of an event in a single observation, i.e., in a situation of a single consideration of an event, as opposed to that with a long series of trials.

While the subjective definition can be useful in such situations, a major problem with it is that it does not define probability in a unique or objective way. As a result, different persons can potentially come up with different probabilities. In addition, there is no way in which the so-defined probability can be objectively checked (unlike the relative frequency definition that can in principle be checked).

It is important to note that in this book we rely heavily on the relative frequency definition of probability, within the context of the classical interpretation of probability. This definition seems to provide a reasonable practical interpretation of the probability of many events currently of interest in behavioral and social research and applications.

4.3. EVALUATION OF EVENT PROBABILITY

In this section, as in the rest of the chapter, we will use the relative frequency definition of probability to illustrate the evaluation or estimation of the probability of an outcome or event. To demonstrate the concepts involved, we use a simple simulation experiment that can be repeated by anyone, requiring only access to R or any other statistical package capable of the following relatively simple computational activities. However, we stress that the use of any such package is not essential for understanding the topics considered in the rest of this chapter.

We begin by considering perhaps the simplest illustrative experiment involving the tossing of a fair coin. Let us denote by 0 the outcome "heads" and by 1 the outcome "tails." Thus, any time we conduct this random experiment, we obtain an outcome that is either a 0 or 1. Thereby, no other outcome is possible, and exactly one of these two outcomes is presumed to occur at any single time or observation. We assume that any repetition of this experiment is unrelated to any other repetition of it. Hence, if we conduct it n times (n being an integer number), then we would have sampled n times one element from the "population" consisting of the two numbers 0 and 1, denoted for ease of presentation as $\{0, 1\}$. Thereby, we note that after each repetition of this experiment, both 0 and 1 are available as possible outcomes for the next experiment. For this reason, sampling in this way is called *sampling with replacement.*

Once this experiment is carried out n times, with n being a large number, we can evaluate—i.e., estimate—the probability of "tails" using the relative frequency definition of probability provided in Section 4.2. Accordingly, the probability of "tails" is the ratio of the number of experiment repetitions with tails occurring, to the overall number of trials, say n. In this manner, we would use the relative frequency definition of probability in order to estimate the probability of a particular event—obtaining "tails" when tossing the coin in question.

Such an experiment can be readily simulated using R (although as mentioned earlier, this is not essential, as long as one treats the outcomes of the following conducted simulation as given). All we need to do, then, is sample n times with replacement an element from the population $\{0,1\}$, and then divide by n the number of times 1 has appeared as an outcome in this series of trials. This is achieved using the following steps. First, we sample with replacement $n = 100$ times from the population $\{0, 1\}$, using the command 'sample', and create the object 's' that contains the results:

```
> s = sample(0:1, 100, replace = T)
```

In this command, we present the population $\{0, 1\}$ as '0:1', followed by the number of samples taken, 100, whereby we request sampling with replacement by using the subcommand 'replace = T'. In this way, we sample with replacement 100 times from $\{0, 1\}$ and collect all 100 outcomes obtained thereby into the resulting set 's'. This set 's' consists of the numbers 0 and 1, i.e., is a series of 0's and 1's, in the order they occurred during the entire study, and is also called *array*. We emphasize that we sample with replacement, since we wish to make sure that the two possible outcomes—0 and 1—are "available" for each experiment repetition. (The default arrangement in the program R for the 'sample' command is sampling without replacement, which the presently used subcommand 'replace = T' overrides.)

In order to obtain now an estimate of the probability of a "tail," we first obtain the number of 1's sampled. This number is actually the sum of all elements in the array 's' defined above. According to the relative frequency definition of probability, the probability of "tails" is then furnished by dividing the number of 1's by the total number of experiments carried out, i.e., by $n = 100$:

```
> sum (s) / 100
```

which returns

```
[1] 0.47
```

Hence, our estimate of the probability for "tails" with the coin used, based on the sample of 100 observations we utilized, is .47. (Note the use of the command 'sum' to add together all elements of the array *s* of numbers.) We observe that the obtained estimate of .47 is fairly close to the well-known probability of .5 for getting a "tail"—a probability value that would have to be valid based on the assumption that the coin is fair.

We reiterate that this estimate of the probability in question is obtained using the relative frequency definition of probability. As indicated earlier, with the relative frequency definition of probability an assumption was made that the experiment was repeated a large number of times. One can perhaps argue that 100 is hardly a large number, so let us repeat this experiment now with $n = 1,000$, i.e., "run" our experiment 1,000 times. We achieve this in R as follows:

```
> sample (0:1, 1000, replace = T)
```

This leads—in the same way as explained above—to the estimate .496 of the probability of a "tails" outcome. As can be seen this value is now much closer to the probability of .5. If we were to conduct 10,000 repetitions of the same experiment, the estimate would be even closer to .5 (in this case the obtained value would be .503). Indeed, one could potentially continue increasing the number of repetitions of the same experiment, whereupon the estimate would tend to get closer and closer to .5.

This simple simulation of an experiment, carried out with R, demonstrates the relative frequency definition of probability and its utility in practical settings. Of course, if no statistical software were to be available, one could potentially conceive of tossing the coin $n = 100$ times, then $n = 1,000$ times, and finally $n = 10,000$ times, and proceeding as above—dividing the number of times "tails" has occurred by the total number n of tosses.

Having defined probability and illustrated it empirically, we are now ready for a discussion of basic event and probability relationships.

4.4. BASIC RELATIONS BETWEEN EVENTS AND THEIR PROBABILITIES

Based on the probability concept defined in Equation (4.1) or (4.2) as the ratio of two nonnegative numbers, it follows that probability can never be negative. Similarly, since we divided in those definitions a number (numerator) by another (denominator) that is never smaller than the former, probability also cannot ever be larger than 1. That is, by definition the following double inequality always holds:

(4.3) $$0 \leq \Pr(E) \leq 1,$$

for any event E. Thereby, the impossible event—at times also called the "empty event" and denoted as Ø—is associated with a probability of 0, and the certain event is associated with a probability of 1. (As we will find out later in the book, these are however not the only events with a probability of 0 and 1, respectively.)

Let us consider now two events, denoted by A and B. For instance, when rolling a dice, let A be the event that "The number one turns up" and B the event that "An even number turns up." Obviously, A and B cannot occur simultaneously, since when rolling a dice only one number turns up, which cannot be both one and at the same time an even number. Such events are called *mutually exclusive* (denoted simply as "m.e."). Consider next the *union* of these two events, denoted as $C = A \cup B$, or simply "A or B." The event C will occur if A or B occurs, i.e., if one *or* an even number turns up when rolling the dice.

An important relationship that can be shown for mutually exclusive events is the following:

(4.4) $$\Pr(C) = \Pr(A \text{ or } B) = \Pr(A \cup B) = \Pr(A) + \Pr(B).$$

In other words, the probability of the union of two m.e. events is the sum of their probabilities. This definition can also be directly extended beyond just two m.e. events. Indeed, if $A_1, A_2,..., A_k$ (with $k > 2$) are k m.e. events, then

$$\Pr(A_1 \text{ or } A_2 \text{ or } ... \text{ or } A_k) = \Pr(A_1) + \Pr(A_2) + ... + \Pr(A_k).$$

For a given event A, its *complement* is defined as the event that A does not occur, sometimes denoted "not A." For instance, if when rolling a dice the event of interest is A = "An even number turns up," then the complement of A is the event D = "not A" = "An *uneven* number turns up." Obviously, if D = "not A" is the complement of A, then

$$(4.5) \qquad \Pr(D) = 1 - \Pr(A).$$

This is because A and D are evidently m.e., and in addition their union is the certain event, i.e., $\Pr(A$ or "not A") $= 1$ (see also Equation (4.4)).

In many empirical situations, one may be interested in two events A and B that are not necessarily m.e., and in particular in their occurrence simultaneously. The event consisting of this simultaneous occurrence is called the *intersection* of the two events and is denoted by $F = AB$, or alternatively as $A \cap B$. We stress that the occurrence of F is tantamount to that of both A and B occurring in a given experiment. We note also that if A and B are m.e., then F is the empty event that never occurs, and then $\Pr(AB) = \Pr(F) = \Pr(\emptyset) = 0$.

The probability of the intersection of two events, $A \cap B$, is related to that of the union of two general events A and B (i.e., events that need not be m.e.) in the following way:

$$(4.6) \qquad \Pr(A \text{ or } B) = \Pr(A \cup B) = \Pr(A) + \Pr(B) - \Pr(AB).$$

The reason is that the probability of the intersection of A and B would be counted twice when adding $\Pr(A)$ and $\Pr(B)$. That is, we need to compensate for this double counting by subtracting $\Pr(AB)$ from the sum of the latter two probabilities. The validity of Equation (4.6) can be graphically demonstrated using so-called Venn diagrams, with an example displayed in Figure 4.1, which are widely used to facilitate understanding of probability of events. It is important to note that Equation (4.4) is a special case of Equation (4.6), which holds when $F = AB$ is the empty event.

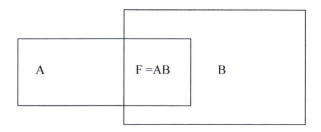

FIGURE 4.1.
Venn diagram for the probability of the intersection F of the events A and B ($F = AB$).

In the remainder of this chapter, we will use on several occasions the probability relationships discussed in this section.

4.5. CONDITIONAL PROBABILITY AND INDEPENDENCE

A type of probability that is of particular relevance in statistical applications in the social and behavioral sciences is that of *conditional probability*. This is the probability of an event occurring on the assumption that another event (with positive probability) has occurred. The importance of this probability can be seen in the above dice-rolling example by asking the following question: "If a dice was rolled and it is known that an even number has turned up, what is the probability that it was the number two?"

We note that this question is different from the ones we have asked so far in the present chapter. In particular, the last question is based on the assumption that some additional information is available about the event, viz., that the number on the dice was an even number. We have not had access to any additional information earlier in this chapter, whether of this or another kind, when asking questions about the probability of certain events. Obviously it is essential to utilize, as opposed to waste, such information when responding to questions about probability of events like the last posed question. This information amounts to a condition under which an answer to such a question is sought. In the example described at the beginning of this Section 4.5, an important condition is presented by the fact (or knowledge) that the rolled dice turned up with an even number; given this knowledge, the question was raised as to what the probability is of the number being two.

4.5.1. Defining conditional probability

Responding to the last raised question is accomplished using the concept of conditional probability. This is a probability for an event, knowing that a certain condition (e.g., another event) has occurred.

To facilitate working out conditional probability for a particular event given the occurrence of another event, let us denote by B the event that an even number turned up on top of the dice, and by A the event that the number two turned up. The last raised question asks about the *conditional probability*, denoted $\Pr(A \mid B)$, of the number on top of the rolled dice being two on the condition (i.e., given) that the number having turned up is even. This conditioning is symbolized by the vertical bar, '|', followed by the condition under which the event before that bar (viz., A here) is being considered. The condition itself (i.e., the conditioning event) is placed after the bar (viz., B here). We emphasize that conditional probability is only then defined, when we condition on an event that is not associated with a probability of zero—otherwise conditional probability is meaningless. (This requirement is fulfilled in the opening example of the present section.)

We reiterate that the currently considered probability, $Pr(A \mid B)$, is not of the kind of probabilities that we have been discussing so far in this chapter. The latter probabilities are called *unconditional* or *marginal*, since we consider them outside of any connection to another event—i.e., we do not condition on any other event(s). In particular, we can readily work out for the above dice-rolling example that $Pr(A \mid B) = 1/3 = .33$ (rounded off to two decimals), since there is only one favorable event out of three possible, viz., the number two turning up, out of the numbers two, four, and six possibly turning up. At the same time, $Pr(A) = 1/6$, and hence is a different probability (keep in mind that $Pr(B) > 0$ here). In fact, it can be shown more generally that $Pr(A \mid B)$ can be determined by the following relationship:

$$(4.7) \qquad Pr(A \mid B) = Pr(AB) \ / \ Pr(B).$$

This equation is often used as a formal definition of conditional probability (assuming $Pr(B) > 0$). Equation (4.7) can also be simply rewritten alternatively in the following way:

$$(4.8) \qquad Pr(AB) = Pr(B).Pr(A \mid B),$$

which represents the probability of the intersection of two events—i.e., of their joint occurrence—as the product of a marginal and a conditional probability in the right-hand side of (4.8). Equation (4.8) represents a fundamental expression of joint probability in terms of two other types of probabilities— marginal and conditional—and is used quite often in various forms in statistics and its applications.

If in addition $Pr(A) > 0$, we can similarly consider conditional probability with regard to the event A:

$$(4.9) \qquad Pr(B \mid A) = Pr(AB) \ / \ Pr(A).$$

Then, combining this equation with Equation (4.8), we obtain

$$(4.10) \qquad Pr(AB) = Pr(A).Pr(B \mid A) = Pr(B).Pr(A \mid B).$$

Thus, Equation (4.10) presents two different ways of expressing the joint probability for two events, A and B (such that they are associated with positive probabilities each)—viz., as in the two right-hand sides of (4.10). Either way, we stress that in Equation (4.10) we have two expressions of the *joint probability* $Pr(\text{``}A \text{ and } B\text{''})$ *as the product of corresponding marginal and conditional probability* (assuming we condition each time on an event with positive probability).

To exemplify this discussion, consider the event A = "picking at random a girl from a student population of third graders" and B = "picking at random a third-grade student who has an IQ score that is higher than 105." Then the joint occurrence of these two events, A and B, is AB = "picking at random a girl with an IQ score higher than 105 (when sampling from a population of third graders)." Equation (4.10) allows us now to re-express this probability in two ways (the symbol '$\times$' is used next to denote multiplication):

Pr(picking at random a girl with IQ>105)

= Pr(picking at random a girl | selected student has IQ>105) $\times$
     Pr(selected student has IQ > 105)

= Pr(picking at random a student with IQ > 105 | selected student is a
     girl) $\times$ Pr(selected student is a girl)

In this way, we were able to "decompose" the probability of a joint occurrence of the two events in question into the product of simpler (i.e., not joint event occurrence) probabilities.

4.5.2. Event independence

The preceding discussion naturally leads us to a related important probability concept, that of event independence. Two events, A and B (with positive probabilities), are defined as *independent* if conditioning on either of them does not change the probability of the other event. This can be denoted as:

(4.11) $\qquad\qquad \Pr(A \mid B) = \Pr(A), \text{ or } \Pr(B \mid A) = \Pr(B).$

We note in passing that only one of the two equations in (4.11) needs to hold in order for the other to hold as well (as long as both events are with positive probability). We also observe that when two events are independent, their joint probability is the product of their marginal probabilities:

$$\Pr(AB) = \Pr(A).\Pr(B).$$

The concept of independence becomes especially important when obtaining samples from studied populations. In particular, one needs to ensure then that samples are selected in such a way that they are independent of one another.

4.6. BAYES' THEOREM

The concept of conditional probability is at the heart of a widely used formula in applications of statistics in the behavioral and social sciences, the *Bayes' formula*, also often referred to as *Bayes' theorem*. The theorem is named after

Thomas Bayes, a famous 17th-century English mathematician. To illustrate the principles behind this formula, let us suppose that we were interested in using a cognitive test for the purpose of diagnosing a particular learning disability in first graders. For this test we are interested in evaluating:

(i)   its *sensitivity*, that is, its true positive rate, i.e., Pr(test is positive | child has a learning disability); as well as

(ii) its *specificity*, that is, its true negative rate, i.e., Pr(test is negative | child has no learning disability).

These probabilities can be worked out with Bayes' formula, which can be obtained using earlier developments in this chapter. To this end, first let us consider two events A and B with positive probability each. Then, from Equations (4.9) and (4.10) we obtain,

$$(4.12) \qquad \Pr(A \mid B) = \Pr(AB) \, / \, \Pr(B) = \Pr(A).\Pr(B \mid A) \, / \, \Pr(B).$$

However, since the event BA and the intersection of B with the event "not A" are m.e. and in their union render B,

$$(4.13) \qquad \Pr(B) = \Pr(BA) + \Pr(B \text{ and "not } A").$$

Hence, from Equations (4.12) and (4.13) it follows that

$$(4.14) \quad \Pr(A \mid B) = \Pr(A).\Pr(B \mid A)/[\Pr(BA) + \Pr(B \text{ and "not } A")].$$

Using for the denominator again Equation (4.10), we finally obtain the Bayes' formula (for the currently considered events A and B):

$$(4.15) \qquad \Pr(A \mid B) = \frac{\Pr(B \mid A).\Pr(A)}{\Pr(B \mid A).\Pr(A) + \Pr(B \mid not\_A).\Pr(not\_A)}.$$

In behavioral and social research, the event A is often used in the form of a "state of nature," and its probability Pr(A) is referred to as a "prior probability." Unlike it, the probability Pr($A \mid B$) given some event B of interest, is called "posterior probability," i.e., the reassessed or modified probability for the event A after obtaining the knowledge that event B has occurred. The probability of B under A is also often referred to as "likelihood."

To illustrate this discussion, consider now the diagnostic test example in more detail. Let us suppose that in a studied population of first graders, 5% of the children have learning difficulties (event A) and 95% have no learning difficulties (event "not A"). That is, Pr(A) = .05 and Pr(not A) = .95.

Next let us assume that based upon past research we knew that the sensitivity and specificity of a diagnostic test for learning difficulties was 72% and 65%, respectively. That is, if B is the event "positive diagnosis" of learning difficulties, then in case a child has such indeed, $\Pr(B \mid A) = .72$. Similarly, from the specificity of this test being .65, it follows that $\Pr(\text{not } B \mid \text{not } A) = .65 = 1 - \Pr(B \mid \text{not } A)$. Therefore, $\Pr(B \mid \text{not } A) = 1 - \Pr(\text{not } B \mid \text{not } A) = 1 - .65 = .35$.

If we have now the result obtained from testing a certain child with this instrument, and the result suggests the child has learning difficulties, then the probability the child indeed is having such difficulties is according to Bayes' formula ('$\times$' denotes multiplication next):

$$\Pr(A \mid B) = .72 \times .05 \,/\, (.72 \times .05 + .35 \times .95) = .098.$$

This probability result can be readily obtained with R as follows (note the use of '*' for multiplication):

```
> Pr.AunderB = .72*.05 / (.72*.05 + .35*.95)
```

which renders a value of .098 as the probability of the child having learning difficulties.

We note in passing that we used R here in the form of a "calculator," in which role also any other statistical software could be used; needless to say, the calculations performed here by R can be alternatively obtained with any handheld calculator.

The formula provided in Equation (4.15) is actually a special case of the general Bayes' formula, which is also often called Bayes' theorem. This special case is obtained when only two events are considered, viz., A and "not A." The general Bayes' formula for a set of m.e. events $A_1, \ldots, A_k$ is as follows (note the analogy of the following expression to the right-hand side of Equation (4.15)):

$$(4.16) \qquad \Pr(A_j \mid B) = \frac{\Pr(B \mid A_j).\Pr(A_j)}{\sum_{j=1}^{k} \Pr(B \mid A_j).\Pr(A_j)}.$$

That is, upon obtaining knowledge that event B has occurred, the prior probability for the jth event A_j is modified to the expression in the right-hand side of Equation (4.16) ($j = 1,..., k$). As indicated earlier, the Bayes' theorem is of fundamental relevance for a whole branch of statistics, called *Bayesian statistics*. Given the introductory nature of the present book, this topic is not considered further—for more specialized treatments on this branch of statistics the reader is referred to Smith (2010) or Swinburne (2005).

Based on the concepts presented in this chapter, we move next to a discussion of various distributions of variables studied in the behavioral and social sciences.

Probability Distributions of Random Variables

5.1. RANDOM VARIABLES

In most social and behavioral science research, we are typically interested in examining a variety of subject characteristics and their potential relationships (cf. Raykov & Marcoulides, 2011). These individual characteristics (or more generally, characteristics of units of analysis composed of persons) are typically referred to as "variables." Although previous chapters relied on an intuitive understanding of this term, we now define a *variable* as follows: A variable is a behavior-related characteristic that takes individual-specific values in a given sample (population) and as such is generally not expected to be equal across studied persons. In other words, *variable* is a concept that is the opposite to that of *constant*.

We are not interested really in studying constants in the social and behavioral sciences, since they do not vary across individuals (or more general units of analysis). Hence, constants typically do not contain information of relevance when behavioral phenomena are of concern. We mention, though, that some special mathematical constants will be important for us in subsequent discussions, such as the numbers $e = 2.718...$, and $\pi = 3.1415...$. As one may recall, the former number is used as the natural logarithm base, whereas the latter number represents the ratio of the circumference of a circle to its diameter. These two constants play a major role in applications of statistics, as we will see later in the book.

Whenever variables are discussed throughout the remainder of this text, we will imply that they are of a particular kind. Specifically, variables typically of interest in the behavioral and social sciences have the property that their values in a given group of subjects (sample or population) are unknown before a study is carried out, which involves collection of data from the persons on their characteristics under consideration. These values become known only after the observation (experiment, study) is conducted and data are collected on the variables and studied subjects. Variables of this type are called *random variables* (RVs). In other words, a RV is such a variable whose individual scores do not exist prior to the actual conducting of the study for which it is of relevance, but become available only after that study has been carried out.

There are two main types of RVs in social and behavioral research—discrete and continuous. A discrete random variable can take on only a countable number of particular distinct values, whereas a continuous variable takes an infinite number of possible values between any two lying in its range. In other words, a continuous random variable is not defined at specific values but is instead defined over an interval of values. In empirical research, it is customary to consider as approximately continuous a RV that can take on a relatively large number of values (e.g., 15 or more), while one considers as discrete a RV that can take only a limited number of values—e.g., two or just a few more. For instance, the answer on an algebra problem—true or false—is an example of a discrete RV. On the other hand, an IQ score obtained from an intelligence test is an example of a variable that for most practical purposes could be treated as a continuous (approximately continuous) RV. The distinction between discrete and continuous RVs becomes especially important in applications of statistics for the purposes of modeling the relationships between studied variables, as we will be doing later in this book. Under such circumstances, different methods are best applicable according to whether we are dealing with discrete response variables or with continuous (response, outcome, dependent) variables.

5.2. PROBABILITY DISTRIBUTIONS FOR DISCRETE RANDOM VARIABLES

The *probability distribution* for a discrete random variable y is defined as the set of numbers that equal the probability $Pr(y)$ for each possible value of y in the domain of that variable, i.e., in the set of scores that the RV y could attain. The probability distribution for a given discrete RV can be provided or represented by a table, graph, or just a formula showing the probability with which y attains each and every one of its possible values. In a given sample, we can obtain the relative frequencies that represent (estimate) these particular probabilities.

5.2.1. A start-up example

To begin discussing probability distributions of discrete RVs, we use the following example. Consider the previous experiment consisting of tossing two fair coins, whereby the result obtained on one of them does not influence that of the other. Let us consider the number of "tails" that occur thereby.

This number is obviously a RV, denoted y in the following discussion. This is because we do not know its value—which could be 0, 1, or 2—until after the experiment has actually been conducted. Given that y is a RV, the natural question then is "What is its distribution?" That is, the question asks for the probabilities with which it takes on its possible values—0, 1, and 2. With some reflection and use of pertinent concepts and results from Chapter 4, we can readily determine the probability distribution of y as given in Table 5.1.

Based on Table 5.1, for example, it is quite evident that the probability of $y = 0$ is .25. In other words, when tossing two fair coins, the probability that no "tails" occur is $1/4$. Using R one can easily represent these probabilities graphically if need be. To this end, we first create an array (set or grid) of the scores of y, and an array with the corresponding probabilities, $Pr(y)$. This can be done with the command 'concatenate', or $c(.)$ for short, where within brackets we list the numbers we wish to assign to the array created in this way (note the symbol Pr.y that we use next for $Pr(y)$):

```
> y = c(0, 1, 2)
> Pr.y = c(.25, .50, .25)
```

With these two commands, we create two arrays—the first containing the values that the RV y of interest can take, and the second containing the probabilities with which y takes these values. We can now provide a graph with these probabilities by using the R command 'plot':

```
> plot(y, Pr.y)
```

The resulting graph is displayed in Figure 5.1.

We note readily that the sum of all probabilities across the values that the RV y can take is 1. In fact, this is a generally valid observation for any discrete RV. Similarly, none of its probabilities is negative or larger than 1. In this considered example (as well as generally; see Chapter 4), the probabilities of an event that represents the union of two or more mutually exclusive events

Table 5.1 Probability distribution of the discrete random variable y (y = possible value, $Pr(y)$ = probability for taking the value y).

y	Pr(y)
0	.25
1	.50
2	.25

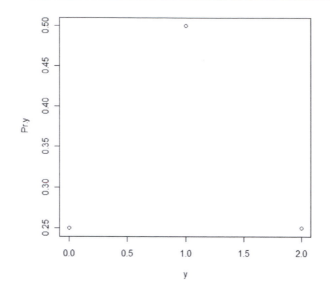

FIGURE 5.1.

Graph of the probabilities of the random variable y, the number of tails when tossing two fair coins (independently of one another).

is the sum of their probabilities. For example, the probability of the RV y taking the value of 1 or 2 is

$$\Pr(y = 1 \text{ or } 2) = .50 + .25 = .75.$$

We stress that in the graph displayed in Figure 5.1 we have represented the theoretical probabilities for the values of the RV y. With a much larger number of independent trials (each consisting of tossing two fair coins, as above), the relative frequency with which 0, 1, and 2 "tails" occur will approximate these probabilities. The larger the number of trials, the better the approximation will be (in general; see for instance the example experiment we used in Section 4.3 of Chapter 4).

5.2.2. The binomial distribution

The above-considered coin-tossing example introduced a context in which a particular type of a discrete RV distribution is applicable, the so-called binomial distribution. The *binomial distribution* is defined as the distribution of the number y of "successes" in a series of n independent trials with two possible outcomes each—denoted for simplicity as 0 and 1 (with the latter value commonly referred to as "success")—whereby the probability of success p is the same in all trials ($n > 0$). For example, in a class with n students, the number of correct responses on a given algebra task—graded as correct vs. incorrect—would follow a binomial distribution, assuming that students work independently and all have the same probability p of solving correctly the particular algebra task.

As seen from this informal definition of a binomial RV, in order to speak of such a variable we need to be given two numbers—often called the *parameters* of this distribution. These are the number of trials n and the probability p of success. Once we know these two parameters n and p, we can speak of an RV having the binomial distribution if the RV can take on the values 0, 1,..., n (and no other) with specific probabilities; the latter are the probabilities for 0, 1,..., n successes in n trials that are independent of one another and with the same probability of success. More formally, if y is a RV following the binomial distribution with parameters n and p, which can be symbolically represented as

$$y \sim \mathrm{Bi}(n, p) \,,$$

then the probability associated with each of them can be shown mathematically to be (e.g., Roussas, 1997):

$$(5.1) \qquad \mathrm{Pr}(y) = \frac{n!}{y!(n-y)!} \, p^y (1-p)^{n-y} \quad (y = 0,\ 1,...,\ n).$$

In Equation (5.1), for any integer k we denote by $k! = 1.2 \ldots (k-1).k$ the product of all integer numbers up to k, including k (whereby $k!$ is referred to as "k factorial," and by definition we set $0! = 1$). For example, 3! would simply be $3 \times 2 \times 1 = 6$.

Although one could hand-calculate these probabilities, we can instead easily obtain them and graph them using R. This software implements the formula provided in (5.1) by using the command 'dbinom'. There are three "arguments" to this command, i.e., three entities that we need to provide R with, in order for R to be in a position to execute this command. Specifically, these are (i) the values of y that are of interest, (ii) the total number of values y could obtain (less 1, for 0), and (iii) the probability p of success at each of the independent trials involved.

To illustrate the definition of the binomial distribution and use of the corresponding R command 'dbinom', let us return to the context of the algebra task example given above. Suppose that we have a class of 10 students who work independently and that the probability of each one of them solving the task is .7. Then we can obtain with R a graph of the probabilities of the RV defined as the number of students with correct solutions of the task, denoted y, as follows. First, we need to generate the set of possible numbers of students with correct answers—viz., 0, 1,..., 10. This is easily done with the command

```
> y = 0:10
```

In this way, we create as an array, or grid for the graph—denoted y here—the set of all possible values that can be taken by the RV y. Then for each possible value of y we need to work out the corresponding probabilities for as many students providing the correct answer, using Equation (5.1). This as mentioned is readily implemented in R and invoked with the command

```
> dbinom(y, size = n, prob = p)
```

where we need to enter the number n (in our example, 10) and the probability p (in our example, .7). (As an aside at this point, the name of the command, 'dbinom', could be in a sense decoded as "distribution of a binomial variable." Technically, 'dbinom' could be seen also as standing for "density of a binomial variable," keeping in mind that the set of its probabilities could be considered the counterpart of the density of a continuous random variable, a concept which is discussed later in this chapter.)

For the currently considered algebra task example, the following command is thus needed:

```
> Pr.y = dbinom(y, size = 10, prob = .7)
```

We can view the probabilities computed in this way by just entering at the R prompt 'Pr.y':

```
> Pr.y
```

The last command produces the following series of probabilities (note the prefix in brackets at the beginning of each output row, indicating the serial number of the probability following next in this set of altogether 11 probabilities—for each of the numbers 0 through 10):

```
[1]  0.0000059049 0.0001377810 0.0014467005 0.0090016920 0.0367569090
[6]  0.1029193452 0.2001209490 0.2668279320 0.2334744405 0.1210608210
[11] 0.0282475249
```

From the provided output, we easily see that the probability of no students correctly solving the task is .000 (rounded off to the third decimal place), for six students correctly solving the task is .200 (rounded off), while that for just three students solving it correctly is .009 (rounded off)—these are the first, seventh, and fourth numbers, respectively, from left to right in this output.

To plot next these probabilities against the possible values of the RV y, we use the 'plot' command as before:

```
> plot(y, Pr.y, type = "h")
```

where we employ the last subcommand 'type' to request vertical lines connecting the probability point on the graph with the horizontal line (abscissa).
This yields the graph displayed in Figure 5.2.

   An interesting property of the binomial distribution is that it becomes
more and more symmetric, for a given probability p, with increasing number
of trials, n. For instance, the graph of the binomial probabilities for $n = 100$
with $p = .7$ is much more symmetric, and displayed in Figure 5.3. In order
to obtain this graph, we first create an array with the 101 numbers from 0 to
100, for instance using the command

```
> y = 0:100
```

Then we furnish the associated probabilities using the command

```
> Pr.y = dbinom(y, size = 100, prob = .7)
```

Finally we plot these probabilities against their corresponding y's (as done
above), which leads to the graph in Figure 5.3 that as mentioned looks much
more symmetric than that in Figure 5.2.

   Like any distribution used in this book, a RV y that is binomially distrib-

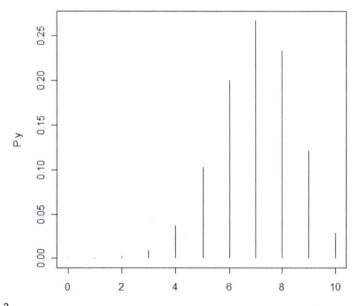

FIGURE 5.2.
Graph of the binomial probabilities (5.1) for $n = 10$, and $p = .7$.

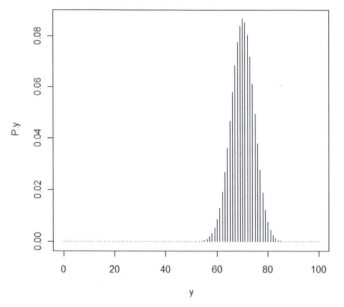

FIGURE 5.3.

Graph of the binomial probabilities for $n = 100$ and $p = .7$.

uted has a mean and variance or standard deviation, which are its respective measures of central tendency and variability (see Chapter 3). They can be shown to equal correspondingly (e.g., Agresti & Finlay, 2009)

$$(5.2) \qquad \mu_y = np, \text{ and}$$
$$\sigma_y^2 = np(1-p).$$

We note that we can determine the mean and variance (standard deviation) in Equations (5.2) if we know only the probability of success in each of the trials, p, and their number, n. If we do not know this probability, but only the number n of trials in a given sample (viz., its size), we may estimate p from the sample as the relative frequency

$$(5.3) \qquad \hat{p} = \#\text{successes}/\#\text{trials},$$

and then substitute it into Equation (5.2). In this way, we will render estimates of the mean and variance:

$$(5.4) \qquad \hat{\mu} = n\hat{p}, \; \hat{\sigma}^2 = n\hat{p}(1-\hat{p}).$$

(e.g., Agresti & Finlay, 2009). These estimates provide empirical information about the population mean and variance, and may be of relevance in a particular study.

5.2.3. The Poisson distribution

With a large number of trials, n, the binomial distribution becomes awkward and unwieldy to deal with. In particular, its probabilities are hard to evaluate precisely then. In such cases, this distribution can be approximated quite well by another distribution for a nonnegative discrete RV, if the probability p of success in the binomial trials is small (for details see below). The approximating distribution is that of the number of events of a prespecified nature that occur during a given time period. For instance, the number of cases of a rare noncontagious disease occurring in a school district during a given year, or the number of airplane accidents occurring on a given day, could be argued to follow the *Poisson distribution*.

More specifically, a nonnegative discrete RV follows the Poisson distribution under the following conditions: (a) events occur one at a time (i.e., no two events occur at the same time); (b) events occur independently of one another; and (c) the expected number μ of events (mean, or rate of occurrence) in a given time period is the same as that number during any other time period of the same length.

We note that while the binomial distribution is limited from below and above—since for a given number n of trials one cannot have more than n successes—the Poisson distribution is limited only from below by 0 but not from above. In particular, the distribution of a RV y following the Poisson distribution with a mean μ, symbolized $y \sim Po(\mu)$, is obtained by knowing the probabilities with which y takes its values. These probabilities are defined as follows:

(5.5) $$Pr(y) = \mu^y e^{-\mu} / y! \ (y = 0, 1, 2, ...),$$

where $e = 2.71828...$ is a special constant that we know as the base of the natural logarithm. With Equation (5.5) in mind, we reiterate that the Poisson-distributed RV y can take the value of 0 with a positive probability, and any other positive whole (integer) number with a corresponding probability.

The probabilities given by Equation (5.5) can be easily obtained with R using the command 'dpois' (for "distribution of a Poisson variable" or "density of a Poisson variable"—see earlier discussion in this chapter). A graph of the Poisson distribution can also be readily furnished by this software. To this end, as with the binomial distribution, we first obtain the array of values that this RV can obtain—for which we wish to get its probabilities—then compute the associated probabilities, and finally, graph them against the former values.

To illustrate this discussion, if $\mu = 3$ is the rate of events occurrence, i.e., the mean of the RV y under consideration (see below), the following commands are needed to graph this Poisson distribution, Po(3), for the first 11 possible scores, viz., zero through 10:

```
> y = 0:10
> Pr.y = dpois(y, 3)
> plot(y, Pr.y, type = "h")
```

This command sequence furnishes the probability distribution graph displayed in Figure 5.4.

A random variable with the Poisson distribution has the interesting property that its mean and variance each equal μ (e.g., Roussas, 1997), that is,

$$(5.6) \qquad \mu = \sigma_y^2 = \mu.$$

From Equation (5.6) we note that unlike the binomial distribution, the Poisson distribution is a "single-parameter" distribution. Indeed, all we need to know in order to produce its probabilities is the expected number of events per unit time (i.e., its mean μ). In this feature the Poisson distribution differs from the binomial distribution, for which we needed to know both its parameters n and p in order to determine the probabilities to take particular values.

Since we usually do not know the mean and variance of the Poisson distribution, for given sample data we can estimate the expectation μ by the number of events per unit time, and then plug it into Equation (5.6):

$$(5.7) \qquad \hat{\mu}_y = \hat{\sigma}^2 = \hat{\mu}.$$

To illustrate this discussion, consider the following example. A certain noncontagious disease occurs in a given school district at the rate of .5 cases per

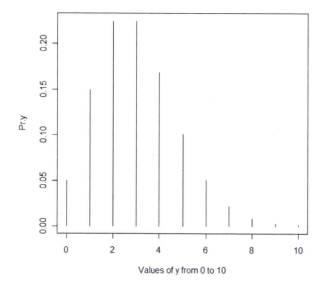

FIGURE 5.4.

Graph of the Poisson probabilities (5.5) (for 0, 1, . . . , 10, and $\mu = 3$).

year. We wish to find out the probability that in a given year there will be two cases of this disease in the district. To accomplish this, we can use the formula (5.1) via the simple command:

```
> dpois(2, .5)
```

which returns

```
[1] .07581633
```

That is, the sought probability is .076 (rounded off to third decimal).

The Poisson distribution becomes even more useful as a means of approximation of the binomial distribution with large n and small probability p of success (specifically with $n \geq 100$ and $p \leq .01$). This approximation is quite good if then $np \leq 20$. In that case, rather than compute the binomial distribution probabilities, one can simply work out the Poisson probabilities—for 0, 1,..., n—with a mean $\mu = np$ (Ott & Longnecker, 2010).

To illustrate, consider the following example. A new medicine aimed at reducing blood pressure in elderly adults has been found to be associated with a probability of .005 for a particular side effect, such as dizziness, say. In a clinical trial, 200 aged persons receive the medicine. What is the probability that none of them will experience dizziness? This probability is readily worked out with R by observing that since 200 > 100, .005 < .01 and 200 × .005 = 1 < 20, the Poisson distribution is a good approximation of the binomial probability of relevance here (with '×' denoting multiplication). Then the sought probability is found out as follows (see preceding example):

```
> dpois(0, 200*.005)
```

which yields .368 (rounded off to third decimal place). Thus, one can say that the probability that none of the persons studied will experience dizziness is just over a third. Conversely, it could be said that with a probability of nearly two-thirds at least one elderly person will experience dizziness during the trial of this medicine.

5.3. PROBABILITY DISTRIBUTIONS FOR CONTINUOUS RANDOM VARIABLES

A continuous RV has the property that its possible values form whole intervals, ranges, or continua, as opposed to discrete RVs that can take only distinct values. In empirical behavioral and social research, one may argue that most variables could be seen as discrete. However, when they take a relatively large number of values (say, 15 or more), they can be considered for many empirical purposes as (approximately) continuous.

For continuous RVs, it is not possible to assign probabilities to single values they can take. This is because, at least theoretically, there are infinitely many such possible values (in fact, infinitely many more values than are countable). Therefore, instead of the tables or graphs representing probabilities for discrete RV values as earlier in the chapter for the discussed binomial and Poisson distributions, we now use a different concept to refer to the distribution of a continuous RV. This is the notion of a "probability density function" (pdf, for short, also called at times "density curve" or "pdf curve"). The pdf is typically used to represent the probabilities with which a continuous RV can take on values within certain intervals. Such a function for a continuous RV is presented in Figure 5.5, and denoted *f* in the rest of this book, when no confusion can arise.

Continuous RVs do not need to have symmetric pdf's, similar to the one displayed in Figure 5.5. Rather, they can also have nonsymmetric density curves. Nonsymmetric pdf's are commonly called "skewed"—displaying asymmetry either to the right or to the left (see also Chapter 3). Specifically, when their right tail is longer than the left, they are called "positively skewed"; alternatively, if their left tail is longer than the right, they are called "negatively skewed." Many random variables in empirical research have nearly symmetric pdf's, however. As we will see in the next chapter, this phenomenon can be

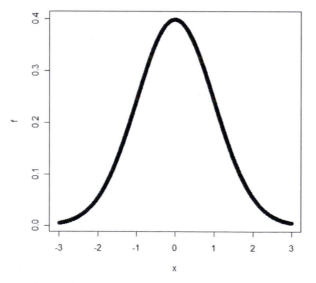

FIGURE 5.5.

Probability density function (pdf, density curve) for a continuous random variable.

explained with an important result in statistics, called the central limit theorem.

Each pdf can be seen as enclosing a certain area between its curve and the horizontal axis of its graph. How large is this area? An important and widely followed convention in statistics and its applications is that *the area under the pdf (density curve) of a continuous RV is assumed to equal one*. This convention is quite reasonable, as the counterpart of a related property for a discrete RV, specifically that the sum of all probabilities for the values it can take is equal to one (see Section 5.2).

Probability density functions resemble in form histograms (see Chapter 2). In particular, the probability of a considered continuous RV obtaining a value within a given interval equals the area under its pdf curve and between the ends of the interval. Specifically, if y is a continuous RV and (a, b) a given interval (in the range of values that y can take, with $a < b$), then $\Pr(a < y < b)$ is the area under the pdf of y that is enclosed between the numbers a and b.

Hence, if one were interested in finding out what the probability is for a continuous RV y to obtain a value in a fairly small interval surrounding (closely) a given number, x say, this probability is approximated by $f(x).\Delta$, where Δ is the length of the considered interval. By letting Δ go to zero, we readily observe that *the probability of a RV y to obtain a prespecified value in its range is zero*. Nonetheless, it is possible that y indeed takes on that particular value x_0, say. This is an instructive example of an event that is not the empty one, which has, however, also a probability of zero (see Chapter 4). Conversely, the probability of this RV taking on a value other than x_0 is one. Similarly, this is an example of an event other than the certain event, which has a probability of one (since one cannot be really certain that the RV y will not take the value x_0).

We mention in passing that while it might be tempting to view $f(y)$ as the probability of a continuous RV y, to take the value y, it would be an incorrect interpretation! The value $f(y)$, for a given number y, cannot be interpreted meaningfully in any different manner than saying that it is the height of the pdf of the RV y at the value y—since the probability of the event E: "The RV y takes the value of y" is zero.

With the preceding discussion in mind, we deal in the next section with a fundamental distribution for continuous RVs, the so-called normal distribution.

5.3.1. The normal distribution

Many variables of interest in the behavioral and social sciences have a distribution with a pdf that approximates well a bell-shaped curve like the one displayed in Figure 5.5. In particular, the scores we obtain from many measuring instruments in these sciences—usually resulting as sums of the scores on their elements, such as items, questions, components, tests, or testlets—often approximate such a distribution well. For example, the scores resulting from an intelligence test or from a college aspiration scale for high school students would likely have this feature. To be more specific, these distributions can be approximated well by the normal distribution. As it turns out, this distribution plays a fundamental role in statistics and its applications; we discuss it next, beginning with a definition.

5.3.1.1. Probability density function

There are infinitely many normal distributions possible for a continuous RV under consideration. Any one of them has a pdf (density curve) that is described by the following function, or curve, for appropriate values of the two parameters μ and σ^2, which will soon be given specific meanings ($\sigma^2 > 0$ is assumed throughout this book for the variance of any continuous RV):

$$(5.8) \qquad f(y) = \frac{1}{\sqrt{2\pi}\sigma} e^{-(y-\mu)^2/2\sigma^2},$$

where the value y is unrestricted, i.e., $-\infty < y < \infty$. That is, in practical terms, as the score y ranges from a very small to a very large number, the function $f(y)$ defined in the right-hand side of Equation (5.8) describes the density curve of the normal distribution with parameters μ and σ^2 (notice the appearance in (5.8) of the constants π and e mentioned earlier in the book). This distribution is commonly denoted as $N(\mu, \sigma^2)$, and the fact that the RV y follows it is represented symbolically as $y \sim N(\mu, \sigma^2)$. We will frequently use this notation in the remainder of the book. Also, whenever we refer to a "normal distribution" or "normal curve" (with a given mean and variance), we will mean in particular the pdf defined in Equation (5.8).

As an aside at this point, Equation (5.8) also allows us to see that all we need to know in order to create (produce) the normal distribution with mean μ and variance σ^2, is the values of these two parameters. In this sense, once we estimate the mean and variance for a population distribution on a given normal variable using data on it from an available sample, all information needed to produce this distribution (based on the sample) is contained in the estimates of these two parameters. In other words, the mean and variance are sufficient statistics with regard to the variable distribution as long as it is normal (e.g., Roussas, 1997).

5.3.1.2. Graphing a normal distribution

We can readily obtain with R a graph of the normal distribution pdf (normal pdf) for any given pair of parameters μ and σ^2. For example, to obtain this graph of the normal distribution with a $\mu = 100$ and $\sigma = 15$, which is approximately the distribution of the scores resulting from many intelligence tests, we proceed as follows: (i) create a "grid" ("net," or array) of scores for y, at which we (ii) compute the right-hand side of Equation (5.8), and then (iii) plot the grid and this set of corresponding scores. These three activities are accomplished with the following three consecutive R commands:

```
> y = seq(55, 145, .05)
> f.y = dnorm(y, 100, 15)
> plot(y, f.y)
```

The first of these commands, as mentioned, makes available for the next two commands or activities the sequence of all numbers between 55 and 145 that are .05 units apart—starting with the smallest, 55, and ending with the largest, 145. (Later in this chapter, we elaborate on why it is meaningful to choose 55 and 145 here.) The second command calculates, using the right-hand side of Equation (5.8) with $\mu = 100$ and $\sigma = 15$, the values of the pdf of the normal distribution $N(100, 225)$ at all these numbers in the array (sequence of numbers) produced by the first command and denoted y. The last command plots each of the values in the array y and its corresponding value of the pdf, $f(y)$, for the normal distribution under consideration. The triple of these commands produce the graph presented in Figure 5.6.

We note in passing that if we wanted to display the pdf of this distribution also for scores lower than 55 and larger than 145, we could reflect that in the

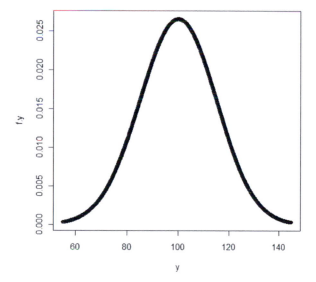

FIGURE 5.6.
Graph of the density curve (pdf) for the normal distribution $N(100, 225)$.

first command above that created the grid for the graph. However, as we will soon see, the probability at lower scores than 55 is practically zero, as it is for scores larger than 145 (for this particular distribution, $N(100, 225)$).

Using the above three command lines, one can similarly create the graph of the pdf of any normal distribution $N(\mu, \sigma^2)$ of interest—all we need to do is just substitute in these three lines its parameters, μ and σ^2 (and modify correspondingly the two end points of the underlying graph grid; see below).

5.3.1.3. Mean and variance of a normal distribution

What do these parameters μ and σ^2 actually mean? The first, μ, is the mean (expectation) of the RV with the distribution $N(\mu, \sigma^2)$, while the second, σ^2, is the variance of the RV following this distribution, as shown in more advanced treatments (e.g., Roussas, 1997). As to the mean, we can in a sense "see" it by examining the graph displayed in Figure 5.6. Indeed, the pdf of the distribution $N(100, 225)$ presented there is centered around 100, which equals its mean μ.

We also note that the normal distribution is *symmetric around its mean μ*. This is easy to see for the distribution presented in Figure 5.6, and more generally can be deduced by examining Equation (5.8). Specifically the exponent in its right-hand side is highest when y = μ, and furnishes the same value for any y above the mean as it does for its mirror image around the mean μ, viz., for the value $\mu - (y - \mu)$. This is precisely the feature of *symmetry* of a function $f(y)$ around a particular number—in this case, μ. Due to this feature, the mean is also equal to the median for any normal distribution.

While the mean μ represents the central location of the distribution, as follows from its symmetry around μ, the variance σ^2 reflects the degree to which the distribution is flat versus peaked (in its central part). In particular, flatter distributions are associated with larger σ^2, while more peaked ones with smaller σ^2. (For our purposes in this book, this can be readily seen graphically, by plotting as above several different normal distributions with the same mean but varying σ's.) The degree to which a distribution is excessively flat or peaked is also reflected in its *kurtosis*. In particular, using the Greek words *lepto* (which means thin or peaked) and *platy* (which means wide or flat), distinctions between *leptokurtic* and *platykurtic* distributions can be made. When a distribution has such a shape that does not enable one to make a clear distinction between the leptokurtic and platykurtic cases, it is generally referred to as *mesokurtic* (where the Greek word *meso* means middle). Such a term implies a compromise between the two cases of peaked versus flat distributions. For example, normal distributions are considered to be meso-kurtic (i.e., they are not leptokurtic or platykurtic). We note that these descriptive aspects of a distribution are related to the so-called moments of a distribution. In particular, the mean, variance, skewness, and kurtosis are the four moments of main interest of a distribution. Of course, since a normal distribution is symmetric, it has no skewness; in other words, its third (central) moment is zero.

We will revisit a related feature of the normal distribution later in the chapter, in the context of probability of a normally distributed RV obtaining a value within certain intervals of its range of scores.

5.3.1.4. The standard normal distribution

Even though there are infinitely many normal distributions, one of them has obtained special relevance. This is the *standard normal distribution*, denoted $N(0,1)$, with a mean of zero and variance of one. The pdf of this distribution was actually graphed in the earlier Figure 5.5 in this chapter. This distribution is also commonly tabulated in many introductory statistics textbooks (e.g., Agresti & Finlay, 2009, p. 592).

To obtain for illustrative purposes a graph of the pdf of the standard normal distribution, as indicated earlier in the chapter we can use the following three commands:

```
> y = seq(-3, 3, .005)
> f.y = dnorm(y, 0, 1)
> plot(y, f.y)
```

We thus create with the first command a thinner grid than the one used earlier, due to the much smaller variance of the distribution of interest here, $N(0,1)$, and our desire to produce a smooth curve (i.e., a curve appearing smooth to the naked eye). The remaining two commands are the same as those used above in Section 5.3, with the only difference that the one producing the pdf values f.y needs to use arguments that are valid for the present case, viz., mean of zero and standard deviation of one (as the second and third of its arguments). These three commands produce the graph displayed in Figure 5.7, for completeness of the current discussion. As we see from it, most scores assumed by an RV following a standard normal distribution can be expected to lie within the interval -3 and 3. The reason is an important fact about the probability of a score from such a distribution to be at least a certain distance away from the mean, which we will discuss in detail later in the chapter.

The standard normal distribution leads us naturally to a very useful concept in empirical behavioral and social research, which we next turn to.

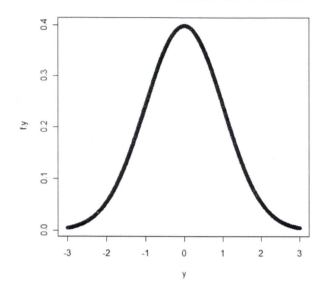

FIGURE 5.7.
Probability density function of the standard normal distribution, $N(0,1)$.

5.3.2. z-scores

The reason the standard normal distribution plays such a central role among the normal distributions is the fact that one can "move" to it and back from any other normal distribution, using a simple standardization formula. In particular, it can be shown that if the RV y is normally distributed with any mean and variance μ and σ, i.e., $y \sim N(\mu, \sigma^2)$, then the so-called z-score,

$$(5.9) \qquad\qquad z = (y - \mu)/\sigma,$$

follows the standard normal distribution, $N(0,1)$. Conversely, if $x \sim N(0,1)$ is a standard normal RV, then the RV $y = \mu + \sigma x$ will have the distribution $N(\mu, \sigma^2)$ (e.g., King & Minium, 2003).

More generally, the z-score is defined for any random variable, regardless of its distribution (as long as its variance is positive, as assumed throughout this book). Further, we stress that Equation (5.9) produces a z-score for any given variable and any subject (unit of analysis). That is, any studied subject (or aggregate of such, if being the unit of analysis) has a z-score on any variable under consideration. This score is computed as in Equation (5.9). We also notice that the z-score equals the number of standard deviations (σ) that the original y score is away from (i.e., below or above) the mean, μ. Also, we will keep in mind that unlike raw scores (y) often obtained on measures in the behavioral and social sciences, the z-scores can be negative (viz., when $y < \mu$) and will usually not be whole numbers.

Equation (5.9) would be applicable if we knew the population mean μ and variance σ^2 on a variable under consideration. Since populations values will rarely be obtainable in empirical research, in an available sample (group) the z-scores are estimated as

(5.10)
$$\hat{z}_{y,i} = \frac{y_i - \hat{\mu}_y}{\hat{\sigma}_y} = \frac{y_i - \bar{y}}{s_y},$$

$i = 1, 2,..., n$. (Frequently in behavioral and social research, the caret above z is left out when estimated z-scores are used.) In Equation (5.10), we attach deliberately both subindexes y and i to the z-score. We do so in order to emphasize that these are individual scores on a given random variable, y, of interest—as mentioned, every subject has a z-score on any variable of concern (for which the variance is positive).

The z-scores have obtained quite some prominence in empirical behavioral and social research mostly due to the fact that different variables in these disciplines are typically measured using different scales whose units are not readily comparable with one another, if at all. These units of measurement are in addition often arbitrary and perhaps meaningless, if not irrelevant. This makes comparison of subject performance across variables (e.g., subtests, components, subscales) very difficult, if not impossible. To allow some comparability of individual scores across variables or measures, the z-scores can be utilized. This enhanced comparability derives from the fact that the z-scores are "pure" numbers, which do not reflect the original units of measurement. Rather, they only reflect the individual score deviations from the mean, which deviations are evaluated in terms of the original standard deviation.

For instance, consider the case where a student has a score of 15 on an algebra test and a score of 25 on a geometry test. Is the student doing better in algebra or in geometry? This question cannot be answered, in general, based only on these available raw scores. The reason is that usually tests are based on a different number of items and we do not know here how many items each test had. However, if we go to z-scores, some comparability becomes possible, if one is willing to take as informative in this regard the knowledge of how the student fares relative to peers (classmates or schoolmates). Specifically, suppose the z-score of the same student on the algebra measure was .75, while the z-score on the geometry measure was -.25. We note that these z-score values can be readily computed using Equation 5.10, once the sample mean and standard deviation have been obtained. Using these z-scores, we could now say that the student is .75 standard deviations above the mean on algebra, but .25 standard deviations below the mean on geometry. That is, the student is doing considerably better than average in algebra but worse than average in geometry.

5.3.3. How to obtain z-scores in empirical research

The z-scores for any variable of interest in empirical studies are readily furnished by R, using the formula:

```
> z = (y - mean(y))/sd(y)
```

To illustrate, consider the earlier MTA example (see also Example 2.2 in Chapter 2), with $n = 36$ students being examined for their mathematics test–taking anxiety. (As mentioned earlier, the complete data set is available in the file CH2_EX22.dat.) For the anxiety score in that data set—the variable denoted 'y' in it—the last indicated R command yields the following z-scores (after entering at the R prompt just 'z'; note that thereby 36 scores are printed on the screen):

```
> z
```

```
 [1] -1.98472359 -1.50357848 -1.02243337 -0.54128825 -0.06014314  2.10500987
 [7] -1.26300592 -1.02243337 -0.30071570 -0.06014314  0.42100197 -0.54128825
[13] -0.30071570  0.42100197  0.42100197  0.18042942 -0.06014314  0.90214709
[19] -1.02243337 -1.50357848 -0.54128825  1.38329220  0.90214709  1.86443731
[25] -1.02243337 -1.02243337 -0.06014314  0.42100197  0.42100197  0.90214709
[31]  1.38329220  1.38329220 -0.54128825  0.18042942 -0.06014314  1.14271964
```

It is instructive to look at the mean and variance of these 36 scores. According to the previous discussion, the mean should be zero and the variance one. To furnish the mean of the above z-scores, after just entering 'mean(z)' at the R prompt ('>'), one will get

```
[1] -2.878858e-17
```

This is a very small number, which for all practical purposes can be treated as zero. Specifically, it is formally equal to $-2.878858 \times 10^{-17}$ (where '×' denotes multiplication). We note in passing that the software R—like many other available statistical software—uses the so-called scientific notation to represent large or small numbers. In this notation, powers of 10 are denoted formally by 'e' followed by the actual power. That is, the number -2.878858e-17 is the same as the number $-2.878858 \times 10^{-17}$. (The symbol e displayed here should not be confused with the constant $e = 2.718...$ mentioned earlier in the book; the latter constant plays a fundamental role for the pdf of the normal distribution, as can be seen from the above Equation (5.8).)

To render the variance of the z-scores, after just entering 'var(z)' at the R prompt, one obtains

```
> var(z)
[1] 1
```

which is what it should be, according to our earlier discussion in this chapter.

5.4. THE NORMAL DISTRIBUTION AND AREAS UNDER THE NORMAL DENSITY CURVE

As mentioned previously, a widely followed convention in statistics and its applications is that the area under the normal curve is assumed (set) to be one, for any normal distribution. (In fact, this is assumed for any distribution that has a pdf—which all continuous RV distributions of relevance in this book do.) This convention allows us to make quite informative statements about the probabilities of certain events, in particular about possible values that a normally distributed RV can take. We discuss such probabilities in the rest of this section.

We begin by noting the following fact. It can be shown mathematically that the area under the normal curve, which is enclosed by the interval ($\mu - \sigma$, $\mu + \sigma$)—corresponding to one standard deviation below and above the mean—is approximately 68%. We can actually easily work this out with R empirically, for any normal distribution whose mean and variance are known, or by using alternatively tables for normal probabilities (see next section). We employ for this aim the R command 'pnorm'—which may be viewed as standing for "probability for the normal distribution." This R command calculates the area under the normal curve, which is to the left of a given number stated subsequently.

To illustrate, suppose we want to find out what the area is under the normal curve that lies within the interval ($\mu - \sigma$, $\mu + \sigma$) for the normal distribution with a mean of one and variance of five (i.e., with a standard deviation of $\sqrt{5}$). To work out the area under the normal curve and within $\sqrt{5}$ units from the mean of one, we use the R command 'pnorm' that has three arguments—i.e., three numbers that we need to provide R with in order to enable the software to respond to our question. These numbers are (in this order): (i) the score in question—we want the area to the left of that score and under the normal curve; (ii) the mean; and finally (iii) the standard deviation of the normal distribution under consideration. In the present example, this leads to the following command (the response we obtain from R is given immediately below the command):

```
> pnorm(1+sqrt(5), 1, sqrt(5))
[1] 0.8413447
```

That is, just over 84% of the entire area under the normal curve for this distribution, $N(1,5)$, is to the left of the point one plus one standard deviation (i.e., to the left of $\mu + \sigma$ in this example). We note in passing that in R, like in other software, square root is accomplished with the command 'sqrt(.)', with the number to be square-rooted given within parentheses.

The last calculated probability implies that the area above $\mu + \sigma$ and under the curve of the distribution $N(1, 5)$ is the complement of this probability to the entire area under that normal curve, i.e., $1 - .8413447 = .1586553$. Due to the symmetry of the normal distribution (see, e.g., Figure 5.6 or the formula of the normal pdf in Equation (5.8), and our earlier discussion in this chapter), it follows that the area under the normal curve and between $\mu - \sigma$ and $\mu + \sigma$ is $.8413447 - .1586553 = 0.6826894$, or just over 68% as mentioned above.

This percentage is actually correct in general for any normal distribution, and we just illustrated it here in a particular example using the distribution $N(1,5)$. A simple illustration of this general result, which is quite useful in empirical work, can be given as follows. Suppose one has administered a measure, such as an intelligence test, which is known to have (approximately) a normal distribution in a large group of students. What is the probability of picking at random a student with an IQ score being positioned no more than one standard deviation away from the mean? In other words, what is the probability of picking at random a student with a z-score smaller than one in absolute value?

This is the same as asking the earlier question in this section, viz., what is the area under the normal curve that is enclosed within one standard deviation from the mean. And the answer we first gave above is .68 (as shown for the general case in more advanced treatments, and demonstrated above for the distribution $N(1,5)$). That is, if one were to keep picking at random students from that large group, in the long run about two out of every three students will *not* have an IQ score that is more than one standard deviation higher or lower than the mean on this measure. (Usually IQ scores have a mean of 100 and a standard deviation of 15, as we indicated above.)

The discussion so far in this section dealt only with the question of what the area was under the pdf curve of a normal distribution and within one standard deviation from the mean. It can be similarly shown that the area under the normal curve and within two standard deviations from the mean is approximately 95%. We can illustrate this general result on our earlier example with the $N(1,5)$ distribution by using R as follows (output provided beneath command):

```
> pnorm(1+2*sqrt(5), 1, sqrt(5))
[1] 0.9772499
```

Once we have this area under the curve (up to two standard deviations below the mean), the area under the normal curve and within two standard deviations from the mean is calculated in this example with R simply as

```
> 0.9772499-(1-0.9772499)
[1] 0.9544998
```

Note that here we used R to conduct simple computations, such as the subtraction of the two obtained numbers. (We can of course use any of a number of other statistical software for the same goal.) That is, the area under the pdf curve of the normal distribution of interest and within two standard deviations from the mean is just above 95%. This percentage is valid not only in the presently considered example, but also in the general case of any normal distribution, as mentioned above.

Further, it can be generally shown that the area under the normal curve and within three standard deviations is just above 99%. In our current example with the distribution $N(1,5)$, we again obtain this area with R using the following two computational steps:

```
> pnorm(1+3*sqrt(5), 1, sqrt(5))
[1] 0.9986501
```

```
> 0.9986501 - (1-0.9986501)
[1] 0.9973002
```

For our earlier IQ example with repeated sampling from a large group of student IQ scores, these findings imply that in the long run about one out of 20 students would have an IQ score further away from the mean than two standard deviations, i.e., would have a z-score larger than 2 or smaller than -2. Further, about five out of 2,000 students would have a score further away than three standard deviations from the mean, i.e., a z-score larger than 3 or smaller than -3.

We stress that the general interpretations given in this section do not depend on a particular normal distribution but are valid for any considered normal distribution. This is because we did not refer in these interpretations to the mean and standard deviation of a particular normal distribution being assumed. Also, the last general finding shows that in a normal distribution nearly all scores lie within three standard deviations from the mean, i.e., have a z-score that is not larger than three in absolute value. Hence, unless the group studied is very large, one would be really surprised to find a score that far or even further away from the mean, i.e., with such a large or an even larger z-score in absolute value terms.

5.5. PERCENTILES OF THE NORMAL DISTRIBUTION

What proportion of scores that a normal RV could obtain may be expected to lie below (or above) a prespecified number? This type of question is of substantial interest when one is concerned with finding out, for instance, how high a given student's score on a test of interest is relative to the scores of the student's peers. For example, if someone has a score of 105 on an intelligence test, what is the percentage of scores among his or her peers that are higher than 105? Questions like these are also of particular relevance in the process of diagnosing possible learning difficulties or problems, as well as in many other empirical settings in the behavioral and social sciences.

As it turns out, such questions can be answered using the concept of a *percentile*. For a given normal distribution and proportion p $(0 < p < 1)$, the *100pth percentile* for this distribution is the score y with the property that $(100p)\%$ of the population values on this variable fall below y. For example, the 50th percentile, i.e., the $100(1/2)$th percentile, is the median of the distribution. As can be seen from Equation (5.8), and indicated earlier in this chapter, the median of a normal distribution is the same as its mean (since this distribution is symmetric around its mean, where its pdf attains its highest value, as mentioned before). Furthermore, the 25th percentile is the median of all scores below the mean, and the 75th percentile is the median of all scores above the mean. (See discussion of the boxplot and its lower and upper hinges in Chapter 3.)

We can readily use R to work out percentiles of particular distributions of interest. To this end, we utilize its command 'qnorm'. This command has also three "arguments," i.e., three numbers we need to give to R when employing it. The first argument is the probability or proportion p of concern. Once we have settled on which percentile we want to work out, this number becomes known. For instance, if we are interested in the 40th percentile, evidently $p = .4$. The second and third arguments are the mean and standard deviation of the normal distribution under consideration. That is, if we are interested in the $(100p)$th percentile for the $N(\mu, \sigma^2)$ distribution, the three arguments are p, μ, and σ, and are to be provided to R in this order.

We illustrate this discussion with the following two examples.

Example 5.1. Suppose an IQ test score has a distribution $N(100, 225)$ in a large group of third graders (population of interest). What is the score that cuts out to the right 5% of the area under the pdf of this distribution?

This question asks about the 95th percentile of the given normal distribution, since to the left of the requested number are 100% − 5% = 95% of the scores in the population of concern. We obtain this percentile with R as follows (the result is again given underneath the used command 'qnorm'):

```
> qnorm(.95, 100, 15)
[1] 124.6728
```

That is, if a student has a score of at least 125, he or she is among the top 5% of his or her peers in terms of IQ score on the test in question.

> **Example 5.2.** Consider a scale measuring anxiety in an elderly population that is known to follow approximately the normal distribution $N(40, 25)$. What is the highest score on this scale that would still be lower than the top 90% of the scores in the population?

Here we are interested in finding the 10th percentile of the distribution $N(40, 25)$. Using R with the command 'qnorm' yields (result given below command):

```
> qnorm(.1, 40, 5)
[1] 33.59224
```

That is, the sought score is 33. In other words, any anxiety score lower than 34 would have the property that at least 90% of the elderly population scores are higher than it.

5.6. USING PUBLISHED STATISTICAL TABLES TO WORK OUT NORMAL PROBABILITIES

An alternative to this software-based approach for working out percentiles is the following. As indicated earlier in the chapter in a more general context, if y is a standard normal RV, then $a + by$ is also a normal RV with mean a and standard deviation b, where a and b are prespecified constants. Hence, if for a given number p $(0<p<1)$ we are interested in the $100p$th percentile of the distribution $N(\mu, \sigma^2)$ with known mean and variance, all we need to do are the following two steps: First, find out what the $100p$th percentile is of the standard normal distribution. Second, multiply this percentile with σ and add μ. The result will be, according to the just cited general statement, the $100p$th percentile for the distribution $N(\mu, \sigma^2)$ of interest in the first place. Use of this approach to evaluation of percentiles of a normal distribution is substantially facilitated by the wide availability of the percentiles of the standard normal distribution, which essentially does step 1 of this procedure. In particular, tables with these percentiles are commonly provided in the appendixes to most introductory statistics textbooks. We do not pursue this topic further here, due to the wide availability of R and other statistical software, and we mention it in this final section of the chapter merely for historical reasons.

6

Random Sampling Distributions and the Central Limit Theorem

6.1. RANDOM SAMPLING DISTRIBUTION

Empirical studies conducted in the social and behavioral sciences are generally interested in examining phenomena in very large populations that cannot be completely accessed and exhaustively studied. For example, if a new teaching method showing fourth-grade children how to perform number division were developed and we wanted to compare it to an already established method, we cannot easily study the entire population of fourth graders taught by the new method. While somewhat conceivable, any attempt to study the entire population would be impractical if not impossible, excessively resource- and time-demanding, and for a number of reasons (to be expanded on later) just not worthwhile attempting—at least not currently. To resolve this problem, we usually resort to (i) taking a sample from a population of interest and (ii) studying each member of the sample. Thereby, it is necessary that the sample resemble (i.e., be representative of) the population of concern as well as possible, since otherwise our conclusions may well be incorrect if not misleading.

6.1.1. Random sample

The above-mentioned representativeness may be accomplished by taking a *random sample* from the population of interest, a concept we define more precisely later in this section. Ensuring sample representativeness is so important an issue that there is even a specific branch of statistics dealing with it, referred to as sampling theory (e.g., Lohr, 1997). Sampling theory is concerned in part with ways to draw samples that possess optimal properties so as to be as representative as possible of the population of interest (at a given sample size). Some of these ways include so-called clustered sampling, simple random sampling, systematic sampling, and stratified sampling. For the purposes of this introductory book, we will only be dealing with simple random samples. In the remainder of the book, therefore, whenever mention is made of a sample, we will presume that it is a simple random sample (see below for a more precise definition).

In certain circumstances in social and behavioral research, all subjects (units of analysis) from a population may indeed be exhaustively studied, as for instance when a census is conducted. Nevertheless, these are usually very expensive investigations that are infrequently or relatively rarely carried out. In this book, we will not be discussing them, but as mentioned will only be dealing with the case of studies that are based on simple random samples from large populations. As was done in some previous discussions, we will denote the number of subjects (units of analysis) in the population as N, and those in the sample as n. Usually, n is much smaller than N, which is assumed to be a finite number, however large it may be. In the special case that $n = N$, we are dealing with a census. Most of the time in contemporary behavioral and social science research, $n < N$, or in fact more likely $n << N$ (a symbol used to denote that n is much smaller than N).

Before we move on, we give a more precise definition of the concept of random sample, which is essential for the remainder of the book. A *sample* of n measurements (subjects, units of analysis) selected from a population under study is said to be a *random sample* if it has the same probability of being selected from the population as any other sample of the same size. That is, a random sample is a "draw" (selection) in a random fashion from a population under consideration. This implies that every subject in a population of interest is given an equal chance of being selected into the sample. Hence, a random sample is not characterized by any systematic feature that would make it different from any other possible draw from the studied population, which draw would consist of the same number of subjects (measurements, units of analysis). We mention in passing that in sampling theory, a random sample defined in this way is usually referred to as "simple random sample." (We will use the reference "random sample" throughout the remainder of the book.)

A random sample may be obtained using tables with random numbers that are commonly provided in many statistics texts (e.g., King & Minium, 2003). Alternatively, one may wish to use tabled values obtained by using a computerized random number generator. Either approach would be feasible if both N and n were not very large (especially as far as N is concerned), and there is a listing available of all population members from which the sample is selected using such a table. A table with random numbers has the property that any number in it is random—i.e., any one of its numbers can be chosen as a starting point in the search for elements from the population to be drawn into the sample. Thereby, one can move in any direction any number of steps without violating the property of the next chosen number in this way being random as well. For much larger studies this process is usually automated, and its details are beyond the confines of this introductory book (e.g., Kish, 1997). Thus, as mentioned above, for the remainder of the book we assume that a random sample from a studied population is available to us, which we can proceed with in our analytic and modeling activities.

6.1.2. Sampling distribution

If we consider taking a random sample of subjects from a studied population and administer to them a particular measure (test, scale), such as an intelligence test or a depression scale, what would be the mean of the resulting IQ scores or depression scores? We cannot answer this question before we actually carry out these activities and average the individual scores obtained thereby. Even if we knew what the mean was in the population, we have no way of predicting with certainty what the mean would be of the IQ scores in any random sample of size n that we could take from the population (when $n < N$). Similarly, we could not predict with certainty the value of the mode of these scores, their median, or any other descriptive index we discussed earlier in this book.

As discussed in Chapter 3, any such descriptive index obtained from a sample would be a good example of a statistic. As will be recalled, a *statistic* is a function of the scores on a given variable of interest that are obtained in a sample of subjects from a population under consideration. All descriptive indexes we considered before—such as the measures of central tendency and variability—are therefore statistics. This is because they are functions of the studied variable values in the sample—i.e., their values result after carrying out certain computational activities on the scores in the available sample, such as summing, averaging, squaring, and so on.

This discussion demonstrates that before we actually obtain the sample we cannot know the value in it of any statistic of interest. Hence, a statistic is itself a random variable (RV). Indeed, its value becomes known only after a sample is obtained from a studied population. This value is typically referred to as a "realization" of the RV. Therefore, before analyzing correspondingly the sample data, we can only consider a statistic of interest as a RV.

However, as we discussed earlier in the book and demonstrated in a number of examples, a RV has a probability distribution. For a given statistic, such as the mean, say, we call its probability distribution the *sampling distribution* of that statistic. Hence, the sampling distribution of a given statistic is the distribution of the set of all possible values that it can obtain across all possible samples at a given size (n), which we could get from the population of interest. This set of values depends obviously on the size n of the samples that we take thereby. Therefore, any statistic has a sampling distribution for any given sample size that may be of interest.

In order to look at the concept of a sampling distribution from a slightly different point of view, let us suppose that we are given a population we are interested in—e.g., all second graders in a particular state. Let us also assume that we are concerned with a test of writing ability for all second graders. We could think of each student in the population as having a score on this test, which score however we unfortunately do not yet know. In a sense, this score is hidden from us, unless of course we actually studied with the test the entire population—which as indicated before, is something that would most of the time not be done in real-life empirical research. Next suppose we decide to draw a sample of $n = 50$ students from this population—i.e., we fix the size of the sample. We observe that there are very many possible samples of this size that we could obtain. For example, if the population contained 100,000 children, it can be shown mathematically that there are in total ('$\times$' is used next to denote multiplication)

(6.1) $$100000!/(50! \times 99950!)$$

possible samples. Although this is clearly an extremely large number, we could of course readily compute it, out of curiosity, using R with the following command (result is given beneath it):

```
> choose(100000, 50)
[1] 3.247911e+185
```

This resultant number approximately equals 3×10^{185}, which is a number written with 185 zeros. We also need to keep in mind that since we are interested in obtaining a random sample, any one of these approximately 3×10^{185} samples is equally likely to be drawn.

Now suppose we were interested only in the mean of each sample drawn. In other words, suppose we were only interested in the random variable (RV) $\bar{y}$, which is defined as the average of the writing ability scores y in a random sample (see also Chapter 3). It is clear then that depending on the selected sample, the realization of this RV $\bar{y}$ in it could be any one of up to about 3×10^{185} distinct possible numbers—a mean for each of the possible samples. (Of course, we do realize that not all of these mean numbers need to be different from one another, at least in general.) Next consider these 3×10^{185} scores $\bar{y}_j$ ($j = 1,...$, 3.247911×10^{185}, i.e., one for each sample) as representing themselves a set of numerical data. Denote this set by $Y = \{\bar{y}_j$ for $j = 1, 2,...$, $3.247911 \times 10^{185}\}$; we stress that Y contains approximately 3×10^{185} elements that as noted above need not all be distinct from one another. This set of data, Y, like any set of numbers, has a distribution, which as previously illustrated we know how to obtain—e.g., using the software R as discussed in Chapter 2. This distribution is referred to as the *random sampling distribution* (RSD) of the RV under consideration here, viz., the RV defined as the mean $\bar{y}$ at the sample size of 50. More generally, the RSD is defined as the distribution of a RV under consideration—e.g., a statistic—across all possible random samples of a given size from the studied population. If we chose a different number as a sample size—for example, if we chose $n = 100$—then along exactly the same lines we see that there is also a random sampling distribution of the resulting set of sample averages across all possible samples of size 100. This would be the RSD of the mean $\bar{y}$ at a sample size 100. And so on—for any given sample size n ($n < N$), there is a RSD of the mean $\bar{y}$ at that sample size.

We chose in the preceding discussion the mean as the object of our considerations mostly because of its popularity in empirical behavioral and social research. In fact, we could just as easily have chosen any other statistic (i.e., function of the sample data) to consider—e.g., the variance, standard deviation, range, and so on. Hence, there is a random sampling distribution, at a given sample size, for any statistic that we may be willing to consider in an empirical setting.

A major gain in adopting the concept of RSD, as we have done in this chapter, is the following realization: since the values of a statistic of interest, such as the mean, across all possible samples with a fixed size need not be the same, there is inherent variability in essentially any statistic that we could consider in a given sample. (Of course, there would be no such variability if a particular constant were chosen as a special case of a statistic, but we exclude this trivial case from consideration.) This emphasizes the fact that the value of any statistic that we could obtain in a given sample from a population under consideration, *need not repeat itself in any other sample from that population*, which we might have as well taken (drawn or selected). That is, the specific score we obtain on a statistic of concern in a given sample from a studied population is only one of potentially very many possible scores that one could obtain with that statistic had another sample of the same size from that population been drawn.

6.2. THE RANDOM SAMPLING DISTRIBUTION OF THE MEAN

The random sampling distribution (RSD) of the mean, or sample average, $\bar{y}$ plays a special role in statistics and its applications. The reason is that it is the subject of a particular and essential result that has widespread applicability, the so-called central limit theorem. (We will be particularly concerned with this theorem in Section 6.3.) For now, let us focus again on the previous observation that any statistic we might be interested in a given sample from a studied population can be seen as a random variable (RV). As a RV, that statistic has a probability distribution and it depends on the size of the sample in an interesting way. Yet what does this dependency actually look like?

Before we address this question in more detail, let us consider some of its aspects, specifically as far as the RSD of the mean is concerned. In particular, let us determine what is the actual central tendency and variability for this RSD. That is, what are the mean and variance for the RSD of the sample average?

6.2.1. Mean and variance of the random sampling distribution of the mean

In order to answer these questions, let us first step back and expand on some related important concepts. To obtain the mean of a probability distribution (random variable), it greatly helps to reconsider what that distribution or RV is composed of. We noted earlier that the RSD of the sample average is the distribution—across samples of a given size—of the averages of the values in all possible samples at that size from a specified population. Hence, the mean of the random sampling distribution of the sample averages (at a given sample size) is actually the mean of all sample averages.

However, each of these averages is itself a random variable, since we do not know its value before the pertinent sample is drawn. An important result in statistics, which for ease of presentation we will not be concerned with mathematically deriving here, is that the mean of a sum of random variables is the sum of their means (e.g., King & Minium, 2003). That is, if Y_1, Y_2,..., Y_m are m given RVs, then the mean of their sum, $\mu_{Y_1 + Y_2 + ... + Y_m}$, is equal to the sum of their means μ_{Y_1}, μ_{Y_2},... ,μ_{Y_m}:

(6.2) $$\mu_{Y_1 + Y_2 + ... + Y_m} = \mu_{Y_1} + \mu_{Y_2} + ... + \mu_{Y_m}.$$

Using this result, it can be shown that if for a given random variable of interest y we denote its population mean as μ_y, then the mean of the statistic defined as the sample average (at a given selected sample size), $\mu_{\bar{y}}$, is in fact equal to μ_y, that is,

(6.3) $$\mu_{\bar{y}} = \mu_y.$$

In other words, the average of the sample averages is the same as the population mean (e.g., Roussas, 1997). Similarly, it can be shown that the variance of this statistic is

(6.4) $$\sigma_{\bar{y}}^2 = \sigma_y^2 / n.$$

That is, while the mean of the RV defined as the sample average (at a given sample size) is the same as the population mean, the variance of this RV is n times smaller than the population variance of the original variable y of interest. In other words, taking the average of a sample reduces the original variance n times, where n is the size of the sample in question. Therefore, the sample average as a random variable is much less varied—in particular with large samples—than any individual observation or score on the variable of interest. Specifically, the larger the sample, the less varied is the sample average relative to any individual observation (score).

Since the mean of the random variable defined as the sample average is the same as that of the original variable of interest y, from the preceding discussion it follows that the higher the sample size is, the closer (probabilistically) the sample average to the population mean of y. Hence, whenever one is interested in the population mean of a RV—e.g., the score on a test of arithmetic ability—taking a large sample from the population of concern will render in its average a score that has a distribution with an important property. Specifically, this distribution will be quite compactly positioned around the population mean of that variable.

This result, which is based on Equations (6.3) and (6.4), is the reason why there is so much interest in statistics and its applications in the sample mean. As this result suggests, one can have quite some confidence in the mean of a large sample from a studied population, as an index informing about the population mean on a variable of interest.

We refer to the sample average in a given sample as an *estimate of the population mean*, and to the statistic sample average (outside of the context of a particular sample) as an *estimator of the population mean*. We reiterate the earlier noted difference—the former is a number, the latter is effectively a formula or a statistic in general, as we indicated earlier in the book. We obtain an estimate when we substitute empirical data into that estimator formula.

6.2.2. Standard error of the mean

Equation (6.4) can be alternatively represented as

$$(6.5) \qquad\qquad \sigma_{\bar{y}} = \sigma_y / \sqrt{n},$$

which results after taking the square root (positive) from both sides of Equation (6.4). Equation (6.5) states that the standard deviation of the random sampling distribution of the mean (at a given sample size, n) is the standard deviation of the original random variable of interest divided by the square root of the sample size.

It is instructive to note here that Equation (6.5) has also obtained considerable prominence in statistics and its applications. The reason for this attention is that it represents a measure of the variability of the sample means around the population mean, but evaluated in the same units of measurement as the original units—i.e., in the units of measurement underlying the original variable y of concern. The right-hand side of Equation (6.5) is also frequently referred to as the *standard error of the mean* (i.e., the standard error of $\bar{y}$), particularly when provided in output generated with most statistical software.

More generally, when one estimates other unknown quantities that describe particular features of distributions of interest, *the standard error of the estimate (estimator) is the standard deviation of the random sampling distribution of the estimate (estimator) across repeated sampling at the given sample size from the studied population.* These unknown quantities are themselves of particular interest, and as mentioned earlier are typically called *parameters.* Perhaps the most well-known examples of parameters are the mean, standard deviation, and variance, but there are many more that could also just as easily be considered. For instance, the inter-quartile range, the range, the median, and the mode of a given variable in a studied population are all parameters characterizing its distribution.

As we mentioned before, in a given sample the parameters are evaluated (i.e., estimated) using appropriate functions of the sample data, viz., corresponding statistics. The remainder of this book deals with a number of such statistics that are used as estimators of important parameters usually of special interest in applications of statistics in the social and behavioral sciences.

6.3. THE CENTRAL LIMIT THEOREM

Section 6.2 emphasized the importance of the mean and variance of the random sampling distribution of the mean. While these are two key aspects of this distribution, they do not inform us about what its shape actually is. In particular, they do not tell us whether that distribution is symmetric or not, or whether it is particularly peaked and/or flat. In other words, these mean and variance quantities provide us with no practically useful information about the skewness and kurtosis of the distribution (i.e., the third and fourth moments of the distribution). The latter queries are responded to by an essential result in statistics known as the central limit theorem (CLT).

To discuss the CLT, we will use again the concept of random sampling distribution (RSD). To this end, let us consider the RSD of the mean (average) of the scores on a variable of concern in a given sample of size n from a studied population. Next, suppose we begin to change n—initially consider a fairly small n, then a larger n, then an even larger n, and so on, each time increasing n. Would there be any particular effect of this successive increase in sample size upon the RSD of the mean? In particular, as n becomes larger and larger, how does the shape of this distribution change, if it does at all? We consider these issues in greater detail below.

6.3.1. The central limit theorem as a large-sample statement

As indicated above, the answer to the last-posed question is provided by the central limit theorem (CLT). The CLT states that as n increases, the random sampling distribution of the sample average (mean) approximates better and better a normal distribution. (This will be the case as long as the original variable distribution has a finite variance, as is assumed throughout the book.)

We note that while Equations (6.3) and (6.4) are valid for any sample size n, the CLT is a limiting statement. In other words, the CLT is a statement that is valid as n increases without any limit or bound. Statements that hold when sample size increases without bound are commonly called *asymptotic* or large-sample statements. That is, Equations (6.3) and (6.4) are valid for any n—whether fixed or increasing without limit—but the CLT is valid only when n is very large (theoretically, beyond any finite number).

In other words, Equations (6.3) and (6.4) are finite sample statements, while the CLT is an asymptotic statement—i.e., one that obtains validity for very large sample sizes. Thereby, at any n, small or large, the mean and variance of the RSD of the sample average (mean) are provided by Equations (6.3) and (6.4). To put it differently, the mean and variance properties reflected in (6.3) and (6.4) are valid for any sample size—regardless of whether the sample size is small or large, fixed or increasing—while the CLT is a statement that is only concerned with the shape of the RSD of the mean for very large sample sizes.

6.3.2. When is normality obtained for a finite sample?

It may be interesting to consider whether—and if so, when—the normal distribution statement in the CLT is valid at a finite sample. We observed that while the CLT makes such a statement for an increasing (as opposed to finite) sample size, this last question asks about the magnitude of a finite sample size at which normality can be claimed for the RSD of the mean.

In order for normality to hold at a fixed, finite sample size, the distribution of the original variable y of interest need itself be normal to begin with. That is, if we consider the RSD of the mean at a fixed sample size n for a given normally distributed RV, y, then this RSD is normal for any size of n—not just for n being very large as stated by the CLT. Thereby, Equations (6.4) and (6.5) hold also for any finite value of n, no matter how large or small.

6.3.3. How large a sample size is sufficient for the central limit theorem to be valid?

The CLT does not require any particular form of the distribution of the original variable y. That is, y could be discrete or continuous, symmetric or not, and as long as the sample size n is sufficiently large the random sampling distribution of the sample average (mean) will be very close to normal.

Yet how large does the sample size n really need to be, in order for the RSD of the sample mean to be practically indistinguishable from normal? This depends on the degree to which the distribution of the original RV y is non-normal (i.e., on the extent to which this initial distribution deviates from normal). As we mentioned earlier, if this deviation is nonexistent, i.e., if y is normal to begin with, then the RSD of the sample mean is normal at any n, with the mean and variance of the RSD being given by Equations (6.4) and (6.5). However, if the distribution of the RV y is very nonnormal to start with—e.g., discrete, such as binomial—then n may need to be relatively large in order for the RSD of the mean to approximate the normal distribution well.

Numerous simulation studies have been conducted and published in the statistics literature suggesting that if the distribution of the initially considered RV y is symmetric, the CLT may obtain practical relevance already at $n < 30$. Accordingly, if the distribution is not deviating a great deal from the normal and is nonsymmetric, then an n around 30 or slightly above may be needed for the CLT to obtain practical relevance. When the distribution of y is very nonnormal, then a sample size well beyond 30 may be needed in order for the CLT to obtain relevance.

Let us now turn to an example to illustrate the preceding discussion about the CLT.

Example 6.1: Suppose that a patient's diastolic blood pressure is normally distributed with a mean $\mu = 85$ mm and variance $\sigma^2 = 16$ mm^2. Assuming we took four measurements of the patient's blood pressure within a several-hour time period on a given day, what is the probability that the average of these measurements will be under 90 mm, thus indicating the patient does not have high blood pressure? (This example assumes high blood pressure is indicated when diastolic blood pressure is above 90 mm.)

Here we are interested in the RSD of the sample average (mean). Let us denote by y the diastolic blood pressure at a given point in time—within the few hours that this patient was measured—which is obviously a RV. Then $\bar{y}$ would be the mean of the four blood pressure measurements taken on the patient. According to the earlier discussion in this section, since the initial variable of concern, y, is normally distributed, so is also its mean, $\bar{y}$. That is, the RSD of the mean is normal even though we have in this case only a sample of $n = 4$ observations. Equations (6.3) and (6.5) give the mean of this RSD as $\mu_{\bar{y}} = \mu_y$ = 85 and standard deviation of

$$\sigma_{\bar{y}} = \sigma_y / \sqrt{4} = 4 / 2 = 2.$$

We now need to work out the probability of the event $E = \{ \bar{y} < 90 \}$ (using curly brackets to denote event defined within them). To this end, we can use R as in the preceding chapter, since we actually know the mean and variance of the normal distribution of relevance as given here, viz., correspondingly 85 and 2:

```
> pnorm(90, 85, 2)
[1] 0.9937903
```

That is, the probability of the mean being under 90 is .994 (rounded off to third decimal place). Hence, even four repeated measurements under the currently considered circumstances give a fairly high probability of concluding someone does not suffer from high blood pressure, when they in fact do not have this condition. (This is of course based on the assumption that the pressure measurements are normally distributed to begin with, an assumption that we made at the beginning of our example discussion.) We thus conclude that the specificity of these diastolic blood pressure measurements is fairly high for the current example settings.

6.3.4. The central limit theorem for sums of random variables

The CLT can be extended to a number of different sample statistics. For instance, there is a version of the CLT for the sample median, and a version of the CLT for the sample standard deviation. These versions represent fairly complicated statements, and their specifics go well beyond the scope of this book. In the remainder of the book, many of the statistics that we will be dealing with will be either averages or sums of random variables—the observations available from samples. As it turns out, there is also a version of the CLT for sums of variables, which we will then be referring to.

To introduce this particular CLT version, we first note that as indicated before, each random sample of n measurements can be considered itself being a set of n random variables. In fact, each of these measurements, before being collected, is a RV in its own right. Indeed, before the variable(s) of interest is evaluated on each element of the sample—i.e., prior to us taking a look at the sample data—we do not know the values of the measurements in the sample. Therefore, we can treat the sample measurements as random variables.

Denote the sample scores as usual $y_1, y_2, \ldots, y_n$, and their sum $y_1 + y_2 + \ldots + y_n$ as Σy. We stress that $y_1, y_2, \ldots, y_n$ as well as their sum denoted for simplicity Σy are all RVs.

Under these circumstances, the CLT for sums of random variables makes the following statement (e.g., Ott & Longnecker, 2010). If $y_1, y_2, \ldots, y_n$ represent observations on a studied variable from a population with a mean μ and finite variance σ, then the mean and standard deviation of their sum are correspondingly:

(i) $\mu_{\Sigma y} = n\mu$, and

(ii) $\sigma_{\Sigma y} = \sqrt{n}\sigma$.

In addition, when the sample size n is large, the RSD of Σy will be approximately normal (with the approximation improving as n increases). If the population distribution is normal, then the RSD of Σy is exactly normal for any finite sample size n.

We emphasize that here we are concerned with a different RSD than the one introduced earlier in this chapter. Specifically, in this subsection we are dealing with the RSD of the sum of random variables, rather than with the RSD of the sample average.

6.3.5. Revisiting the random sampling distribution concept

As we have emphasized on several occasions in this chapter and book, we use sample statistics to evaluate—or obtain an idea about, loosely speaking—the corresponding unknown population quantities of interest, referred to as parameters. This process of evaluation was called earlier *estimation*, and the results obtained were referred to as *estimates* of the population parameters. For example, we use the sample mean to estimate the population mean. Similarly, we use the sample variance or standard deviation to estimate the population variance or standard deviation, respectively. Also, we use the sample median to estimate the population median. We emphasize that the population parameters are intrinsically unknown (unless of course we observe the entire population, which would rarely be the case in most empirical research situations). We make here the important observation, however, that even after we estimate these parameters based on a sample, no matter how large the sample size, strictly speaking *their population values still remain unknown* (unless of course the sample is identical to the population, a case excluded from consideration here). We do have their estimates then, however, which give us some approximate idea what the magnitude of the values of the population parameters could likely be.

Since the population parameters will remain unknown, the natural question that arises at this point is how good the sample estimates are as quantities informing us about the unknown population parameters. The concept of the random sampling distribution (RSD) for a given statistic can be of particular help in answering this question with regard to the pertinent parameter. Specifically, the RSD tells us about the variability of the sample estimates of this parameter across repeated sampling from the population of interest (at the given sample size). If we know in addition some properties of the RSD—e.g., that its mean coincides with the population parameter of interest—then we can make certain probabilistic statements about ranges of plausible values for the corresponding population parameter.

How these statements will be specifically arrived at is the topic of subsequent chapters. We can however mention here that if the RSD is on average centered on the population parameter and is in addition a distribution with a relatively small variance, we would expect that most of its values—across repeated sampling at a given size from the population—would be close to the population parameter. For example, we already know from our earlier discussion in this chapter that the mean of the RSD of the sample mean equals the population mean μ_y, and that the standard deviation of this RSD is $\sigma_y / \sqrt{n}$. This means that the RSD of the sample average is "centered" on the population mean, μ_y, and that with large samples the variability of the sample mean will be very limited. Hence, if a relatively large sample is available from a studied population, the sample mean will have fairly high probability of being close to the population mean. How this probability could be specifically evaluated will be the topic of later chapters.

6.3.6. An application of the central limit theorem

We mentioned earlier in this chapter that the CLT is a statement that does not restrict the original variable distribution (i.e., the population distribution of the studied variable y). Hence, the CLT also applies when this distribution is even binomial. Such an instance of a binomial distribution would be the probability of k correct answers ("successes") on an algebra test question in a class of students, each with the same probability to correctly solve it and working independent of one another. Let us denote this probability by π. Using the CLT, it follows that with large samples the distribution of the number of correct responses will approximate the normal distribution with an appropriate mean and variance. To make this statement more precise, let us denote by $y_1, y_2,..., y_n$ the results obtained by the n students representing a sample from a studied population. That is, each of these random variables obtains the score of one if the corresponding student has correctly solved the problem and zero otherwise. Then the sum of these random variables, Σy, is the number of correct responses in the sample.

We now recall that, as discussed earlier in this section, the CLT is valid also for sums of random variables. In particular, we stated before that with large samples Σy is approximately normal with a mean $n\mu_y$ and standard deviation $\sqrt{n}\sigma_y$. As indicated in Chapter 5, however, $\mu_y = \pi$ and $\sigma_y = \pi(1 - \pi)$ for the binomial variable in question. Hence, for a large sample, the number of successes (in a series of independent trials with the same probability of success in each) is approximately normal with a mean equal to $n\pi$, and standard deviation $n\pi(1 - \pi)$. In Chapter 5, we also mentioned that this normal approximation is quite good when $n\pi$ and $n(1 - \pi)$ exceed 20 (see also Agresti & Finlay, 2009). This will be the case with moderately large samples if the probability of success is neither very small nor very large. This approximation can be used to work out probabilities related to the binomial distribution (see Chapter 5).

6.4. ASSESSING THE NORMALITY ASSUMPTION FOR A POPULATION DISTRIBUTION

The normal distribution is very convenient for many purposes in the behavioral and social sciences. In addition, this distribution has been also extensively studied. Its properties are well understood and examined, and are thus available to researchers in cases where they are dealing with distributions that are normal, or approximately so, in studied populations. For this reason, it is important to have easily applicable ways to ascertain whether a distribution of a random variable under consideration is normal.

How could one find out, however, whether the distribution of a RV (e.g., a statistic) in question is normal in a population of concern? There is a relatively straightforward graphical procedure that allows one to assess whether a distribution can be relatively well approximated by a normal distribution, which we describe in this section. To this end, suppose the random sample consists of the n observations $y_1, y_2, \ldots, y_n$. In order to apply this graphical procedure, we need to first rank order them (this can be done easily with R or using any other available statistical software). Denote by $y_{(1)} \leq y_{(2)} \leq \ldots \leq y_{(n)}$ the rank-ordered sequence of original scores in ascending order. For instance, if we have the following sample of obtained anxiety scores,

(6.6)   22, 23, 28, 29, 25, 17,

then their rank-ordered sequence is obviously

(6.7)   17 < 22 < 23 < 25 < 28 < 29,

or, in other words,

(6.8) $y_{(1)} = 17, y_{(2)} = 22, \ldots, \text{and } y_{(6)} = 29.$

In a sample of size n, for the purposes of graphical examination of normality, $y_{(1)}$ is treated as the $[(1 - .5)/n]$th percentile, $y_{(2)}$ as the $[(2 - .5)/n]$th percentile,..., and $y_{(n)}$ as the $[(n - .5)/n]$th percentile. We stress that these are all sample percentiles.

If the distribution from which the sample came is normal, it can be argued that each one of these percentiles should be close to its corresponding percentile from that normal distribution, denoted $z_{.5/n}, z_{1.5/n},..., z_{(n-.5)/n}$, respectively. Hence, if we graphically represent the points $(z_{.5/n}, y_{(1)}), (z_{1.5/n}, y_{(2)}),...$, and $(z_{(n-.5)/n}, y_{(n)})$, they should fall closely along a line in case the population distribution is indeed normal. Whether or not this is the case on the graph, represents a simple graphical procedure for ascertaining normality. We will often refer to this type of graph in subsequent chapters and so it is useful to assign it a particular name, with which it is also quite well known in the literature.

Definition: The graph of the points $(z_{.5/n}, y_{(1)}), (z_{1.5/n}, y_{(2)}),..., (z_{n-.5/n}, y_{(n)})$, is called *normal probability plot* (NPP).

The construction of a NPP is readily accomplished with R. To this end, one can use the command 'qqnorm(.)', whereby one gives within parentheses the array of numbers that make up the available sample. We illustrate this activity with the following example.

Example 6.2: The following 20 scores from an intelligence test (referred to as IQ scores below) are obtained on a sample from a studied population of elderly adults:

89 92 121 100 91 94 128 84 84 101 93 105 110 67 111 104 102 108 116 87

Could one consider as plausible the claim that the distribution of this text is normal in the studied population?

First we need to read into R this sequence of scores and create thereby an array (set) of scores, denoted x below, which is to be used subsequently with the command 'qqnorm' in order to produce the NPP. As mentioned earlier in the book, the creation of this array is easily accomplished with the command

```
> x = c(89  92 121 100  91  94 128  84  84 101  93 105 110  67 111 104  102
108 116 87)
```

Once the data are read in this way, we obtain the NPP as follows:

```
> qqnorm(x)
```

which yields the graph displayed in Figure 6.1.

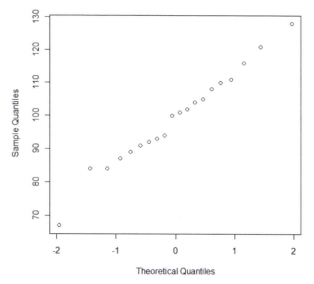

FIGURE 6.1.
Normal probability plot for 20 IQ scores.

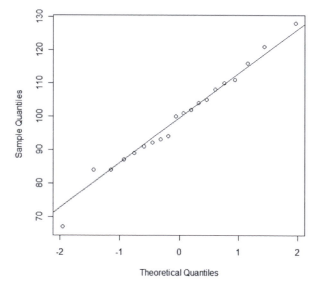

FIGURE 6.2.
Normal probability plot with superimposed line for the above 20 IQ scores.

From Figure 6.1, it would appear that the scores approximately fall along a diagonal line in this NPP. Such a judgment can be facilitated using the command 'qqline', which will superimpose a line upon this set of points:

```
> qqline(x)
```

which produces for the above set of 20 IQ scores the plot in Figure 6.2. From Figure 6.2, it seems clear that the deviations from the line are not large enough to warrant a claim of nonnormality, given the relatively limited sample size of $n = 20$. (It would be reasonable to expect some nonnormal appearance with such a relatively small sample—e.g., Raykov & Marcoulides, 2008.) Therefore, it may be suggested that the normality assumption is plausible for the population of test scores from which the sample of the 20 IQ scores in this example came.

While we realize that there is a certain degree of subjectivity involved in assessing normality using the outlined simple graphical procedure in this section, a number of more advanced methods have also been proposed in the literature (e.g., see Marcoulides & Heshberger, 1997; Roussas, 1997). These methods provide ways to examine more objectively a claim that a given sample of scores came from a population following a normal distribution.

7

Inferences about Single Population Means

7.1. POPULATION PARAMETERS

The previous chapters in the book focused on various concepts dealing mainly with descriptive statistics. As we mentioned earlier, however, there is another branch of statistics, called *inferential statistics* (IS), that is of particular relevance when one is interested in drawing conclusions about populations but typically cannot study each member of them. In such cases, all one has access to are samples obtained from the populations of interest. It is under such circumstances that IS becomes especially helpful for making particular generalizations. This is because the main objective of inferential statistics is to make inferences about studied populations using information from the available samples. Specifically, populations of concern in behavioral and social research are usually characterized by numerical indexes that are generally unknown, called *parameters*. For example, as noted before, the mean, mode, proportion, variance, and standard deviation are all parameters. Most problems that IS deals with are at least related to if not focused on inferences about one or more parameters of specifically studied population(s). As an illustration of this introductory discussion, let us consider the following two examples.

> **Example 7.1**: Consider a test of reading ability for second graders that is administered at the beginning of the academic year in a given US state. Its population mean, denoted μ, is unknown, and we are interested in making inferences about this parameter, i.e., about the average reading ability score in this state's population of second graders.

> **Example 7.2**: Let π denote the proportion of scores on a reading ability test for elementary school students in a particular state, which are below a standard that is used to designate need of remedial assistance. This proportion, π, is also a parameter, and one may well be interested in drawing conclusions about it.

Once we have identified population parameters of interest, the next important question is how to obtain a good indication about each of them using empirical data. That is, how can we effectively make inferences about these unknown parameters in the populations under consideration, by using data from available samples that typically are small portions or subsets from these populations? These are the issues that will be addressed in the next sections of this chapter and again in later parts of the book.

7.2. PARAMETER ESTIMATION AND HYPOTHESIS TESTING

There are two general types of methods for making inferences about population parameters, namely, estimation and hypothesis testing. *Estimation* is concerned with answering questions about the value of a population parameter. In contrast to estimation, *hypothesis testing* is mainly concerned with determining whether a population parameter fulfills a certain condition. For example, if we are primarily interested in evaluating the population mean μ of reading ability in the population of second graders in the state of California in a given year, then we are concerned with estimation of the parameter μ. Alternatively, if we are attempting to determine whether the proportion of students in the state of Michigan who are in need of remedial assistance is below 10%, then we can be interested in hypothesis testing. Thus, it should be evident from these simple examples that estimation and hypothesis testing have different concerns. Additionally, they also use largely different procedures to accomplish their aims. Their unifying theme, however, is the use of information in available samples for making conclusions (inferences) about population parameters that are unknown.

7.3. POINT AND INTERVAL ESTIMATION OF THE MEAN

When we are interested in estimating the mean μ on a variable of interest in a population under consideration, there are two avenues that can be pursued. One of them is to seek a single value that is in some sense most informative about the mean. This value is called a *point estimate* of the mean. The second path is to seek a range of plausible values for the population mean μ. This range is called an *interval estimate* of the mean or *confidence interval* (CI) for the mean. We discuss these two possibilities in turn next.

7.3.1. Point estimation

As we already indicated earlier in the book, we can use the sample average as an estimate of the population mean. That is, if $y_1, y_2, ..., y_n$ are the sample observations on a random variable y of interest, then this estimate is

(7.1) $\hat{\mu} = (y_1 + y_2 + ... + y_n)/n = \bar{y}.$

Equation (7.1) in fact defines a point estimator of the population mean μ, as we mentioned previously. In other words, Equation (7.1) provides a generally valid algorithm, or procedure, of how to obtain a point estimate of the mean based on a given sample. We furnish this estimate by substituting into its right-hand side the individual observations obtained in the available sample. The sample average in Equation (7.1) seems to be a very reasonable estimate in many situations, as long as there are no "outliers" like data entry errors or extremely large/small observations that do not belong to the population of interest. However, the right-hand side of Equation (7.1) does not indicate how good the resulting mean estimate really is. In particular, we do not know how close the value of $\hat{\mu}$ in a given sample is to the population parameter μ that is the value of actual interest.

More generally, we can certainly say that since any selected sample is not going to be identical to the population, a sample average is in general not going to be exactly equal (other than by sheer coincidence) to the population mean. Since we can in effect assume that an estimate is not going to be equal to the population mean (no matter how large the sample—but presumed smaller than the population, of course), the critical question is *how far away* $\hat{\mu}$ *is from* μ. The quantity μ is the one of real concern in this whole development, and we unmistakably observe that the last question is a fundamental query about the quality of estimation. In fact, this question applies to any estimate (estimator) of any parameter, and not just that of the mean as considered here. There is no doubt that a sample estimate does provide information about the population parameter. However, since we are also pretty certain that they will not equal each other, a critical question about estimation quality in empirical research pertains to how far the estimate is from that parameter.

7.3.2. Interval estimation

The last-mentioned question is effectively tied to the magnitude of the distance between a sample estimate and the population parameter it evaluates. Such an important question concerning distance can be addressed using interval estimation. The essence of *interval estimation* is the construction of a range of plausible values about the population parameter, which is more generally referred to as *confidence interval* (CI). This confidence interval is constructed by using information obtained from the sample. Considering in particular the case of estimating the mean, this question in essence asks about an interval that contains plausible values for the mean of a random variable of concern in the studied population.

We can construct such a CI by using the central limit theorem (CLT) introduced in the previous chapter. Accordingly, for large n (perhaps at least 30 or so), the sample average $\bar{y}$ is approximately normal, with a mean being the population mean μ and standard error equal to $\sigma/\sqrt{n}$ (see detailed discussion provided in Chapter 6). Although the CLT will be frequently used throughout the remainder of this chapter, for ease of presentation we initially assume that the population standard deviation σ is known. In a subsequent chapter, we will give up this somewhat unrealistic assumption.

As was mentioned in Chapter 6, the area under the normal curve and within two standard deviations from the mean is approximately 95% of the entire area under that curve, which is conventionally assumed to be one. Hence, if we repeatedly sample from a studied population, the interval $(\mu - 2\sigma/\sqrt{n}, \mu + 2\sigma/\sqrt{n})$ will enclose approximately 95% of all resulting sample averages. As it turns out, there is in fact a closely related way of using the CLT for the purpose of interval estimation of the population mean μ. The reason is that the CLT asserts for a large sample size n the normality of the sample average, namely the fact that $\bar{y} \sim N(\mu, \sigma^2/n)$.

With this in mind, let us now try to find such a value c, for which a symmetric interval around the population mean would enclose precisely 95% of the sample averages $\bar{y}$. That is, we are seeking a value c for which the following probability holds

$$(7.2) \qquad \Pr(\mu - c \cdot \sigma/\sqrt{n} < \bar{y} < \mu + c \cdot \sigma/\sqrt{n}) = .95,$$

where "Pr" denotes probability (a dot is used in Equation (7.2) to denote multiplication; see also Chapter 4). We note that the left-hand side of Equation (7.2) actually can be slightly algebraically modified by subtracting μ and dividing by $\sigma/\sqrt{n}$ all three sides of the double inequality contained in it, leading to

$$(7.3) \qquad \Pr[-c < (\bar{y} - \mu)/(\sigma/\sqrt{n}) < c] = .95.$$

As was discussed in Chapter 6, the quantity $(\bar{y} - \mu)/(\sigma/\sqrt{n})$ is actually the z-score pertaining to the sample average $\bar{y}$. According to the CLT, with large samples this z-score is normally distributed and thereby follows the standard normal distribution:

$$(7.4) \qquad z = (\bar{y} - \mu)/(\sigma/\sqrt{n}) \sim N(0,1).$$

Hence, the sought value of c is in fact that value whose mirror image around 0, viz., $-c$, cuts off 2.5% to the left of the area under the standard normal curve. As will be recalled from Chapter 5, since the pdf of the standard normal distribution is symmetric, it follows that the two numbers c and $-c$, which are mirror images of each other, cut together 5% away from that area. That is, the area below $-c$ and above c is 5% of the entire area under the standard normal curve. Due to this property of c, we can readily use the software R and specifically its function 'qnorm' (see Chapter 4) to work out its specific value as follows (with result furnished by R given immediately under this command):

```
> qnorm(.025, 0, 1)
[1] -1.959964
```

That is, $-c = -1.96$ (rounded off to second decimal place). Hence, from Equation (7.2) it follows that

$$(7.5) \qquad \Pr(\mu - 1.96 \cdot \sigma/\sqrt{n} < \bar{y} < \mu + 1.96 \cdot \sigma/\sqrt{n}) = .95.$$

We can now alternatively modify the double inequality contained in the left-hand side of Equation (7.5), in order to obtain an expression in terms of the unknown mean, μ, which is of actual concern to us. To this end, we subtract from all three sides of this double inequality first μ, then $\bar{y}$, and finally multiply the result by (-1) (thereby changing the direction of the inequalities involved). These three steps lead to the following result

$$(7.6) \qquad \Pr(\bar{y} + 1.96 \cdot \sigma/\sqrt{n} > \mu > \bar{y} - 1.96 \cdot \sigma/\sqrt{n}) = .95,$$

which is the same as

$$(7.7) \qquad \Pr(\bar{y} - 1.96 \cdot \sigma/\sqrt{n} < \mu < \bar{y} + 1.96 \cdot \sigma/\sqrt{n}) = .95.$$

Equation (7.7) in actual fact asserts that the interval

$$(7.8) \qquad (\bar{y} - 1.96 \cdot \sigma/\sqrt{n}, \ \bar{y} + 1.96 \cdot \sigma/\sqrt{n})$$

is associated with a probability of .95 of enclosing the population mean. Therefore, the interval provided in (7.8) can be considered to be an interval estimate of the population mean. As mentioned above, a popular name for such an interval is *confidence interval*. That is, Equation (7.8) represents a confidence interval (CI) for the mean, μ, at the used probability level of .95. (We will soon introduce a more appropriate name for this level, calling it "confidence level.")

There are three aspects of the CI in (7.8) that need to be further clarified here. First, the two endpoints—that is, the lower and upper limits—of the interval estimate of the mean μ are expressed in terms of the sample average $\bar{y}$. Hence, they depend on its sample value in empirical research. That is, these two endpoints are themselves random variables. This is because before we draw the sample, the sample average is unknown and hence the CI endpoints $\bar{y} - 1.96 \cdot \sigma/\sqrt{n}$ and $\bar{y} + 1.96 \cdot \sigma/\sqrt{n}$ are also unknown. Indeed, it is only after the sample is drawn that they become known to us (since only then can we work out the sample average, $\bar{y}$). Therefore, in general every sample gives rise to a different CI, unless for two samples under consideration their sample averages happen to be identical (which in general would be quite unusual). Thus, if we draw r samples (with $r > 0$), we will have in general r different resulting confidence intervals of the same population parameter—in this case the population mean μ of the studied variable.

Second, we cannot be certain that the CI will cover the population mean μ for a given sample from a population under consideration—and in empirical research we are typically dealing with only a single sample from a studied population. In fact, Equation (7.7), on which the interval estimate (7.8) is based, only says that in a series of many samples drawn from that population, 95% of the resulting intervals (7.8) will cover the population mean μ (for further details see Chapter 4 and the pertinent probability definition in terms of relative frequency). Thereby, we do not know for which 95% of all these samples their associated CI will in fact cover μ.

Third, it is essential to also keep in mind the right-hand side of Equation (7.7), viz., the number .95. This number, based on the relative frequency interpretation of probability (see Chapter 4), reflects the degree of confidence we have in covering the population mean μ across a large number of repeated samples of the same size from the studied population. For this reason, this probability number is commonly called a "confidence level." As a result, the interval presented in (7.8) is typically referred to as a *confidence interval (CI) at the 95%-confidence level* (abbreviated as 95%-CI), or alternatively as an *interval estimate of the mean μ at the confidence level .95*.

In this connection, we readily observe that had we instead been interested in finding a confidence interval for the mean at the .99 confidence level, we would need to seek another number c^* using the corresponding equation

$$(7.9) \qquad \Pr(\mu - c^* \cdot \sigma / \sqrt{n} < \bar{y} < \mu + c^* \cdot \sigma / \sqrt{n}) = .99.$$

Following exactly the same developments as those given above in connection with Equation (7.2), we could then easily use R as follows in order to find this number c^*:

```
> qnorm(.005, 0, 1)
[1] -2.575829
```

That is, $c^* = 2.58$ (rounded off to second decimal place) would have resulted. Hence, the 99%-confidence interval (99%-CI) for the population mean μ would be

$$(7.10) \qquad (\bar{y} - 2.58 \cdot \sigma / \sqrt{n}, \ \bar{y} + 2.58 \cdot \sigma / \sqrt{n}).$$

Similarly, if we wanted to obtain a 90%-CI of the population mean μ in the first instance, the needed number c^{**} would be obtained with R as follows:

```
> qnorm(.05, 0, 1)
[1] -1.644854
```

that is, $c^{**} = 1.64$. Then the resulting 90%-CI would be

$$(7.11) \qquad (\bar{y} - 1.64 \cdot \sigma/\sqrt{n}, \ \bar{y} + 1.64 \cdot \sigma/\sqrt{n}).$$

We reiterate that for a fixed sample we do not know whether any of the CIs discussed in this section would definitely cover, or contain, the population mean μ. It is also important to note that as the confidence level increases so does the width of the CI. This shouldn't be surprising, since as the confidence level increases we in effect want to be *more confident* that we cover the population mean μ (in a series of repeated samples). Finally, we again emphasize that all our developments up to this point in the chapter were based on the assumption that the standard deviation σ of the original RV of interest, y, was known. As mentioned previously, we will relax this assumption later in the book.

7.3.3. Standard normal distribution quantiles for use in confidence intervals

Looking at the intervals (7.8), (7.10), and (7.11), we see that the lower and upper end of each of these three CIs has the same structure. The only difference between them lies in the value c with which we multiply the standard error of the mean, $\sigma/\sqrt{n}$, before adding and subtracting the result from the sample average $\bar{y}$. In the first considered instance, this number c was determined to be 1.96, then 2.58, and finally 1.64 (for the confidence levels of 95%, 99%, and 90%, respectively). Thus, it should be clear that this value c in effect governs the *width* of the corresponding CI. In this sense, the value c plays a very important role in determining the length of the CI. For this reason, this number c is usually represented in statistics using a special symbol (at least whenever the assumptions of normality of the sample mean and known variance of a variable y of concern can be made). The special symbol used is $z_{\alpha/2}$, thereby letting us state that

$$c = z_{\alpha/2},$$

where α is a number between zero and one (i.e., $0 < \alpha < 1$). This number α is the complement to 100% of the used confidence level, expressed as a fraction. That is, this number would be $\alpha = .05$ if a 95%-CI is sought, $\alpha = .01$ if a 99%-CI is needed, and $\alpha = .10$ if a 90%-CI is to be constructed.

The last equation, $c = z_{\alpha/2}$, states that this important value c is the point that cuts off to the right the fraction $\alpha/2$ from the area under the standard normal curve, and thus cuts off to the left the fraction $(1 - \alpha/2)$ of that area.

This number, $z_{\alpha/2}$, is often referred to as the $(1 - \alpha/2)$th *quantile of the standard normal distribution*. (Obviously, this is the $100(1 - \alpha/2)$th percentile of this distribution, in our earlier terminology, but it seems to be more easily referred to as its $(1 - \alpha/2)$th quantile—this is also the reason for the frequent use in the literature of the symbol $z_{\alpha/2}$.)

With this notation, we now obtain the following general form of the $(1 - \alpha)100\%$-confidence interval for the population mean, for any α $(0 < \alpha < 1)$:

$$(7.12) \qquad (\bar{y} - z_{\alpha/2} \cdot \sigma / \sqrt{n},\ \bar{y} + z_{\alpha/2} \cdot \sigma / \sqrt{n}).$$

We can construct this CI in (7.12) for the population mean on a given variable y of interest, any time we know sample size, confidence level, and the standard deviation of the RV y under consideration. Although we will make frequent reference to the CI in (7.12) throughout the remainder of the book, for now we simply emphasize that it provides the CI for the population mean at any confidence level (as determined by this number α). We also note in passing that the critical number α has yet another, related and very important interpretation that we will deal with in the next section when discussing the topic of hypothesis testing.

To illustrate the above developments up to this point of the chapter, let us consider the following example involving a writing ability test.

> **Example 7.3 (writing ability testing):** A writing ability test is known to have a population variance of 225 and a mean value that is unknown in a studied population of third graders from the state of Hawaii. In a sample of $n = 120$ students representative of that state's third graders, the sample average score on the test is found to be 26. What range of scores would provide 95% confidence in covering the mean of this writing test score in repeated sampling (at this size) from this population?

This question asks about a 95%-CI for the mean of the writing ability test score. Denoting this test's score by y here, we observe that at the used sample size of $n = 120$ the CLT is probably going to hold (or at least provide a good approximation to the associated normal distribution). Hence, it would be reasonable to use the normal approximation for the sampling distribution of the average $\bar{y}$. With this in mind, the earlier Equation (7.8) provides us with the sought 95%-CI for the mean of the writing ability test score as

$$(\bar{y} - 1.96 \cdot \sigma / \sqrt{n},\ \bar{y} + 1.96 \cdot \sigma / \sqrt{n}).$$

Based on the above given values, we can readily use the calculator capacity of R in order to determine numerically as follows the lower and upper endpoints (limits) of this CI:

```
> 26-1.96*15/sqrt(120)
[1] 23.31616


> 26+1.96*15/sqrt(120)
[1] 28.68384
```

That is, the 95%-CI for the unknown population mean is found to be (23.32, 28.68). In other words, we are 95% confident that the population mean could be a number somewhere between 23.32 and 28.68 (see also discussion earlier in this section for a stricter interpretation of this interval in the context of repeated sampling). Of course, since the left and right endpoints of this CI are not whole numbers yet the writing test is likely to produce scores that are whole numbers only, one can round them off to the lower and upper number, respectively. In this way, we obtain the interval

$$(23, 29),$$

which is associated with a confidence level of at least 95%. We note that anytime we make a CI wider, we actually enhance the associated confidence level. This is because we can then be even more confident that we will enclose the mean within the wider interval (i.e., we will enclose it more often across repeated sampling from the studied population).

In conclusion of this section, we stress that unlike ordinary estimation procedures (viz., those often used in everyday life or in informal discussions), inferential statistics provides us with ways to evaluate the quality of the individual (point) estimates obtained with its methods. In particular, the merit of a point estimation procedure is reflected in the width of the CI that can be obtained using appropriate methods of inferential statistics. We elaborate further on this issue next.

7.3.4. How good is an estimate, and what affects the width of a confidence interval?

As we conveyed above, a confidence interval represents a range of values that are plausible for a population parameter of interest, such as the mean or standard deviation. Thereby, any of the values enclosed in the interval is just as plausible as any other value in that interval for the given confidence level, viz., $100(1 - \alpha)\%$. For instance, if the interval (a, b) (with $b > a$) is obtained as a confidence interval for a given parameter at a particular confidence level, then any number q between a and b is just as plausible a candidate for the population value of that parameter as is any other number r with the property $a < r < b$. Conversely, any number below a, and any number above b, is *not* plausible (at the given confidence level) as a population value of the parameter. That is, any number $u < a$, or any $v > b$, is not a good candidate then for a population value of the parameter.

We also mentioned earlier that the quality of a parameter estimate is reflected in the width of the resulting confidence interval. Specifically, in general terms, it is obvious that the narrower the CI is, the higher the precision is with which the unknown parameter has been estimated. Hence, if there may be more than one interval estimation procedure for a parameter of concern, the method producing the smallest CI at a given confidence level (and sample size) has the highest quality.

Let us now take a second look at Equation (7.8) and notice again that the width of the CI depends on three quantities. The following discussion in this subsection assumes that when we consider the effect of any one of these three quantities, the other two remain fixed.

We mentioned previously the effect of one of these quantities, the confidence level. Indeed, as indicated, higher (smaller) confidence level leads to wider (narrower) CIs. In this connection, it is worthwhile emphasizing that a general notation for the confidence level is as a $(1 - \alpha)100\%$-CI, where $0 < \alpha < 1$. Hence, the smaller α is, the wider the CI. The reason is that smaller α's go together with higher percentage $(1 - \alpha)100\%$, and thus with a higher confidence level. This is because a higher confidence level leads to a larger $z_{\alpha/2}$ value, in the role of the critical value c in our earlier developments of the CI construction process. Indeed, as will be recalled, we subtracted and added c times the standard error of the mean, to the sample average $\bar{y}$ in order to obtain the pertinent CI. Hence, we see that the smaller α is—and hence the higher the confidence level—the further "out" (i.e., away from the mean of the distribution $N(0,1)$) we need to go in order to find this quantile $z_{\alpha/2} = c$. Therefore, the smaller α is, the larger the value c is that we need to multiply with the standard error of the mean and subtract/add to the sample mean, in order to render the pertinent CI; this leads obviously to a wider CI.

A second factor that affects the width of the CI is the sample size, n. Specifically, the larger the sample size, the smaller the standard error of the mean and thus the shorter the CI (since then the smaller the multiplier of c is, viz., $\sigma/\sqrt{n}$—see earlier Equation (7.8)). This statement is valid more generally, i.e., also when we conduct interval estimation of other population parameters. That is, the larger the sample, the more precise our inference will be, since we obtain a shorter interval of plausible population values. This observation is the motivation of the frequently found recommendation in statistical and applied literature to work with samples that are as large as possible. Large samples are tantamount statistically to large amounts of information about population parameters. Intuitively, the reason is that then the sample is closer to the studied population, and hence there is higher potential for better inferences about the parameters of concern. We will revisit the effect of sample size from a slightly different perspective in the next subsection.

The last quantity that affects the width of a CI is the magnitude of the variance of the original studied variable, y. Looking at any of the CIs provided in Equations (7.8), (7.10), or (7.11), the larger this variance σ is, the wider will be the associated CI. As it turns out, in some experimental studies it is possible to control the magnitude of σ, in fact even reduce it. In contrast, for most observational or nonexperimental studies (also sometimes referred to as correlational studies), there are limited, if any, possibilities to accomplish this aim. A detailed discussion of such possibilities is beyond the scope of this introductory book, and we direct the reader to more advanced treatments on the matter (e.g., Shadish, Cook, & Campbell, 2002).

7.4. CHOOSING SAMPLE SIZE FOR ESTIMATING THE MEAN

The number of subjects included in a sample, n, has a number of important implications whenever empirical studies are conducted. One of them is obviously the amount of resources (time, effort, cost) associated with obtaining the sample and studying the individuals—or in general, the units of analysis—in the sample. Usually, obtaining larger samples can be a very costly undertaking. On the other hand, having a limited sample size has the potential of ending up with very low estimation quality (i.e., rendering very imprecise inferences). This is because the width of the associated CIs would likely be fairly large, as was discussed in the previous section. In the present section, we will be concerned with a procedure that can be used to obtain the least possible sample size necessary to ensure a certain level of precision of estimation of the mean of a variable in a studied population.

This procedure depends on two quantities that need to be decided upon before it is used. To discuss these quantities, we return to the previously introduced concept of the width of a CI, which is closely related to a notion often used in the behavioral and social sciences, and especially in various kinds of surveys. This is the notion of "tolerable error." Typically, tolerable error (TE) is defined as the width of a CI at an appropriate confidence level. Often in social and behavioral research (e.g., in surveys), investigators can reason in favor of a particular value of TE that they consider acceptable. We stress, however, that the determination of a TE is typically based upon subject-matter considerations, and it is substantive researchers who are best equipped with the knowledge, skills, and experience needed to make such decisions.

Once a TE is elected, the next step in the procedure to determine sample size, n, is to decide on the confidence level to be used. Very high confidence levels (e.g., in excess of 99%) are hard to argue for, since usually they lead to very wide CIs. On the other hand, choosing a very small confidence level, such as 30%, leads to CIs that would cover the population parameter a very limited proportion of times in repeated sampling. For instance, choosing 30% as a confidence level effectively means that the population parameter (e.g., the mean) is covered only about a third of the time in repeated sampling. This is a very poor coverage for most practical goals. Primarily due to an often-followed convention, confidence levels of 95% and 90%, and in some situations 99%, have been widely considered acceptable. (We stress, however, that a CI at any level can be constructed using the procedure outlined in Section 7.3, assuming of course that the corresponding α is between zero and one.)

Keeping all the above issues in mind, let us return to our earlier concern with interval estimation of the population mean on a variable of interest. For ease of presentation, let us denote the elected tolerable error as E. In other words, E is the width of interest of the CI at a chosen confidence level $(1 - \alpha)100\%$ $(0 < \alpha < 1)$. As before, let us assume we know the standard deviation σ of the measure y of concern (e.g., the score on an ancient history test). Then looking at the general form (7.12) of the CI for the mean, shows that its width is

(7.13) $$E = 2z_{\alpha/2}\sigma/\sqrt{n}.$$

Hence, if we also know the confidence level, we can determine the smallest sample size n at which the tolerable error would be equal to E. This can be accomplished by algebraically solving Equation (7.13) in terms of n, which leads to

(7.14) $$n = \left[\frac{2z_{\alpha/2}\sigma}{E}\right]^2.$$

Looking at Equation (7.14), one can readily see that it critically depends on knowledge of the standard deviation σ of the variable of interest, y. Of course, in most empirical behavioral and social research studies one will not know σ with a reasonable degree of certainty. If any knowledge about σ is available from prior research, and that knowledge can be considered trustworthy, it may be used in Equation (7.14). Alternatively, when no such prior knowledge about σ is available, one could use an earlier-discussed relationship between the range and the standard deviation to approximate the population value of σ. Specifically, we mentioned in Chapter 3 that the range is generally about four times the standard deviation for a given random variable (recall that the range is the difference between the largest and the smallest observation in an available sample). Thus, when there are no extreme observations (i.e., abnormal or outlying observations), one can substitute the ratio $r/4$ for σ in Equation (7.14) and proceed with determining the sought (approximate) sample size n. We illustrate this discussion with the following example.

> **Example 7.4:** Suppose it is known that scores on a studied depression scale are normally distributed in an adult population of interest, and that in a given sample its recorded observations fall between 2 and 26. How many persons does one need to measure with this scale, in order to achieve a tolerance error of two units (points) at a confidence level of 95% when evaluating the population depression mean?

Here we do not know the standard deviation of the random variable y of interest. However, we know that the range of the depression score is $26 - 2 = 24$. Hence, according to the preceding discussion, a sensible estimate of the standard deviation of y would be

$$(26 - 2)/4 = 24/4 = 6.$$

Then substituting the value 6 for σ in Equation (7.14), we obtain with R:

```
> (2*1.96*6/2)^2
[1] 138.2976
```

That is, we would like to use a sample size of $n = 139$ students. We note in passing that we round off to the next higher integer rather than the next lower, in order to accomplish better precision of estimation. As indicated above, the reason is that the larger the sample size, the higher the quality of estimation that we thereby achieve.

7.5. TESTING HYPOTHESES ABOUT POPULATION MEANS

7.5.1. Statistical testing, hypotheses, and test statistics

As we mentioned at the beginning of this chapter, a second type of statistical inference is *hypothesis testing* (HT), also called at times *statistical hypothesis testing*. HT can be used when there is a claim about the value of a population parameter, and one wants to evaluate the empirical evidence contained in an available sample that is consistent with the claim (or, conversely, that contradicts the claim). For example, suppose that based on prior research in a substantive area a college aspiration scale is claimed (conjectured) to have a mean of 18 in a studied population of high school seniors. A researcher may then wish to examine such a hypothesis in relation to the alternative that its mean is not 18. A way to accomplish this aim statistically is to evaluate in a given sample from the population the degree to which obtained empirical data contradicts a given hypothesis—e.g., the mean being equal to a prespecified number, like 18 here. This evaluation includes also that of the degree to which the available data is consistent with the hypothesis negation, or an alternative statement of particular interest—e.g., that the mean is not equal to 18 in this example.

When proceeding with HT, as just indicated there are two competing hypotheses that need to be considered simultaneously, with one of them getting selected in the end. One of these is the hypothesis that is usually of research interest, referred to as the *research hypothesis*. In our above example, this hypothesis states that $\mu \neq 18$, where μ denotes the population mean of the college aspiration scale. We formally call this the "alternative hypothesis" and denote it symbolically as H_a: $\mu \neq 18$. In other empirical settings, this hypothesis may have a somewhat different form, as discussed later in the chapter. The negation of this hypothesis, $\mu = 18$ in our case, is simply called the *null hypothesis* and symbolized as H_0: $\mu = 18$. (In other settings, the null hypothesis may have a somewhat different form that is not overlapping with the statement of the alternative hypothesis. We will indicate such null hypotheses later in the chapter.)

The goal of HT then is, informally speaking, to evaluate the empirical evidence in favor of each of these two hypotheses, which is contained in the available sample from a studied population. The result of this process is then considered by the investigator, and a decision is made as to whether to reject or not the null hypothesis.

To carry out HT, we need a specific procedure accomplishing this evaluation of sample evidence in favor of (or against) each of the two hypotheses mentioned, H_a and H_0. This procedure is referred to as a *statistical test*. Its aim is to evaluate the magnitude of the "distance" between the data and the particular null hypothesis. A measure of this distance is the *test statistic*. The test statistic, as its name suggests, represents itself a statistic (i.e., it is a function of the sample observations). That is, a test statistic is the result of specific computational activities carried out on the sample observations. The purpose of these activities is to express the distance between the data and the null hypothesis in a way that inferences concerning the validity of the claim being examined about a parameter of concern can be made. (The specifics of this process are discussed in detail later in this chapter.)

To return for a moment to our earlier example of the study of college aspiration, suppose that in a sample of $n = 36$ high school seniors the pertinent scale score mean estimate is 22.5 (recalling that the population mean value was assumed to be equal to 18, according to the null hypothesis). Thus, as a simple version of the distance between the null hypothesis and the available sample, one could consider the difference $22.5 - 18 = 4.5$ points. This difference of 4.5 points can be thought of as a simple version of a test statistic.

Unfortunately, this simple version of a test statistic as a measure of the distance between null hypothesis and data has some important problems. First, it fails to account for the instability of the sample average $\bar{y}$ that would be obtained across repeated sampling from the studied population. Consequently, this simple distance measure is certain to lead to a different value in another selected sample. Additionally, and just as importantly, we cannot judge when its values are sufficiently large in order to warrant rejection of the null hypothesis. Hence, more sophisticated versions of a distance measure are needed to account for the sampling variability in the test statistic used, in order to allow more accurate judgments to be made. This is the goal of our discussion in the next subsections.

7.5.2. Rejection regions

As indicated before, in addition to the two nonoverlapping hypotheses and a test statistic, we need a rule to determine when to consider the empirical evidence provided by a sample as sufficient to reject the null hypothesis. Roughly speaking, this will have to occur when the distance between this hypothesis and the sample data is sufficiently large to warrant such a decision. Determining when this is the case is tackled next.

A convenient approach to resolving this issue is to consider the distance between null hypothesis and sample data large enough, when the values of the test statistic under consideration fall within an extreme region. For convenience, we will call this region the *rejection region*. The rejection region represents the set of sufficiently "distant" values of the test statistic relative to the null hypothesis. These are values that are quite unlikely to be observed for the test statistic, if one were to assume the null hypothesis were true. As such, the test statistic values from the rejection region warrant a conclusion that the sample data contains enough evidence against the null hypothesis. That is, this evidence warrants the consideration that the null hypothesis is worthy of being rejected.

The determination of the rejection region is an activity that is specific to each test statistic and posited null and alternative hypotheses, and makes use of certain key assumptions. These assumptions ensure that the test statistic has a known distribution. Thereupon, one chooses the extreme part or parts of this distribution—relative to the null hypothesis and in favor of the alternative—as constituting the rejection region.

7.5.3. The "assumption" of statistical hypothesis testing

One noteworthy assumption that must be made in order to conduct hypothesis testing is that the null hypothesis is correct unless there is sufficient evidence in the sample that warrants its rejection. Let us reflect a little further on this last statement. An initial observation to consider when testing a hypothesis is that we are in fact operating in a situation characterized by uncertainty. This is because we are dealing with a conjecture about an unknown population parameter(s) and must make a decision about a statement that we do not know is correct or not, to begin with. In such a situation, it is reasonable to make an assumption and then see whether the assumption (and its implications) is consistent with the available data in the studied sample. This is precisely what the above assumption of the null hypothesis being correct—in a sense, until proven wrong—accomplishes. Specifically, in such a situation of uncertainty about the null and alternative hypotheses being examined, this assumption is what allows us to move forward and make headway. (It is important to note that if we were certain about any of the two hypotheses under consideration, we would not need to conduct hypothesis testing at all.)

Let us now return to the college aspiration study mentioned previously. Informally at this stage, one can consider values of the sample average that are sufficiently distinct from 18 as warranting rejection of the null hypothesis, which is stated as $H_0: \mu = 18$. But what needs next to be assessed is how much larger or smaller than 18 would be considered distinct enough from H_0. The answer to this question can be furnished by the test statistic (which we still need to come up with) and on knowledge of its distribution. This is the distribution under the null hypothesis, that is, under the assumption that H_0 is true. As emphasized earlier, this is the same assumption upon which the whole process of statistical testing is based. The rejection region in the example study thus comprises all scores that are sufficiently distant from 18 (in either direction), in accordance with the distribution of the test statistic under the assumption that H_0 is true.

The next important assumption to consider is that of normality of the sample mean of the original variable of interest, y. As emphasized previously, the distribution of many variables in behavioral and social research approximate the normal distribution well. Thus, the assumption of normality of y is not unreasonable in many empirical cases.

Another vital assumption to bear in mind concerns our knowledge of the standard deviation σ of the studied RV y. For instance, suppose the variance of the college aspiration measure was 144 in the studied population. This assumption of known variance will be helpful to us in order to get started since it allows us to immediately connect the discussion here with that earlier in the chapter and in Chapter 6. (We stress that we will relax this assumption later in the chapter, but for now proceed based on this assumption in order to simplify the following discussion.)

As indicated in Chapter 6, when a random variable y is normally distributed with a mean μ and variance σ^2, the associated z-score

(7.15) $$z = (y - \mu)/\sigma$$

is standard normal, i.e., follows the distribution $N(0,1)$. Given the standard normal distribution of z, the question now is which possible scores on it could be considered sufficiently different (larger or smaller) from its mean, so as to warrant rejecting the null hypothesis about its value.

To answer this question we must capitalize on our knowledge of what the value of μ is under the null hypothesis being tested. In our earlier empirical example, the null hypothesis tested stated that $H_0: \mu = 18$. Obviously, if this hypothesis were true, the z-score in Equation (7.15) with $\mu = 18$ substituted in it, would follow a normal distribution $N(0,1)$. However, as mentioned in Chapter 6, 95% of the scores on a standard normal variable can be expected to fall within 1.96 standard deviation from the mean of zero (i.e., to fall within the interval $(-1.96, 1.96)$). That is, scores on z that fall outside this interval are in a sense unusual since they occur only at a rate of one to 20. This is because they collectively make up the remaining 5% of the area under the standard normal curve.

This reasoning suggests that z scores falling outside the specified interval are associated with a probability up to .05 (5%) to occur. This is a rather small probability. Indeed, if the null hypothesis were to be correct, then we would have high expectation that the z-score in Equation (7.15) would fall between -1.96 and 1.96. If this z-score then turns out to be larger than 1.96 or smaller than -1.96, we would be dealing with an event that has very small probability or likelihood under the null hypothesis. Obtaining such a finding would constitute evidence against the tested null hypothesis. In that case, we would be willing to reject this hypothesis, i.e., consider H_0 disconfirmed.

Returning again to our empirical example with the college aspiration scale, we first note that at the used sample size of $n = 36$ the sample average may be considered (approximately) normal due to the central limit theorem. Making this normality assumption, and recalling from Chapter 6 that the sample mean $\bar{y}$ has variance that equals the ratio of the variance of the studied random variable y to sample size n, it follows that the z-score of the sample average 22.5 is equal to

$$(22.5 - 18) / (12/6) = 2.25$$

(see Equation (7.15) under H_0). Since this score of 2.25 is well outside the specified interval $(-1.96, 1.96)$, we consider the available data to contain evidence that sufficiently strongly points against the null hypothesis of the mean being 18. Hence, we can view this evidence as warranting rejection of the null hypothesis $H_0: \mu = 18$. That is, we can suggest—using statistical hypothesis testing reasoning—that the mean of the college aspiration measures is different from 18 in the studied high school senior population.

If we take another look at Equation (7.15), we notice that it is determining the distance between a particular score y on the studied random variable y

and its mean μ, which is free of the original units of measurement. The reason is that this difference—which is the numerator in Equation (7.15)—is divided there by the standard deviation σ. By conducting this division, we in a sense account for the variability of the score y in the population of interest. With this in mind, the right-hand side of Equation (7.15) with $\bar{y}$ in place of y in fact measures the distance between the data ($\bar{y}$) and the null hypothesis H_0: μ = 18. Therefore, the z-score in Equation (7.15) does not really share the earlier discussed limitations of the simple version of a test statistic, i.e., the one being the simple difference between sample average and hypothetical value 18. With this in mind, the z-score provided by Equation (7.15) with $\bar{y}$ in place of y can be considered a desirable test statistic.

As it turns out, we also obtain in this z-score a ratio whose distribution is known if the null hypothesis is true. Specifically, this ratio follows the standard normal distribution. Knowledge of this distribution allows us to identify its areas that are associated with very small probability. This permits us to consider a score falling in those areas as sufficiently inconsistent with the null hypothesis so as to warrant its rejection. The set of all these scores—the corresponding areas with limited (small) probability under the null hypothesis—constitute the rejection region.

7.5.4. A general form of a z-test

The preceding discussion allows us now to present the general form of a test statistic for testing the hypothesis that the mean of a studied variable y is a prespecified number, denoted μ_0, if its variance σ is known. In the general case, the pertinent null hypothesis is H_0: $\mu = \mu_0$, and the alternative is H_a: $\mu \neq \mu_0$. In analogy to the earlier discussion, we reject the null hypothesis if the observed sample average $\bar{y}$ is sufficiently far from the hypothetical value μ_0 (i.e., is sufficiently larger or smaller than μ_0).

To determine whether this is the case in a given data set, we use as before the corresponding z-score as a test statistic (at times referred to as z-test statistic):

$$(7.16) \qquad z = \frac{\bar{y} - \mu_0}{\sigma / \sqrt{n}}.$$

Specifically, if this z-score falls outside of the interval (-1.96, 1.96), we reject the null hypothesis H_0; otherwise we treat H_0 as retainable, i.e., we do not reject it. As earlier in this chapter, these developments are based on the assumption of the sample average following a normal distribution and a known standard deviation σ of the variable y of concern.

Equation (7.16) represents the general form of what is referred to as a *z-test* for testing the null hypothesis of the population mean on a studied variable y being equal to a given number, μ_0. We stress that this z-test is applicable when knowledge about the standard deviation σ of y is available.

Looking at Equation (7.16), we see the test statistic in its right-hand side as resulting from specific calculations carried out on the sample observations $y_1, y_2, \ldots, y_n$. That is, this z-test statistic is a function of the sample data. More generally, *test statistics* are such functions of the sample data, which evaluate its distance from the null hypothesis, in the direction of the alternative hypothesis considered. Thereby, they do this evaluation in a way that accounts for the variability in the collected data.

An important general feature of a test statistic, in order for it to be useful for the purpose of statistical hypothesis testing, is that it is associated with a completely known distribution if the null hypothesis were true. This distribution is referred to as test statistic distribution under H_0, at times also called simply a "null distribution." We use the latter to find out which scores of the test statistic are associated with very limited probability should the null hypothesis be true. As indicated earlier, the collection of these scores represents the rejection region of relevance when testing a null hypothesis and a rival alternative hypothesis. In our above college aspiration scale example, the rejection region consists of the areas under the standard normal curve that contain z-scores larger than 1.96 or smaller than -1.96, if we are willing to consider scores that are more than two standard deviations away from the mean as sufficiently rare under H_0 so as to warrant rejection of this null hypothesis.

7.5.5. Significance level

We defined above the concept of a rejection region by identifying scores on the test statistic that are extreme or in a sense unlikely under the null hypothesis, i.e., scores that are associated with limited or small probability to occur should the null hypothesis be true. We have not specified, however, in the general case what exactly would be considered "limited probability."

In our pertinent considerations, we often referred to probabilities under .05 as small. This number, .05, is frequently used in this role in hypothesis testing, but it is not the only one that can be argued for. More generally, such a boundary—like .05 here—below which we are willing to consider a probability as small, is called "significance level" and is often denoted as α. We will give an alternative definition for *significance level* later in this chapter, but for now we simply note that it is the highest value between zero and one with the property that any probability smaller than it is considered small in the above sense for the purpose of hypothesis testing. That is, if in an empirical setting we obtain a test statistic value with the property that the probability is less than α to get a score on this statistic that is at least as inconsistent with the null hypothesis and falls in the direction of the alternative, then we will consider the null hypothesis as rejected.

In most applications, $\alpha = .05$ is usually chosen. There are also empirical cases, however, where $\alpha = .01$ can be a reasonable choice, or alternatively when $\alpha = .1$ is sensible to select. Strictly speaking, there is no restriction on the particular choice of α as a number between zero and one, and its selection typically depends on the research question as well as the circumstances under which the inference is to be made. Another principle to follow when choosing the significance level α in empirical research is that its selection should not depend on the data that is to be subsequently analyzed. That is, if one looks first at the data, and in particular some test statistics of possible interest, and then chooses the significance level, incorrect conclusions may well be drawn from the statistical test results that can be seriously misleading when interpreted substantively. For this reason, the choice of α should be made prior to examining the analyzed data.

7.6. TWO TYPES OF POSSIBLE ERROR IN STATISTICAL HYPOTHESIS TESTING

7.6.1. Type I and Type II errors

As we mentioned earlier in this chapter, when carrying out statistical hypothesis testing we are expected to make a decision for either the null hypothesis or the alternative hypothesis. We make this decision depending on the available sample data, and thus in a situation of uncertainty. Specifically, we do not know whether H_0 or H_a is true in the population. (If we knew it, we would not need to get involved in any hypothesis testing–related activities.) Hence, we can speak of a "true state of affairs" that represents the population situation: in the population either H_0 or H_a is true. We stress that we have defined H_0 and H_a as nonoverlapping, and thus it is not possible that they are both correct. The true state of affairs is typically unknown, however. Based on the data, and using an appropriate test statistic (and associated assumptions), we make a decision—either rejecting H_0 and hence effectively considering H_a as retainable, or considering H_0 as retainable and thus effectively rejecting H_a. Hence, we can commit two different types of errors, referred to as Type I and Type II and discussed in detail next.

A Type I error is committed whenever we reject H_0 based on the sample data, but this hypothesis is in fact true in the studied population. That is, we commit a Type I error any time the null hypothesis is actually true, but using the sample data we make a decision to reject this hypothesis. This will be specifically the case whenever the sample data happens to yield a test statistic falling in the associated rejection region, whereas H_0 is actually true in the population. Since sample data are random, in principle there is no restriction on the value of the test statistic in a sample—and so there is nothing that precludes it from falling in the rejection region also when H_0 is in fact true in the studied population (but we are not aware of this).

Alternatively, a Type II error is committed when the alternative hypothesis H_a is correct in the population, but based on the sample we fail to sense this and decide not to reject H_0. That is, a Type II error is committed whenever the alternative hypothesis is true but the empirical data happens to yield a test statistic value *not* falling in the rejection region, thus leading us to the decision of retaining the null hypothesis.

Table 7.1 presents all four possible outcomes, indicating these two error types. The four possible outcomes result by crossing the two decisions possible—reject or do not reject (i.e., retain) the null hypothesis—with the two possibilities regarding the status of the null hypothesis in the population, viz., H_0 being actually true in reality or alternatively being false in the population under investigation.

We emphasize that we do not know the true state of affairs (otherwise we are done and do not need statistical hypothesis testing) and that we have to make our decision to reject the null hypothesis H_0 or retain it using random data. Therefore, we can attach probabilities to each one of the four possible outcomes in Table 7.1. Let us denote by α the probability, or rate, for committing a Type I error. (We will soon see why this is a correct choice of notation.) Further, denote by β the probability/rate of committing a Type II error. One would naturally want to minimize (i) the probability/rate α of making a Type I error *and* (ii) the probability/rate β of committing a Type II error. If we could only find a test statistic that accomplishes requirements (i) and (ii), it would be a perfect choice.

However, this simultaneous minimization of both probabilities for making a Type I error and a Type II error is not possible. In fact, anything we do to minimize the Type I error α actually leads to an increase of the Type II error

Table 7.1 Four possible outcomes in statistical hypothesis testing and the two errors that can be committed.

Decision	True State of Affairs (Population) with Regard to Null Hypothesis H_0	
	True	*False*
Reject H_0	Type I error	Correct decision
Do Not Reject H_0	Correct decision	Type II error

β, and vice versa. This is because making the Type I error small in fact decreases the probability of the null hypothesis being rejected, and this will also have to hold for the cases when it is incorrect. That is, suppressing the Type I error leads to an increase of the Type II error. One similarly sees the reverse as well—suppressing the Type II error leads in effect to increasing the Type I error.

To resolve this dilemma, the methodology of statistical hypothesis testing provides us with the following procedure. First, one controls the Type I error by not allowing it to exceed a certain relatively small number, such as .05. Once having ensured this, one chooses a test statistic (statistical test), which has the lowest possible probability for a Type II error. A special branch of statistics called *test theory* has been developed, with one of its goals being the development of formal means allowing finding of such optimal test statistics. Although a detailed discussion of test theory is beyond the confines of this book, we mention that all statistical tests used in this book possess the property of being optimal in this sense.

We reiterate that while there is no objective rule to determine α, a widely followed and commonly accepted convention is to use $\alpha = .05$. However, in certain circumstances, different values for α can be used, as indicated above. Most often in those cases one seems to use either $\alpha = .01$ or $\alpha = .1$ (or some other small value that is in principle equally plausible to use instead).

7.6.2. Statistical power

We mentioned earlier in this chapter that the probability of a Type II error (denoted as β) is the probability to miss a potentially important finding in a given empirical study by deciding to retain the null hypothesis H_0 when it is in fact false. For example, one commits a Type II error when in the population the mean on a particular algebra knowledge test is not equal to a prespecified number μ_0 as stipulated in a tested null hypothesis, but in the available sample the value of the test statistic—like that in Equation (7.16)—does not fall in the rejection region and hence one considers the null hypothesis as retainable.

The complement to the probability of making a Type II error, i.e., $1 - \beta$ is thus the probability of rejecting the null hypothesis when it is in reality false. Partly due to this revealing interpretation, the difference $1 - \beta$ is called *statistical power*, or just *power* for short. We stress that power is associated with a given testing procedure (test statistic), and thus if the test statistic is changed there will likely be a change in the corresponding power. Furthermore, power is associated with particular null and alternative hypotheses, and even for a given null hypothesis it will probably be different for other alternative hypotheses considered in tandem with the null hypothesis.

Similarly, as sample size increases so does power (of a meaningful test statistic). This relationship can be relatively straightforwardly shown formally for many statistical tests, but in general it can be argued for on grounds of the following intuitive observation. Specifically, as sample size increases, the sample becomes more and more like the population. Hence, if the null hypothesis is incorrect in the population to begin with, once sample size increases beyond a sufficiently large number, the associated test statistic value should point to rejection of the null hypothesis. This will be due to the sample resembling then well enough the population, in order for the statistical procedure to correctly sense that the null hypothesis is false there. Last but not least, we stress that we naturally want all our hypothesis testing procedures to have the highest possible, or optimal, statistical power.

7.6.3. Type I error and significance level

If we now revisit our earlier discussion on how to determine the rejection region(s) for a given test statistic, we will notice that we did it under the assumption of the null hypothesis H_0 being true. (We had to make this assumption in order to make headway—if we do not make the assumption, it will not be in general possible to work out the needed distribution of the test statistic.) That is, the rejection region(s) was associated with limited probability under the null hypothesis. Further, when the test statistic value fell in that region(s), we were willing to consider it as evidence warranting rejection of H_0. That limited probability was not to exceed the significance level α. Hence, the significance level was in fact the probability of rejecting H_0, worked out under the assumption of H_0 being true.

This is, however, precisely the probability of committing a Type I error—the probability of rejecting H_0 when it is in fact true. Therefore, the earlier defined significance level α is the probability of committing a Type I error, which we subsequently also referred to as α (see preceding subsection). Hence, this is indeed a correct notation for two quantities that are actually identical.

We stress that the Type I error depends on the test statistic used. Thereby, we emphasize that if we change the test statistic for a given pair of null and alternative hypotheses considered, we will in general need to change the definition of the rejection region in order to ensure the same prespecified significance level α (i.e., the Type I error probability).

7.6.4. Have we proved the null or alternative hypothesis?

We pointed out on a number of occasions that when carrying out statistical hypothesis testing we are operating in a situation of uncertainty. In fact, we need to make, then, a decision about the "true state of affairs" in a studied population, based on information from only part of it—the sample—which typically is a fairly small fraction of the population. Because we are functioning in this situation of uncertainty, our decisions may be incorrect. This is the reason we may commit one of two types of errors—Type I or Type II error. (We note in passing that we cannot commit both types of errors, as they are mutually exclusive possibilities.) Hence, even though there may be apparently overwhelming evidence in a given sample in support of the null hypothesis and the sample may be very large, as long as it is not identical to the population we cannot claim that we have definitively proved the validity of the null hypothesis.

We thus see that statistical hypothesis testing (and more generally statistics as a science itself) is not a means of determining the true state of affairs. This can only be accomplished when the entire studied population of interest is exhaustively studied, i.e., when each and every one of its members is evaluated on all variables of concern. Any time we use sample data—with a sample not being identical to the population—we do not have any guarantee that a null hypothesis found to be retainable based on that data is actually true in the population.

Looked at from another perspective, we always run the risk of committing a Type II error—the null hypothesis being wrong but based on our statistical procedure (test statistic value in the available sample) we decide to retain it. Due to this fact, we cannot prove the validity of the null hypothesis using statistical hypothesis testing, as long as the sample is not identical to the studied population. Conversely, the question may be raised as to whether we can prove the alternative hypothesis, in case we decide to reject the null hypothesis. Again, no matter how strongly the sample data points against the null hypothesis and in favor of the alternative hypothesis under consideration, no statistical procedure can prove the null hypothesis as wrong and thus the alternative as correct. The reason again is the fact that it is possible—using statistics on a sample that is not identical to the population studied—to commit a Type I error. Accordingly, even if we reject the null hypothesis, no matter how large the sample is (as long as it is not identical to the entire population), the null hypothesis may in fact be correct in the population.

This discussion shows that when we are using statistical procedures on samples that are not identical to populations under consideration, we are not in a position to place complete trust in our decision about either the null or alternative hypothesis. That is, whether we reject the null hypothesis or retain it, we cannot claim we have proved it as wrong or correct, respectively. Similarly, we cannot claim that we have proved the alternative hypothesis in case the null hypothesis is rejected. We can be certain in our decisions of this type only when we have examined the entire population of interest.

So then, why study and use statistics for the purpose of hypothesis testing?

The reason is that statistical hypothesis testing procedures, as made available to us by the discipline of test theory, make optimal use of available data and minimize the possible inferential errors that could be committed. These are the errors that can be committed when making decisions about hypotheses of interest in situations of uncertainty. These situations arise any time we have examined only samples representing parts of populations of actual relevance to research questions in the empirical sciences. When we have to make a decision, then, between a null and alternative hypothesis, i.e., a choice for just one of them, it is only logical that we could end up with an incorrect choice.

7.6.5. One-tailed tests

The statistical tests we have discussed so far assumed that the alternative hypothesis of interest (research hypothesis) only stated the population mean μ as unequal to a prespecified number, μ_0. Symbolically, such alternatives are of the form $H_a: \mu \neq \mu_0$. This circumstance effectively leads us to consider as pertinent to H_a two potential directions of deviation from the null hypothesis $H_0: \mu = \mu_0$, viz., μ being either larger or smaller than μ_0. For this reason, such alternative hypotheses H_a are called *two-tailed* or *two-sided alternative hypotheses* (or *two-tailed/sided alternatives*, for short). The preceding discussion in Section 7.5 was thus concerned with a statistical testing procedure for examining the null hypothesis H_0 when tested against this two-tailed alternative H_a. Accordingly, the generally valid z-test in Equation (7.16) is called a *two-tailed test* (assuming normality of the observed variable mean $\bar{y}$ and knowledge of the standard deviation σ of the studied random variable y).

However, often in empirical behavioral and social research one is interested in testing more specialized, directional research hypotheses against the same null hypothesis $H_0: \mu = \mu_0$—for instance, such directional alternative hypotheses as $H_a: \mu > \mu_0$ or $H_a: \mu < \mu_0$. Consider an educational scientist who is interested in examining as a research hypothesis the statement that the mean on a trigonometry test in a studied population is larger than 22, in tandem with the null hypothesis that it equals this number. Conversely, consider a clinician interested in testing the hypothesis that the population mean on a newly developed anxiety scale is not higher than 26, alongside the null hypothesis that it equals this number.

Due to such alternative hypotheses being concerned only with a particular direction of deviation from the null hypothesis, they are called *one-tailed (one-sided) alternative hypotheses*. Correspondingly, the tests used to examine them are also called *one-tailed tests*. What would a one-tailed statistical test look like then, for the null hypothesis $H_0: \mu = \mu_0$ versus the alternative $H_0: \mu > \mu_0$, assuming as throughout this chapter normality of the mean $\bar{y}$ of the underlying random variable y and knowledge of its standard deviation σ? We have already laid the groundwork needed for developing such a test earlier in this chapter, and hence we can capitalize on it when responding to this question next.

As illustrated previously in the chapter, in order to develop a statistical test we need a test statistic to measure the distance, in the direction of the alternative hypothesis, between the data and the null hypothesis. In analogy to the preceding developments in the two-tailed alternative hypothesis case, as such a test statistic we can again choose the z-ratio in Equation (7.16). We restate that equation next (associated with the same number) for completeness of this discussion:

(7.16)
$$z = \frac{\bar{y} - \mu_0}{\sigma / \sqrt{n}}.$$

This test statistic plays an instrumental role for the developments in the remainder of this section.

7.6.5.1. Alternative hypothesis of mean larger than a prespecified number

Using the test statistic in Equation (7.16), how could we come up with a rejection region for the case we are testing the null hypothesis H_0: $\mu = \mu_0$ against the alternative H_a: $\mu > \mu_0$? We emphasized earlier that when developing a rejection region, we are interested only in deviations from the null hypothesis that are in the direction of the alternative.

Since we are concerned here with the alternative hypothesis of the population mean being larger than a prespecified value, μ_0, the rejection region would consist of all sufficiently large values of z as defined in Equation (7.16). How large, however, is large enough? As we pointed out earlier in this chapter, one can obtain an answer to this question when finding out which scores on the test statistic z in (7.16) are so much larger than the hypothetical value μ_0, that they are associated with fairly small probability to be observed if the null hypothesis H_0 were to be true. All these values of z would constitute the rejection region of concern here.

Given that the test statistic z in Equation (7.16) follows a standard normal distribution (with large samples, as assumed at the outset of this chapter unless the studied RV y is normal to begin with), we need to find those values of z that fulfill two requirements. First, they comprise an area under the standard normal curve that is 5% of the entire area under the normal curve. Second, this area is farthest away from the hypothetical value μ_0 in the direction of the alternative. That is, we are searching here for all those values that comprise the uppermost 5% of the area under the standard normal curve. According to our discussion in Chapter 6, this is the part of the area under the normal curve that is cut out (to the right) by the 95th percentile. Hence, the area under the normal curve and above this percentile, which we denoted $z_{.05}$ earlier, is the rejection region we are searching here.

We can easily determine this percentile with R using again the command 'qnorm':

```
> qnorm(.95, 0, 1)
[1] 1.644854
```

That is, if in a given empirical setting the z-ratio (7.16) turns out to be larger than this cutoff value 1.645, we reject the null hypothesis H_0: $\mu = \mu_0$ and consider the one-sided alternative H_a: $\mu > \mu_0$ as retainable. In other words, we do not reject H_0 unless $z > 1.645$. We illustrate this discussion next with an empirical example.

> **Example 7.5 (depression study)**: A researcher studying depression is interested in testing the hypothesis that the average depression level for a new depression scale is 25 in their state, i.e., H_0: $\mu = 25$, versus the alternative that it is actually higher, i.e., H_a: $\mu > 25$. In a sample of 200 persons, the average turns out to be 26.13. Assuming the population variance on this scale is 225, is there sufficient evidence in the study to warrant rejection of the null hypothesis and suggest that the population depression level is higher than that corresponding to the score 25 on this scale?

Here we are interested in a one-sided alternative, H_a, and hence need to use the last-discussed, one-tailed z-test. Indeed, given the sample size of $n = 200$, the assumption of normality of the sample average $\bar{y}$ may be considered reasonable, owing to the central limit theorem (see Chapter 6). The z-test statistic (7.16) yields here the following value that we readily obtain with R:

```
> z = (26.13 - 25)/ (15/sqrt(200))
> z
[1] 1.065374
```

Since this value is smaller than the critical value of 1.645, we conclude that we do not have sufficient evidence in the sample to warrant rejection of the null hypothesis that the state depression level equals 25. We can thus consider as retainable the null hypothesis of this level being 25 in the researcher's state.

7.6.5.2. Alternative hypothesis of mean smaller than a prespecified number

Similar to what was done above, we can also develop a one-tailed test for examining the null hypothesis H_0: $\mu = \mu_0$, versus the alternative stating that the mean is lower than this hypothetical value μ_0, viz., H_a: $\mu < \mu_0$. Specifically, we easily realize that the rejection region of concern would consist of all scores of the z-ratio (7.16) that are sufficiently smaller than μ_0. They comprise collectively the area of 5% under the standard normal curve and farthest away to the left of μ_0. Given the symmetry of the standard normal distribution about zero, it follows that these are all those z-test statistic values from Equation (7.16), which are smaller than -1.645.

That is, if in a given empirical setting the standard deviation of a random variable y under consideration is known (and it can be assumed that its sample average is normally distributed), and one is interested in testing the null hypothesis H_0: $\mu = \mu_0$ versus the alternative H_a: $\mu < \mu_0$, we reject the null hypothesis if

$$(7.16) \qquad\qquad z = \frac{\bar{y} - \mu_0}{\sigma / \sqrt{n}}$$

is smaller than -1.645. Otherwise, we consider H_0 as retainable. We illustrate this discussion with the following example.

> **Example 7.6 (general mental ability testing):** A general mental ability test is known to have a mean of 95 and variance of 185 for the population of tenth graders in a given US state. A study in a neighboring state enrolls $n = 450$ tenth graders, for whom the average performance on the test is 93.45. Based on the empirical evidence, can it be suggested that high school sophomores in the latter state have a lower mean on this test than their neighbor state sophomores, knowing that the test variance is also 185 in this state?

Here we are interested in testing the null hypothesis H_0: $\mu = 95$ about the population mean versus the one-tailed alternative that it is smaller, i.e., H_a: $\mu < 95$. To this end, according to the preceding discussion in this section, we examine the z-ratio (7.16) and check if it is lower than -1.645. We can readily achieve this with R as follows:

```
> z = (93.45-95)/(sqrt(185)/sqrt(450))
> z
[1] -2.41742
```

Since this test statistic result is lower than the upper boundary of the rejection region, viz., -1.645, its value falls within the rejection region. For this reason, we reject the null hypothesis H_0: $\mu = 95$ in favor of the one-tailed alternative H_a: $\mu < 95$. We consider this result as empirical evidence suggesting that in the state in question the mean of the general mental ability test is lower than in its neighboring state.

7.6.5.3. Advantages and drawbacks of one-tailed tests

As can be surmised from the preceding discussion, one-tailed tests have the property that they have higher power than two-tailed tests since they focus all their sensitivity in a single tail of the distribution of the test statistic under the null hypothesis. Technically, this is seen by realizing that their rejection region is closer to the hypothetical mean than for the two-tailed tests (since 1.645 is closer to the mean of zero for the z-distribution of relevance than 1.96). Hence, when the alternative is actually true in the population, even smaller deviations from the null hypothesis would be sufficient for sensing an incorrect null hypothesis, i.e., rejecting it, than for the two-tailed tests.

On the other hand, however, one-tailed tests have no sensitivity for violations of the null hypothesis that are in the opposite direction to the alternative hypothesis considered. For instance, if the alternative is $H_a: \mu > \mu_0$, a sample average that is smaller by any amount than μ_0 is not counted by the corresponding one-tailed test as possible evidence against the tested null hypothesis $H_0: \mu = \mu_0$. The reason is that such a sample average does not lead to a test-statistic value falling in the rejection region, which consists here of all z-scores above 1.96.

Thus, one needs to be very careful in one's considerations when determining whether a one-tailed or a two-tailed test is needed in a given empirical setting. Therefore, if one wishes to avoid missing an important violation of the null hypothesis, one would probably more often consider using two-tailed tests, if not routinely choose them. Conversely, if one is really interested only in a particular deviation from the null hypothesis (viz., if one is willing to test only if the mean is larger, or only smaller, than the hypothetical mean value), and in addition there are no intolerable consequences from missing out a deviation in the opposite direction, then one may decide to use a corresponding directional, one-tailed test. This decision will usually depend on the subject matter, available theoretical knowledge in it, particular empirical circumstances, and the actual research question.

7.6.5.4. Extensions to one-tailed null hypotheses

The one-tailed tests we discussed earlier were characterized by the feature that their null hypotheses were of the form $H_0: \mu = \mu_0$, i.e., focused only on a single prespecified value μ_0 of the population mean. For this reason, sometimes such hypotheses are called *simple*, or *point hypotheses*. Being concerned only with a single value, they require the researcher to choose it very carefully, in order to make optimal use of their data for the purpose of hypothesis testing.

In some empirical situations, however, researchers may not have sufficient information to develop such precise null hypotheses, or they may not be interested in simple (point) null hypotheses to begin with, as these may not be particularly informative. In those circumstances, one may instead be interested in examining one-tailed null hypotheses, e.g., H_0: $\mu \leq \mu_0$ or conversely H_0: $\mu \geq \mu_0$, with an alternative hypothesis being its corresponding negation, i.e., H_a: $\mu > \mu_0$ or H_a: $\mu > \mu_0$, respectively. (We note that since we are considering in this chapter continuous random variables, the probability of the variable y taking a particular value—such as μ_0—is zero; hence, it is immaterial whether we include the equality sign in the null or in the alternative hypothesis.) We refer to a hypothesis like H_0: $\mu \leq \mu_0$ or H_0: $\mu \geq \mu_0$ as a composite hypothesis (and similarly for an alternative hypothesis), since it encompasses a whole range of values rather than a single one.

The preceding developments have also paved the way for developing a test for composite null hypotheses, on the assumption again of known variance of the underlying random variable y and normality of the associated sample mean $\bar{y}$. Specifically, also here we can use the z-ratio (7.16) as a test statistic. With it in mind, for each of the above pair of null and alternative hypothesis to be tested, we need to find next the pertinent rejection region. As illustrated on a few occasions earlier in this chapter, one can readily see here that the rejection region would be the set of scores on the test-statistic z in Equation (7.16), which is sufficiently away from the null hypothesis and in the direction of the alternative tested. In actual fact, as can be easily argued for, we can use the same rejection regions as developed above for testing composite null hypotheses against one-sided alternatives. Specifically, if the null hypothesis tested is H_0: $\mu \leq \mu_0$ against the alternative H_0: $\mu > \mu_0$, the rejection region consists of the uppermost 5% of the area under the standard normal curve, i.e., above 1.645. Conversely, if the null hypothesis tested is H_0: $\mu \geq \mu_0$ against the alternative H_0: $\mu < \mu_0$, the rejection region consists of the lowest 5% of the area under the standard normal curve, i.e., below -1.645. We illustrate this activity next with an example.

Example 7.7 (scale of educational motivation): An educational motivation scale is known to have a variance of 125 in a studied population of high school juniors. In a sample of $n = 235$ students, its average is determined to be 37.64. A researcher is concerned with the question whether there is sufficient evidence in the sample to suggest that its mean is not higher than 40, coming up with this particular number based on research unrelated to the available sample data.

In this example, we are interested in testing the null hypothesis H_0: $\mu \leq 40$ versus the alternative H_a: $\mu > 40$. According to the preceding discussion, the rejection region consists of all z-scores that are larger than 1.645. We first examine the associated z-ratio (7.16), which we can obtain with R as follows:

```
> z = (37.64 - 40)/(sqrt(124)/sqrt(235))

> z

[1] -3.248891
```

Since the value of the test statistic is lower than 1.645, it falls outside of the rejection region for testing the null hypothesis H_0: $\mu = 40$ versus the alternative H_a: $\mu > 40$. We thus conclude that the evidence in the available sample is not sufficient to warrant rejection of the null hypothesis H_0: $\mu \leq 40$, which we thus can consider retainable.

7.6.5.5. One- and two-tailed tests at other significance levels

The preceding discussion was concerned only with using the $\alpha = .05$ significance level. However, the same approach can be followed with any other significance level chosen. For example, if $\alpha = .01$ is decided for as a significance level (before looking at the data to be analyzed), all preceding developments in this Section 7.6 remain valid, with the only modification that the boundary point defining the rejection region—also typically referred to as critical point or cutoff—corresponds to this significance level of .01 rather than that pertaining to $\alpha = .05$.

As we worked out earlier in this book, the cutoff for the case of a two-tailed alternative at a significance level $\alpha = .01$ can be readily determined with R as follows:

```
> two.tailed.cut.off.at.level.01 = qnorm(.995,0,1)

> two.tailed.cut.off.at.level.01

[1] 2.575829
```

Therefore, if we are testing the null hypothesis H_0: $\mu = \mu_0$ against the alternative H_0: $\mu \neq \mu_0$ at a significance level of $\alpha = .01$, the rejection region consists of all z-scores from Equation (7.16) that are below -2.58 and all z-scores above 2.58 (rounded off to second decimal place). Similarly, if we are using a significance level of $\alpha = .1$, then the cutoff for the case a two-tailed alternative is

```
> two.tailed.cut.off.at.level.1 = qnorm(.95,0,1)

> two.tailed.cut.off.at.level.1

[1] 1.644854
```

That is, if we are testing the null hypothesis H_0: $\mu = \mu_0$ against the alternative H_0: $\mu \neq \mu_0$ at a significance level of $a = .1$, the rejection region consists of all z-scores from Equation (7.16) that are below -1.645 and all z-scores above 1.645.

Only slight changes are needed in this approach if we are interested in testing a simple or one-tailed (composite) null hypothesis against a one-tailed alternative hypothesis at significance levels other than .05. Specifically, if we are willing to test H_0: $\mu = \mu_0$ or H_0: $\mu \leq \mu_0$ against the alternative H_a: $\mu > \mu_0$ at the significance level $\alpha = .01$, then the rejection region consists of all z-scores for the sample average that are larger than 2.33, as found readily with R:

```
> qnorm(.99, 0, 1)
[1] 2.326348
```

Conversely, if we are willing to test H_0: $\mu = \mu_0$ or H_0: $\mu \geq \mu_0$ against the alternative H_a: $\mu < \mu_0$ at the same significance level, the rejection region consists of all z-scores from Equation (7.16) that are smaller than -2.33. Alternatively, if testing the same null hypotheses against the alternative H_a: $\mu < \mu_0$ at the significance level $\alpha = .1$, then the rejection region consists of all z-scores from (7.16) that are smaller than -1.28:

```
> qnorm(.1,0,1)
[1] -1.281552
```

If thereby the alternative is H_a: $\mu > \mu_0$ (and the null hypothesis is simple or stating the alternative tail), then the rejection region consists of all z-scores from (7.16) that are higher than 1.28.

These developments and our earlier discussion in this chapter lead us easily to a more general observation. If the simple (point) null hypothesis H_0: $\mu = \mu_0$ is to be tested against the two-tailed alternative H_a: $\mu \neq \mu_0$ at the significance level α, the rejection region consists of all z-scores from Equation (7.16) that are smaller than $-z_{\alpha/2}$ or larger than $z_{\alpha/2}$. Alternatively, if the simple (point) or composite null hypothesis H_0: $\mu = \mu_0$ or H_0: $\mu \leq \mu_0$ is to be tested against the one-tailed alternative H_a: $\mu > \mu_0$ at the significance level α, the rejection region consists of all z-scores from Equation (7.16) that are larger than z_α. If the null hypothesis H_0: $\mu = \mu_0$ or H_0: $\mu \geq \mu_0$ is to be tested against the one-tailed alternative H_a: $\mu < \mu_0$ at the significance level α, the rejection region consists of all z-scores from Equation (7.16) that are smaller than $-z_\alpha$.

7.7. THE CONCEPT OF P-VALUE

The discussion of statistical testing in this chapter was concerned predominantly with the determination of a rejection region for a given test statistic when testing a null versus an alternative hypothesis of interest. Another, essentially equivalent way of proceeding then is through use of the notion of a *p-value*, also at times referred to as *level of significance of a test statistic value.* This approach is widely used in applications of statistics in the behavioral and social sciences, and more generally in empirical settings when testing statistical hypotheses.

The *p*-value can be viewed, like the test statistic, as a measure of the degree to which the sample data is *in*consistent with a tested null hypothesis. However, unlike the test statistic, very small—rather than large—*p*-values are indicative of serious inconsistencies of data and null hypotheses. In this case, the latter may be rejected. Alternatively, if the *p*-value is not very small, the null hypothesis may be retained.

More specifically, to define the concept of a *p*-value, we need to make the assumption that the tested null hypothesis is true. Under this assumption, the *p*-value is defined as the probability to obtain such a value on the used test statistic, which is at least as *in*consistent with the null hypothesis (and in agreement with the alternative hypothesis) as is the value of this test statistic in the actually available sample. That is, the *p*-value is the probability to obtain a test statistic value that is in agreement with the alternative and at least as strongly contradicting the null hypothesis as is the sample test statistic value, if the null hypothesis were to be true.

A straightforward way to obtain the *p*-value is to make use of the distribution of the test statistic under the assumption of validity of the null hypothesis. (This distribution is frequently referred to as *distribution under the null*, for short.) For an available sample, we can then work out the value of the used test statistic and determine the critical area under the curve of its distribution under the null hypothesis. This area consists of all test statistic values that are at least as inconsistent with the null hypothesis and in the direction of the alternative, as is the particular test statistic value in the available sample.

What do we do next with the *p*-value obtained, in order to carry out statistical hypothesis testing? Since the *p*-value gives a probability of a result at least as inconsistent with the null hypothesis, if the latter were to be true, then we can reason as follows. If the *p*-value is small enough, we can reject that hypothesis. Otherwise, we can retain the null hypothesis. Yet how small is small enough for us to proceed in this way? This question does not have an answer that follows from some statistical or mathematical deductions. Usually, the threshold for "smallness" is chosen to be .05, which as mentioned earlier equals what may be considered conventional significance level (unless there are reasons to choose a different value for significance level). Further, we mentioned earlier that the significance level equals the Type I error rate that we wanted to keep small in order to control this error probability. The conventional choice of $\alpha = .05$ ensures this as well (but we stress that there may be reasons in an empirical study to choose a different significance level, as indicated before in this chapter). That is, if the *p*-value is smaller than the significance level (e.g., .05), we reject the null hypothesis. If the *p*-value is not smaller than the significance level, we consider the null hypothesis as retainable. Therefore, the only remaining question is how to work out the *p*-value in a given empirical setting where we have a data set available and are interested in testing a given null hypothesis versus an alternative hypothesis.

Working out the *p*-value using specifically designated command procedures, based on the reasoning earlier in this subsection (see also below), is implemented in widely circulated statistical analysis software, such as R, for nearly all statistical tests used in this book. The only exception is the *z*-test we have been dealing with in this chapter, which makes the assumption of known variance of the underlying random variable, *y*. (This assumption is most of the time considered not fulfilled in empirical research, and for this reason there are no automatic procedures of obtaining the associated *p*-values with these programs.) Beginning with the next chapter, we will routinely use the software-implemented procedures for determining *p*-values associated with analyzed sample data, but in the rest of this chapter we will instruct R to work them out for us. We illustrate this discussion next by revisiting the earlier college aspiration example in Section 7.5 (for completeness, we include its text below and refer later to it as Example 7.8).

> **Example 7.8 (college aspiration scale):** A researcher is interested in testing if a college aspiration scale has a mean of 18 in a studied population of high school seniors, which scale is known to have a variance of 144 there, versus the alternative that its mean is not 18. In a sample of $n = 36$ seniors the college aspiration score average—i.e., the mean estimate—is 22.5. What would be reasonable for the researcher to conclude with regard to the null hypothesis H_0: $\mu = \mu_0 = 18$ versus the alternative H_a: $\mu \neq \mu_0 (= 18)$ of interest?

As discussed above, all we need to do now is only evaluate the *p*-value associated with the sample value of the test statistic used, rather than the rejection region as earlier in this chapter. That is, we use here (a) the same test statistic (7.16) that of course follows the same distribution under the null hypothesis, viz., the standard normal $N(0,1)$; as well as (b) the same value of the test statistic for the available sample (see Equation (7.16)), viz., $22.5 - 18/\sqrt{(144/36)} = 2.25$. The only difference in our current testing approach is that we need to work out the *p*-value associated with this sample result, 2.25, which is the used test statistic value.

To this end, we first note that we are dealing here with a two-tailed alternative, H_a. Hence, we need to work out the probability of obtaining a sample value that is at least as large as 2.25, or alternatively at least as small as -2.25. (Due to the symmetry of the standard normal distribution around zero, any test statistic value larger than 2.25 is a mirror image of another possible one that is smaller than -2.25, and therefore just as inconsistent with the null hypothesis.) That is, we need to find out the area under the normal curve that is above 2.25 and below -2.25. To this end, due to symmetry reasons, we can work out the area under the normal curve above 2.25 and multiply it by two, in order to take into account the two-tailed nature of the alternative hypothesis. We achieve this easily with R as follows:

```
> 1-pnorm(2.25, 0, 1)
[1] 0.01222447
> 2*(1-pnorm(2.25,0,1))
[1] 0.02444895
```

Therefore, the sought p-value is .024. Since this is smaller than the conventionally used significance level of α = .05, we conclude that if the null hypothesis were to be true, the sample we have observed from the studied population would be associated with an event that would be very rare. For this reason, faced with the necessity to make a choice between the null hypothesis H_0: μ = 18 and the alternative hypothesis H_a: $\mu \neq 18$ here, we decide for the latter. This is because we interpret the empirical finding associated with a p-value of only .024 as strong evidence against the null hypothesis. We thus reject the claim that in the population the mean on the used college aspiration scale is 18. (We note that this is the same decision we arrived at via use of the pertinent rejection region earlier in the chapter, as one would expect.)

The discussed testing approach is appropriate when the alternative hypothesis is two-tailed, as in the last example considered. If the alternative were instead to be determined as one-tailed before looking at the data, a minor modification would be needed in the presently outlined procedure. The reason is that with one-tailed alternatives, we are considering deviations from the null hypothesis only in the direction of the tail of the specified alternative hypothesis, since only such deviations count as evidence against the null hypothesis. For instance, suppose we had settled in the last example, before looking at the data, on the one-sided alternative H_a: $\mu > \mu_0$, with the same null hypothesis as above. Then, in order to work out the p-value associated with the test statistic value observed in the sample, we need to find only the area beyond, i.e., to the right, of the value 2.25 found in the above example. This area was determined easily earlier with R to be

```
> 1-pnorm(2.25, 0, 1)
[1] 0.01222447
```

i.e., half the p-value when testing the two-tailed hypothesis. Since in the sample we observed an average that was in compliance with the alternative tail, as

22.5 > 18, given this small p-value we would decide to reject the null hypothesis. However, if in the sample the average were to be less than 18 (e.g., 16.85), given that this result is not in agreement with the alternative we would decide for retaining the null hypothesis without even having to look at the p-value. This is because none of the evidence we have in the sample would point in favor of the alternative, and so we cannot decide for the alternative hypothesis. (Note that, as indicated earlier, we would decide to retain the null hypothesis no matter how much smaller than 18 the sample average is.)

The described testing approach, as mentioned before, is often referred to for short as a *one-tailed test* and the p-value associated with it as a *one-tailed p-value*. We emphasize that to obtain this value we halved the p-value that pertains to the testing problem when dealing with a two-tailed alternative. However, we use this halved p-value to make a decision in favor of the null or alternative only if the test statistic value in the given sample is in agreement with the alternative hypothesis. By analogy, the process of testing a null hypothesis versus a two-tailed alternative is called a *two-tailed test*, and the resulting p-value is also referred to as a *two-tailed* p-value.

The discussed procedure for working out the p-value is directly applicable also in the case when the null is a more general hypothesis, such as H_0: $\mu < \mu_0$. (At times, this hypothesis is also called a *one-tailed null hypothesis*. Note that then the alternative hypothesis has to be one-tailed as well.) The reason is that in the preceding developments leading up to this procedure we never used the fact that the null was a simple hypothesis. Hence, the same reasoning is applicable when the null is a composite (one-tailed) hypothesis.

To illustrate this discussion, consider the last college aspiration example, but suppose we were interested to begin with in testing the null hypothesis that the population mean on the used scale is no larger than 18, versus the alternative that it is larger than 18. That is, we wish to test here the null hypothesis H_0: $\mu \leq 18$ against the alternative H_a: $\mu > 18$. (We reiterate that we need to have settled on the null and alternative hypotheses, as well on the significance level, before looking at the data or the results of any analyses carried out on it.) Proceeding as above, given the sample finding of a z-value of 2.25 associated with the observed sample average of 22.5, we need to work out the area under the standard normal curve and beyond 2.25. As elaborated earlier in this subsection, the associated p-value is readily found with R as follows:

```
> 1-pnorm(2.25, 0, 1)
[1] 0.01222447
```

Given this p-value of .01 (rounded off), which is smaller than the conventionally used significance level of .05, we can reject the null hypothesis that the population mean is no higher than 18 in favor of the alternative that it is larger than 18.

In conclusion, we stress that if the null hypothesis to begin with was H_0: $\mu = 18$ and the alternative H_0: $\mu < 18$, then the mean obtained in the available sample would not be in the direction of the alternative (as $22.5 > 18$). In that case, we would directly consider the null hypothesis as retainable, and there would not be any need to work out the pertinent p-value.

7.8. HYPOTHESIS TESTING USING CONFIDENCE INTERVALS

In the preceding Sections 7.6 and 7.7, we used test statistics and associated p-values to examine research hypotheses. A criticism that can be raised against this testing approach when the null is a simple hypothesis, such as H_0: $\mu = \mu_0$, is that this type of very precise hypothesis can be argued to be most of the time incorrect in studied populations to begin with. In addition, as indicated earlier, the statistical power increases toward 1 (being a probability) with increasing sample size as well. Hence, one may argue, whether this null hypothesis is rejected or not is a matter of how large a sample is used.

An alternative approach to statistical hypothesis testing when simple null hypotheses are of concern is based on the use of confidence intervals introduced in Section 7.3 of this chapter. As we clarified there, a confidence interval (CI) represents a range of plausible values for a population parameter (e.g., the mean). Suppose one were interested in testing the simple null hypothesis H_0: $\mu = \mu_0$ against the alternative H_0: $\mu \neq \mu_0$. Denote the confidence interval at 95% confidence level as (l, u), where l and u are its lower and upper endpoints. (We recall that their values are sample-dependent.)

Our preceding discussion in this chapter suggests that when testing a null hypothesis like H_0, we are in a sense asking the following question: "Given the sample, is the hypothetical value for the parameter of interest—i.e., μ_0—a plausible value for this parameter in the population?" For example, given the data, does the μ_0 look like a possible value for the mean μ in the studied population? Yet the CI is a range of plausible values by definition, i.e., in fact the CI contains all plausible values, at a confidence level chosen prior to looking at the data, for the population parameter of concern. Hence, by checking if the CI contains the hypothetical value of the parameter, we are in fact performing statistical hypothesis testing. That is, if the CI contains the value of the parameter as stated in the null hypothesis, we can consider it retainable; if it does not contain it, we can reject the null hypothesis.

This reasoning underlies a more rigorous result (e.g., Roussas, 1997) stating that a $100(1 - \alpha)$%-CI can be used in this way to test at a significance level α the null hypothesis stipulating a particular value for an unknown parameter, versus the alternative that the latter does not equal that value. In case of interest in the mean, this result implies that if one were concerned with testing the null hypothesis H_0: $\mu = \mu_0$ against the alternative H_0: $\mu \neq \mu_0$ at significance level α, one can check if μ_0 is contained in the $100(1 - \alpha)\%$-CI, i.e., whether $l < \mu_0 < u$ holds. If this CI contains μ_0, then H_0 is retained, but if the CI does not contain μ_0, i.e., if $l > \mu_0$ or $u < \mu_0$, then H_0 is rejected.

We illustrate this approach to hypothesis testing using the earlier college aspiration scale example (Example 7.8). Assuming conventional significance level of $\alpha = .05$, as discussed in Section 7.3, the general form of the $100(1 - \alpha)\%$-CI in the current setting is presented in (7.12). (We reiterate that here assumed is normality of the sample mean and knowledge of the variance of the underlying random variable y, the score on the college aspiration scale.) The general CI is as follows:

$$(\bar{y} - z_{\alpha/2} \cdot \sigma/\sqrt{n}, \bar{y} + z_{\alpha/2} \cdot \sigma/\sqrt{n}).$$

Thus, for our example, all we need is $z_{\alpha/2}$, which we found in Section 7.3 to be 1.96. Using this value, the 95%-CI for the population mean of the college aspiration scale of concern here is ('$\times$' is used next to denote multiplication)

$$(22.5 - 1.96 \times 12/6, 22.5 + 1.96 \times 12/6),$$

i.e., the sought CI is (18.58, 26.42). Since this 95%-CI does not include the hypothetical value 18 for the mean, this value is not plausible for the population mean. For this reason, we conclude that the sample contains sufficient evidence warranting rejection of the null hypothesis H_0: $\mu = \mu_0 = 18$, in favor of the alternative H_a: $\mu \neq 18$. This is the same decision we arrived at before in the chapter using the earlier discussed means of hypothesis testing, as one could expect.

In conclusion, we emphasize that the discussions in this section are valid for testing statistical hypotheses about any population parameter, not just for the mean—the parameter we were mostly concerned with here. Thereby, we can formally treat the symbol μ as denoting generally any population parameter of interest, and correspondingly μ_0 as a particular value for it. If we then proceed exactly as in this last section, we will be in a position to test any simple hypothesis about a population parameter by using a corresponding level confidence interval for that parameter, against a two-tailed alternative.

8

Inferences about Population Means When Variances Are Unknown

All discussions regarding statistical inference in the last chapter assumed that the variance of the underlying random variable y of interest was known and that its sample mean $\bar{y}$ was normal. Nevertheless, it is rarely the case in empirical behavioral and social research that one can easily assume the variance σ^2 of y as known or possible to evaluate very precisely. For instance, a newly developed measure of neuroticism cannot be typically assumed to have a known population variance. In addition, the population of subjects for which the measure has been developed may be rather heterogeneous. Hence, unless the sample is very large—which may well be hard to achieve with limited resources—it cannot be reasonably assumed that its population variance could be known or evaluated with high precision.

In such situations, it may nonetheless be still of particular interest to carry out statistical inference about population means on studied variables. For these cases, the general idea underlying the z-test discussed in Chapter 7 in fact remains applicable. Specifically, after estimation of the population standard deviation σ of the studied variable y by the sample standard deviation s, and substitution of the latter for σ into the test statistic in Equation (7.16) of that chapter, one can carry out testing and confidence interval evaluation with the same general procedure after paying attention to one important point, which we turn to next. This point has to do with the appropriate consideration of the so-called t-ratio and t-distribution.

8.1. THE *t*-RATIO AND *t*-DISTRIBUTION

When we do not assume knowledge of the standard deviation σ of a studied random variable y, the following suggestion may be made in analogy to the z-test discussed in the previous chapter. Accordingly, the test statistic given in

Equation (8.1) below can be used for testing the null hypothesis H_0: $\mu = \mu_0$ versus the alternative H_a: $\mu \neq \mu_0$ or even one-tailed alternative hypotheses:

$$(8.1) \qquad\qquad t = \frac{\bar{y} - \mu_0}{s / \sqrt{n}}.$$

The ratio in the right-hand side of Equation (8.1), which is frequently referred to as the t-*ratio*, is not identical to the *z*-test statistic presented in Equation (7.16) and used throughout the preceding Chapter 7 (frequently also referred to as *z*-ratio). For this reason, we use a different notation—viz., *t*—to designate the left-hand side of Equation (8.1). Specifically, with this notation we emphasize the fact that in Equation (8.1) we substitute the sample standard deviation *s* for the population standard deviation σ in the earlier Equation (7.16), which standard deviation we do not assume here as known anymore.

While this may seem to be a straightforward substitution leading from Equation (7.16) in Chapter 7 to Equation (8.1) here, it actually entails some important consequences. In particular, due to using the estimate *s* of the standard deviation of *y* in Equation (8.1), the resulting test statistic *t* in it does not follow a standard normal distribution under the null hypothesis of the mean being equal to μ_0, but instead follows a different distribution. The distribution of the right-hand side of Equation (8.1) under the assumption $\mu = \mu_0$, that is, under the null hypothesis, is referred to as the t-*distribution*. A more complete reference to it, which is used at times in the literature, is as *Student's* t-*distribution*—bearing the pseudonym "Student" used by the British statistician William S. Gossett in the early 20th century.

As shown in more advanced treatments (e.g., Roussas, 1997), the test statistic *t* in Equation (8.1) possesses this *t*-distribution when *y* is normally distributed, and a fairly close distribution when *y* is coming from a symmetric distribution. As is the case with the normal distribution, a concept that we used throughout the last two chapters, there are infinitely many *t*-distributions. Each one of these distributions differs from any other of the class of *t*-distributions by an associated quantity that is called *degrees of freedom*, commonly denoted as *df*. This quantity, *df*, is always an integer number, i.e., a whole positive number. The concept of degrees of freedom plays a special role for many test statistics used in empirical research, and for this reason we discuss it next in greater detail.

8.1.1. Degrees of freedom

The *degrees of freedom* (denoted alternatively *d*) reflect the number of independent pieces of information about a random variable *y* of concern that are available in a given study. Initially, we start with *n* such pieces contained in the *n* observations on *y* that comprise the available sample, $y_1,..., y_n$. However, to obtain the *t*-ratio in Equation (8.1), we need to estimate the unknown population mean μ, which we do with the sample average $\bar{y}$. That is, we obtain in this way information about the population mean, or in other words we extract this information from the sample—viz., from the initial n independent sources of information about the random variable y. Hence, estimation of the population mean μ is tantamount to utilizing one of the initial n pieces of information available in a given sample. As a result, $n - 1$ independent pieces of information remain about y. For this reason, the degrees of freedom (df) associated with the *t*-ratio in Equation (8.1) are $df = d = n - 1$.

This procedure of obtaining the degrees of freedom associated with a statistic in question remains valid also when many other unknown parameters or a set of such are of interest. Specifically, to obtain then the degrees of freedom we subtract the number of estimated parameters from the initial number of independent pieces of information about a variable under consideration, as available in a given study. (As an aside at this point, a study may involve more than one sample, i.e., a sample from each of several distinct populations, and all samples are then taken into account when determining the degrees of freedom associated with a particular statistic.) We will utilize and discuss this degree of freedom calculation procedure on a few particular occasions in the remainder of the book.

8.1.2. Properties of the *t*-distribution

Returning to the *t*-ratio in Equation (8.1), as pointed out above it possesses a *t*-distribution with $n - 1$ degrees of freedom, when given is a sample of n observations, $y_1,..., y_n$. This definition reveals an important feature of the *t*-distribution, viz., that it has a shape that depends on the number of subjects studied, i.e., on the number of subjects in the sample. Another property of the *t*-distribution is that it approaches the standard normal distribution with increasing sample size, and hence with degrees of freedom. This feature can be shown using more advanced methods (e.g., Roussas, 1997). We elaborate empirically upon this property of the *t*-distribution in Section 8.2 below.

Since to obtain the *t*-ratio in Equation (8.1) we substitute the sample estimate s of the standard deviation σ of the underlying random variable y, we in a sense transfer the sampling variability of the estimate s into (8.1). (Recall that the empirical standard deviation s is a random variable whose value depends on the drawn sample—see, e.g., Chapter 3.) Thus, for another sample with the same size from the same population of interest, the value of s will in general be different. That is, there is inherent variability that underlies the empirical (sample) value of s. This variability is passed over to the *t*-ratio in Equation (8.1), since the statistic s is an integral part of it. This added variability to the *t*-ratio relative to the *z*-ratio in Equation (7.16) of Chapter 7, which does not utilize the sample standard variance s, represents a major way in which the two test statistics differ from one another. In particular, this added variability leads to the fact that the *t*-ratio in Equation (8.1) follows a distribution different from the standard normal, which as pointed out in the preceding chapter is the distribution of the *z*-ratio (7.16) (see Chapter 7).

It has been shown in the literature that the variance of a random variable *x* following a *t*-distribution with *df* degrees of freedom is (for *df* > 2; e.g., Rao, 1973)

$$(8.2) \qquad Var(x) = df/(df-2).$$

From Equation (8.2), it is seen that the variance of the *t*-distribution is always larger than one, which is the variance of the standard normal distribution $N(0,1)$. Therefore, the probability density function (pdf) of the *t*-distribution is somewhat flatter and "shorter" than that of the standard normal—due to the fact that the area under the curve of the normal distribution is one as well.

We illustrate this flatness feature using graphs of the standard normal and several *t*-distributions, which we can obtain readily using R. As before, first we create a "net" (or "grid," array) of very closely positioned points on the horizontal axis, then compute both the density function values of the standard normal and the *t*-distribution with degrees of freedom *df* = 3, say, and superimpose these two pdf's. We note thereby that the pdf, or density curve, of the *t*-distribution is obtained with the command 'dt', whereas that of the standard normal is obtained with the command 'dnorm'. The overlay of the two graphed distributions is accomplished with the command 'lines', placing in gray color the pdf of the *t*-distribution (by using the subcommand col = "gray"). All these activities are achieved consecutively with the following five R commands:

```
> x = seq(-4, 4, .005)
> d.n = dnorm(x)
> plot(x, d.n)
> d.t = dt(x, 3)
> lines(x, d.t, col = "gray")
```

These commands lead to the graph displayed in Figure 8.1 (the gray curve appears thereby as thinner than the default black curve).

We notice from Figure 8.1 a characteristic property of the *t*-distribution. Specifically, its tails are thicker than those of the standard normal distribution, and thus it rises to a lower level. As pointed out before, the reason for this is the fact that the area under the pdf of either distribution is one, due to the earlier-mentioned pertinent convention for any pdf (see Chapter 5). This tail-thickness property of the *t*-distribution relative to the standard normal distribution results from the substitution of the imprecise sample estimate *s* for σ

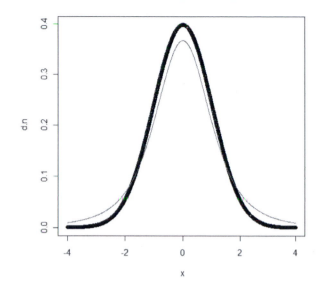

FIGURE 8.1.

Graphs of the densities of the standard normal distribution (thick line) and the *t*-distribution with $df = 3$ degrees of freedom (thin line).

into the formula for the *z*-ratio (7.16) (see Chapter 7), in order to obtain the *t*-ratio in (8.1) as mentioned earlier in this chapter.

The difference between the *t*-distribution and the standard normal distribution diminishes, however, with increasing sample size *n*. Then also the degrees of freedom *df* increase, since $df = n - 1$, as pointed out before. In Figure 8.2, the pdf of the *t*-distribution with $df = 8$ degrees of freedom is overlaid with the standard normal. As seen from that figure, there are much smaller differences now between the two distributions relative to their differences in Figure 8.1. (Figure 8.2. is obtained via the same sequence of commands leading to Figure 8.1, with the only difference that the curve `d.t = dt(x, 8)` is now used instead of the earlier curve `d.t = dt(x, 3)`. Similarly, in the following Figure 8.3, the line `d.t = dt(x, 20)` is used instead in order to obtain the pdf of the *t*-distribution with $df = 20$; see below.)

Continuing in the same way, Figure 8.3 shows the pdf of the *t*-distribution with $df = 20$ degrees of freedom, where for most practical purposes the differences between the standard normal and that *t*-distribution are minimal if of relevance. More generally, these differences become less and less pronounced as sample size *n* increases (and thus degrees of freedom $df = n - 1$ do so as well; practically, there is little difference between the two considered distributions for $df > 30$.)

The three Figures 8.1 through 8.3 enable us also to recognize another important property of the *t*-distribution. While having fatter tails than the

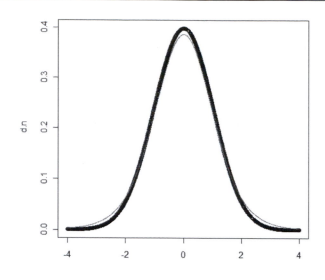

FIGURE 8.2.

Graphs of the densities of the standard normal distribution (thick line) and the *t*-distribution with *df* = 8 degrees of freedom (thin line; the size of the figure frame is the same as that of Figure 8.1).

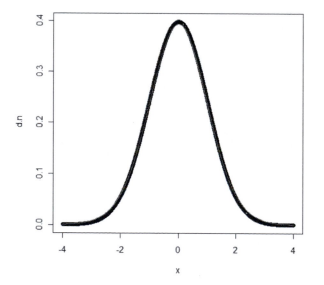

FIGURE 8.3.

Graphs of the densities of the standard normal distribution (thick line) and the *t*-distribution with *df* = 20 degrees of freedom (thin line; the size of the figure frame is the same as that of Figures 8.1 and 8.2).

standard normal $N(0,1)$ for any finite sample, the t-distribution with df degrees of freedom ($df > 2$) is also symmetric around zero, like any normal distribution. It will be useful to keep this symmetry feature in mind for the remainder of this chapter.

8.2. HYPOTHESIS TESTING ABOUT THE MEAN WITH UNKNOWN STANDARD DEVIATION

Having highlighted the differences between the t-distribution and the standard normal distribution in the last section, we now return to our main concern in this chapter. Specifically, we would like to carry out statistical inference about a population mean from a normally distributed random variable y of interest, whose population standard deviation σ is unknown. We stress that such a scenario is quite common in empirical research, since we typically do not know the population variance (and hence the standard deviation) of most random variables of concern.

Under those circumstances, as pointed out above we can use the t-ratio defined in Equation (8.1). Since we now know the distribution of this t-ratio, viz., a t-distribution with $df = n - 1$ degrees of freedom (n denoting sample size as usual), in all our inferential activities we can proceed as in the case with a known standard deviation σ but referring eventually to this t-distribution. That is, whenever a percentile (quantile) is needed, we have to use those of the pertinent t-distribution rather than standard normal distribution as we did throughout Chapter 7, where we assumed that σ was known. By analogy to the quantiles of $N(0,1)$, we denote these of the t-distribution as $t_{\alpha,df}$, for given significance level α and degrees of freedom df. We stress that we now use two subindexes attached to the symbol of the t-distribution for designating its quantiles, viz., α and df. This is because the t-distribution itself depends on df (and thus on sample size), a property that is not shared with the distribution $N(0,1)$ of the z-ratio in Equation (7.16) (see details provided in Chapter 7) or with any other normal distribution.

8.2.1. Percentiles of the t-distribution

We can easily obtain the percentiles of the t-distribution using the software R with the command 'qt(p, d)'. We stress the notational analogy to the earlier used command 'qnorm(p, μ, σ)' for obtaining the percentiles of the normal distribution with mean and variance μ and σ^2, respectively. In the command needed here, 'qt(p, d)', for p we enter the probability pertaining to the percentile in question and for d the associated degrees of freedom, i.e., sample size less one. For instance, if we are interested in the 95th percentile of the

t-distribution with $df = 3$ degrees of freedom, we obtain it as follows (result given beneath command):

```
> qt(.95, 3)
[1] 2.353363
```

That is, the number 2.353 (rounded off to the third decimal place) cuts off to the right 5% of the area under the density curve of the t-distribution with three degrees of freedom. We note that this percentile of the t-distribution is larger than the corresponding 95th percentile of the standard normal distribution, $N(0,1)$, which we know from before is 1.645. The reason is, as pointed out earlier, that the tails of the t-distribution are thicker than those of $N(0,1)$. Thus, given the small sample size, we need to go further out—that is, away to the right from zero—in order to find the same percentiles of the t-distribution relative to the corresponding percentiles of the standard normal distribution.

8.2.2. Confidence interval and testing hypotheses about a given population mean

As indicated in Chapter 7, of particular interest are confidence intervals (CIs) for population means. In the present chapter, the CIs of means are also of special relevance in the empirical settings of concern where we do not know the population standard deviation of a studied variable, or personal characteristic, y. Given the earlier discussion in this chapter, by analogy to the case when we assumed we knew the standard deviation σ of y (see Chapter 7), we obtain $(1 - \alpha)100\%$-CIs intervals for population means by using the corresponding quantiles $t_{\alpha, d}$ of the t-distribution in lieu of the same quantiles of the z-distribution ($0 < \alpha < 1$). In particular, the $100(1 - \alpha)\%$-CI for the population mean, when the standard deviation of the studied variable y is unknown but instead estimated from the sample, is (compare with the CI defined in (7.12) in Chapter 7):

$$(8.3) \qquad (\bar{y} - t_{\alpha/2, \, df} \cdot s/\sqrt{n}, \; \bar{y} + t_{\alpha/2, \, df} \cdot s/\sqrt{n}).$$

Using this CI, we can carry out—just like in Chapter 7 (Section 7.8)—hypothesis testing about population means in situations where the standard deviation of y is unknown. This approach to hypothesis testing, which we exemplify below, does not provide a p-value associated with a given sample and the test statistic value obtained in it. We can readily furnish such a p-value for a tested null hypothesis versus an alternative hypothesis, however, using the t-ratio in Equation (8.1). Since this ratio plays an instrumental role in the present testing approach, the resulting statistical test is often referred to as "t-test for the mean."

To carry out a t-test for a given mean value μ_0, i.e., to test the null hypothesis $H_0: \mu = \mu_0$ versus the alternative $H_0: \mu \neq \mu_0$, we employ with R the command 't.test':

```
> t.test(y, mu = mu0)
```

As seen from the last line, this command has two "arguments," i.e., two entities that need to be supplied to the software in order for it to carry out the t-test in question. The first argument is the data, i.e., the variable y for which we are testing a hypothesis with regard to its mean (as usual, μ denotes the mean of y in the studied population). We discussed earlier in the book how we can read data into R. Once we do so, any variable (variable name) in a given data set can be used for 'y' in the 't.test' command, as long as a research question can be addressed by a t-test carried out with regard to its mean.

The second argument, denoted mu = mu0 in the last stated R command, is the hypothetical value μ_0 of concern in the null hypothesis tested. Thereby, the particular hypothetical value (number) is entered in place of 'mu0'. For instance, if we wish to test the null hypothesis $H_0: \mu = 22$ versus the alternative $H_a: \mu \neq 22$, for a variable denoted 'y' in a data file that has been read into R, the above command is as follows (note that the name of the variable appears as the first argument, while 'mu' is spelled out this way in the left-hand side of the second argument of the following command):

```
> t.test(y, mu = 22)
```

We exemplify this discussion using the mathematics test–taking anxiety (MTA) data set first introduced in Chapter 2 (Example 2.2; the data are available in the file CH2_EX22.dat). Suppose we want to test the null hypothesis that in the studied population of high school freshmen the mean anxiety score was 27.5, versus the alternative that it was a distinct number (whatever it might be then). That is, we are interested here in testing $H_0: \mu = 27.5$ versus the alternative $H_a: \mu \neq 27.5$. We assume again that the anxiety scores are stored in the variable denoted 'y' in the available data set.

In order to test this null hypothesis, we first need to read the data into R. To accomplish this, as mentioned in Chapter 2 we need to assign a name to the data file after reading it in, which we here choose to be 'mta'. We then read in the data with the following command (note the path name used next on a particular computer where the data are stored, which name need not be the same in other applications with the same data):

```
> mta = read.table("C://data/CH2_EX22.dat", header = T)
```

Once the data are read in, a "data frame" is created where the variables are not immediately available for our purposes to R. To make them so, we attach the data to the R engine:

```
> attach(mta)
```

We are now ready to test the above null hypothesis H$_0$: $\mu = 27.5$ against the alternative H$_a$: $\mu \neq 27.5$. We achieve this, as indicated earlier, with the R command 't.test', where we now substitute 27.5 for 'mu0' in its second argument:

```
> t.test(y, mu = 27.5)
```

This command produces the following output:

```
        One Sample t-test
data:  y

t = -6.1346, df = 35, p-value = 5.135e-07
alternative hypothesis: true mean is not equal to 27.5

95 percent confidence interval:
 21.84356 24.65644
sample estimates:
mean of x
    23.25
```

This R output contains a substantial amount of information, which we discuss in detail next. First, the test statistic—the t-ratio defined in the earlier Equation (8.1)—has the value of -6.13 here. Second, the degrees of freedom are $df = 36 - 1 = 35$. Third, the associated p-value is $p = 5.14 \times 10^{-7}$. The obtained p-value is a very small number and hence is below the usual preset significance level of $\alpha = .05$. As a result, we can reject H$_0$: $\mu = 27.5$ and decide for the alternative hypothesis of the mean being a different number in the studied population of high school freshmen. We also note that the output contains the 95%-confidence interval (8.3) for the population mean. This interval is (21.84, 24.65). Since it does not contain the hypothesized value 27.5, we can alternatively conclude that the null hypothesis can be rejected, and thus that the alternative hypothesis of this mean being distinct from 27.5 can be decided for. (We note that for the purpose of hypothesis testing, we need only follow one of the two analytic avenues indicated here—use of the p-value, or of the CI.)

8.2.3. One-tailed *t*-tests

The discussed testing approach needs some modification if a one-tailed test is to be carried out, as we indicated in Chapter 7. Specifically, if we had started out before looking at the data with the intent to test the same null hypothesis H_0: $\mu = 27.5$ but against the one-sided, directional alternative H_a: $\mu < 27.5$, we would need to examine first the sample average. This average was found earlier and is also stated in the final two lines of the last presented R output as 23.25. Thus, the sample average is in the direction of the alternative, since it is smaller than 27.5. Therefore, all we need to do now is halve the *p*-value reported in the R output. Given that this *p*-value was found above to be a very small number, its half is even smaller and hence smaller than any reasonable preset significance level, such as .05, say. Therefore, in this case we would reject the null hypothesis and decide for the alternative stating that the mean is smaller than 27.5.

On the other hand, if before looking at the data we chose to test the null hypothesis H_0: $\mu = 27.5$ against the alternative H_a: $\mu > 27.5$, we again would need to first check the sample mean. Since it is now not in the direction of the alternative hypothesis (as 23.25 is smaller than 27.5 stipulated in the alternative hypothesis), we would retain the null hypothesis rather than the alternative hypothesis, as discussed in detail in Chapter 7.

We reiterate that we need to decide before looking at the data for a specific null hypothesis and an alternative hypothesis to be tested. That is, before looking at the data set (or doing any analysis of it), we must decide what exactly the null hypothesis H_0 and the alternative hypothesis H_a are. Only then may we proceed as discussed in this section. If we first look at the data and use information from it to choose the specific form of the null and/or alternative hypothesis—in particular, decide which of the two possible tails the one-tailed alternative should have—then seriously misleading results can follow. The reason is that we would be "testing" then with a given data set a hypothesis that has been determined at least in part by the features of that very same data set. Such an approach is in general bound to yield incorrect results. This is because it capitalizes on chance effects at work in the available sample, which are due to the ever-present sampling error (the difference between available sample and studied population, in any study that is not a census), and hence the ensuing results cannot be trusted.

8.2.4. Inference for a single mean at another significance level

The above discussion was based on the assumption that we settled, before looking at the data, on the significance level $\alpha = .05$ (i.e., the probability of Type I error—see Chapter 7). The testing principle underlying the approach used, however, is directly applicable when we preselect another significance level. For example, if we wanted to carry out statistical inference using the significance level $\alpha = .01$ to begin with (i.e., we chose $\alpha = .01$ before looking at the data), then we need to add this information as a third argument to the above R command 't.test'. To this end, we can use its subcommand 'conf.level $= .99$', since the confidence level corresponding to a significance level of .01 is $(1 - .01)100\% = 99\%$. The command 't.test' then looks as follows for the last-considered example:

```
> t.test(y, mu = 27.5, conf.level = .99)
```

and provides the following output:

```
        One Sample t-test
data:  y
t = -6.1346, df = 35, p-value = 5.135e-07
alternative hypothesis: true mean is not equal to 27.5
99 percent confidence interval:
 21.36297 25.13703
sample estimates:
mean of x
    23.25
```

We notice that the p-value is not changed, since our data and test statistic are not changed either. If we were to test the simple null hypothesis H_0: $\mu = 27.5$ versus the alternative H_a: $\mu \neq 27.5$, to begin with, we need to compare the p-value reported by R to the chosen different significance level, which is .01. Since the reported p-value of 5.135×10^{-7} is smaller than .01, we reject the null hypothesis and decide for the alternative.

Similarly, if we were interested in the first instance in one-tailed tests, we proceed in full analogy to the case of $\alpha = .05$ discussed in detail in the previous subsection 8.5.3. We note in passing that the CI produced thereby will be different in case the significance level $\alpha = .01$ is preset. In fact, the 99%-CI for the population mean will be wider than before, since we will be using here a higher confidence level (viz., 99% rather than 95% as earlier).

In conclusion of this section, we emphasize that while we made in it the assumption of normality of the studied random variable y, the t-tests and confidence intervals discussed in it yield trustworthy results also with minor to mild deviations from normality. More serious deviations from normality can be handled with alternative methods that go beyond the confines of this introductory book (e.g., Ott & Longnecker, 2010; Roussas, 1997). Further, we stress that the significance level for any statistical test, and hence the implied confidence level associated with a confidence interval of interest, needs to be decided upon (i.e., chosen) before looking at the data. If this choice is done after the data are inspected, it is possible that seriously misleading results can be arrived at.

8.3. INFERENCES ABOUT DIFFERENCES OF TWO INDEPENDENT MEANS

So far in this chapter, we have been concerned with inferences about a single population mean. We have emphasized thereby that in order to carry out the associated statistical tests, we must know a priori the specific hypothetical value of the mean that we test about with them. Many times in empirical behavioral and social research, however, this knowledge is not available, or there is no particular value for the mean that would be of substantive interest. In addition, very often one is interested in inferences involving not one but more than a single population and their means. For instance, one may well be interested in finding out how the means on a studied variable differ in an experimental and a control group (populations), or for male and female subjects, or for different socioeconomic groups, and so on.

In this section, we deal with settings where we are concerned specifically with two populations (groups) under consideration. We consider two cases: (a) when the populations of interest are independent of one another, and (b) when they are related to one another. In case (a), we will assume that we have obtained two random samples from either of the two distinct populations, with corresponding sizes n_1 and n_2, and we will use the fact that these samples are also independent of one another. Our following developments will be based on the next important result that will permit us to obtain a measure of the distance between null hypothesis and data from the available samples from these populations, and thus a test statistic for testing population mean equality. (For a detailed demonstration of this result, see Roussas, 1997.) The result states that for independent normal random variables the normal distribution is preserved when they are subtracted from one another or added to each other.

Result 8.1: If $y_1 \sim N(\mu_1, \sigma_1^2)$ and $y_2 \sim N(\mu_2, \sigma_2^2)$ are two independent normally distributed random variables, then their difference and their sum are also normally distributed, each with the following means and variances:

(a) $y_1 - y_2 \sim N(\mu_1 - \mu_2, \sigma_1^2 + \sigma_2^2)$, and
(b) $y_1 + y_2 \sim N(\mu_1 + \mu_2, \sigma_1^2 + \sigma_2^2)$.

We point out that unlike the means, the variance of both the sum and the difference of the two random variables is the same, viz., the sum of their variances. This is because irrespective of whether one takes their sum or difference, the random variability of any of the two resulting variables, viz., $y_1 - y_2$ and $y_1 + y_2$, is superimposed on that variability of the other variable.

Result 8.1 can be used together with the central limit theorem (CLT), if need be, to find out the distribution of the difference of two sample means in the setting we are interested in this section. Here we are dealing with two random samples from two unrelated populations, and $\bar{y}_1$ and $\bar{y}_2$ denote their sample averages (means). As we know from Chapter 6, their means and variances are correspondingly μ_1 and σ_1^2 / n_1 (for $\bar{y}_1$) as well as μ_2 and σ_2^2 / n_2 (for $\bar{y}_2$). Since the two samples are independent, however, so are their sample averages $\bar{y}_1$ and $\bar{y}_2$. Thus, using Result 8.1, we see that the mean and variance of their difference are correspondingly

$$(8.4) \qquad \mu_{\bar{y}1-\bar{y}2} = \mu_{\bar{y}1} - \mu_{\bar{y}2} = \mu_1 - \mu_2, \text{ and}$$
$$\sigma^2_{\bar{y}1-\bar{y}2} = \sigma^2_{\bar{y}1} + \sigma^2_{\bar{y}2} = \sigma^2_1 / n_1 + \sigma^2_2 / n_2,$$

where $\mu_{\bar{y}1-\bar{y}2}$ and $\sigma^2_{\bar{y}1-\bar{y}2}$ denote the mean and variance, respectively, of the difference in sample means, $\bar{y}_1 - \bar{y}_2$. Hence, for the standard deviation $\sigma_{\bar{y}1-\bar{y}2}$ of this mean difference, $\bar{y}_1 - \bar{y}_2$, it follows that

$$(8.5) \qquad \sigma_{\bar{y}1-\bar{y}2} = \sqrt{\sigma^2_{\bar{y}1} + \sigma^2_{\bar{y}2}} = \sqrt{\sigma^2_1 / n_1 + \sigma^2_2 / n_2}.$$

We summarize the last developments in the following result, which will be of particular importance in the remainder of this Section 8.4.

> **Result 8.2:** The random sampling distribution of the difference of two sample averages (means), $\bar{y}_1 - \bar{y}_2$, has the following three properties:
>
> (i)   it is approximately normal for large samples (and is normal for any sample size when each of the random variables y_1 and y_2 is so),
> (ii) its mean is the difference between the two population means (see first of Equations (8.4)), and
> (iii) the standard error of the difference of the two sample averages is $\sigma_{\bar{y}1-\bar{y}2} = \sqrt{\sigma^2_1 / n_1 + \sigma^2_2 / n_2}$.

This result allows us to carry out statistical inference with regard to the difference in two independent population means, following the same principles underlying the inferences about single population mean that were discussed earlier in this chapter.

8.3.1. Point and interval estimation of the difference in two independent population means

We first address the question what the best numerical guess, or estimate, would be for the difference in the means, μ_1 and μ_2, of two independent populations. As a point estimate of their difference, $\mu_1 - \mu_2$, obviously one can use the difference in their sample averages, $\bar{y}_1 - \bar{y}_2$, since the point estimate of μ_i is $\bar{y}_i$ ($i = 1, 2$; see Chapter 2). Hence, whenever we wish to obtain an idea of how much two populations might differ in terms of their means, we can simply subtract the averages obtained in the available samples from these populations.

As pointed out earlier in this Section 8.3, we use the same principles employed earlier in the chapter for interval estimation of the population mean difference $\mu_1 - \mu_2$. In order to proceed, we assume that (a) both populations are normally distributed (with respect to the studied variable y, or personal characteristic, in either of them), and (b) the variances of y are the same in the two populations, i.e., $\sigma_1^2 = \sigma_2^2 = \sigma^2$, say. (We do not assume that they are known, only that they are equal, whatever common population value they may have.) The last assumption of identity of the two variances can be readily used to obtain an estimate of this common variance, σ^2. Indeed, since the two populations have the same variances, each of the samples provides an estimate of this common variance. Hence, we can pool the two sample estimates into one estimate of the common variance, σ^2.

To this end, we need to first sum the squared individual deviations from the means in each sample. From Chapter 2, this sum from sample 1 is $(n_1 - 1)s_1^2$, with s_1^2 denoting the variance estimate from that sample. Similarly, the sum of squared individual mean deviations from sample 2 is $(n_2 - 1)s_2^2$, with s_2^2 denoting the variance estimate from it. Adding them together, we obtain the pooled sum of squared individual mean deviations as

$$(8.6) \qquad\qquad (n_1 - 1)s_1^2 + (n_2 - 1)s_2^2.$$

In order to furnish now an estimate of the common variance, σ^2, we need to divide the sum of individual mean deviations from both samples, (8.6), by the associated degrees of freedom (df). To find these df, we use the procedure discussed in Section 8.2 when considering the t-distribution and how its degrees of freedom were determined.

To work out the appropriate degrees of freedom here, we note that in order to render the critical sum in (8.6), we need to estimate the mean in each of the populations. Hence, we lose two degrees of freedom from the initial $n_1 + n_2$ available independent observations (pieces of information) on the studied variable y that we have access to with the two samples. That is, the relevant degrees of freedom are here $n_1 + n_2 - 2$. Hence, the sought estimate of the common variance, σ^2, is:

$$(8.7) \qquad\qquad s_p^2 = \frac{(n_1 - 1)s_1^2 + (n_2 - 1)s_2^2}{n_1 + n_2 - 2}.$$

This estimate (8.7) is often referred to as "pooled variance estimate," as indicated by the used subindex. Thus, the corresponding estimate of the common standard deviation σ is

$$(8.8) \qquad s_p = \sqrt{\frac{(n_1 - 1)s_1^2 + (n_2 - 1)s_2^2}{n_1 + n_2 - 2}}.$$

Now that we have an estimate of the common standard deviation σ, from Result 8.2, point (iii), we obtain the following estimate of the standard error of the difference in the two sample averages:

$$(8.9) \qquad \hat{\sigma}_{\bar{y}_1 - \bar{y}_2} = s_p \sqrt{1 / n_1 + 1 / n_2}.$$

We note that the right-hand side of Equation (8.9) is obtained by substituting s_p as the common estimate of the variances appearing in the formula for the standard error of the difference in two sample means in Result 8.2, (iii). We also mention in passing that the estimate in Equation (8.7) is actually a weighted average of the estimates of the common variance, σ^2, that are obtained from each of the samples. Thereby, either of these estimates is weighted proportionately to the size of the sample that it comes from—viz., by the weight $(n_i - 1)/(n_1 + n_2 - 2)$ for the ith sample ($i = 1, 2$).

With the estimate in Equation (8.9) of the standard error of the difference in the two sample means of concern, we can now use the same logic underlying the derivation of the confidence interval (8.3) earlier in this chapter, in order to obtain a confidence interval for the difference of two independent population means, $\mu_1 - \mu_2$, at a given confidence level $(1 - \alpha)100\%$ $(0 < \alpha < 1)$. Accordingly, with Equations (8.3) and (8.9) in mind, we obtain this CI as follows:

$$(8.10) \qquad \left(\bar{y}_1 - \bar{y}_2 - t_{\alpha/2, n_1 + n_2 - 2} s_p \sqrt{\frac{1}{n_1} + \frac{1}{n_2}}, \; \bar{y}_1 - \bar{y}_2 + t_{\alpha/2, n_1 + n_2 - 2} s_p \sqrt{\frac{1}{n_1} + \frac{1}{n_2}} \right).$$

We can also use this confidence interval for the purpose of statistical testing about two population means, as discussed in the next section.

8.3.2. Hypothesis testing about the difference in two independent population means

As was done in Section 8.2, we can use the CI (8.10) for statistical inferences about two independent population means. In particular, when interested in testing the null hypothesis that the two means are the same, i.e., H_0: $\mu_1 = \mu_2$ (or, equivalently, H_0: $\mu_1 - \mu_2 = 0$) versus the alternative that they are not, i.e., H_a: $\mu_1 \neq \mu_2$ (or H_a: $\mu_1 - \mu_2 \neq 0$), we can utilize the CI (8.10) and check if it covers zero. In that case, we retain H_0; otherwise, we reject the null hypothesis and decide for H_a. If we are willing to furnish a p-value associated with the mean difference in the available samples, we use correspondingly the following test statistic that is rendered using the same principle underlying the t-ratio in Equation (8.1) earlier in the chapter:

$$(8.11) \qquad t = \frac{\bar{y}_1 - \bar{y}_2}{s_p \sqrt{\dfrac{1}{n_1} + \dfrac{1}{n_2}}}.$$

Analogous to our discussion in Section 8.1, the test statistic in Equation (8.11) follows under the null hypothesis the t-distribution with $n_1 + n_2 - 2$ degrees of freedom. Hence, the pertinent p-value (with a two-tailed alternative, as currently considered) is twice the area under the density curve for this t-distribution, which is positioned above the absolute value of the t-ratio (8.11) when the corresponding statistics from the two available samples are substituted into it. When a one-tailed alternative is considered to begin with (i.e., is decided for before one looks at the data), the p-value of relevance then is half the two-tailed p-value. This halved p-value is to be used for decision making with respect to the tested hypotheses only if the sample averages differ in a way complying with the alternative hypothesis; if they do not, one considers the null hypothesis as retainable.

The outlined approach is also directly applicable when one is interested in testing for a prespecified difference other than zero of the two population means. Suppose this difference is δ, a value that a researcher comes up with before looking at the data ($\delta \neq 0$). That is, we are interested in testing the null hypothesis, $H_0: \mu_1 - \mu_2 = \delta$ versus the alternative that they do not differ by δ, viz., $H_a: \mu_1 - \mu_2 \neq \delta$. To this end, we can still use the $(1 - \alpha)100\%$-CI in (8.10) for inferences about the population mean difference, at a prespecified confidence level $(1 - \alpha)100\%$ ($0 < \alpha < 1$). Specifically, if δ is covered by the CI (8.10), we retain the null hypothesis; if δ is not covered by this CI, we reject the null hypothesis, thus deciding for the alternative.

If of interest is to obtain a p-value associated with the sample mean difference, we use the correspondingly modified test statistic from Equation (8.11):

$$(8.12) \qquad t = \frac{\bar{y}_1 - \bar{y}_2 - \delta}{s_p \sqrt{\dfrac{1}{n_1} + \dfrac{1}{n_2}}}.$$

With respect to one-tailed tests, as indicated before, we divide the resulting p-value and use it further only if the sample mean difference is in the direction of the alternative tested. Otherwise, we consider the null hypothesis as retainable.

Before we illustrate the statistical inferences discussed in this section, we note that they yield trustworthy results also with some deviations from the assumption of normality and that of equal variances, especially when the studied variable distributions in the two populations are symmetric and sample sizes are fairly similar. We demonstrate next the above developments using the following examples.

Example 8.1: A new method for teaching number division is to be compared with an established one. Two random samples of fourth graders are assigned at random to an experimental and control group. The experimental group is taught number division using the new method, while the control group is taught using the old method. At the end of the study, a test of number division ability is administered to both groups. (The data are provided in the file CH8_EX81.dat, where 'y' denotes the test score and 'g' group membership; thereby, g = 1 for the control group and g = 0 for the experimental group.) A researcher is concerned with answering the question whether there are any group differences, i.e., teaching method differences, with regard to mean number division ability.

We respond to this question by carrying out a *t*-test for equality of the means of the two populations involved. We first read into R the data as follows (note the path, which needs to be modified when the data set resides in a different subdirectory):

```
> nda = read.table("C://data/CH8_EX81.dat", header = T)
> attach(nda)
```

To test the null hypothesis H_0: $\mu_1 - \mu_2 = 0$ versus the alternative H_a: $\mu_1 - \mu_2 \neq 0$, we use again the R command 't.test' with a slightly changed "argument" relative to its earlier application in this chapter. We still need to indicate the variable of interest, here also denoted 'y', but now we need to include in addition information pertaining to group membership. Since this information is contained in the variable denoted 'g', we have to include reference to the latter in the command. This is accomplished as follows:

```
> t.test(y~g)
```

For now, we only say that the '~' sign can be interpreted in this context as relating the variable before it to that after it. That is, we wish to use the *t*-test with regard to the variable 'y', once it is placed in relation to the variable 'g', i.e., group membership. The last R command yields the following output.

```
        Welch Two Sample t-test
data:  y by g
t = 0.323, df = 37.036, p-value = 0.7485
alternative hypothesis: true difference in means is not equal to 0
95 percent confidence interval:
-2.011203  2.774049
sample estimates:
mean in group 0 mean in group 1
        23.60870          23.22727
```

As we see from this output, the associated p-value of .75 is substantially higher than the conventional significance level of .05. For this reason, we retain the null hypothesis being tested. Alternatively, we could examine the corresponding 95%-CI, which is rendered here as $(-2.01, 2.77)$ and thus contains the zero point. This finding suggests alternatively that the null hypothesis can be retained. We can interpret the result as lack of sufficient evidence in the analyzed data set, which would warrant rejection of the null hypothesis of no method effect (i.e., no population mean differences). In other words, it seems that the new method is about as effective as the old one in teaching number division for fourth graders (at least as far as mean ability is concerned, as reflected in the number division test used). (We note in passing that the particular version of the t-test used by R by default, the so-called Welch two-sample test, is applicable also when the assumption of equal variances is violated; see next section.)

If before looking at the data our research question asked, to begin with, whether the new method led to better average performance, then we could respond to it by testing the null hypothesis of no mean differences versus the alternative of the mean in the experimental group being higher. To this end, we would first examine the mean difference in the available samples, which in this case is in the direction of the alternative since the average test score in the experimental group (23.61) is larger than that score in the control group (23.23). With this in mind, we would then halve the p-value obtained, .75, leading to a p-value of .38 for the presently performed one-tailed t-test. Since the latter p-value is higher than a conventional significance level of .05, we would retain the null hypothesis of no mean differences in the two groups, and thus of no differential method effect upon number division ability.

Conversely, in case we were interested in the first instance in testing the null hypotheses of no group mean differences versus the alternative that the old method of teaching number division was still associated with a higher mean on the division test used in this study, again we would first examine if the means in the two samples complied with this alternative hypothesis. Since they do not (in the example), we would conclude that there is no sufficient evidence in the available data set that would warrant rejection of the null hypothesis of no mean differences, i.e., of no differential method effect on number division ability.

As a last illustration, suppose that before looking at the data we were interested in testing the null hypothesis that the experimental group mean would be larger than the control group mean by four units on the number division test, versus the alternative that their difference would not be four. In this case, we would be concerned with testing the null hypothesis $H_0: \mu_1 - \mu_2 = 4$ against the two-tailed alternative $H_a: \mu_1 - \mu_2 \neq 4$. We could easily respond to this question (at the conventional confidence level .95) by examining whether the 95%-CI obtained for this data set covers the hypothetical value of four. Since this CI is $(-2.01, 2.77)$, as found out from the last presented R output, we see that four is not covered by the CI. For this reason, we would reject the null hypothesis of the two means differing by four units on the used test, and conclude that they differ by another number of units on the test.

8.3.3. The case of unequal variances

As we mentioned earlier in this chapter, the t-ratios in Equations (8.11) and (8.12) follow the t-distribution with $df = n_1 + n_2 - 2$ under the assumption of the variance of the studied variable y being the same in the two populations under consideration. When this is not the case, one faces a situation that cannot be easily handled with the help of an exact method. An alternative, approximate method was developed by Welch and Satterthwaite in the middle of the past century. This procedure consists of using the same interval estimation and hypothesis testing approach as in the case of variance equality, but with different degrees of freedom. The latter are approximated with the following formula (e.g., Ott & Longnecker, 2010):

$$(8.13) \qquad df = \frac{(n_1 - 1)(n_2 - 1)}{(1 - c)^2 (n_1 - 1) + c^2 (n_2 - 1)},$$

where

$$(8.14) \qquad c = \frac{s_1^2 / n_1}{s_1^2 / n_1 + s_2^2 / n_2}.$$

Thereby, if the degrees of freedom following from Equation (8.13) are not an integer number, their estimate is rounded down to the nearest integer.

One may reason that it might well be difficult to argue in a given empirical setting in favor of the equality of two population variances on a random variable of interest. We could examine for equality the two population variances using an appropriate statistical test (discussed in the next chapter), in which case the null hypothesis would be H_0: $\sigma_1^2 = \sigma_2^2$, or alternatively H_0: $\sigma_1^2/\sigma_2^2 = 1$ (assuming of course $\sigma_2^2 \neq 0$, as would typically be the case in empirical research). However, it could also be argued that such a point hypothesis would unlikely be strictly correct and would be rejected with a large enough sample (as statistical power approaches then one, as we mentioned earlier in the book). Thus, it may seem unreasonable in general to make the assumption of equal variances, since according to this reasoning that assumption is almost always incorrect.

Accepting this view, one could set out in practice to use always the last discussed approximate method by Welch and Satterthwaite when interested in examining population mean differences. This is in fact the approach implemented in R, and the software does not assume equality of the variances but always proceeds as if they were different—the latter being clearly the more general case. An alternative would be first to test for equality the two population differences and then proceed with either method—depending on the outcome of that variance test (see next chapter). However, such a two-step procedure has been criticized in the literature as unnecessarily including two tests on the same data set—a potential problem with controlling the Type I error rate. Instead, one could always proceed with the Welch/Satterthwaite approximate method for testing two independent mean differences. This is a widely followed view, which we accept in the remainder of this book. As pointed out, it is also implemented as the default option in the command 't.test' in R, and the last use of this command demonstrated its application on an empirical example.

8.4. INFERENCES ABOUT MEAN DIFFERENCES FOR RELATED SAMPLES

The methods discussed in the last section are appropriate only for the case of two independent populations. In many empirical settings, however, one often obtains data from two related samples—for example, when repeated measurements are taken twice on the same units of analysis, or when subjects are examined that are to some degree related to one another (e.g., siblings, couples, husbands and wives, etc.). Conducting inferences about mean differences for two related groups (populations) is the subject of this section.

We begin by observing that the methods employed in Section 8.3 made an essential use of the fact that the samples were drawn from two independent populations. This is because they appropriately accounted for the fact that the variance of the difference of the sample means was the sum of the variances of the two sample means. When the samples are not independent, however, this relation does not hold anymore, but instead the variance of the mean difference depends also on the degree to which the two samples are related to one another. Hence, using methods from Section 8.3 in the case of related samples would waste important information about their relationship and lead in general to incorrect results as well as possibly misleading substantive interpretations.

Empirical settings where related samples are used, such as two repeated assessments on the same subjects (units of analysis), have the potentially important advantage that they can better evaluate, i.e., more precisely estimate, their mean difference. This is because in a sense one of the measurements can be taken as a control or benchmark against which the other measurement can be compared with higher precision. This often leads to higher power to detect mean differences, at a given sample size, in studies with repeated samples than in studies with independent samples. A similar advantage can accrue in settings where pairs of related subjects are available, and thus a more precise evaluation of their differences on a studied variable may become possible.

For example, in a study of the effectiveness of a new method for teaching an algebra topic relative to an already established method for teaching it, a random sample of students may be paired on the basis of their scores on an intelligence test administered before the teaching methods. Placing then into pairs students who are as similar as possible with regard to their resulting IQ scores, e.g., after rank ordering them, and then randomly assigning one of the students in the pair to the new method and the other student to the old method, yields a set of matched pairs of students who are very much alike—within the pairs—as far as intelligence is concerned. This makes it less likely that observed differences in their algebra test scores at the end of the study would be the result of uncontrolled intelligence differences.

8.4.1. The sampling distribution of the mean difference for two related samples

The random sampling distribution of the mean difference for two related samples is described by a modification of Result 8.1, which is valid for the case of related samples (e.g., Roussas, 1997). Accordingly, if y_1 and y_2 denote the random variables used in that result, with corresponding means and variances denoted μ_1, μ_2, σ_1^2, and σ_2^2, then with large samples the difference in the sample means $\bar{y}_1 - \bar{y}_2$ is approximately normal with mean and standard deviation given by the following two equations (with the same notation as in Result 8.1):

$$\mu_{\bar{y}1-y2} = \mu_1 - \mu_2, \text{ and}$$
$$(8.15) \qquad \sigma_{\bar{y}1-y2} = \sqrt{\frac{\sigma_1^2 + \sigma_1^2 - 2\sigma_1\sigma_2\rho}{n}}.$$

In Equations (8.15), n is the number of pairs of measurements or subjects (units of analysis), and ρ is a measure of the amount of dependence between the two samples (we will discuss in detail this index, called "correlation," in Chapter 11).

For example, if in a study of the effect of an anxiety-lowering drug, 25 patients are measured before and after they take it, then one is dealing with $n = 25$ pairs of interrelated measurements. In this case, there would be two interrelated samples of 25 scores each—one sample with 25 pretrial anxiety scale scores, and another sample of 25 posttrial scores on the same subjects. Alternatively, if wives and husbands in 40 families are asked for their opinion on a particular political issue, we will have $n = 40$ pairs of responses that represent two related samples—one consisting of the wives' responses, the other of the husbands' responses.

With Equations (8.15), statistical inference about the mean difference in two related groups is carried out along the same lines and using the same principles as elaborated in Section 8.2 of this chapter, after an important observation is made first. If y_1 and y_2 denote the random variables representing the scores on the variable of concern (e.g., anxiety scores) in the first and second samples, then the null hypothesis of no mean difference, H_0: $\mu_1 = \mu_2$, is equivalent to the null hypothesis H_0^*: $\mu_1 - \mu_2 = 0$. Next, if we denote as $D = y_1 - y_2$ the difference in the two random variables of concern, then this equivalent hypothesis H_0^* is a hypothesis about the mean of this difference score D, viz., H_0^{**}: $\mu_D = 0$, where μ_D denotes the mean of D. However, the last null hypothesis H_0^{**}: $\mu_D = 0$ is precisely of the kind we have dealt with in Section 8.2. Indeed, H_0^{**} is a hypothesis about a single mean, and specifically asserting that this mean is 0. In addition, the second of Equations (8.15) gives us the standard deviation of the sampling distribution of this mean, viz., of the difference D. This standard deviation is actually the standard error of the mean of D. Hence we have now all that we need in order to carry out statistical inference with respect to the mean of the random variable D. The reason is that we reduced the original question about the mean difference for two variables, to a question about the mean of a single variable. For the latter question, all developments in Section 8.2 are directly applicable.

Hence, inferences about the mean difference in two related population means can be conducted based on the confidence interval (see (8.3)):

$$(8.16) \qquad (\bar{D} - t_{\alpha/2, n-1} \cdot s_{\bar{D}}, \ \bar{D} - t_{\alpha/2, n-1} \cdot s_{\bar{D}}),$$

where $n - 1$ are the degrees of freedom of the pertinent t-distribution and s_D is the standard deviation (standard error) of the mean difference score $\bar{D}$. This standard error is presented in the second equation of (8.15). We note that s_D is the estimate of the standard deviation of the difference score, divided by $\sqrt{n}$, and can thus be readily obtained in an empirical setting by taking simply the standard deviation across subjects of their difference scores D, after evaluating these scores first, and then dividing the resulting standard deviation estimate by $\sqrt{n}$. These computational activities are implemented in statistical analysis software, in particular in R. We illustrate with the following example.

Example 8.2: In a study of a new anti-depression drug, the scores using an established depression scale of $n = 30$ subjects were obtained before and after taking the drug. (Their data are contained in the file CH8_EX82.dat, where the variable named 'y1' denotes the depression score before the trial, while the variable 'y2' designates that score after the trial.) Is there any evidence for improvement, as a possible result of using this anti-depression drug?

If we denote the mean depression score before and after the trial by μ_1 and μ_2, respectively, this research question is concerned with testing the null hypothesis H_0: $\mu_2 = \mu_1$ versus the alternative hypothesis H_1: $\mu_2 < \mu_1$. In order to test these hypotheses, we first read in the data with R and focus on the pretrial and posttrial depression score variables y1 and y2, which we can use subsequently for our testing purposes (note the path):

```
> dep = read.table("C://data/CH8_EX82.dat", header = T)
> attach(dep)
```

As we elaborated earlier, since the null hypothesis to be tested is equivalent to H_0^*: $\mu_D = 0$ for the mean μ_D of the difference score D = y2 − y1, all we need to do here is test the latter null hypothesis about a single mean being zero versus the one-tailed alternative H_a^*: $\mu_D > 0$. As discussed in detail in Section 8.2, this is accomplished readily using the command 't.test', whereby we give as first argument the difference y2 − y1 and as a second argument mu = 0. This is because the hypothetical value of the mean of the differences score is here zero (the results of this command are presented immediately after it):

```
> t.test(y2-y1, mu = 0)
        One Sample t-test

data:  y2 - y1
t = -5.4771, df = 29, p-value = 6.741e-06
alternative hypothesis: true mean is not equal to 0
95 percent confidence interval:
-2.838387 -1.294947
sample estimates:
mean of x
-2.066667
```

These results include in particular the 95%-CI for the mean of the difference score D of interest here. This interval is $(-2.838, -1.295)$, and is thus entirely below the hypothetical mean of zero—as one would expect under the alternative hypothesis H_a^*. We can thus suggest that we can reject the null hypothesis H_0^* in favor of the alternative H_a^*. Hence, we can interpret this finding as evidence against the claim of no mean differences in depression before and after the trial, which evidence is in favor of the statement that the depression level after the drug trial is lower.

Inferences about Population Variances

The last few chapters have been entirely concerned with inferences about population means. In many empirical situations in behavioral and social science research, however, variability in a studied variable is just as relevant as is its mean or central tendency. An important result in statistics states that when a random variable is normally distributed, the sample mean and variance estimator are unrelated (e.g., Roussas, 1997). As a consequence, all methods dealing with inferences about population means discussed up to this point in the book do not provide any information in relation to drawing inferences about population variability on a variable of concern.

The variability of studied variables represents the degree of individual differences on them, which differences are often of special substantive interest in their own right. For example, variability in a given intelligence measure can be of particular concern to educational researchers and psychologists when examining intellectual development (and possible delays in it) in early childhood. As another example, variance on a mathematics ability test informs us about the potency of the resulting score (test score) to discriminate among students. This is an important characteristic of the ability measure in its own right.

When samples are available from examined variables in populations under investigation, their data can be utilized in order to also make inferences about the degree of individual differences in the populations. To this end, we can use statistical methods that have been specifically developed to address this concern. These statistical methods will be discussed in the present chapter.

9.1. ESTIMATION AND TESTING OF HYPOTHESES ABOUT A SINGLE POPULATION VARIANCE

9.1.1. Variance estimation

As elaborated in Chapter 2, when given a sample $y_1, y_2,..., y_n$ from a studied variable y in a population under consideration, we can estimate its variance with the sample variance s^2 defined as follows:

$$s^2 = \frac{1}{n-1}[(y_1 - \bar{y})^2 + (y_2 - \bar{y})^2 + \ldots + (y_n - \bar{y}^2]$$

(9.1)

$$= \frac{1}{n-1} \sum_{i=1}^{n} (y_i - \bar{y})^2.$$

We also mentioned in Chapter 2 that the sample variance s^2 is an *unbiased* estimator of the population variance σ^2. This implies that across repeated sampling, at a given sample size, the average of the resulting sample variances s^2 will equal the population variance σ^2. This is an important property that we would like a considered parameter estimator to possess.

9.1.2. The random sampling distribution of the sample variance

The sample variance s^2 is obviously itself a random variable, as we pointed out earlier in the book. That is, there is inherent variability in s^2, since the expression in the right-hand side of Equation (9.1) is sample-dependent. In other words, the value of s^2 in a given sample need not be the same as its value in another sample. Given this instability of s^2, the natural question that arises at this point is the following: "What is the random sampling distribution (RSD) of the sample variance, s^2?"

This question asks what the distribution is of sample variance estimates across many repeated samples, at a given size, from a population of interest. As can be shown (e.g., Roussas, 1997), the RSD of the following multiple of the sample variance

(9.2) $(n-1)s^2/\sigma^2$,

is of a kind that we have not yet encountered in the book. Specifically, when sampling from a normal population—i.e., when the initial variable of interest y is normally distributed—then the expression (9.2) follows across these repeated samples the so-called chi-square distribution with $df = n - 1$ degrees of freedom (denoted as usual df or d).

To illustrate graphically this discussion, Figure 9.1 contains the graphs of the probability density functions (pdf's) of the chi-square distribution with degrees of freedom ranging across several choices from 1 through 40 (viz., for $d = 1, 2, 3, 5, 10, 15, 25, 40$; see label of ordinate/vertical axis for pertinent pdf). The series of graphs displayed in Figure 9.1 shows that with increasing degrees of freedom, the shape of the chi-square distribution approaches a symmetric curve. In general, however, the right tail of the chi-square pdf is longer than the left, leading to what is referred to as "positive skewness" that this distribution exhibits (e.g., Chapter 3).

Another interesting property of the chi-square distribution is that it can

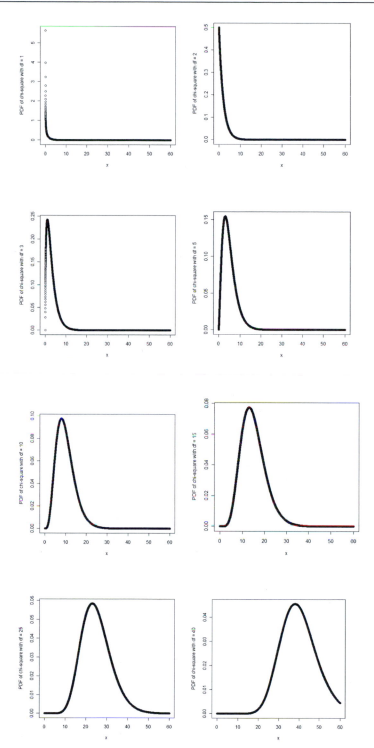

FIGURE 9.1.
Probability density functions of the chi-square distribution with $d = 1, 2, 3, 5, 10, 15,$ 25, and 40 degrees of freedom.

take only positive values (for any positive degrees of freedom). This is due to the ratio in (9.2) being positive for any available sample. Furthermore, the mean and variance of this distribution are $\mu = df$ and $\sigma^2 = 2df$—i.e., equal the degrees of freedom and twice these, respectively (e.g., Roussas, 1997).

We note in passing that each of the chi-square pdf curves presented in Figure 9.1 can be readily obtained with the following three combined R commands. We notice that these are similarly obtained as other pdf's considered earlier in the book—observe the use now of the command 'dchisq(x,d)' to obtain the value of the chi-square distribution with d degrees of freedom at the value x:

```
> x = seq(0, 60,.005)
> p.x = dchisq(x, d)
> plot(x, p.x, ylab = "PDF of chi-square with df = d")
```

whereby one consecutively updates the inputted value of the degrees of freedom from 1, to 2, 3, 5, 10, 15, 25, and finally to 40. We use thereby the corresponding labeling for the vertical axis, using the subcommand 'ylab' of the command 'plot'.

9.1.3. Percentiles of the chi-square distribution

Like the earlier discussed t-distribution, the percentiles of the chi-square distribution are easily obtained with R using the command 'qchisq(p, d)', where p is the probability corresponding to the 100pth percentile in question and d is the degrees of freedom of the distribution under consideration. This 100pth percentile, given the degrees of freedom df, is symbolized $\chi^2_{p,df}$ for notational convenience. For example, the 95th percentile of the chi-square distribution with $df = 5$ degrees of freedom is obtained with R as follows (result given beneath command line):

```
> qchisq(.95, 5)
[1] 11.07050
```

i.e., $\chi^2_{.95,5} = 11.07$. In other words, the area under the pdf of the chi-square distribution with 5 degrees of freedom, which is above (beyond) the number 11.07, represents 5% of the entire area under the pdf of this distribution. (We recall from our earlier discussion in the book that by convention this entire area is assumed to be 1, as is the area under the pdf of any distribution having a pdf.)

9.1.4. Confidence interval for the population variance

In order to obtain a confidence interval (CI) of the population variance, we will use the above-mentioned result stating that for a normally distributed variable y the inverse function of the sample variance presented in (9.2) follows the chi-square distribution with $df = n - 1$. Based on the earlier given definition of a percentile, we see that for an α between zero and one the following probability equality holds:

$$(9.3) \qquad \Pr\{\chi^2_{\alpha/2,df} < (n-1)s^2/\sigma^2 < \chi^2_{1-\alpha/2,df}\} = 1 - \alpha.$$

Equation (9.3) states that $(\chi^2_{\alpha/2,df}, \chi^2_{1-\alpha/2,df})$ could be viewed as a $(1 - \alpha)100\%$-CI for the expression $(n - 1)s^2/\sigma^2$. We are, however, interested in a CI for the variance, σ^2, rather than the multiple of its inverse function, which is represented by the ratio $(n - 1)s^2/\sigma^2$. Hence, in order to obtain a $(1 - \alpha)100\%$-CI for σ^2 we manipulate the two inequalities involved in the probability in the left-hand side of Equation (9.3) using straightforward algebra. To this end, we divide all sides involved by $(n - 1)s^2$ and invert the resulting two inequalities, to obtain such for the variance itself. These rearrangements furnish the following equation:

$$(9.4) \qquad \Pr\{(n-1)s^2/\chi^2_{1-\alpha/2,df} < \sigma^2 < (n-1)s^2/\chi^2_{\alpha/2,df}\} = 1 - \alpha.$$

Equation (9.4) is obviously interpretable as stating that the interval

$$(9.5) \qquad ((n-1)s^2/\chi^2_{1-\alpha/2,df}, (n-1)s^2/\chi^2_{\alpha/2,df})$$

represents the sought $(1 - \alpha)100\%$-CI for the population variance σ^2.

This CI in expression (9.5), for a given confidence level, can be readily obtained with R. To this end, assuming the data for the sample from the random variable y is in a variable named 'y', and denoting as usual by l and u the lower and upper endpoints of the CI in (9.5), we use the following two corresponding commands:

```
> l = (n-1)*var(y)/qchisq(1-a/2, n-1)
> u = (n-1)*var(y)/qchisq(a/2, n-1)
```

In an empirical setting, we substitute in them the corresponding significance level for α and the size of the available sample for n.

We illustrate this discussion by using data from the depression drug trial example considered in the last chapter (Example 8.2, with data found in the file CH8_EX82.dat). Suppose we were interested here in obtaining a 95%-CI for the pretrial depression score variance. Let $\alpha = .05$ for this illustration, and recall that the sample size in that example was $n = 30$. Hence, the last two stated R commands are as follows for this example (their results are presented beneath each of them; notice that, as above, the symbol 'l' used next is meant to be the letter *l* rather than the number 1):

```
> l = 29*var(y)/qchisq(.975, 29)
[1] 5.343127
> u = 29*var(y)/qchisq(.025, 29)
[1] 15.22396
```

Therefore, the sought 95%-CI for the pretrial depression score variance is (5.34, 15.22). We interpret this finding as suggesting with a high degree of confidence that the population pretrial depression variance may be between 5.32 and 15.22.

9.1.5. Testing hypotheses about a single variance

The confidence interval provided with expression (9.5) can also be used to test hypotheses if need be, at the significance level α, about the value of the population variance on a studied variable. Thereby, the same principle is used as earlier in the book. Specifically, we check how this CI relates to the hypothetical value or the tails of the alternative and null hypotheses, and correspondingly make a decision for one of them. More specifically, we consider the following testing problems defined by their pertinent null and alternative hypotheses.

1. $H_0: \sigma^2 = \sigma^2_0$, $H_a: \sigma^2 \neq \sigma^2_0$

Here we check if the CI (9.5) covers the hypothetical value σ^2_0. If it does, we retain the null hypothesis; otherwise we reject it.

2. $H_0: \sigma^2 = \sigma^2_0$, $H_a: \sigma^2 > \sigma^2_0$; or $H_0: \sigma^2 = \sigma^2_0$, $H_a: \sigma^2 < \sigma^2_0$.

If the CI (9.5) is entirely within the null hypothesis tail, we retain H_0; if the CI is entirely within the alternative hypothesis tail, we reject H_0. If the CI, however, covers the hypothetical value σ^2_0, decision is suspended; in another study with a larger sample, it may be the case that the CI will be entirely within one of the tails, in which case we proceed as just outlined. If no decision is reached, we interpret the CI as suggesting with high confidence that the population variance may be between the numbers representing its lower and upper endpoints.

To illustrate this discussion, let us return to the last depression example (pretrial depression score; Example 8.2 from Chapter 8). If before looking at the data our hypotheses to be tested were $H_0: \sigma^2 = 12$ versus $H_a: \sigma^2 \neq 12$, then at the significance level $\alpha = .05$ we can retain H_0. This is because the above-found 95%-CI, (5.34, 15.22), contains this hypothetical value. However, if our hypotheses (settled on before looking at the data) were instead H_0: $\sigma^2 = 18$ versus H_a: $\sigma^2 > 18$, we would retain H_0. In case they were H_0: $\sigma^2 = 10$ and H_a: $\sigma^2 > 10$ (again, settled on before looking at the data), then we would suspend judgment, suggesting that the available data did not contain sufficient evidence allowing us to decide for either of the hypotheses. We would then only interpret the CI as suggesting with high confidence that the population depression variance may be between 5.34 and 15.22.

9.2. INFERENCES ABOUT TWO INDEPENDENT POPULATION VARIANCES

The relationship between two population variances will be of interest when research questions ask how the degrees of individual differences on a given variable compare to one another across two studied unrelated populations. This relationship will also be of concern when, as we discussed in Chapter 8, an assumption of the t-test that we used there is to be examined. As will be recalled, that assumption stipulated equality of the variances of a measure under consideration, i.e., the random variable y, across the two groups involved—for example, males and females, or experimental and control groups. This type of question is addressed using inferences about the ratio of two independent population variances, which are the subject of this Section 9.2. Before moving on with such inferences, however, we need to discuss another important distribution that will be of instrumental relevance thereby.

9.2.1. The *F*-distribution

Inferences about the relationship between two variances are made possible by an important result presented in the statistical literature (for further mathematical details on this result, see for example Roussas, 1997). This result allows us to define a new distribution that we have not yet dealt with in the book. Accordingly, when random samples of sizes n_1 and n_2—with data on a studied variable y—have been drawn from two independent normal populations, the ratio of their sample variances s_1^2 and s_2^2 and population variances σ_1^2 and σ_2^2, given as

$$(9.6) \qquad \frac{s_1^2 \, / \, s_2^2}{\sigma_1^2 \, / \, \sigma_2^2}$$

follows across repeated sampling at these sizes a distribution referred to as an F-distribution. The ratio (9.6) is also frequently referred to as an F-ratio and denoted by $F(df_1, df_2)$ (or just F if no confusion can arise).

Like all types of distributions discussed so far, there are infinitely many F-distributions, and each one of them has specific values for two quantities that are referred to as its degrees of freedom and usually denoted df_1 and df_2. Thereby, df_1 is the degrees of freedom associated with the sample variance estimate in the first sample, s_1^2, i.e., $n_1 - 1$; and similarly df_2 is the degrees of freedom associated with the sample variance estimate in the second sample, s_2^2, i.e., $n_2 - 1$.

To illustrate graphically this discussion, in Figure 9.2 the graphs of the pdf's of the F-distributions are displayed, with degrees of freedom ranging across several choices (see label of vertical axis for pertinent pdf).

The graphs displayed in Figure 9.2 suggest the following two properties of

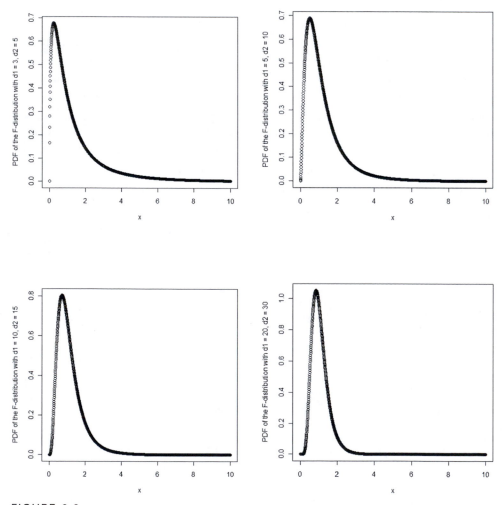

FIGURE 9.2.

The probability density functions of several F-distributions (see vertical axis label for pertinent degrees of freedom).

the F-distribution, which are more generally valid and resemble those of the chi-square distribution discussed earlier in the chapter. (A third property is discussed further below.)

1. The F-distribution is such of a positive random variable. This is because the F-ratio (9.6) contains in its numerator and denominator positive quantities, for any pair of samples under consideration.
2. The F-distribution is nonsymmetric.

We note in passing that the graphs in Figure 9.2 can be readily furnished with R using the following commands (see earlier discussion on obtaining the graphs in Figure 9.1 with respect to explanation of commands and subcommands, and note next the use of the command 'df(x,d1,d2)' for obtaining the value of the pdf of the distribution $F(df_1, df_2)$ where d1 and d2 stand for df_1 and df_2):

```
> x = seq(0, 10,.005)
> p.x = df(x, 3, 5)
> plot(x, p.x, ylab = "PDF of the F-distribution with d1 = 3, d2 =  5")
> p.x = df(x, 5, 10)
> plot(x, p.x, ylab = "PDF of the F-distribution with d1 = 5, d2 =  10")
> p.x = df(x, 10, 15)
> plot(x, p.x, ylab = "PDF of the F-distribution with d1 = 10, d2 =  15")
> p.x = df(x, 20, 30)
> plot(x, p.x, ylab = "PDF of the F-distribution with d1 = 20, d2 =  30")
```

9.2.2. Percentiles of the F-distribution

The percentiles of the F-distribution are similarly readily obtained with the R command 'qf(p, d1, d2)'. To invoke their computation, all we need to supply R with is the probability p corresponding to the $100p$th percentile in question, and the two degrees of freedom quantities that are denoted in this command by d1 and d2. For example, if we are interested in obtaining the 95th percentile of the pertinent F-distribution of the ratio (9.6) in a study with a pair of samples of sizes 55 and 62 from two independent populations, then this percentile would be obtained as follows (result given beneath command):

```
> qf(.95, 54, 61)
[1] 1.544803
```

That is, the area under the pdf curve of the F-distribution with $df_1 = 55$ and $df_2 = 62$ that is to the left of 1.54, is 95% of the entire area under that curve—which is conventionally set at one.

There is another interesting property that characterizes the F-distribution, as such of a random variable defined in terms of the ratio of two variances. This property derives from the fact that in its definition the choice of the first or top variance is essentially arbitrary. Therefore, if for a given α ($0 < \alpha < 1$) we denote by $F_{\alpha, df1, df2}$ the αth percentile of the F-distribution with fixed degrees of freedom, then

$$(9.7) \qquad F_{\alpha, df1, df2} = 1 \,/\, F_{1 - \alpha, df2, df1}$$

holds (note that the order of the degrees of freedom is reversed in the right-hand side of Equation (9.7) relative to its left-hand side). That is, the $100p$th and $100(1 - p)$th percentiles of the F-distribution are "inverse symmetric" to one another, in the sense of Equation (9.7). Returning for a moment to our last example, we can see a particular demonstration of Equation (9.7) by multiplying, using R, the 95th with the 5th percentiles of the F-distribution (with reversed degrees of freedom):

```
> qf(.95, 54, 61)*qf(.05, 61, 54)
[1] 1
```

That is, the product of the 95th and 5th percentiles in question here—with reversed degrees of freedom—is precisely 1, which means that they are "inverse symmetric" in the above sense (see Equation (9.7)).

9.2.3. Confidence interval for the ratio of two independent population variances

Suppose we have samples of sizes n_1 and n_2 from two independent normal populations and wish to obtain a range of plausible values for the ratio of their variances. According to the preceding discussion in this Section 9.2, the F-ratio in Equation (9.6) follows then a F-distribution with degrees of freedom $df_1 = n_1 - 1$ and $df_2 = n_2 - 1$. Therefore, by the definition of percentiles, for a given α between zero and one,

$$(9.8) \qquad \Pr\{F_{1-\alpha/2, df1, df2} < \frac{s_1^2 \,/\, s_2^2}{\sigma_1^2 \,/\, \sigma_2^2} < F_{\alpha/2, df1, df2}\} = 1 - \alpha,$$

where Pr denotes probability. After some straightforward rearrangements on the left-hand side of Equation (9.8) (dividing all sides of the two involved inequalities by the ratio $s_1^2 \,/\, s_2^2$ and inverting the latter as well as the degrees of freedom order), we obtain using also Equation (9.7)

$$(9.9) \qquad P\{\frac{s_1^2}{s_2^2}F_{\alpha/2, df2, df1} < \frac{\sigma_1^2}{\sigma_2^2} < \frac{s_1^2}{s_2^2}F_{\alpha/2, df1, df2}\} = 1 - \alpha.$$

Equation (9.9) can be interpreted as saying that the interval

(9.10)
$$\left(\frac{s_1^2}{s_2^2}F_{\alpha/2,df2,df1},\ \frac{s_1^2}{s_2^2}F_{\alpha/2,df1,df2}\right)$$

is a $100(1-\alpha)\%$-confidence interval for the ratio $\dfrac{\sigma_1^2}{\sigma_2^2}$ of the two population variances of concern. The lower and upper endpoints of this CI can be readily obtained with R in full analogy to the way we obtained these limits of the CI in expression (9.5) for a single population variance in subsection 9.1.4 of this chapter.

The CI in expression (9.10) provides a range of plausible values for the ratio of the variances of a studied random variable, y, in two independent populations. As such, it could also be used to test various hypotheses about this ratio if need be, as we have demonstrated earlier in the book in cases with CIs for other parameters. This can also be readily accomplished with R, using its command 'var.test'. To this end, we need to specify the variable 'y' from a given data file's variables, whose variances are of interest, and the variable 'g' containing information about group membership. Then the full command is analogous to that for testing equality in two independent population means, 't.test', which we discussed in the preceding chapter:

```
> var.test(y ~ g)
```

The output produced by this command contains the p-value associated with the test of the null hypothesis $H_0: \sigma_1^2 = \sigma_2^2$ against the alternative $H_a: \sigma_1^2 \neq \sigma_2^2$, as well as the confidence interval (9.10) for their ratio.

We illustrate this discussion with the data from the teaching method comparison study we used in Section 8.4 of the last chapter. (As will be recalled, the data are contained in the file CH8_EX81.dat.) Unlike our concerns in that section of Chapter 8, here we have a different focus. Specifically, we are interested in examining whether the individual differences, i.e., variances, of the division ability test score are the same in the experimental and control groups (populations). To this end, after reading the data into R and extracting the needed variables (recall, 'y' denotes in that data file the relevant test score and 'g' group membership), the above-mentioned command 'var.test' produces the following output:

```
> nda = read.table("C://data/CH8_EX81.dat", header = T)
> attach(nda)

> var.test(y~g)
```

```
        F test to compare two variances
data:  y by g
F = 0.472,  num df = 22,  denom df = 21,  p-value = 0.08748
alternative hypothesis: true ratio of variances is not equal to 1
95 percent confidence interval:
 0.1971765 1.1199362
sample estimates:
ratio of variances
        0.4719963
```

We see that the F-ratio (9.6) equals here .472, and that the 95%-CI for the ratio of the variances is (.20, 1.12). Since it includes one, the hypothetical value of interest that represents population variance equality, we do not reject the null hypothesis that the variances of the number division test scores are the same under both teaching methods, viz., the new and old methods. That is, discrepancies in effectiveness between the new and old methods, if any, do not seem to be affecting the individual differences in number division test scores.

We may note in passing that although the experimental group has less than half the variance of the control group, since we have relatively limited samples from either group (viz., 15 students in each) the 95%-CI is relatively wide and covers the value of one, which represents the equality of the two group variances. Thus, this is just an illustrative example where possibly the lack of power due to relatively small sample sizes leads to a finding of the null hypothesis not being rejected. We will return to and elaborate on this and several related issues in a later section of the book.

Analysis of Categorical Data

The previous chapters were predominantly concerned with quantitative data and continuous random variables. This type of data typically arises in empirical studies where one uses interval or ratio scales for measurement purposes. Often in empirical behavioral and social science research, however, collected data may be on a nominal scale (such as data on gender, political party membership, religious affiliation, or ethnicity) or alternatively on an ordinal scale—for instance when collecting information on military rank, academic rank, or end-of-year class ranking order. The resulting data encountered in such situations are frequently referred to as categorical data. We deal in this chapter with methods for analyzing such data.

10.1. INFERENCES ABOUT A POPULATION PROBABILITY (PROPORTION)

In Chapter 4 we discussed the binomial distribution. This was the distribution of the number y of "successes," e.g., correct answers in a series of n independent trials that each had the same probability π of success. If we denote the outcome of any trial as 0 in case of an "unsuccessful" result and as 1 for a "successful" result, then we can consider the jth trial outcome as a random variable. We denote it y_j and notice that it can take on the value of 1 with a probability π, and the value of 0 with probability $1 - \pi$ ($j = 1,..., n$). Then the above random variable y defined as the number of successes in this series of trials is obviously the sum of these n random variables, i.e., $y = y_1 + y_2 + ... + y_n$. As will be recalled, we mentioned in Chapter 4 that the ratio y/n can be used as an estimate of the probability π of success. That is,

(10.1) $$\hat{\pi} = y / n$$

is an estimator of the unknown probability of success on any of the trials.

In more advanced treatments (e.g., Roussas, 1997), it has been shown that the estimator $\hat{\pi}$ defined in Equation (10.1) possesses a number of desirable optimality properties that we will make use of here. In particular, with a large number n of trials considered, the estimator $\hat{\pi}$ is (i) approximately normally distributed, (ii) unbiased, (iii) approaches the true probability π with increasing n, and (iv) exhibits the smallest variability possible. This approximation of the distribution of $\hat{\pi}$ with increasing n can be seen from the central limit theorem (CLT), if applied to an individual trial outcome as the initial random variable of concern. This CLT application also tells us that the mean of y and the standard error associated with it are correspondingly (e.g., Ott & Longnecker, 2010)

$$(10.2) \qquad \begin{aligned} \mu_{\hat{\pi}} &= \pi, \text{ and} \\ \sigma_{\hat{\pi}} &= \sqrt{\pi(1-\pi)}/n. \end{aligned}$$

Similarly, from the CLT it also follows that with a large number n of trials the distribution of the number of successes y in them is itself approximated by the normal distribution with the following mean and standard deviation:

$$(10.3) \qquad \begin{aligned} \mu_y &= n\pi, \text{ and} \\ \sigma_y &= \sqrt{n\pi(1-\pi)}. \end{aligned}$$

This distribution approximation result can be used to obtain a test statistic for testing the null hypothesis that the probability of success on a given trial is a prespecified number π_0, i.e., $H_0: \pi = \pi_0$, versus the alternative $H_a: \pi \neq \pi_0$ or a one-tailed alternative (see below). Indeed, since the number of successes, y, is normally distributed for a large n with mean and variance stated in Equations (10.3), the ratio

$$(10.4) \qquad X = \frac{y - n\pi_0}{\sqrt{n\pi_0(1-\pi_0)}}$$

follows the standard normal distribution, i.e., $X \sim N(0,1)$. Hence, with respect to X we can rely on the results from Chapter 5 allowing us to make inferences about a population mean, which in this case is the mean of X. In particular, with a given significance level α ($0 < \alpha < 1$), for a two-tailed test—i.e., when the alternative H_a is two-tailed—we reject the null hypothesis H_0 if the test statistic in Equation (10.4) falls in the pertinent rejection region, that is, if $X > z_{\alpha/2}$ or $X < z_{1-\alpha/2}$. For a one-tailed test—that is, when the alternative H_a is one-tailed (e.g., $H_a: \pi < \pi_0$ or $H_a: \pi > \pi_0$)—we check first if the sample estimate (10.1) of π is in agreement with the alternative. If this is the case, we halve the π-value associated with the two-tailed alternative, and see whether the resulting probability is smaller than the significance level α: if it is, we reject the null hypothesis, otherwise we retain it. If the sample estimate (10.1) is not in the direction of the alternative under consideration, we retain the null hypothesis.

This hypothesis testing procedure can be readily carried out with R using the command 'prop.test(y, n, π_0)', where as mentioned before 'y' stands for the number of successes in a series of n independent trials with probability of π_0 for success in each. We illustrate next with an example.

Example 10.1: In a short high school course using a computerized method of teaching, 50 students are taught an algebra topic and at the end examined to assess their knowledge level. Let us assume that students have the same probability of passing the exam and are examined independently of each other. Thereby, suppose that 15 students failed their exam. Would this result represent sufficient evidence to claim that the probability of passing the exam is at least .65, versus the claim that it is .65?

Here we are concerned with testing the null hypothesis H_0: $\pi = \pi_0$, against the alternative H_a: $\pi > \pi_0$, where $\pi_0 = .65$. We use the above-mentioned R command 'prop.test' as follows (output is provided immediately after it):

```
> prop.test(35, 50, .65)

   One-sample proportions test with continuity correction
data:  35 out of 50, null probability 0.65
X-squared = 0.3516, df = 1, p-value = 0.5532
alternative hypothesis: true p is not equal to 0.65
95 percent confidence interval:
 0.5521660 0.8171438
sample estimates:
  p
0.7
```

We see that the sample estimate of probability for passing the exam, i.e., "success" in this setting, is .7 and complies with the alternative hypothesis H_a of interest. Hence, we halve the reported p-value of .55 and obtain the relevant one-tailed p-value here as $p = .28$. Assuming we use the conventional significance level $\alpha = .05$, since $.28 > .05$ we do not reject the null hypothesis. We stress that R also provides a confidence interval for the proportion π, which represents a range of plausible values for this proportion that can be of importance in empirical research.

In conclusion of this section, we note that as discussed in Chapter 4 the normality approximation—on which the developments in the present section were based—would be satisfactory for most practical purposes when the number n of trials (sample size) is so large that both $n\pi$ and $n(1 - \pi)$ are at least five. When this is not the case, for instance when n is not sufficiently large, more advanced methods can be used within the framework of the so-called theory of exact tests. For further details on these methods, the reader is referred, for example, to Agresti (2002).

10.2. INFERENCES ABOUT THE DIFFERENCE BETWEEN TWO POPULATION PROBABILITIES (PROPORTIONS)

In many empirical settings a researcher may be interested in comparing two population probabilities for success. For instance, this would be the case when one is interested in comparing the probability of passing an exam between two groups receiving computerized versus traditional instruction, assuming students have the same probability of success on the exam and are independently evaluated. In such situations, we are dealing with two random variables y_1 and y_2 that each follow a binomial distribution. Suppose we have n_1 independent observations (trials) in the first population where the probability of success is π_1, and n_2 independent observations (trials) in the second population where the probability of success is π_2. We can estimate these probabilities, as in the preceding section, by their corresponding empirical proportions of success:

(10.5) $$\hat{\pi}_1 = y_1 / n_1 \text{ and } \hat{\pi}_2 = y_2 / n_2.$$

Using the central limit theorem, as in the last section, it can be shown that with large sample sizes n_1 and n_2 the random sampling distribution of the difference $\hat{\pi}_1 - \hat{\pi}_2$ can be approximated by the normal distribution with the following mean and standard deviation:

(10.6) $$\mu_{\hat{\pi}1-\hat{\pi}2} = \pi_1 - \pi_2, \text{ and}$$
$$\sigma_{\hat{\pi}1-\hat{\pi}2} = \sqrt{\pi_1(1-\pi_1) / n_1 + \pi_2(1-\pi_2) / n_2}.$$

This approximation would be satisfactory for most practical purposes when each of the four products $n_1\pi_1$, $n_1(1 - \pi_1)$, $n_2\pi_2$, and $n_2(1 - \pi_2)$ is at least five.

The preceding developments can be directly applied when one is interested in testing hypotheses about the difference between two independent population proportions. Specifically, suppose we were interested in testing $H_0: \pi_1 = \pi_2$, versus the alternative $H_a: \pi_1 \neq \pi_2$, or a one-tailed alternative (see below). With the normal approximation mentioned of the difference in the empirical proportions of success $\hat{\pi}_1$ and $\hat{\pi}_2$, the test statistic here

(10.7) $$X = \frac{\hat{\pi}_1 - \hat{\pi}_2}{\sqrt{\dfrac{\hat{\pi}_1(1-\hat{\pi}_1)}{n_1} + \dfrac{\hat{\pi}_2(1-\hat{\pi}_2)}{n_2}}}$$

follows (approximately) a standard normal distribution, i.e., $X \sim N(0,1)$. Hence, with a given significance level α ($0 < \alpha < 1$), for a two-tailed test—

i.e., when the alternative H_a is two-tailed—we reject the null hypothesis H_0 if $X > z_{\alpha/2}$ or $X < z_{1-\alpha/2}$. For a one-tailed test—that is, when the alternative H_a is one-tailed, such as H_a: $\pi_1 < \pi_2$ or H_a: $\pi_1 > \pi_2$—we check first if the difference in the empirical estimates (10.5) is in agreement with the alternative. If so, we halve the π-value associated with a two-tailed alternative, and examine whether the resulting probability is smaller than the significance level α. If it is, we reject the null hypothesis, otherwise we retain it. If the difference in the estimates (10.5) is not in the direction of the alternative considered, we do not reject the null hypothesis.

This testing procedure can be readily conducted with R using the command 'prop.test(c1, c2)', whereby in c1 and c2 the pairs of numbers of successes and trials (n_i, y_i) are provided for each of the two groups involved ($i = 1, 2$; see below how to define formally c1 and c2). We illustrate next with an example.

> **Example 10.2:** In a study aimed at evaluating the effectiveness of a new method for teaching multiplication to second graders, two random groups of 40 pupils each are randomly assigned to the new or an already established method of teaching. Let us assume that students have the same probability of passing the exam and are being examined independently of each other. Thereby, suppose that 12 students from the group exposed to the new method failed their exam, while 14 students from the group taught with the old method failed. Would these results represent sufficient evidence to claim that students exposed to the new method have a higher probability of passing the exam?

To get started, let us denote by π_1 and π_2 the probability of passing the exam in the new method group and in the old method group, respectively. We wish to test the null hypothesis of equal probabilities, H_0: $\pi_1 = \pi_2$, versus the one-tailed alternative that the new method group has higher probability of passing the exam, viz., H_a: $\pi_1 > \pi_2$. We use then R in the following way. First, we need to provide the data to the software. To this end, one of the simplest ways is to communicate to R two pairs of relevant statistics—the first pair containing the numbers of successes in both groups, and the second pair containing the numbers of students in each group. In our example, the first pair is (28, 26), whereas the second pair is (40, 40). We communicate this to R by creating these pairs employing the earlier used command 'c', for 'concatenate':

```
> c1 = c(28,26)
> c2 = c(40,40)
```

We are now ready to carry out the test of interest here via the command 'prop.test(c1,c2)' as mentioned above; the output produced by it is provided beneath this command:

```
> prop.test(c1,c2)


Two-sample test for equality of proportions with continuity correction

data:  c1 out of c2
X-squared = 0.057, df = 1, p-value = 0.8113
alternative hypothesis: two.sided
95 percent confidence interval:
 -0.1799779  0.2799779
sample estimates:
prop 1 prop 2
 0.70   0.65
```

Since the estimate of the probability of passing the exam, i.e., the empirical frequency of success, in the new method group is larger than that in the old method group, the data complies with the alternative H_a of concern in this example. We can thus proceed by halving the reported p-value of .81, obtaining a one-tailed p-value of .42 (rounded off). At a conventional significance level of .05, this p-value is larger than it, and therefore we retain the null hypothesis H_0. Hence, the available data does not contain sufficient evidence warranting rejection of the hypothesis that both groups have the same probability of success on the exam. This may be due to both methods being about equally effective in teaching multiplication to second-grade students.

10.3. INFERENCES ABOUT SEVERAL PROPORTIONS

Often in empirical studies the number of categories that a researcher is examining on a random variable of interest is larger than two. For instance, the result of a particular licensure test may be pass, fail, or undecided—e.g., when there is not sufficient evidence to make a pass or fail decision. Another example might include the results of a test to identify students exhibiting mild, moderate, or severe reading difficulties. In such situations, the so-called multinomial distribution plays an important role and is discussed next.

10.3.1. The multinomial distribution

This setting can be dealt with using an extension of the binomial distribution, the *multinomial distribution* (MND). In general, the MND assumes that a random variable y_j defined as outcome of a particular measurement—e.g., an experiment, answer to a question, or ability test result—is observed on n subjects (units of analysis), $j = 1,..., n$. These measurements or observations are assumed to be independent of each other. In addition, the probability that in a single trial the ith outcome will be observed is denoted π_i ($i = 1,..., k$, k = number of outcomes), whereby $\pi_1 + \pi_2 + ... + \pi_k = 1$ holds. For this setup, it can be shown that the probability distribution of the number of observations resulting in each of the k outcomes considered, which follows the MND, is as follows (Agresti & Finlay, 2009):

(10.8)
$$\Pr(n_1, n_2, ..., n_k) = \frac{n!}{n_1 n_2!...n_k!} \pi_1^{n_1} \pi_2^{n_2}...\pi_k^{n_k},$$

where the left-hand side is the probability of n_i outcomes of the ith type ($i = 1,..., k$, $k > 2$), with $n_1 + n_2 + ... + n_k = n$, and n denotes as usual sample size. The probabilities defined in Equation (10.8) are often referred to as *multinomial probabilities*. We mention in passing that as indicated earlier $n!$ $= 1.2 ... (n - 1).n$ is the product of all integers smaller than n, and n itself, whereby 0! is defined as 1.

To illustrate this discussion, let us return to the above licensure exam example. In it, the probabilities associated with the multinomial distribution, also referred to in this case as a *trinomial distribution*, are as follows:

(10.9)
$$\Pr(n_1, n_2, n_3) = \frac{n!}{n_1! n_2! n_3!} \pi_1^{n_1} \pi_2^{n_2} \pi_3^{n_3},$$

where n_1 = number of passes, n_2 = number of fails, and n_3 = number of undecided; thereby, the sum of the probabilities π_1, π_2, and π_3 for these three outcomes is $\pi_1 + \pi_2 + \pi_3 = 1$. For instance, the probability to have in a group of seven examinees two passes, three fails, and two outcomes with no decision on a licensure test, whereby the probabilities for these outcomes are correspondingly .3, .4, and .3, is

(10.10)
$$\Pr(2,3,2) = 7!/(2!3!2!).3^2.4^3.3^2 = .011.$$

That is, if this experiment were repeated many times, about 11 in 1000 of them, in the long run, would result in two passes, three fails, and two with no decision.

10.3.2. Testing hypotheses about multinomial probabilities

Suppose that based on substantive considerations, e.g., prior research, one is in a position to come up with fixed hypothetical values for the outcome probabilities π_1, π_2,..., π_k in a multinomial experiment with k outcomes ($k > 2$). Let us denote these values by π_{01}, π_{02},..., π_{0k}, respectively. Based on the available data, how could one test the hypothesis of the outcome probabilities being equal to these hypothetical values, i.e., how would one go about testing the null hypothesis H_0: $\pi_1 = \pi_{01}$,..., $\pi_1 = \pi_{0k}$?

To answer this question, we need the concept of *expected number of out-*

comes for each type of outcome, i.e., for each outcome denoted 1, 2,..., k, for notational simplicity. (In the above licensure example, one could denote the outcome pass by 1, fail by 2, and no decision by 3, say. We do not impart any numerical features to these numbers, however—i.e., we will not treat them as "real" numbers in this section.) This concept of expected number of outcomes responds to the query what number of outcomes of a particular type one would anticipate to observe under H_0, if one were to make a given number of repetitions (observations) of the experiment in question. For example, if there were 100 examinees, and we hypothesize that the probabilities for the outcomes 1, 2, and 3 are .25, .50, and .25, respectively, we would expect to observe 25 passes, 50 failures, and 25 with no decision. More generally, if n denotes the number of trials, that is, number of repeats of the considered experiment with k outcomes, or sample size, then $n\pi_i$ is the expected number of outcomes of the ith type ($i = 1,..., k$). We denote these expected numbers by E_i; that is, $E_i = n\pi_i$ is the number of expected outcomes of type i in a series of n independent repetitions of the multinomial experiment under consideration ($i = 1,..., k$).

More than 100 years ago, the British statistician Karl Pearson developed the following so-called chi-square statistic for testing the null hypothesis H_0: $\pi_1 = \pi_{01},..., \pi_k = \pi_{0k}$:

$$(10.11) \qquad\qquad \chi^2 = \sum_{i=1}^{k} \frac{(n_i - E_i)^2}{E_i}.$$

He showed that for large n it follows the chi-square distribution with $k - 1$ degrees of freedom, when the null hypothesis is true (e.g., Rao, 1973). We note that if the tested null hypothesis H_0 is correct, we would anticipate the observed number of outcomes of type i to be close to the expected number E_i of outcomes of this type ($i = 1,..., k$). In that case, the test statistic in Equation (10.11) will be "small." Conversely, if H_0 is not correct, some of the terms in the right-hand side of Equation (10.11) will be "large." As a result, overall this test statistic would be expected to be large. How large a value for this χ^2 statistic is large enough, however, to be considered evidence warranting rejection of the null hypothesis H_0 to be tested?

As we mentioned in Chapter 8, the mean of the chi-square distribution equals its degrees of freedom. Hence, if the null hypothesis H_0 is correct, it could be expected that the magnitude of the test statistic in Equation (10.11) would be similar to $k - 1$. Thus, if this test statistic is much larger than $k - 1$, we would be willing to reject H_0. More specifically, when using a significance level α, the rejection region for testing H_0 would consist of all those scores that the test statistic (10.11) could take, which are beyond the $100(1 - \alpha)$th percentile of the chi-square distribution under H_0. That is, we would reject H_0

if $\chi^2 > \chi^2_{1-\alpha, k-1}$, with the last symbol denoting the $100(1 - \alpha)$th percentile of the chi-square distribution with $k - 1$ degrees of freedom.

This testing procedure can be carried out with the software R as follows. First we enter the data, using the 'c' command (for 'concatenate') as earlier in the chapter. We submit to R thereby one row containing the numbers n_1, n_2,..., n_k of observed outcomes of each of the k types of concern. Then we enter a second row, using the same command, containing the hypothetical probabilities π_{01}, π_{02},..., π_{0k}. Having done this, we use next the R command 'sum', in order to obtain the right-hand side of Equation (10.11) defining the test statistic of concern here. Once knowing the resulting test statistic value corresponding to our data, we use the command 'pchisq(chi-square, df)' to work out the probability to obtain a value smaller than the test statistic value. Finally, we subtract this probability from 1, in order to furnish the p-value associated with the null hypothesis H_0 being tested.

We illustrate this testing procedure by revisiting and extending the earlier licensure example in this section. Suppose that in a professional licensure exam administered to 98 persons, 28 failed, 48 passed, and for 22 a decision of pass or fail could not be made. Is there sufficient evidence in the data to warrant rejection of the hypothesis that the probability of passing the exam is .5, for failing it .25, and for a no-decision outcome .25? Here we have $n = 98$, $n_1 = 48$, $n_2 = 28$, $n_3 = 22$, and $\pi_{01} = .50$, $\pi_{02} = .25$, $\pi_{03} = .25$. The null hypothesis is H_0: $\pi_1 = .50$, $\pi_2 = .25$, $\pi_3 = .25$. As outlined above, to test this hypothesis we first create two rows—denoted next 'y' and 'p'—with our data and hypothetical probabilities, respectively, by 'concatenating' their corresponding values:

```
> y = c(48, 28, 22)
> p = c(.50, .25, .25)
```

With these two lines, we effectively communicate to R our data and hypothesis to be tested. Next we use this software to work out the test statistic value (10.11) and print it to the screen—the result is given beneath the last presented command next:

```
> chi_square = sum((y-n*p)^2/(n*p))
> chi_square
[1] 6.102564
```

We need next the p-value associated with this test-statistic value or 6.102, which we obtain as mentioned above, noting that the pertinent degrees of freedom are $df = 3 - 1 = 2$:

```
> 1-pchisq(6.102, 2)
[1] 0.04731159
```

At a conventional significance level of $\alpha = .05$, which we are also willing to use here, the finding of this p-value being smaller than this level warrants rejection of the null hypothesis H_0. We thus conclude that there are at least two probabilities for pass, fail, or undecided, which are not equal to the tested probabilities of .50, .25, and .25, respectively (as prescribed by the null hypothesis).

We point out that the test statistic in the above Equation (10.11) is best used for testing the null hypothesis under consideration in this section when the overall number of observations, n, is large. It has been argued that there could be no single and generally applicable rule concerning the appropriate number of observations and expected number of outcomes in this sense, but there is a popular rule of thumb that may be followed in empirical research. Accordingly, the distribution of the test statistic in Equation (10.11) would be approximated well by the chi-square distribution with $k - 1$ degrees of freedom, if (a) there is no expected number of outcomes E_i that is less than one, and (b) fewer than 20% of all expected number of outcomes E_i are smaller than five ($1 \leq i \leq k$). When requirement (a) or (b) is not the case in an empirical setting, then combination (i.e., collapsing) of some categories may be carried out if the resulting larger category is of substantive interest to consider in the study. Alternatively, "exact tests" could be utilized, which are outside the confines of this book (for details, see e.g., Agresti, 2002).

We note that the testing approach used in this section can be employed also for testing a specific probability distribution—like the Poisson distribution, say—as underlying a multinomial experiment with a prespecified number of outcomes. To accomplish this, one works out first the expected numbers of outcomes E_i using the assumption of the null hypothesis distribution ($i = 1,..., k$); if the parameters of this distribution are unknown, they must be first estimated from the data and their estimates used then to determine these expected numbers of outcomes. The distribution of the test statistic in Equation (10.11) is then the same as above, viz., chi-square, with the only difference that one needs to subtract one additional degree of freedom for each parameter estimated. That is, with q parameters to estimate first ($q > 0$), the degrees of freedom of its chi-square distribution will be $df = k - q$. All other details pertaining to carrying out the corresponding null hypothesis test remain the same as above in this section.

10.4. TESTING CATEGORICAL VARIABLE INDEPENDENCE IN CONTINGENCY TABLES

Suppose a multinomial experiment or study is carried out and we wish to examine whether the probabilities of the possible outcomes depend on another categorical variable of interest, such as gender, religious or political party affiliation, or socioeconomic status. For instance, in the licensure exam setting in the preceding section, one may be interested in testing the hypothesis that the probabilities for the "pass," "fail," and "no decision" outcomes are related to the gender of the examinees. In that case, one would be interested in testing the hypothesis that the probability distribution across these three types of outcomes is independent of gender. In other words, of concern would be the null hypothesis stipulating that the distribution of the categorical variable exam outcome is the same for male as for female examinees. The alternative hypothesis would simply be its negation, i.e., exam outcome and gender are related, or in other words that there is an association between them.

More generally, these types of questions arise when one is dealing with two categorical variables, denoted x and y, say, rather than just a single one as discussed so far in this chapter. If one of the variables—such as x—can take k possible category values, while the other, say y, can take q possible values, then one can consider the cross-table, or cross-tabulation, resulting from simultaneously examining both variables x and y. These cross-tabulations are of particular relevance when one is willing to test the hypothesis of no association between the two qualitative variables, x and y, and are discussed next.

10.4.1. Contingency tables

In a cross-tabulation, which is also commonly referred to as *contingency table* (CT) for the variables x and y, there are kq cells of possible outcomes when both categorical variables are considered together. The set of these cells with the probabilities of an outcome falling into each of them, is called *probability distribution* of the pair of variables, x and y.

To illustrate, suppose we were interested in examining whether gender and licensure exam outcome are independent. Assume that for a total of $n = 172$ examinees, there were 45 passes, 23 fails, and 12 undecided among the males, while among the females there were 55 passes, 22 fails, and 15 undecided. Then the associated CT has two rows—one for each gender—and three columns, viz., for passed, failed, and no decision. This CT will thus have $2 \times 3 = 6$ cells, and its cells will be filled with the actual number of males or females who passed, failed, or for whom no decision could be reached. This CT is presented in Table 10.1. The remainder of this chapter will be concerned with a method for examining the hypothesis of independence of the row and column variables, e.g., of gender and exam outcome in the example represented by the CT in Table 10.1.

10.4.2. Joint and marginal distributions

This is the first time in the book when we consider two random variables together—denoted x and y, say. Up to this moment, our discussions were in

Table 10.1   Contingency table for licensure exam outcome by gender.

	Pass	Fail	No Decision	Total
Males	45	23	12	80
Females	55	22	15	92
Total	100	45	27	172

a sense *unidimensional*, since we considered only one variable—say y—at a time. In this section, however, we are interested for the first time in pairs of variables, x and y, which are categorical, or qualitative.

When we consider a pair of random variables x and y simultaneously, rather than one at a time, we are interested in their *joint distribution*, or in the *bivariate distribution* of x and y. This is a distribution that is distinct from the one of interest when examining any of the variables on its own—only x or only y. The latter unidimensional distribution, for a variable considered one at a time (e.g., y), is called *marginal distribution*. The joint and marginal distributions play special roles in the test for underlying variables' independence, a topic that we next turn to.

10.4.3. Testing variable independence

To examine whether two categorical variables x and y of interest are related or not, we can use a relatively minor modification of the approach followed in the preceding section. In fact, we will use for this aim the same test statistic defined in Equation (10.11), after working out appropriately the expected numbers of outcomes to fall into each of the cells of the associated contingency table. For simplicity of reference, we call these expected numbers *expected (cell) frequencies*, as opposed to the observed (cell) frequencies that are the numbers of outcomes to fall into each of the cells. The population probabilities for an observation (outcome) in any of the cells will be called *cell probabilities*.

To proceed, let us denote by n the number of subjects studied on both variables x and y. Designate further by n_{ij} the observed frequency for the cell that is the crossing of the ith possible value on the first categorical variable x with the jth possible value on the second variable y, for $i = 1,..., r$, and $j = 1,..., c$, where r and c denote the number of values that x and y can take, respectively. For example, in the earlier licensure exam setting, in case we use the formal notation 1 for males and 2 for females, as well as 1 for "pass," 2 for "fail," and 3 for "not decided," as before, then n_{11} would be the number of males who passed the exam, while n_{23} would be the number of females for whom no decision (pass or fail) could be reached.

We next symbolize by $n_{i.}$ the number of outcomes with the ith value of the first variable, x ($i = 1,..., r$). Similarly, let $n_{.j}$ designate the number of outcomes with the jth value on the second categorical variable, y ($j = 1,..., c$). Obviously, the $n_{i.}$'s give the frequencies with which the random variable x takes its values. At the same time, the $n_{.j}$'s are the frequencies with which the random variable y takes its values. That is, while the n_{ij}'s represent the observed cell frequencies corresponding to the joint distribution of both variables, x and y (i.e., when they are both considered together), the $n_{i.}$'s are the observed frequencies that correspond to the marginal distribution of x and the $n_{.j}$'s present the observed frequencies for the marginal distribution of y. For this reason, the $n_{i.}$'s and $n_{.j}$'s are called *observed marginal frequencies*, correspondingly for the variables x and y. We use the data in Table 10.1 to illustrate these frequencies, where we attach their symbols to the entries of the cells of the table, as presented in Table 10.2.

Using all these observed frequencies—i.e., the observed cell and marginal frequencies n_{ij}, $n_{i.}$, and $n_{.j}$—we can estimate the population probabilities for each of the two categorical variables to take their values (outcomes). To this end, let us denote these probabilities by $\pi_{i.}$ and $\pi_{.j}$, respectively ($i = 1,..., r$, and $j = 1,..., c$). That is, $\pi_{i.}$ is the population probability of x to take a value in its ith category, and $\pi_{.j}$ is the population probability of y to take a value in its jth category. Further, denote by π_{ij} the population probability of x taking a value in its ith category and of y taking a value in its jth category, i.e., for an outcome falling in the (ij)th cell of the contingency table generated by the simultaneous consideration of the variables x and y.

Based on the earlier developments in this chapter, in particular in Section 10.2, we can estimate these probabilities in the following way (see Equation (10.1); e.g., Agresti, 2002):

(10.12) $$\hat{\pi}_{i.} = n_{i.} / n \text{ and } \hat{\pi}_{.j} = n_{.j} / n,$$

$i = 1,..., r$ and $j = 1,..., c$. We next note that if the null hypothesis of independence of x and y is correct, then this would imply from the probability-related discussion in Chapter 4 that $\pi_{ij} = \pi_{i.} \pi_{.j}$. In fact, the latter equation is equiva-

Table 10.2   Contingency table for licensure exam outcome by gender, with the generic notation n_{ij}, $n_{i.}$, and $n_{.j}$ for cell frequencies and for marginal frequencies ($i = 1, 2; j = 1, 2, 3$).

	Pass	Failed	No Decision	Total
Males	$n_{11} = 45$	$n_{12} = 23$	$n_{13} = 12$	$n_{1.} = 80$
Females	$n_{21} = 55$	$n_{22} = 22$	$n_{23} = 15$	$n_{2.} = 92$
Total	$n_{.1} = 100$	$n_{.2} = 45$	$n_{.3} = 27$	$n = 172$

lent to the null hypothesis of independence, and we can formally use the notation H_0 for it in the remainder of this chapter. That is, the hypothesis of independence of x and y is tantamount to the null hypothesis

$$(10.13) \qquad H_0: \pi_{ij} = \pi_{i.}\,\pi_{.j} \text{ (for all possible pairs of } i = 1,..., r \text{ and } j = 1,..., c).$$

Since in order to proceed with hypothesis testing we need to work out the distribution of a selected test statistic under the null hypothesis, we have to find next the expected cell frequencies on the assumption of H_0 being true. With this assumption, based on the discussion in Chapter 4, it follows that we can estimate the population cell probabilities by the product of the pertinent population marginal probabilities for the two variables involved, x and y. That is,

$$(10.14) \qquad \hat{\pi}_{ij} = \hat{\pi}_{i.}\,\hat{\pi}_{.j} = (n_{i.} / n)(n_{.j} / n),$$

$i = 1,..., r$ and $j = 1,..., c$. Then the expected cell frequencies E_{ij} will be evaluated empirically, that is, estimated, by multiplying with sample size—i.e., total number of observations—the estimated cell probabilities in Equations (10.14), i.e., as

$$(10.15) \qquad E_{ij} = n\hat{\pi}_{ij} = n_{i.} n_{.j} / n \ (i = 1,..., r; j = 1,..., c).$$

Having obtained the expected cell frequencies, it follows from the discussion in the preceding Section 10.3 (see Equation (10.11) and immediately preceding and succeeding discussion) that one can test the null hypothesis (10.13) of independence using the test statistic

$$(10.16) \qquad \chi^2 = \sum_{i,j=1}^{r.c.} \frac{(n_{ij} - E_{ij})^2}{E_{ij}},$$

where the sum is over all $r.c$ cells of the CT generated by the variables x and y. This test statistic (10.16), as mentioned earlier, follows for large n the chi-square distribution with $df = (r - 1)(c - 1)$ degrees of freedom when the null hypothesis of independence is true (e.g., Rao, 1973). Testing this null hypothesis in an empirical setting is thus completed by checking if the value of (10.16) then is higher than the $100(1 - \alpha)$th percentile, for a given significance level α, of the chi-square distribution with $df = (r - 1)(c - 1)$ degrees of freedom.

The outlined testing procedure is readily carried out with the software R. To this end, first we need to communicate the data to it. We accomplish this using a new command, 'matrix', where we concatenate all rows of the sample contingency table. (A 'matrix' is here a reference to a rectangular array of numbers, or a table of numbers.) Subsequently, we use the R command 'chisq.test'. We illustrate with the previously discussed example of licensure examination, using the data provided in Table 10.1.

To this end, first we communicate to R the data using the command 'matrix' as follows:

```
> lis.exam = matrix(c(45, 23, 12, 55, 22, 15), nrow = 2, byrow = T)
```

This command initially enters the six cell observed frequencies in Table 10.1 into a single row with six elements, using the 'concatenate' command, or 'c'. To inform R, however, that these six numbers come from a contingency table with two rows and three columns, we use the subcommand 'nrow = 2'— stating that we have two rows in the resulting table. We then request from R to treat the first provided three cell frequencies as coming from row 1 and then the remaining as coming from the second row of the contingency table of concern here. That is, these six numbers are presented above row-wise. This is signaled to the software using the subcommand 'byrow = T'. This subcommand effectively states "it is true that the numbers are given row by row." We can always print the resulting matrix to the screen to assure ourselves that R has correctly represented internally the data to be analyzed subsequently:

```
> lis.exam
     [,1] [,2] [,3]
[1,]   45   23   12
[2,]   55   22   15
```

Hence, the internal representation of the data, achieved with the last preceding R command, is indeed correct (cf. Table 10.1). Now that we have the data read into R, we test the null hypothesis of interest as indicated above, viz., with the 'chisq.test' command (its result is provided beneath the command):

```
> chisq.test(lis.exam)
        Pearson's Chi-squared test
data:  lis.exam
X-squared = 0.5209, df = 2, p-value = 0.7707
```

These results indicate a fairly high p-value, definitely higher than any reasonable significance level α that could have been preset here. For this reason, we do not reject the null hypothesis of licensure exam outcome being unrelated to gender. We conclude that there is not sufficient evidence in the data to warrant a suggestion that the male and female distributions of the numbers of pass, fail, and no-decision outcomes are different.

When the null hypothesis of no association between the two categorical variables is rejected, however, it would be appropriate to examine the differences between the observed and expected frequencies in each of the cells of the contingency table considered. These differences are referred to as cell residuals (or just residuals, for short). Their examination—in terms of their sign and magnitude—helps locate the most salient differences that have contributed to the rejection of the null hypotheses. This examination may lead to interesting substantive findings in their own right, and it is thus recommended in case of null hypothesis rejection (e.g., Verzani, 2005).

11

Correlation

The previous chapters were primarily concerned with issues related to analyses of single variables. Specifically, we considered one variable at a time and discussed a number of issues related to the distribution of this variable. Many research questions in the behavioral and social sciences, however, involve at least two studied variables. In particular, the vast majority of inquiries in these sciences pertain to examining the potential relationships between two or more variables measured on a sample of subjects (or units of analyses) or in a population, like in census studies. The remainder of this book provides an introduction to several methods that have been developed to address such research questions and how their application is conducted using the software R. In this chapter, we lay the basic foundations of these methods, which will be particularly helpful when dealing with more general statistical methods of analysis and modeling.

11.1. RELATIONSHIP BETWEEN A PAIR OF RANDOM VARIABLES

One of the simplest ways to address the question of whether two studied variables are related to one another or not is by using the concept of correlation. As its name suggests, this concept is concerned with the degree to which two random variables, say x and y, co-relate or co-vary with one another. That is, this question focuses on the extent to which variability in one of the variables is associated with variability in the other. In other words, an important aspect of this query is whether considered subjects with relatively large values on one of the variables (say x) tend to be among the subjects also with relatively large values on the other variable (y). Conversely, the query might be whether subjects with relatively small values on x tend to be among the subjects with relatively large values on y.

For example, a question that is frequently of interest in the field of educational research asks whether there is any relationship between Scholastic Aptitude Test (SAT) scores and college-freshman-year success. That is, are students with high SAT scores among those who also have high grade point averages (GPA scores) at the end of their college freshman year? This is a typical question about what may be termed a positive relationship between two random variables—SAT and GPA scores here. Another question of interest may be whether the number of hours an elementary school child watches television in a week is related to his or her grades in school. That is, do students who watch television for many hours a week tend to be among those with overall lower grades in school? This is a typical question about what may be termed a negative, or inverse, relationship among two variables.

These and many other queries are concerned with whether there is a relationship between two random variables under consideration, x and y. These questions specifically ask if above average (or below average) scores on x tend to be associated with above average (or below average) realizations on y, as in a positive relationship case; or perhaps conversely, whether below (or above) average scores on x tend to go together with above (or below) average realizations on y for the same subjects or units of analysis, as in a negative relationship case.

All of the above-posited questions are quite different from most of the questions we have been concerned with so far in the book. Specifically, in the previous chapters we addressed many queries about individual random variables, considered separately from other random variables—i.e., we simply looked at them one at a time. For example, in earlier chapters we asked various questions about the graphical representations of scores on a given variable, about central tendency and variability on a specified measure, about probability distributions, or about mean and variance differences in populations for a given variable that was considered separately from other variables of interest in a study. A common feature underlying all these questions was our focus on one variable at a time and various features of its distribution. Those previous questions do differ from the ones we just posed above. Specifically, the current questions are intrinsically concerned with two random variables rather than just one. Their essential feature is that they consider the pair of variables simultaneously. Indeed, a question about the relationship between two variables cannot be meaningfully raised unless one considers a pair of variables at the same time, rather than one at a time.

11.2. GRAPHICAL TREND OF VARIABLE ASSOCIATION

The concept of correlation was developed in order to specifically address questions about certain patterns of variable interrelationships. We define this concept as follows for continuous random variables, and subsequently we empirically illustrate it. *Correlation* is the degree to which there is a linear relationship between two random variables of interest, denoted x and y. This is a qualitative definition of a new concept that we have not dealt with earlier in the book. For this reason, it is fitting to illustrate here its underlying idea with some empirical data.

Example 11.1 (examining the relationship between SAT score and GPA during freshman year of college): In a small study, $n = 14$ freshmen in a university reported their SAT scores given below (denoted x) and their GPAs (denoted y) at the end of their first year of college. We are concerned with the question of whether there is a discernible linear relationship between the variables SAT and GPA. The students' data are as follows (with 'id' = subject identifier, 'x' = SAT score, and 'y' = freshman year GPA score) and are contained in the file CH11_EX1.dat.

id	x	y
1	1520	3.8
2	1330	2.9
3	1460	3.6
4	1250	2.7
5	1270	2.7
6	1310	2.9
7	1450	3.5
8	1530	3.7
9	1560	3.8
10	1470	3.3
11	1510	3.5
12	1370	2.9
13	1550	3.9
14	1260	2.6

Let us formally denote these 14 individual pairs of scores as (x_i, y_i), $i = 1,..., 14$. A convenient graphical representation of them is provided by the *scatterplot*, which consists of as many points in the plane—the commonly used two-dimensional coordinate system—as there are studied subjects (or units of analysis, more generally). Thereby, each of these points represents a pair of scores on the two variables under consideration for the pertinent subject (unit of analysis). In the present SAT example, a scatterplot thus has $n = 14$ points, each representing a student in the study, i.e., a row of the above table of scores. In the graphical plot of these scores, the horizontal (or x-) axis corresponds to the variable x, and the vertical (or y-) axis corresponds to the variable y. For our SAT example, each of its $n = 14$ points represents the data on a single subject. Specifically, on the horizontal axis is his or her SAT (x) score while on the vertical axis is his or her GPA (y) score.

We can readily obtain a scatterplot with R—as illustrated earlier in this book—using the command 'plot' (after of course first reading in the data from the file CH11_EX1.dat):

```
> d = read.table("C://data/CH11_EX1.dat", header = T)
> attach(d)

> plot(x,y)
```

The last command produces the plot displayed in Figure 11.1.

As can be seen from Figure 11.1, there is a *discernible linear trend* between the SAT scores and GPA scores. In particular, freshmen with higher than average SAT scores tend to be among those who have also higher than average GPA scores. Similarly, students with lower than average GPA scores are also among those who have lower than average SAT scores. Yet we note that this relationship is not perfect. Indeed, these 14 paired scores do not exactly lie along a straight line. Specifically, we see three students who differ in their SAT scores, being in the 1300 range, but have the same GPA score of 2.9. (Such a difference would obviously not be possible, should the 14 points be positioned precisely along a straight line.)

While there is no perfect linear relationship between SAT and GPA in this data set, the plot in Figure 11.1 clearly demonstrates a *tendency* of higher scores on one of the variables to be coming from students with higher scores on the other measure as well. Similarly, this *trend* or pattern of relationship

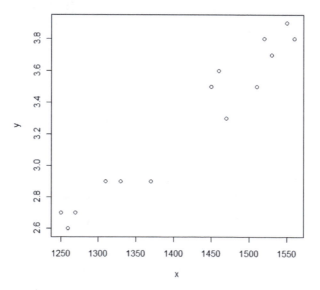

FIGURE 11.1.
Plot of SAT scores (*x*) and GPA scores (*y*) for *n* = 14 college freshmen.

holds also for smaller scores—students with lower SAT scores tend to be among those with lower GPA scores. We emphasize that this is a tendency, i.e., a discernible linear trend, rather than a perfect linear relationship. In actual fact, the observation (of an imperfect relationship) that we just made from Figure 11.1 is characteristic of the vast majority of empirical research in the behavioral and social sciences. In them, one should not really expect to observe often, if ever, perfect (or even close to perfect) linear relationships between studied variables, for at least two main reasons. First, there is usually a considerable amount of *measurement error* involved when evaluating studied variables in these disciplines. This error may contain "pure" measurement error, or error that results from measuring in fact a variable that is not really identical to the one of actual interest (e.g., Raykov & Marcoulides, 2011). Second, relationships between variables of concern in empirical research cannot be realistically expected to be so simple as to be described well by straight-line (linear) functions.

Nonetheless, the knowledge of an *approximate* linear relationship—i.e., of a *discernible linear relationship* as in Figure 11.1—can be very useful in these and many other disciplines. Such a relationship indicates potentially a very important association between two variables of interest. This association is particularly helpful when trying to predict one of the variables based on knowledge of the other, as we will be doing later in the book. In fact, the stronger this association is, the better these predictions are going to be. More-over, knowledge of an existing association between two or more variables—by considering them pairwise, say—allows us to deepen our knowledge about these and other variables. This may well help us answer further and more involved scientific questions, e.g., such pursued with more advanced statistical methods.

11.3. THE COVARIANCE COEFFICIENT

The developments in Section 11.1 provided a qualitative description of the concept of correlation. In particular, Figure 11.1 presented graphically a small data set and allowed us to judge informally whether we were dealing with a discernible linear trend for two studied random variables. This graph or scatterplot permits, however, only a subjective interpretation. Thus, a judgment whether there is such a trend in the graph may well differ across persons. For this reason, it is important to have also an objective measure of variable correlation, which reflects the degree of linear relationship between two variables of interest.

Two objective quantitative measures that can be used for this goal are the covariance coefficient and the correlation coefficient (for short often referred to as "covariance" and "correlation," respectively). To define them formally for a pair of random variables x and y, denote in a studied (finite) population their scores by $x_1, x_2,..., x_N$ and $y_1, y_2,..., y_N$, respectively, and their means correspondingly by μ_x and μ_y. Then their *covariance coefficient*, denoted $Cov(x,y)$, can be defined in the population as

$$(11.1) \qquad Cov(x,y) = \frac{1}{N} \sum_{i=1}^{N} (x_i - \mu_x)(y_i - \mu_y).$$

Populations are rarely available for study, however, and so we typically resort to examining samples from them. In a given sample of size n from a population of interest, with scores on the two variables denoted correspondingly x_1, $x_2,..., x_n$ and $y_1, y_2,..., y_n$, as well as sample means $\bar{x}$ and $\bar{y}$, the covariance coefficient is estimated by

$$(11.2) \qquad c_{x,y} = \frac{1}{n-1} \sum_{i=1}^{n} (x_i - \bar{x})(y_i - \bar{y}).$$

Equations (11.1) and (11.2) show that the covariance is a *symmetric* measure of the relationship between the two variables involved, that is, $Cov(x, y) = Cov(y, x)$. In other words, the covariance treats equally both variables involved, rather than differently from each other. (In the next chapter, we discuss an alternative method for studying variable relationships, which does not handle symmetrically the two variables involved.) In addition, we note that Equations (11.1) and (11.2) bear distinct resemblance to the definition and estimator, respectively, of the variance coefficient (see details in Chapter 3). Specifically, the variance and its estimator as well as estimate result correspondingly from these two equations by setting $x = y$. That is, the variance of any random variable is its covariance with itself.

A main limitation of the covariance coefficient is that it is not readily possible to interpret its value in an empirical study. The reason is that its magnitude depends on the units of measurement underlying the two variables involved, x and y. However, their units are usually hard to interpret themselves in subject-matter terms in the social and behavioral disciplines. Thus, it is not easy to make sense of a finding that a covariance between two studied variables is 3.45 or -5.67, for instance. In fact, the only possible value of a covariance coefficient that can be interpreted unambiguously is zero. In particular, when $Cov(x, y) = 0$, one can state that there is no linear relationship between the two variables x and y. In that case, there is also no discernible linear pattern in their scatterplot.

This interpretational limitation applies both to the population covariance coefficient and its sample estimate. Specifically, even if we knew the population covariance coefficient, for the above reasons it is very hard if at all possible to impart a subject-matter interpretation to its value. This limitation implies also that we cannot say when a covariance coefficient is large or small.

This is the reason why the covariance coefficient is often referred to as a *nonnormed* measure (index) of linear variable relationship. This reference also reflects the fact that the covariance coefficient is unbounded in its magnitude. Indeed, there is nothing that prevents in principle a covariance coefficient to be larger than any given positive number, or conversely smaller than any prespecified negative number.

While the magnitude of a covariance coefficient is difficult to interpret, if it is possible at all, its sign is informative. As can be seen by examining Equations (11.1) and (11.2), a positive covariance coefficient indicates a tendency of larger-than-average x-scores to be associated—i.e., stem from the same subject or unit of analysis—with larger-than-average y-scores. Similarly, smaller-than-average x-scores tend to go together with smaller-than-average y-scores. We refer to such a tendency as a positive association, and we emphasize that it corresponds to a positive covariance. Conversely, Equations (11.1) and (11.2) also show that a negative covariance is indicative of a tendency for larger-than-average x-scores to be associated with smaller-than-average y-scores. Also, smaller-than-average x-scores tend to go together with larger-than-average y-scores then. We refer to such a tendency as a "negative association" and stress that it corresponds to a negative covariance.

This interpretation of the sign of a covariance coefficient cannot completely compensate for the general lack of direct interpretability of its magnitude (value). For this reason, covariance coefficients are less often used on their own in empirical behavioral and social research. (We note that they can be used as starting points in some applications of more advanced statistical methods, such as structural equation modeling; e.g., Raykov & Marcoulides, 2006, 2008.)

Before we move on to a discussion of another relationship index that does not share this limitation of the covariance coefficient, we mention that we can readily estimate the covariance coefficient in a given sample using the software R. To this end, we utilize the command 'cov(x,y)'. For the above SAT example (Example 11.1), we estimate the covariance coefficient between SAT score and GPA score as follows (result given beneath command):

```
> cov(x,y)
[1] 52.37363
```

That is, the estimate provided in Equation (11.2) for the data set of Example 11.1 is 52.37 (rounded off). Hence, the covariance between SAT and GPA scores is positive here. Thus, in this study, students with a higher-than-average SAT score—which is 1417.14—tend to be among those with a higher-than-average GPA score, which is 3.27. (Using the command 'mean', as in Chapter 3, one can readily obtain these sample averages from the available data.) Conversely, freshmen with below-average SAT scores tend to be among those with below-average GPA scores. However, we underscore that we cannot say whether the covariance of 52.37 found in this sample is large (strong), medium, or small (weak). This as mentioned is a main limitation of the covariance coefficient. For this reason, we now move on to a discussion of another, closely related index of linear relationship between a pair of variables. That index has become very popular in the social and behavioral sciences, in part because it is possible also to interpret its magnitude.

11.4. THE CORRELATION COEFFICIENT

We noted in the previous discussion that the covariance coefficient is a non-normed measure of linear relationship. That is, it is not possible to say if its value is large or small, because by definition (e.g., Equation (11.1)) the covariance depends on the units of measurement of the variables involved. As an alternative to the covariance, the correlation coefficient is a normed index of linear relationship between two random variables, denoted x and y, say. Being defined as the covariance coefficient divided by the product of the standard deviations of the two variables, the correlation coefficient is no more expressed in terms of their units of measurement because these are canceled out by this division. (The underlying assumption in this definition is that neither variable has zero variance; see below.) Therefore, the correlation coefficient is free of the measurement units of the two variables in question; i.e., this coefficient is a scale-free index.

More specifically, in a studied population the correlation coefficient between two random variables with positive variances is defined as follows:

$$(11.3) \qquad \rho_{X,Y} = \frac{Cov(X,Y)}{\sqrt{Var(X)Var(Y)}},$$

where $Var(.)$ denotes variance (see Chapter 3, and below in this section). In a given sample of size n, the correlation coefficient can be estimated by

$$(11.4) \qquad \hat{\rho}_{X,Y} = \frac{1}{n} \sum_{i=1}^{n} \hat{z}_{X,i} \hat{z}_{Y,i},$$

that is, by the average product of the corresponding z-scores associated with the variables involved. This estimate is frequently denoted alternatively by $r_{X,Y}$.

Equations (11.3) and (11.4) present what is frequently referred to as the "Pearson product moment correlation coefficient," bearing the name of its originator, Karl Pearson (for continuous random variables; see, e.g., Raykov & Marcoulides, 2011, for a nontechnical discussion of possible correlation coefficients between discrete variables). These two equations also show that since the covariance is a symmetric coefficient, so is also the correlation coefficient. Furthermore, from these equations it is readily observed that the correlation and covariance coefficients are zero at the same time. That is, if there is no linear relationship between the variables x and y, their correlation is zero as is their covariance. Then, as pointed out earlier, there is no discernible linear pattern in the scatterplot of the associated data points (x_i, y_i) ($i = 1,..., n$ or N as in a census). Conversely, if their covariance is zero, so is also their correlation and vice versa, and there is no linear relationship between x and y. In addition, Equations (11.3) and (11.4) indicate that the correlation coefficient is not defined if any of the variables involved has zero variance. That is, if at least one of the variables is a constant—which as pointed out earlier in the book is equivalent to its variance and standard deviation being zero—then their correlation does not exist, while their covariance is zero.

Another important feature of the correlation coefficient also follows from its definition. Specifically, as shown in more advanced sources, the covariance between two variables never exceeds the product of their standard deviations (e.g., Roussas, 1997). Since the covariance is divided by this product in the definition of the correlation coefficient (see Equation (11.3)), it follows that any correlation lies within the closed interval $[-1, +1]$. That is, for any two random variables x and y (with positive variances),

$$(11.5) \qquad\qquad -1 \le \rho_{x,y} \le 1$$

always holds. Inequality (11.5) in actual fact represents two inequalities bounding the correlation from below and from above by -1 and 1, respectively. In addition, it demonstrates that the correlation coefficient is a normed measure of linear relationship between the random variables x and y. The correlation is normed in the sense that its magnitude is never lower than -1 or larger than 1 (assuming of course that the correlation exists for two considered variables, which as mentioned will only be the case if none of them is a constant).

While the correlation coefficient is bounded by -1 and 1, when does it equal these smallest and highest possible values, respectively? It can be shown (e.g., Roussas, 1997) that the correlation coefficient is 1 or -1, if and only if there exists a perfect linear relationship between the two variables involved, x and y. This will be the case if and only if there exist two numbers, a and b, say, with which one of the variables—say y—is expressed as such a perfect linear function in terms of the other, i.e., $y = a + bx$ holds. (Note that then also x can be expressed as a perfect linear function in terms of y, using in general two different numbers in the role of a and b.)

We emphasize that the correlation coefficient, unlike the covariance, is a quantity that has no units attached to its value—i.e., it is a "pure" number. This is a particularly useful feature that helps a great deal in interpreting the correlation in an empirical setting. Specifically, we interpret the correlation coefficient by paying attention to the following questions. First, what is its sign? If it is positive, then larger (or smaller) values on x tend to go together with larger (smaller) values on y; if it is negative, then larger values on x go together with smaller values on y, and conversely. Second, what is its value? Correlations close to 1 or -1, e.g., in the .90s or $-.90$s, are usually considered indicative of a strong linear relationship. The scatterplot of the data shows then the individual points clustered relatively tightly along a line (see below in this section for a graphical illustration). Alternatively, correlations in the .50s through .80s in absolute value are considered indicative of some but not strong linear relationship. The scatterplots of such data sets indicate discernibly a linear trend, yet the points are considerably less closely clustered along a line (see below). Last but not least, correlation coefficients in the vicinity of zero are indicative of a weak or no linear relationship between the variables studied. Under such circumstances, the associated scatterplots do not indicate a discernible linear trend, and for close to zero correlations can be nearly spherical in appearance.

Like the covariance, the correlation coefficient is readily estimated in a given sample with data on two variables, x and y, say, using R. To accomplish this, we use the command 'cor(x,y)'. For the above SAT example (Example 11.1), we estimate their correlation as follows (result given beneath command):

```
> cor(x,y)
[1] 0.9713206
```

That is, the correlation between SAT scores and GPA freshmen scores is fairly strong, estimated at .97. Hence, there is a strong positive linear relationship in this data set between success on the SAT and in the freshman college year. As a result, the pertinent scatterplot (see Figure 11.1) shows a clearly discernible linear pattern. Examining Equations (11.3) and (11.4), this correlation effectively suggests that the rank ordering of the SAT scores is nearly the same as that of the GPA scores—as could be seen using the 'rank(x)' and 'rank(y)' procedures with R.

We illustrate further the concept of correlation by considering several additional examples.

Example 11.2 (SAT and college junior year GPA): The following scores stem from a small study of $n = 12$ college juniors.

id	x	y
1	1460	3.1
2	1250	2.8
3	1270	2.8
4	1310	3.2
5	1450	3.1
6	1530	3.6
7	1560	3.7
8	1470	3.1
9	1510	3.6
10	1370	3.0
11	1550	3.7
12	1260	2.9

The correlation coefficient for these two variables is estimated with R as follows, and their scatterplot is provided in Figure 11.2:

```
> cor(x,y)
[1] 0.8749617
```

```
> plot(x,y)
```

An examination of Figure 11.2 indicates that (a) the correlation is notably weaker than that in Example 11.1, being estimated here at .87 (rounded off);

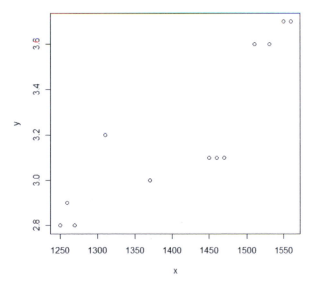

FIGURE 11.2.
Scatterplot of SAT scores (x) and GPA scores (y) in junior college year.

as well as (b) the pertinent scatterplot is not as strongly suggestive of a linear relationship between the two variables studied here relative to the previous example. In particular, the data points in Figure 11.2 do not fall as closely along a line as in Example 11.1. This will be a general finding with correlations in the .50s through .80s range or so.

The next example demonstrates an even weaker correlation, which is in addition negative.

Example 11.3 (hours watching television and score on a test of reading ability): The following data stem from a study with $n = 16$ elementary school students, where the relationship between hours watching television per week and their score on a reading ability test is of interest ('x' = weekly hours of television watching, 'y' = reading ability test score):

id	x	y
1	6	32
2	8	32
3	7	28
4	6	32
5	5	30
6	9	24
7	5	32
8	4	30
9	5	36
10	3	29
11	5	37
12	7	32
13	4	29
14	5	32
15	8	29
16	9	28

For this data set, the estimated correlation coefficient is obtained with R as follows, and the associated scatterplot is displayed in Figure 11.3:

```
> cor(x,y)
[1] -0.3965841

> plot(x,y)
```

This correlation of −.40 (rounded off) is markedly smaller in magnitude than the ones in the preceding two examples, and the plot of the data points

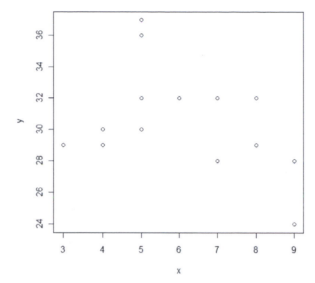

FIGURE 11.3.

Scatterplot for data on weekly hours TV watching (*x*) and a reading ability test (*y*).

is far less clustered along an (imaginary) line. We stress that here we are dealing with a negative correlation—children watching more television tend to have lower test scores. Similarly, due to the negative correlation, there is a negative slope for a possible line through the scatter of points.

11.5. LINEAR TRANSFORMATION INVARIANCE OF THE CORRELATION COEFFICIENT

We mentioned earlier in the chapter that the correlation coefficient is a "pure" number—i.e., a scale-free number. The reason was the fact that in its definition (e.g., see Equation (11.1)) a division was carried out of the covariance between the two variables involved with the product of their standard deviations. This leads to canceling out the effect of the measurement unit in the numerator and denominator, furnishing a scale-free index in the resulting correlation coefficient.

This scale-free feature is the reason why the correlation coefficient does not depend also on a change in the units of measurement of two variables under consideration, if the change is carried out using a linear transformation. In particular, whether we measure height and weight in inches and pounds, respectively, or alternatively in centimeters and kilograms, the same correlation coefficient results between height and weight (in a given sample/population). This is because the units of measurement get canceled out, and thus the new units of measurement—being a multiple of the old ones—do not really matter.

This insensitivity to change in the units of measurement following a linear transformation is a consequence of a more general property of the correlation coefficient. Specifically, the correlation is invariant to linear changes in at least one of the two variables involved. That is, if $X = k_1 + k_2 x$ and/or $Y = q_1 + q_2 y$ are linear transformations of the original variables x and y, with k_1, k_2, q_1, and q_2 being constants (whereby k_2, and q_2 are not zero), then

$$(11.6) \qquad Corr(X, Y) = Corr(x, y),$$

where for notational emphasis $Corr(.,.)$ is used to symbolize correlation of the variables within parentheses (e.g., King & Minium, 2003). We note in passing that the correlation coefficient is not invariant under a nonlinear change of the units of measurement, i.e., a nonlinear transformation of at least one of the two variables involved. However, we point out that in order to carry out such transformations there must be serious reasons to change the units of measurement in this manner. For further details and additional discussions on carrying out such transformations, the reader is referred to more advanced sources (e.g., Agresti & Finlay, 2009; Raykov & Marcoulides, 2008).

11.6. IS THERE A DISCERNIBLE LINEAR RELATIONSHIP PATTERN BETWEEN TWO VARIABLES IN A STUDIED POPULATION?

As indicated on a number of occasions in the book, typically in behavioral and social research for various reasons we are unable to study entire populations, but only samples drawn from them. Hence the question naturally arises whether, based on a given sample, we can infer if in the population that it came from there is no linear relationship between two variables of interest, say x and y. This query asks about inferences with regard to the obtained sample correlation coefficient—specifically, drawing conclusions about it being zero in the studied population or not. As it turns out, the question can be answered via a statistical test about the population value of a correlation coefficient, which we discuss next.

To facilitate such inferences, we need to consider as a null hypothesis the statement of the correlation being zero, i.e., H_0: $\rho_{x,y} = 0$, where $\rho_{x,y}$ denotes the population correlation coefficient between x and y. As an alternative hypothesis we can consider, depending on the research question, H_a: $\rho_{x,y} \neq 0$, H_a: $\rho_{x,y} > 0$, or H_a: $\rho_{x,y} < 0$. It can be shown (e.g., King & Minium, 2003) that under the null hypothesis H_0, the following ratio

$$(11.7) \qquad t = r_{x,y} \frac{\sqrt{n-2}}{\sqrt{1 - r^2_{x,y}}}$$

follows a t-distribution with degrees of freedom $d = n - 2$. This is the fundamental relationship to be used in order to accomplish the hypothesis testing of concern here.

To achieve this aim, first we note from Equation (11.7) that large values of the correlation coefficient lead to large values of t, and conversely small values of $r_{x,y}$ are associated with small values of t. This is precisely what we want from a test statistic most of the time, if it is to be used for the purpose of testing a given null hypothesis. That is, we can use the t-ratio in Equation (11.7) as a test statistic in a t-test when we are willing to ascertain whether there is sufficient evidence in the data warranting rejection of the null hypothesis H_0 of no linear relation between two studied variables. This t-test can obviously be one-tailed or two-tailed, depending on the alternative hypothesis and research question asked. We follow thereby the same testing principles as discussed earlier in the book when we dealt with testing of one- and two-tailed hypotheses. To adopt a widely used reference, if we reject this null hypothesis of zero population correlation coefficient, we can refer to the correlation between the variables in the study as being significantly different from zero, or as *significant* for short. We illustrate with the following example.

Example 11.4 (relationship between reaction time in a cognitive test and GPA score): The reaction time on a cognitive test, in milliseconds (μs), and the GPA scores are obtained from a sample of $n = 56$ freshmen students. Is there a linear relationship between these two variables in the studied freshmen population? (The data are provided in the file CH11_EX4.dat, where 'x' denotes reaction time and 'y' denotes GPA score.)

We can respond to this question using R. To this end, we use the command 'cor.test', as follows (after first reading in the above data; output of testing procedure given after this command):

```
> d = read.table("C://data/L11_EX4.dat", header = T)
> attach(d)

> cor.test(x,y)



Pearson's product-moment correlation

data: x and y
t = -15.8708, df = 54, p-value < 2.2e-16
alternative hypothesis: true correlation is not equal to 0
95 percent confidence interval:
```

```
-0.9449202 -0.8464944
sample estimates:
      cor
-0.907448
```

We see from this output that the correlation coefficient between reaction time and GPA score is negative, estimated at $-.91$, which is a strong correlation. (Recall that what determines whether a correlation is strong, medium, or weak is the absolute value of this coefficient.) That is, there is a clearly discernible linear relationship between reaction time and academic success in freshman year at college. Specifically, there is a marked tendency of students with short reaction times to have high GPA scores and for students with long reaction times to have low GPA scores.

Further, the associated p-value with the t-test statistic (11.7) is very small—less than .001—and in fact smaller than any reasonable preset significance level. Thus, if we were to test the null hypothesis H_0 of no correlation against the two-tailed alternative H_a: $\rho_{x,y} \neq 0$, we would reject H_0 and conclude that there is evidence in the data indicating a discernible linear relationship between reaction time and GPA score. If we were to have settled, before looking at the data, on the alternative H_a: $\rho_{x,y} < 0$—as one could expect on subject-matter grounds in this example—then given that the correlation estimate is in its direction we would halve the reported p-value. Having thus obtained a p-value that is even smaller than the reported one above, i.e., smaller than .001, we would conclude that we could reject H_0 in favor of the hypothesis that there is a negative correlation between reaction time on the used cognitive test and GPA score for college freshmen.

We similarly note that the software R provides with this command 'cor.test' also a confidence interval (CI) at the conventional 95%-CI. This CI stretches here from $-.94$ through $-.85$. In general, the CI of the correlation coefficient is nonsymmetric, due to the fact that the random sampling distribution of the correlation coefficient is itself nonsymmetric in general (unless its population value is zero; e.g., King & Minium, 2003). What underlies then the procedure of obtaining the CI for the correlation coefficient is the so-called Fisher transformation, which is a nonlinear function (e.g., Agresti & Finlay, 2009). This nonlinearity leads to the general lack of symmetry in the resulting CI. The details of how one could use R for obtaining such a CI, along with the underpinnings of the procedure used for this purpose, go beyond the confines of this book. A nontechnical discussion of them can be found, for example, in Raykov & Marcoulides (2011).

We would like to point out here that the CI of the correlation coefficient can also be used to test hypotheses about a correlation coefficient if need be, where the hypothetical value is not zero. For example, if the null hypothesis is H_0: $\rho = \rho_0$, with ρ_0 being a prespecified number (not necessarily zero), versus an appropriate alternative hypothesis corresponding to a research question, we use the same testing principles as discussed earlier in the book (e.g., Chapter 7). For instance, suppose that in the above Example 11.4 we had decided before looking at the data to test the null hypothesis H_0: $\rho_{x,y} = -.80$ versus the alternative H_a: $\rho_{x,y} \neq -.80$. In that case, given that the CI for the correlation coefficient was found to be $(-.94, -.85)$ and did not thus include the hypothetical value of $-.80$, we would reject the null hypothesis H_0 in favor of the alternative hypothesis that the population correlation is not $-.80$.

11.7. CAUTIONS WHEN INTERPRETING A CORRELATION COEFFICIENT

The correlation coefficient is a very popular measure of linear relationship between studied variables in empirical behavioral and social research, and it is very frequently employed in these and related disciplines. For this reason, it is of special importance to be aware of a number of important issues when interpreting its estimates, which we discuss in this section.

First, we emphasize that the correlation coefficient is a measure of *linear relationship* only. Hence, it is possible that two variables have a strong *nonlinear* relationship, yet their correlation coefficient is close to zero. This result would follow from the fact that then there would be limited or no linear trend in the relationship between the two variables involved. We illustrate with the following simple example.

> **Example 11.5 (nonlinear relation associated with small correlation):** The variables x and $y = x^2$ have a perfect curvilinear relationship—i.e., a nonlinear relationship of the strongest possible degree (being a perfect relation). For our purposes here, we first create scores on x easily using the 'seq' command as earlier in the book (note that alternatively we could take for x any set of realizations of a random variable). Then we compute the correlation between x and $y = x^2$ as well as plot their scores. This leads to the following results (note below the use of the sign '$\wedge$' to denote raising a variable to the power following the sign):

```
> x = seq (-5, 5, .05)
> y = x^2

> cor(x,y)
[1] 1.89315e-16

> plot(x,y)
```

We observe that the correlation of x and y, being 1.89315×10^{-16}, is practically zero. The graph of the variables x and y, which is displayed in Figure 11.4, reveals, however, a perfect (nonlinear) relationship between the two variables.

Example 11.5 presents a simple demonstration of the fact that the correlation coefficient informs only about the degree of linear relationship, rather than of any (i.e., possibly nonlinear) relationship. At the same time, this exemplifies that the correlation is insensitive to anything other than the linear relationship between two random variables.

Further, we note that a relatively small value of a correlation coefficient may alternatively be the result of a restriction in the variable range, and not necessarily of lack of a discernible linear association in the studied population between the two variables involved (e.g., Agresti & Finlay, 2009). One could check for restriction of range by examining how the sample standard deviations of studied variables relate to what may be known about them in the population. In addition, one should revisit the data collection procedure, since a ceiling or floor effect may have been operating during the observation process (e.g., Graziano & Raulin, 2009). Similarly, one should examine whether any restriction could have been in place when selecting sample subjects (i.e., drawing the sample from the studied population). In particular, one may have chosen samples from prespecified groups without being aware of a range restriction in effect. This can happen, for instance, when sampling only from students going to college, rather than from all high school seniors in

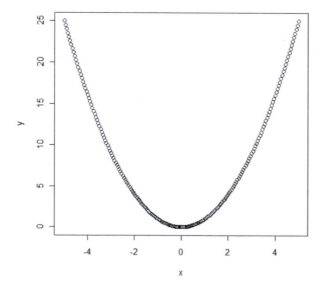

FIGURE 11.4.

Plot of the variables x and y in Example 11.5.

a given state, and subsequently administering the tests or measures under consideration to the sampled students. Also, one should look in addition at the scatterplot of the available data, which may indirectly point to a threshold operating in the sample.

Finally, one of the most frequent misuses of the correlation coefficient occurs when it is interpreted as indicative of causation. Specifically, no causal interpretation is possible based only on knowledge of the correlation of two variables under consideration. As we pointed out earlier, the correlation is a symmetric measure of linear relationship. In particular, irrespective of whether x causes y or vice versa, their correlation is one and the same. In other words, the correlation coefficient does not provide any information about the direction of the relationship between the variables. Hence, no definitive conclusions about causality can be drawn from the examination of a given correlation coefficient—whether in a population of interest or a sample from it. That is, regardless of whether a correlation is large or small, positive or negative, significant or not, no implications can be drawn about the direction of causality with respect to the two variables involved. The reason is that no uniquely interpretable information about causality is contained in the correlation coefficient to begin with, irrespective of whether it is observed in a studied population or only in a sample drawn from it.

Simple Linear Regression

The correlation coefficient was introduced in the previous chapter as a symmetric measure, or index, of linear variable relationship. It was also indicated that this coefficient can be used to make predictions about a given variable, based on knowledge of the value on another variable of a particular individual (or unit of analysis). Such predictions are quite useful in the social and behavioral sciences. When we make predictions of this type, however, we in effect no longer treat the two variables symmetrically. This is because we use one of them to learn about the other. In the present chapter, we will be concerned with studying this type of variable relationship. Specifically, we will use for this aim a particular modeling approach, which is usually referred to as "regression analysis."

12.1. DEPENDENT AND INDEPENDENT VARIABLES

The variable that is of focal interest in a given study is often called a *dependent variable* (DV) or alternatively a *response* or *outcome variable*. This is the variable for which we may also wish to make particular predictions. We will assume in this and the following two chapters that the DV is (approximately) continuous, or can be treated as a continuous random variable. Alternatively, the variable that we use as a means for predicting the DV is called an *independent variable* (IV) or a *predictor*. At times it is also referred to as an *explanatory variable* or *covariate* in the literature—to emphasize that it typically covaries with the DV.

In the remainder of this chapter, we will be concerned with the case when there is just a single predictor, i.e., a single IV variable that is used to predict a DV of interest. The more general case, with two or more predictors (IVs), will be covered in the next chapter. As before, we denote the two variables under consideration by x and y, but we now need to pay attention to which variable is a DV and which an IV. We use throughout the symbol y to denote the DV or response variable and x to denote the IV. That is, we wish to discuss methods for studying the relationship between x and y in such a way that will permit us to predict individual values of y based on knowledge of such values on x.

12.2. INTERCEPT AND SLOPE

In the remainder of this chapter, we will use a *linear* relationship to make predictions about the DV y using the IV x. To this end, we will employ the method of *linear regression analysis*. Specifically, we posit—that is, assume—the linear relationship

$$(12.1) \qquad\qquad y = a + bx + e$$

to hold between the variables x and y, where e denotes a model error term that we discuss next in detail. We refer to Equation (12.1) as a *simple linear regression (SLR) model*.

The term e in the right-hand side of Equation (12.1) plays a special role in this approach to prediction, and is referred to as *model error* or *error term*. A major feature of e whenever the SLR model (12.1) is considered—and generally in a statistical model—is that its mean is zero in a studied population. (We note in passing that the model can always be reformulated in such a way that the mean of e is zero; see Wooldridge, 2008, for a more detailed discussion on this topic.) That is, according to the SLR model (12.1), the relationship between x and y is linear, apart from an unobservable error term that on average vanishes in the population.

Equation (12.1) reveals that we do not assume a perfect linear relationship between y and x, which would have been the case had we not included the error term e in its right-hand side. We do not make the assumption of a perfect deterministic relationship, since as mentioned earlier in the book (e.g., Chapter 11) a perfect relationship is unrealistic to expect most of the time for studied variables in the social and behavioral sciences. Rather than making this unrealistic assumption, the error term e in the model (12.1) accounts for the deviations from perfect linear relationship with regard to the covariability of the variables x and y. That is, e is the part of the model (12.1) that captures the imperfection in the relationship between x and y, in terms of its deviations from a straight line. Thereby, the error term is assumed to be uncorrelated with the IV x (cf. Wooldridge, 2008). In most applications of SLR, in particular for the remainder of this book, it is additionally posited that the error term e is normally distributed, with variance independent of x. The validity of these assumptions can be examined with methods discussed later in the chapter, and some of these assumptions can be relaxed in more advanced models.

We stress that Equation (12.1), with the subsequently discussed assumptions, defines a *model* for the relationship between the two variables involved, the DV y and the IV x. The concept of a model is inextricably connected to the possibility that it may be correct or plausible, but it may conversely be wrong in a particular population of interest. Thus, whenever we come up with Equation (12.1) for two x and y variables under consideration, we are in fact making the assumption that there exist two numbers, a and b, for which (12.1) holds in a studied population.

The SLR model (12.1) obtains its name from the following two facts. First, the parameters of main interest in it—a and b—appear only linearly, i.e., in their first power, in the right-hand side of its defining Equation (12.1). Second, there is only a single explanatory variable, x, involved in it. With respect to the first mentioned property of linearity, we note that it is not important how the explanatory variable x itself is included in the model, but only how its parameters appear in the model. In particular, as we will do later in this chapter, we can add the square and/or another power of x if need be to the right-hand side of Equation (12.1) without altering its linearity feature—as long as the associated parameter with the higher power of x, say c, appears only linearly (see Section 12.6). Indeed, after we do this the model will still be linear, since all that counts for its linearity is whether merely the first powers of its parameters appear in the right-hand side of (12.1) as separate parameters. Whenever this is the case, we refer to a model as *linear*. This linearity property will be upheld also in the models we consider in the next chapter, where their parameters will be involved only in their first power in the pertinent definition equations (as separate parameters). The second of the above-mentioned features expresses the fact that only a *single* independent variable is included in the model (12.1). When we have more than one independent variable in a regression model, we will speak of a *multiple regression model*. Models of this type will be of concern in the next chapter.

Returning to our earlier concerns with prediction of an individual value on the dependent variable y, let us consider now how we could carry it out. Obviously, in general, in order to make a prediction we need to use a relationship. With regard to the two variables of interest, x and y, to predict a value on y that corresponds to a known value on x, say x_0, we need knowledge of the relationship between x and y. In actual fact, such a relationship for these two variables is provided by model (12.1), whenever it is plausible in a population under consideration. We reiterate that as pointed out earlier, when Equation (12.1) is correct as a model for the relationship between x and y, there exist two numbers a and b with this equation. In those cases, employing this model the prediction of an unknown dependent variable value (denoted as y') corresponding to a known predictor value x_0, will be $y' = a + bx_0$, according to the model.

When we are interested in using the SLR model (12.1), we are also typically concerned with its validity in the population. Assuming it is correct there, what could one actually say about a and b? Unfortunately, since we do not know these two numbers, they must be treated as unknown population parameters. As it turns out, they also have very special names—*intercept* and *slope*, respectively. The reason for these names is that since the term *e* is on average zero in the population, when $x = 0$ the average of *y* should be *a* (according to the SLR model). That is, *a* is the height at which the line $y = a + bx$ intersects with the vertical axis, i.e., the y-axis. This is the reason why *a* is called the *intercept*. Similarly, if we consider the averages of *y* for two given values of *x* that are only one unit apart, then these averages differ by precisely *b* units:

$$a + b(x + 1) - (a + bx) = b.$$

That is, *b* represents the degree to which *y* increases on average, or decreases on average, following a change by one unit in the IV *x*. For this reason, *b* is called the *slope*. Figure 12.1 reflects graphically this interpretation of the intercept and slope for an SLR model.

A frequent joint reference to the intercept and slope in the SLR model, which we will also use, is as *SLR model parameters* (or just *model parameters*). We stress that Equation (12.1) represents a population model. That is, whenever this model is proposed, or posited, one assumes that it holds in the population—i.e., the model is assumed to be an adequate means there for the description and explanation of the relationship between the variables *x* and *y*. In fact, there are statistical procedures, discussed later in this chapter, that help examine the validity of this model in the population. We will see next that there is yet another parameter of the SLR model defined in Equation

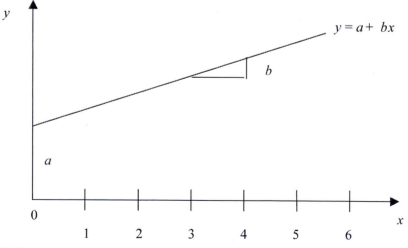

FIGURE 12.1.

Graphical representation of the intercept and slope in a simple linear regression model.

(12.1) that we have not yet mentioned. That parameter plays an important role when evaluating the intercept and slope based on sample data from a studied population, as well as when assessing model adequacy.

12.3. ESTIMATION OF MODEL PARAMETERS (MODEL FITTING)

As we mentioned earlier, advancing model (12.1) as a way of describing the relationship between two random variables x and y in a studied population is tantamount to the assumption of the existence of two real numbers a and b with which Equation (12.1) holds (along with the subsequent distributional assumptions). Given data in a sample drawn from the population, we wish to find these values in such a way that makes model (12.1) as close as possible to the available data. This will only then be the case if the values of the error term e are as small as possible when relating via a and b the individual values for x and y in the sample.

For our following considerations, it will be useful to introduce at this point notation for the individual observed values on both variables of interest. To this end, let us denote by (x_1, y_1), (x_2, y_2),..., (x_n, y_n) their observations on n subjects (or units of analysis) in the given sample from the studied population. Our earlier reasoning in this chapter implies that when we wish to evaluate, that is, estimate, a and b from the sample of data on the random variables x and y, we need to seek for such values of the unknown model parameters a and b, with which the individual deviations

(12.2) $$y_i - a - bx_i$$

are minimal ($i = 1,..., n$). However, some individual deviations (12.2) may be positive while others may be negative. Yet all n individual observations are important to minimize in absolute value, regardless of their sign. This is mathematically conveniently achieved by minimizing—across all possible choices of the unknown parameters a and b—the sum of their squares:

(12.3) $$S = \sum_{i=1}^{n}(y_i - a - bx_i)^2.$$

As we can see from Equation (12.3), S is the sum of the squared deviations between the individual observed scores y_i on the dependent variable y, on the one hand, and what their predictions would be according to the model (12.1), viz., $a + bx_i$, on the other hand ($i = 1,..., n$).

Estimating the model parameters a and b by minimizing the sum of squared individual observations between data and model predictions on the dependent variable is a main part of a major parameter estimation method in statistics. This method is the *least-squares (LS) method*, which has a long history stretching over two centuries. The resulting estimates of the SLR model parameters a and b are referred to as *LS estimates* of the intercept and slope, respectively. It can be shown that these LS estimates result as follows (note the use of caret to denote parameter estimate and bar to denote sample mean):

$$(12.4) \qquad \hat{b} = S_{xy} / S_{xx} \text{ and } \hat{b}_0 = \bar{y} - \hat{b}_1 \bar{x},$$

where $S_{xy} = \sum_{i=1}^{n}(x_i - \bar{x})(y_i - \bar{y})$ and $S_{xx} = \sum_{i=1}^{n}(x_i - \bar{x})^2$ are respectively the covariance and variance of x estimates multiplied by $(n - 1)$. The expressions S_{xy} and S_{xx} are often referred to correspondingly as *sums of cross-products* and *sums of squares* for the two variables in question, x and y. With simple algebraic manipulation (see Chapter 11 for the definition of the correlation and covariance coefficients), we can obtain

$$(12.5) \qquad \hat{b} = S_{xy} / S_{xx} = r_{x,y} \frac{s_y}{s_x},$$

where $r_{x,y}$ denotes the sample correlation between x and y, whereas s_x and s_y designate their standard deviations, respectively.

Equation (12.5) provides a very useful relationship between the concepts of regression and correlation, which is worthwhile emphasizing here. Accordingly, the slope of the SLR model (12.1) is directly related to the correlation between the two variables involved. Specifically, the population slope b is equal to the population correlation coefficient $\rho_{x,y}$ up to the ratio of the standard deviations of the two variables involved. From this it follows that the correlation and slope are identical only when the two variables are equally varied (in the population or sample).

Let us illustrate these initial developments on linear regression by revisiting the data from Example 11.4 provided in Chapter 11. As will be recalled, in that example we were interested in describing the relationship between GPA score and reaction time on a cognitive test. Next, we will be interested in predicting the GPA score for a subject with a known reaction time. (Data are available in the file CH11_EX4.dat.) To estimate the intercept and slope of the SLR model (12.1), which process is frequently referred to as *SLR model estimation* or *model fitting*, one can readily use the software R. To achieve this aim, we can employ the command 'lm'—for 'linear modeling'—in the following way (one could interpret the sign '~' next as saying that the variable on the left is the DV and that on the right as the IV, or alternatively that the former is regressed upon the latter, for the SLR model in Equation (12.1)):

```
> lm(y~x)
```

This command yields the following output.

```
Call:
lm(formula = y ~ x)

Coefficients:
(Intercept)          x
  5.606733    -0.005162
```

According to these results, the estimate of the intercept is $\hat{a} = 5.606733$ and of the slope is $\hat{b} = -0.005162$. It is important to note that since in this example we are dealing with milliseconds as units of measurement on the response variable, it would be desirable to keep as high as possible precision of estimation. Thus, the estimated simple regression model is

$$(12.6) \qquad y = \hat{a} + \hat{b}x = 5.60673 - 0.005162x.$$

We stress that in Equation (12.6) there is no error term. The reason is that (12.6) presents the estimated model rather than a theoretical or population model. We can consider the model in Equation (12.1) as a population model, i.e., as a theoretical model that is advanced before the estimation of its parameters is actually carried out based on sample data. Alternatively, once this estimation is conducted and the estimated intercept and slope parameters are substituted into the right-hand side of Equation (12.1), we no longer have a population model, but only a sample-estimated model. As such, this model no longer has an error term—since by this estimation process the error has been in a sense dealt with.

We can now use the estimated SLR model (12.6) for prediction purposes. Specifically, if we did not know the GPA score for a student with a given reaction time on the cognitive test (the IV, or predictor, in this example), we could predict it using Equation (12.6) as we indicated earlier. (Note that we do not need to predict the y score for any subject for whom the y score is known or both their x and y scores are known.) For instance, if we only knew for a student that his or her reaction time was $x_0 = 475$ μs, then using the estimated SLR regression model (12.6) their predicted GPA score is determined to be equal to (with '$\times$' denoting multiplication)

$$y' = \hat{a} + \hat{b}x_0 = 5.60673 - 0.005162 \times 475 = 3.155.$$

Before we place much trust in this prediction of y, however, we need to address the issue of how well the underlying SLR model indeed fits the analyzed data (i.e., how good the fit of this model is to the analyzed data). We next turn to this model goodness-of-fit question.

12.4. HOW GOOD IS THE SIMPLE REGRESSION MODEL?

We emphasized earlier in the chapter that in order to make headway when interested in prediction, we need to assume the validity of a particular model that we use for this goal after estimating its parameters. However, as is typical when we make an assumption in the empirical sciences, we need to ask how well it is supported by the available data. That is, the question that we need to answer next is: "How good is the regression model that has been assumed to be valid?"—or in other words, "What is the goodness-of-fit of this model to the analyzed data?"

To begin to address this question, we need to return to the population form of the SLR model given in Equation (12.1). As we stressed earlier in the chapter, an essential element of this model is its error term, e. In particular, we readily realize that if the error term is substantial, then the SLR model will not be really a good means of description and explanation of the relationship between the two variables in question, x and y. This observation leads us to the notion of residuals, which we will be concerned with next.

12.4.1. Model residuals and the standard error of estimate

The process of model parameter estimation that we discussed in the previous section also provides a way to address the question of the goodness-of-fit of the postulated SLR model. In particular, we stressed above that in order to estimate its intercept and slope, we minimized the sum of the squared deviations between observed DV scores, y_i, and the predictions $a + bx_i$ about these scores using the model. These differences play an important role in evaluating how good the SLR model is (i.e., what its goodness-of-fit to the data is). Specifically, the individual data-to-prediction differences are referred to as *residuals,* and as we will discuss later in this chapter they are also instrumental when assessing model adequacy. In particular, when fitting the SLR model, each individual is associated with a *residual,* also referred to as an *estimated residual* or *individual residual,* which is defined as the difference between their observed value of y_i and the model predicted $\hat{y}_i$ value (in the rest of the chapter, for convenience, we also use the symbol $\hat{y}_i$ as notation for predicted response value for the ith case):

$$(12.7) \qquad \hat{e}_i = y_i - \hat{a} - \hat{b}x_i = y_i - \hat{y}_i \ (i = 1, ..., n).$$

We note in passing that we could have presented earlier the SLR model (12.1) also at the individual case level, viz., as $y_i = a + bx_i + e_i$, and Equation (12.7) would then give the sample-based estimates of the individual model residuals $e_i \ (i = 1, ..., n)$.

Having defined the residuals $\hat{e}_i$ in Equation (12.7), we realize that they can differ—and usually will differ—considerably across the sample units. Can we come up with an overall average measure of their magnitude? Such a measure is obviously given by the average of the sum of their squares $\sum_{i=1}^{n} \hat{e}^2_i$. This sum of squares is often referred to as the *residual sum of squares* (RSS) and at times denoted as SS_{res} (where the *SS* typically stands for "sum of squares").

The average RSS is obtained by dividing the sum of residual squares by the associated degrees of freedom (df):

$$(12.8) \qquad s^2_e = \frac{\sum_{i=1}^{n}(y_i - \hat{y}_i)^2}{n-2} = \text{RSS} / \text{df} = SS_{res} / \text{df},$$

where $\hat{y}_i = \hat{a} + \hat{b}x_i$ denote for convenience the model-based prediction of the dependent variable value for the *i*th subject (case, or unit of analysis; $i = 1,..., n$). In Equation (12.8), we divide the RSS by $n - 2$, since here df $= n - 2$. The reason is the fact that in order to obtain the right-hand side of Equation (12.8), we need to estimate two parameters, *a* and *b*—since otherwise the predicted values $\hat{y}_i$ cannot be computed. That is, we need to subtract 2 from the initial number of independent observations, *n*, as discussed earlier in the book (Chapter 5), in order to obtain the associated degrees of freedom. Thus, the degrees of freedom are $n - 2$. We emphasize that the degrees of freedom are representative here of the number of independent observations remaining after estimating the intercept and slope. Since we want to obtain an average measure of the individual residuals' magnitude, the most natural measure would be their average square. Given that we have in effect $n - 2$ individual contributions to the RSS, this average measure of error magnitude is provided by the ratio RSS/df, as defined in Equation (12.8).

The square root of s^2_e, i.e., s_e, is called the *standard error of estimate* (SEE) associated with the SLR model (12.1). (As throughout this book, we assume positive square roots being taken or considered.) The SEE represents the sample standard deviation around the regression line, or residual standard deviation of the dependent variable *y*. The SEE can be interpreted as the standard deviation of the response variable scores y_i, which are associated with a given value of the explanatory variable, x_i (under the assumptions of the SLR model; $i = 1,..., n$).

We conclude this section by stressing that there are in fact three estimates, $\hat{a}$, $\hat{b}$, and s_e, which we obtain when fitting the SLR model (12.1). This is because the SLR model is associated with three parameters, namely, the intercept, slope, and SEE—the standard deviation of the population outcome scores at a given value of the explanatory variable. Their estimates are obtained when this model is fitted to sample data.

12.4.2. The coefficient of determination

While the SEE provides information about the size of the average error associated with the utilized SLR model, the SEE is expressed in the original units of measurement. For this reason, the SEE has two important limitations.

First, the units of the SEE—being the original units of measurement of the DV y—are generally difficult to interpret in subject-matter terms, if at all possible in the social and behavioral sciences. Second, there is no limit from above for the magnitude of the SEE (while obviously it is zero from below). As a consequence, it is hard to know in an empirical setting whether the SEE is large or small. Only when it is zero, we know that there is no error in the model, but this will rarely if ever be the case in applied research.

For this reason, it would be desirable to have another measure of model fit, which is scale-free and normed, preferably between zero and one, say. Such a measure is the so-called coefficient of determination, usually referred to as the *R-squared index* and denoted R^2. This measure is commonly defined as the proportion of variance in the dependent variable that is explained in terms of the independent variable via the SLR model (12.1). That is, the R^2 definition is as follows:

$$(12.9) \qquad\qquad R^2 = \frac{S_{yy} - RSS}{S_{yy}}.$$

In Equation (12.9), S_{yy} is the variance of the response variable y multiplied by $(n - 1)$, i.e., $S_{yy} = \sum_{i=1}^{n} (y_i - \bar{y})^2$. At times, S_{yy} is referred to as *total sum of squares* and denoted by SS_{total}. We emphasize that in the numerator of Equation (12.9) we have the difference between the DV variance S_{yy} on the one hand and the residual (or error) sum of squares RSS, on the other hand. That is, the numerator—being this difference—is actually the remainder of what is achieved by the SLR model (12.1) when the goal is to explain variance in the DV y, as it usually is when this model is considered in empirical research. From Equation (12.9), it obviously follows that: (a) $0 \le R^2 \le 1$ holds always; (b) scores of R^2 close to 1 indicate that most variability in the DV y is explained in terms of the IV x via the fitted SLR model; and (c) scores of R^2 close to 0 or even 0 indicate that very little variability in the DV y, if any, is explained in terms of the IV x via the SLR model.

Furthermore, the R^2 index defined in Equation (12.9) can be shown to equal the square of the maximum possible correlation between the DV y and a linear function of the IV x that is of the form $a + bx$ (where a and b can be chosen without any constraint in order to attain this maximal correlation). This correlation coefficient, which equals R, is in general referred to as *multiple correlation*—in particular when there are multiple predictors (see next chapter). In the special case of a single predictor—i.e., an SLR model—the R^2 index can be shown to equal the square of the correlation coefficient between x and y, i.e., $\rho^2_{x,y}$ (in the population, or its sample counterpart in the sample; e.g., King & Minium, 2003). That is, in the SLR model (12.1) of concern in this chapter, the R^2 is

(12.10)
$$R^2 = \rho_{x,y}^2.$$

It can also be demonstrated (e.g., Pedhazur, 1997) that the R^2 index is an "optimistic"—i.e., positively biased—estimator of the population percentage of variance in the DV y that is explained in terms of the IV x via the SLR model (12.1). This positive bias results from the fact that as mentioned the R^2 is associated with the result of an optimization procedure. This is the minimization of the critical sum of squared deviations S in Equation (12.3), which is carried out on the sample data in order to estimate the intercept and slope in the SLR model. However, since a sample is a proper subset of the studied population (unless obtained in a census study), it is expected to differ from the population and it is this difference that is typically referred to as *sampling error*. As a result of the presence of sampling error, the R^2 index obtained in the sample (which is not equal to the population) is in general an overestimate of the population proportion variance in the DV that is explainable in terms of variability in the IV via the SLR model. (This argument also holds in cases with more than one predictor, that is, in multiple regression analysis models, a topic we take up in the next chapter.)

To counteract this bias, the so-called adjusted R^2 index, denoted R_a^2, aims at correcting for the bias and is generally a better estimate of this population proportion of explained variance. For the SLR model, the *adjusted R^2* is defined as follows (Pedhazur, 1997):

(12.11)
$$R_a^2 = 1 - (1 - R^2)(n-1)/(n-2).$$

The multiple correlation coefficient R, the R^2, and the adjusted R^2 can be readily obtained with the software R when the SLR model is fitted to data. To this end, we need to request a "summary" of the output associated with the SLR model (12.1), which we obtain as earlier with the command 'lm'. For the previous reaction time example (Chapter 11, Example 11.4), we obtain these goodness-of-fit indexes using the command 'summary', after creating first an object that is defined as equal to the output produced by the command 'lm'. This object is named next 'slr.ex.11.4' (output presented beneath command):

```
> slr.ex.11.4 = lm(y~x)
> summary(slr.ex.11.4)



Call:
lm(formula = y ~ x)

Residuals:
      Min         1Q      Median          3Q         Max
-4.741e-01  -1.225e-01  -5.682e-05   1.323e-01   3.678e-01
```

```
Coefficients:

            Estimate Std.   Error t value Pr(>|t|)
(Intercept)  5.6067330  0.1452832    38.59   <2e-16 ***
x           -0.0051619  0.0003252   -15.87   <2e-16 ***
---
Signif. codes:  0 '***' 0.001 '**' 0.01 '*' 0.05 '.' 0.1 ' ' 1


Residual standard error: 0.2063 on 54 degrees of freedom
Multiple R-squared: 0.8235,     Adjusted R-squared: 0.8202
F-statistic: 251.9 on 1 and 54 DF,  p-value: < 2.2e-16
```

This output initially shows that the individual residuals range in value from $-.47$ to $.37$. (It can be shown that in the population their mean is zero; e.g., Pedhazur, 1997.) For now, we do not pay attention to the 'standard error', 't-value', and 'Pr' columns in this output, as well as to its last line—we will revisit these output parts again in the next section. The last presented (summary) output shows that the SEE is estimated at 0.2063 and is associated with 54 degrees of freedom (since $n - 2 = 56 - 2 = 54$ here). We cannot really say, however, what this number actually means; that is, by only looking at it we cannot really say whether it is large or small. We could of course compare the magnitude of the SEE to the magnitude (standard deviation) of the DV y, which is the GPA score, and note that on average .21 points from the GPA score variance remain unexplained by the SLR model (12.1) that is fitted. However, even such an observation is not a particularly insightful interpretation when it comes to evaluating how well a used model fits a data set.

For this reason, we examine the R^2 index associated with the SLR model and its adjusted version. The R^2 index is .82 here (rounded off to second decimal place), whereas its adjusted value only marginally differs from it (viz., by less than .01). That is, about 82% of the individual differences (variability) in the GPA score were possible to explain in this data set in terms of reaction time using the SLR model

$$\text{GPA} = a + b. \text{ (Reaction time)} + e.$$

This percentage, 82%, is a fairly sizable proportion explained variance in the used sample, at least relative to what may be considered the majority of current behavioral and social research studies.

In conclusion of this section dealing with overall model fit, we stress that from the definition of the R^2 index it also follows that its numerical value is specific to a fitted model. An SLR model is a rather simple model, and it is possible that if its R^2 is not considered to be high, then an extended model—e.g., a model using additional predictors or nonlinear (e.g., higher) powers of the explanatory variable x—may have substantially higher R^2 values (see Section 12.6 later in this chapter for an example). Before we address aspects of this issue in more detail later in this and in the next chapter, however, we discuss how we can make conclusions about the population values of model parameters and coefficients of determination of SLR models under consideration.

12.5. INFERENCES ABOUT MODEL PARAMETERS AND THE COEFFICIENT OF DETERMINATION

When we fit the SLR model (12.1) to a given data set, we use only data from an available sample rather than from the entire population of actual interest. Hence, the question that naturally arises now is what could be said about the intercept and slope of this model in the studied population itself. A related question asks whether the model is capable of explaining any population variance in the DV in terms of population variance in the IV. These questions request inferences to be made about the population parameters and the R^2 index in the population of concern, based on the available sample and the performance of the SLR model in it. To this end, we need to know what the sampling distributions of the intercept and slope estimators, $\hat{a}$ and $\hat{b}$, are. As shown in more advanced treatments (e.g., Roussas, 1997), when at each value of the IV the scores of the DV follow a normal distribution, these estimators are normally distributed with means being their population values and variances obtainable via appropriate formulas given below.

The slope b of the SLR model (12.1) is of particular interest thereby, since its value pertains to the answer to the question of whether there is a discernible linear relationship between the DV and IV used. It can be shown (e.g., Ott & Longnecker, 2010) that the ratio

$$(12.12) \qquad t = \frac{\hat{b} - b_0}{s_e \sqrt{1 / S_{xx}}}$$

follows a t-distribution with df $= n - 2$ (since we estimate two parameters here—a and b), where b_0 is a hypothetical population slope. Equation (12.12) allows one to readily carry out hypothesis testing about the slope. In particular, when the null hypothesis of no linear relationship between the DV and IV is to be tested, then the test statistic is (note, $b_0 = 0$ holds then)

$$(12.13) \qquad t = \frac{\hat{b}}{s_e \sqrt{1 / S_{xx}}},$$

which follows the t-distribution with df $= n - 2$ under the corresponding null hypothesis H_0: $b_0 = 0$. The associated p-value with this hypothesis is provided in the output produced by the software R in a column titled

"Pr($>$|t|)". Also, a p-value is then provided that is associated with the null hypothesis of the intercept being zero, in the column with the same title (and in the row of the intercept estimate).

For our above example dealing with the relationship between GPA score and reaction time, we see from the R output that the p-values associated with these two null hypotheses of vanishing intercept and slope are very small, practically zero. Hence, we can reject the null hypothesis that the slope is zero, as well as the null hypothesis that the intercept is zero, and conclude that there is evidence in the data for a discernible linear relationship between GPA score and reaction time.

Using the distribution of the test statistic given in Equation (12.13), as earlier in the book (see details in Chapter 6) it can be shown that for a given α ($0 < \alpha < 1$), a $(1 - \alpha)100\%$-confidence interval for the slope is

$$(12.14) \qquad (\hat{b} - t_{\alpha/2, n-2} s_e \sqrt{1/S_{xx}}, \; \hat{b} + t_{\alpha/2, n-2} s_e \sqrt{1/S_{xx}}),$$

where $t_{\alpha/2, n-2}$ denotes the $(\alpha/2)$th quantile of the t-distribution with df $= n - 2$. As discussed earlier, this confidence interval can also be used to test a null hypothesis of the slope being equal to a prespecified number.

A closely related question that is often posed in empirical behavioral and social research is if the SLR model (12.1) "matters." This would be the case when its R^2 index is not zero in the studied population—as otherwise the model will not matter at all since it won't explain any DV variance in terms of IV variance. The corresponding null hypothesis that one needs to test in order to address this question is H_0: $R^2 = 0$, versus the alternative H_a: $R^2 > 0$. If this null hypothesis is to be retained, then it can be suggested that the fitted SLR model does not explain any part of the variance in the DV in terms of the variance in the IV—i.e., there is no linear relationship between the two variables in the studied population. If this null hypothesis is rejected, however, the statistical conclusion would be that there is a discernible linear relationship between the two variables. As developed in more advanced treatments (e.g., Roussas, 1997), this null hypothesis H_0: $R^2 = 0$ can be tested for the SLR model (12.1) using the test statistic

$$(12.15) \qquad F = \frac{S_{yy} - RSS}{s_e^2}.$$

The F-statistic in Equation (12.15) follows under the null hypothesis H_0 an F-distribution with degrees of freedom 1 and $n - 2$ (recall, the F-distribution is characterized by two rather than a single number as degrees of freedom).

The outcome of this test is provided in the last line of the SLR model output obtained with R, when the software is used as outlined earlier in this section. For the above reaction time example (Example 11.4), this test statistic is 251.9 on one and 54 degrees of freedom, and the associated p-value is less than 2.2×10^{-16}, i.e., practically zero. Thus, we reject the null hypothesis H_0: $R^2 = 0$, and suggest that in the population the SLR model (12.1) does matter, i.e., it explains a positive proportion of variance in GPA scores in terms of variability in reaction time.

12.6. EVALUATION OF MODEL ASSUMPTIONS, AND MODIFICATIONS

12.6.1. Assessing linear regression model assumptions via residual plots

We indicated throughout this chapter that in addition to the assumption of (approximately) continuous response variable y, the discussed SLR model and underlying approach of simple linear regression analysis are based on several further assumptions. Specifically, these assumptions are the following:

1. There exists a linear relationship between the variables x and y—i.e., the SLR model (12.1) is correct in the studied population.
2. The error term e is normally distributed, and more specifically the individual errors are independent of one another as well as normally distributed (with zero mean).
3. The variance of the y scores at any given x score, is constant—i.e., it does not depend on the x score.

When these assumptions are correct, the SLR model (12.1) is a useful means of describing the relationship between a predictor and a dependent variable. When the assumptions cannot be considered plausible for a given data set, however, then doubt is cast upon the validity of the SLR model (12.1) in the population under consideration. In that case, a conclusion can be reached that the model does not adequately describe the relationship between the two studied variables, x and y. The set of assumptions 1 through 3 are often referred to as *ordinary least squares* (OLS) assumptions (cf. Wooldridge, 2008, for a more detailed discussion on this topic). This reference results from the fact that when they hold, the classical—i.e., unmodified, or ordinary—least squares principle we employed above can be used to fit the SLR model (12.1) (as well as more general models containing two or more predictors). We note that the OLS parameter estimates do not depend on the normality assumption. In fact, this assumption is only needed when inferences are to be made about model parameters and coefficients of determination in studied populations.

Since the SLR model is based on several assumptions as mentioned, its application is warranted only when they are plausible for an empirical data set and population of concern. Therefore, we need methods that allow us to assess whether this is indeed the case—i.e., whether assumptions 1 through 3 are consistent with available sample data. To this end, one can argue that if these assumptions were to be correct, one would expect that

(i)   a plot of the above residuals $\hat{e}_i$ in Equation (12.7) against the predictor values x_i ($i = 1,..., n$) will produce a band of points that is symmetric around the horizontal line $y = 0$, which band in addition will be of (about) the same width regardless of the value of x;

(ii)   a plot of the residuals $\hat{e}_i$ against the response variable values y_i ($i = 1,..., n$) will produce a band of points that is symmetric around the horizontal line $y = 0$, which band in addition will be of (about) the same width regardless of the value of y;

(iii)   a plot of the residuals $\hat{e}_i$ against the predicted values $\hat{y}_i$ ($i = 1,..., n$) will produce a band of points that is symmetric around the horizontal line $y = 0$, which band in addition will be of (about) the same width regardless of the value of x;

(iv)   the residuals $\hat{e}_i$ should be normally distributed ($i = 1,..., n$).

If these plots do not exhibit the pertinent pattern indicated in (i) through (iv) but instead reveal some other clearly discernible trend or pattern, then it can be argued that at least one of the above three assumptions does not hold. In such cases, the fitted SLR model does not represent a plausible means of data description. Alternatively, if only a very limited number of points violates these assumptions, as judged by the plots, then it could be argued that the corresponding individuals may be "outliers," i.e., possibly result from data entry errors or stem from studied units belonging to a different population from the targeted one (for a nontechnical discussion of the concept of "outlier," see e.g., Raykov & Macoulides, 2008).

The plots described in (i) through (iv) can be readily obtained using the following respective R commands:

```
> plot(x, resid(name of model object))
> plot(y, resid(name of model object))
> plot(fitted(name of model object), resid(name of model object))
> qqnorm(resid(name of model object))
> qqline(resid(name of model object))
```

where 'name of model object' is the name assigned to the object representing the fitted model (see next). Thereby, we use the last two listed commands to obtain first a normal probability plot for the residuals that is then overlaid by a line, thus allowing us to visually assess the extent of their deviation from a straight line. We illustrate the residuals plots (i) through (iv) and their utility in assessing the SLR model assumptions with the following example.

> **Example 12.1**: In a study of the relationship between educational motivation and algebra knowledge, $n = 52$ middle school students are administered established instruments measuring these variables. (The data are presented in the file CH12_EX1.dat.) For our purposes here, we are interested in examining the above plots (i) through (iv) of the residuals associated with the SLR model (12.1) predicting algebra test score (response variable y) using the score on the motivation measure (predictor variable x).

To this end, we begin by assigning the name 'mod.1' to the object defined as the output associated with the SLR model (12.1) for these two variables:

```
> mod.1 = lm(y ~ x)
```

The residual plots of interest are then furnished with the following specific commands:

```
> plot(x, resid(mod.1))
> plot(y, resid(mod.1))
> plot(fitted(mod.1), resid(mod.1))
> qqnorm(resid(mod.1))
> qqline(resid(mod.1))
```

The resulting plots, for the data of Example 12.1, are presented in Figures 12.2 through 12.5.

As can be seen by examining Figures 12.2 through 12.5, the residual plots depicted on them exhibit the patterns indicated in (i) through (iv), which suggest that the SLR model assumptions are not inconsistent with the data. Specifically, the plots displayed in Figures 12.2 through 12.5 do not indicate serious violations of the above OLS assumptions 1 through 3 with regard to the analyzed data. Therefore, it could be suggested that the SLR model (12.1) represents a plausible method of description of that example data set under consideration.

We note that the assessment of model fit using the residual plots (i) through (iv) contains some subjective element that in general cannot be avoided when using these graphical evaluation approaches. In particular, with small samples (e.g., only up to a few dozen, say) some deviations from the straight line in the normal probability graph (iv) could be expected even if the residuals were drawn from a normal distribution. Therefore, it would be

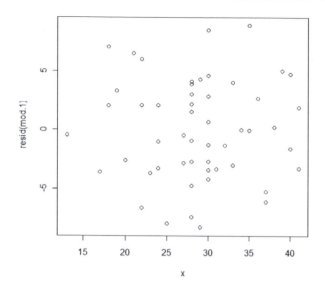

FIGURE 12.2.

Plot of residuals versus predictor (x) values for the simple regression model relating algebra knowledge to motivation (Example 12.1).

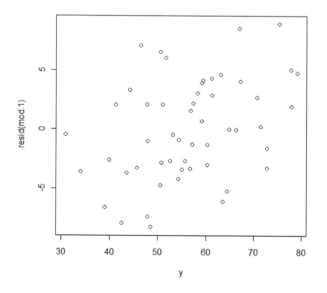

FIGURE 12.3.

Plot of residuals versus response (y) values for the simple regression model relating algebra knowledge to motivation (Example 12.1).

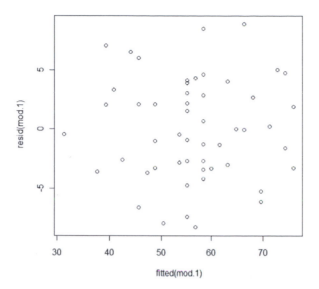

FIGURE 12.4.

Plot of residuals versus fitted values (predicted response values) for the simple regression model relating algebra knowledge to motivation (Example 12.1).

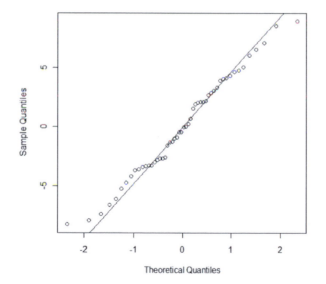

FIGURE 12.5.

Normal probability plot (with overlaid straight line) for the residuals associated with the simple regression model relating algebra knowledge to motivation (Example 12.1).

a good idea to consider only clearly discernible patterns or trends in any of these four examined plots as indicative of possible violations of some of the SLR model assumptions (see also next subsection).

12.6.2. Model modification suggested by residual plots

The preceding discussion in this Section 12.6 demonstrated how we can use the above residuals graphs (i) through (iv) and related ones in ascertaining that a considered SLR model may be a plausible means for description and explanation of a given sample of data. In addition to these aims, the graphs are also helpful in indicating certain violations—if present—of the assumptions underlying the SLR model (12.1) for a particular data set. In fact, these plots can then guide a researcher in his/her search for improved models associated with better fit. In particular, if graphs (i) through (iv) show a clearly discernible pattern or trend—e.g., a pattern of nonlinearity—then the SLR model (12.1) cannot be really considered a plausible means of data description. With such a nonlinear pattern emerging, it is possible that adding a higher power of the predictor variable—such as its square—can improve considerably the model fit. We demonstrate this application of model residual graphs with the following example.

> **Example 12.2 (college aspiration and mathematics ability test score):** In a study of the relationship between college aspiration and mathematics ability, scales of these two variables are administered to $n = 69$ high school seniors. The file CH12_EX2.dat contains their data (with 'x' denoting college aspiration score and 'y' the mathematics test score). We wish to find out whether the SLR model (12.1) is a plausible means of description of their relationship, and if it is not, to determine ways of improving it.

Since the first of the above OLS assumptions 1 through 3 (see subsection 12.6.1) stipulates that a linear relationship between the variables is involved, we can first look at the plot of the data to examine if there may be any particular deviations from linearity, to begin with, in the relationship between aspiration and mathematics ability score. We use the R command 'plot' for this aim, as before, and the result is presented in Figure 12.6 following it:

```
> plot(x, y, xlab = "College Aspiration", ylab = "Mathematics Test Score")
```

Although this graph appears at first glance essentially linear in shape, we notice some bending in the middle part, which does not seem to be very disturbing at this stage. (The above display is also an example how some simple plots—like that of data on two variables—may not always reveal the whole story about variable relationship, as we will soon see.)

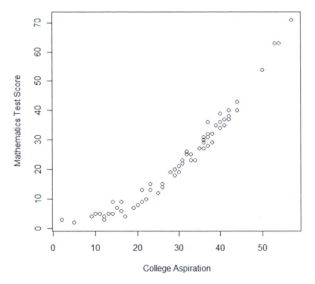

FIGURE 12.6.

Plot of the data from Example 12.2.

We fit next the SLR model (12.1) to these data and create the above plots (i) through (iii) in Figures 12.6 through 12.8 (see output beneath the following two commands):

```
> slr.ex.12.2 = lm(y~x)
> summary(slr.ex.12.2)



Call:
lm(formula = y ~ x)

Residuals:
    Min      1Q  Median      3Q     Max
-5.5756 -2.7389 -0.9553  1.5878 14.5017

Coefficients:
            Estimate Std.  Error t value Pr(>|t|)
(Intercept) -12.83282    1.41261  -9.085  2.7e-13 ***
x             1.21634    0.04366  27.858  < 2e-16 ***
---
Signif.  codes:  0 '***' 0.001 '**' 0.01 '*' 0.05 '.' 0.1 ' ' 1
```

```
Residual standard error: 4.354 on 67 degrees of freedom
Multiple R-squared: 0.9205,      Adjusted R-squared: 0.9193
F-statistic: 776.1 on 1 and 67 DF,  p-value: < 2.2e-16
```

We see that the fitted linear regression model is associated with a fairly high (adjusted) R^2 index, suggesting this model explains a great deal of the variability in the DV y. Similarly, the null hypotheses of vanishing slope and such R^2 are rejected. Indeed, the associated F-statistic in Equation (12.15) is here 776.1 and based on one and 67 degrees of freedom its pertinent p-value is practically zero. This suggests that the linear model matters—i.e., the hypothesis H_0: $R^2 = 0$ in the studied population of high school students can be rejected. Similarly, the slope estimate is 1.22 and its associated p-value is practically zero as well (with its t-value being 27.86), suggesting that the null hypothesis of no linear relationship between college aspiration and math ability test score in the population can be rejected. (As can be seen from the preceding discussion, these two null hypotheses are in fact identical, which is the reason why the p-values associated with their F- and t-statistics cited are identical as well.)

Despite these apparent indications of relatively good overall fit of the SLR (12.1) model, we recall that the R^2 coefficient is by definition an omnibus (overall) index of goodness of fit, as explicated in its definition in Equation (12.9). The reason is that the R^2 is defined as the ratio of two variances yet the latter are themselves overall indexes, rendering thus in their ratio also an overall goodness of fit measure. Hence, by its very definition the R^2 index does not pay attention to (i.e., does not reflect) the extent to which individual observations are fitted (explained) by the model. Therefore, the R^2 may be large even if there may be a few individual residuals that are not well approximated (fitted) by the model and thus invalidate it as a possibly adequate means of description of an entire given data set. In fact, the present is an example of precisely this phenomenon occurring, as we will see shortly.

We therefore examine next the earlier mentioned residual plots (i) through (iii) for this data set, which are presented in Figures 12.7 through 12.10 that we obtain by using the following R commands:

```
> plot(x, resid(slr.ex.12.2), ylab = "Model residuals")
> plot(y, resid(slr.ex.12.2), ylab = "Model residuals")
> plot(fitted(slr.ex.12.2), resid(slr.ex.12.2), xlab = "Fitted  Values",
      ylab = "Model residuals")
> qqnorm(resid(slr.ex.12.2))
> qqline(resid(slr.ex.12.2))
```

The plot in Figure 12.7 exhibits distinctive nonlinearity, with notably large residuals (relative to the magnitude of the response variable y) at smaller-

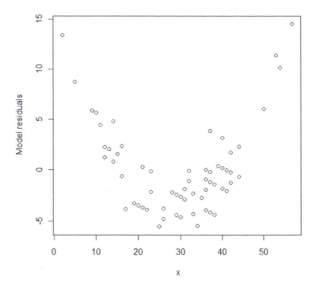

FIGURE 12.7.

Plot of residuals against predictor values (Example 12.2).

than-average and at larger-than-average college aspiration scores (i.e., for $x < 10$ or $x > 50$, say). Similarly, there are notably negative residuals for the students with average college aspiration scale scores (i.e., x scores in the 20s and 30s). Since the model residuals depicted along the vertical axis are the differences between observations and model predictions, the fitted SLR (12.1) in fact underpredicts the mathematics ability scores for students with large or with small aspiration, while it overpredicts these scores for students with average aspiration. This finding should not be unexpected, however, given the somewhat nonlinear appearance of the graph of the original data in the above-displayed Figure 12.6. A similar result is observed in the remaining two of the above residual plots (ii) and (iii), which are presented next as Figures 12.8 and 12.9. The plot displayed in Figure 12.8 also demonstrates that the fitted model underpredicts the mathematics ability for students with scores on this test in the 50s and 60s, as well as those with very low scores, while accomplishing a relatively good prediction for students with such scores in the 20s and 30s. Similarly, the plot in Figure 12.9 shows that for small and for large predicted values the model is associated with considerable residuals, unlike for predicted response values with intermediate magnitude.

Furthermore, the residuals associated with the fitted SLR model can hardly be considered normally distributed, as judged by their normal probability plot presented in Figure 12.10. In particular, as could be expected from the preceding plots, there are marked deviations from normality for large and for small residuals. The magnitude of these deviations leads us to suggest that also the

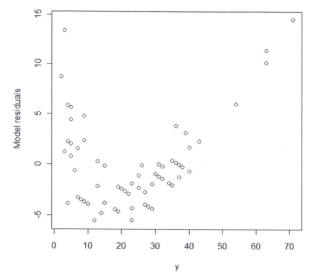

FIGURE 12.8.
Plot of residuals against response variable values (Example 12.2).

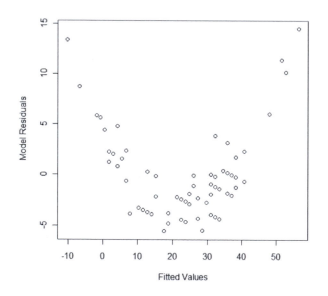

FIGURE 12.9.
Plot (iii) of residuals against predicted (fitted) response values (Example 12.2).

normality assumption is clearly violated for this model when fitted to the data from Example 12.2.

Hence, all residual plots (i) through (iv) in Figures 12.6 through 12.9 for the numerical example under consideration (Example 12.2) indicate serious violations of the SLR model (12.1), and specifically of its assumptions. In

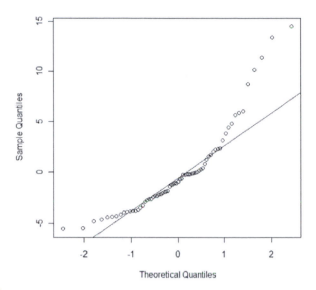

FIGURE 12.10.

Normal probability plot for the residuals of the simple linear regression model (Example 12.2).

particular, there is evidence suggesting that the linearity and residual normality assumptions do not hold. Thus, despite the relatively high (adjusted) R^2 index of the fitted linear model and the significance of all test results obtained with it—in particular for the slope and this R^2 index—we conclude that the SLR model does not provide a plausible means of data description.

The present Example 12.2 at the same time demonstrates clearly the fact that a high overall fit index, such as the adjusted R^2, is no guarantee for a well-fitting model. In particular, even though a model may be associated with a high adjusted R^2 index, there may be a considerable number of subjects for which it provides less than satisfactory fit. This fact underscores the relevance of also evaluating the model residuals as a matter of routine, when fitting simple regression models. (This conclusion remains valid also for more complex regression models, such as those containing nonlinear powers of used predictors or multiple predictors, which are discussed later in this chapter and the next.)

The residual plots in Figures 12.7 through 12.10 show marked violations from the straight line for smaller-than-average x scores as well as for larger-than-average x scores. This finding can be interpreted as suggesting that the relationship between aspiration and mathematics ability, as captured in their scale/test scores x and y, may in fact be quadratic rather than linear. That is, the SLR model (12.1) may actually have an omitted term, the square of the predictor x. (Such models with omitted terms are often referred to as "misspecified models.") As a response to this suggestion, we can modify the earlier fitted SLR model to this example data by introducing a new variable that is defined as equal to the square of this predictor. To this end, we use the command

```
> x2 = x^2
```

Next, in order to fit the data from Example 12.2 better, we extend the SLR model to include the squared reaction time—i.e., consider the extended model

$$(12.16) \qquad\qquad y = a + bx + cx^2 + e^*,$$

where for convenience the symbol e^* denotes the error term of this model (thus, not to be assumed equal to the error term e in the SLR model (12.1)) and the same notation is used for the intercept and coefficient in front of x. In agreement with our earlier discussion in Section 12.1 of this chapter, we emphasize here that model (12.16) is also a linear regression model, just like (12.1) is. The reason is the fact that its parameters a, b, and c appear in the right-hand side of its defining equation (12.16) only linearly. That is, despite the inclusion of the square of the explanatory variable x into the latter model, it remains a linear regression model.

We fit this model to the data using R in the following way, whereby to emphasize its feature of including the square of the mathematics test score (x) we formally refer to the resulting R-object as 'model.qt' (for 'model with quadratic term') in the remainder of this chapter. To invoke fitting this model to the data, we add the variable denoted 'x2'—the squared explanatory variable—after the symbol '~' used in the model fitting command 'lm' next, with the ensuing output provided beneath commands used:

```
> model.qt = lm(y~x+x2)
> summary(model.qt)
```

```
Call:
lm(formula = y ~ x + x2)

Residuals:
     Min       1Q    Median        3Q       Max
-3.62493  -1.43378   0.08254   1.08254   5.51978
```

```
Coefficients:
              Estimate Std.   Error t value Pr(>|t|)
(Intercept)   2.102148   0.997868   2.107    0.0390 *
x            -0.050921   0.071370  -0.713    0.4781
x2            0.022105   0.001206  18.337   <2e-16 ***
---
Signif.  codes:  0 '***' 0.001 '**' 0.01 '*' 0.05 '.' 0.1 ' ' 1


Residual standard error: 1.777 on 66 degrees of freedom
Multiple R-squared: 0.987,       Adjusted R-squared: 0.9866
F-statistic:  2498 on 2 and 66 DF,  p-value: < 2.2e-16
```

We notice that the residuals associated with the fitted model (12.16) are markedly smaller than those pertaining to the SLR model (12.1) fitted earlier. In particular, here they range between -3.62 and 5.52, while for the former model they ranged between -5.58 and 14.50. While it is not immediately seen as an easy task to interpret the magnitude of the individual residuals of a given model (except of course to relate it to that of the original dependent variable scores), when we have more than one model fitted to the same set of observed variables (data set) we can informally compare the models by comparing the magnitude of their residuals with one another. Such a comparison does not give us, however, an overall idea about the relative fit of the models, which can be readily obtained by comparing their overall indexes.

Returning to the example study of the relationship between college aspiration and mathematics ability, we see that the R^2 index of the fitted model (12.16) is significant (see last line of output) since the p-value associated with the F-statistic pertaining to the null hypothesis of this index being zero in the population is very small—practically zero. This means that model (12.16) matters—i.e., it explains a significant proportion of response variance. (This is not an unexpected finding, since we know from the earlier discussion in this chapter that the linear model (12.1) matters, and hence the model that adds one more explanatory term to it—viz., the variable 'x2'—would have to matter as well.)

At the same time, we notice the markedly higher R^2 index of the model (12.16) than that index of the earlier fitted linear model, with the same relationship holding for their adjusted R^2 indexes. This suggests that model (12.16) is an improvement over the earlier model (12.1) as far as overall fit to the analyzed data is concerned. In order to examine if this is also the case in the studied population that is of actual interest, we check in the last presented output if the coefficient of the quadratic term of the model (12.16) is significant, i.e., test the hypothesis H_0: $c = 0$. Since the p-value associated with the quadratic parameter estimate $\hat{c} = .022$ is very small—practically zero—this

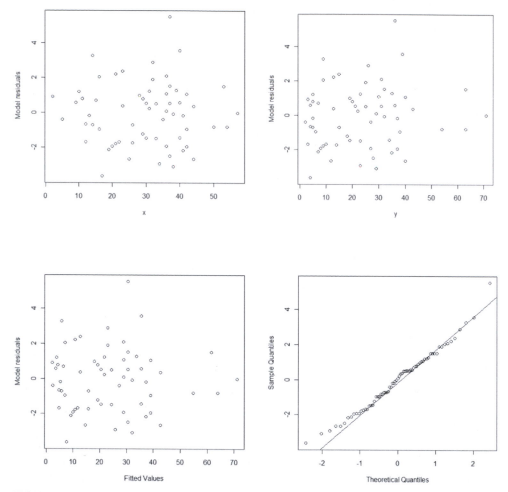

FIGURE 12.11.

Residual plots (i) through (iii) and normal probability plot for the quadratic model (12.16) fitted to the data of Example 12.2 (see labels on axes to differentiate between plots).

null hypothesis can be rejected. This suggests that as far as overall fit goes, model (12.16) is indeed an improvement upon the SLR model (12.1) as a means of description of the relationship between college aspiration and mathematics ability in the high school student population in question.

While similarly to the SLR model the last fitted model (12.16) is associated with fairly high overall fit indexes, it is unclear whether the latter model is associated with good local fit, i.e., whether it fits the analyzed individual subjects' data well. As we saw earlier in this section, a high R^2 index is not a guarantee for good local fit (i.e., individual data fit), and so we would now like to see how model (12.16) fares at the level of the subject data. To this end, we examine the above residual plots (i) through (iv) for model (12.16), using the same commands as before (but now applied on the R-object 'model.qt'; see Figure 12.11 for all four plots).

In the first three of these residual plots, there are no noticeable patterns—unlike those in the earlier Figures 12.7 through 12.10 for the previously fitted SLR model (12.1). This finding of no noticeable patterns in the residual plots (i) through (iii) would be expected with well-fitting models that represent plausible means of data description and explanation. In addition, the normal probability plot for the residuals of model (12.16) does not suggest any marked deviations from the normality assumption. Specifically, this model's residuals are relatively close to the fitted line, and their limited deviations from it do not exhibit any particular pattern (compare with the normal probability plot of the residuals associated with the SLR model (12.1) when fitted to this data set; e.g., Figure 12.10).

The example used throughout this section provided a clear demonstration of the relevance of carefully examining residual plots, such as the above graphs (i) through (iv), whenever the SLR model (12.1) is fitted to data. The example also illustrated the fact that these and related residual plots can be used to both guide a researcher to assess its fit to the analyzed data as well as in his or her search for better fitting models if need be—like the extended model presented in (12.6).

In conclusion of this section, we also saw with this example and our pertinent discussion how these aims of (i) assessment of model fit at the level of individual data through residual plots, and (ii) model improvement based on information about possible misfit obtained from these plots can be readily accomplished with the software R.

13

Multiple Regression Analysis

The previous chapter introduced linear regression modeling with a single response and a single explanatory variable. However, very few phenomena of interest in the behavioral and social sciences can be described well using only a single independent variable. Indeed, phenomena typically studied in these disciplines generally tend to be multifactorially determined. For this reason, their description and explanation require the consideration of more than a single explanatory variable. In these cases, the extension of the simple linear regression model in Equation (12.1) in Chapter 12 to two or more independent variables becomes relevant. This modeling approach is commonly referred to as multiple regression analysis (MRA). MRA is of special importance for statistics and its applications in behavioral and social research, due to the fact that many analytic methods can be considered at least related to special cases of the general model underlying MRA (e.g., see Raykov & Marcoulides, 2008).

13.1. MULTIPLE REGRESSION MODEL, MULTIPLE CORRELATION, AND COEFFICIENT OF DETERMINATION

Multiple regression analysis (MRA), like simple regression analysis, is based on two types of variables: (i) explanatory variables or independent variables, which we denote as $x_1, x_2,..., x_k$ (with $k > 1$); and (ii) an outcome variable, or response (dependent variable), denoted as y. These explanatory variables can be of any nature, and they are often for short referred to as "predictors" in the rest of the book (without any causality related implications, as in the last chapter). That is, the predictors $x_1, x_2,..., x_k$ can have any scale and distribution. However, similar to Chapter 12, the response or outcome variable y in MRA is assumed to be a continuous variable (or at least approximately so; we thus assume throughout this chapter and the next that y is a continuous variable).

By analogy to the simple linear regression (SLR) model discussed in the last chapter, the goal of MRA is to find weights b_1, b_2,..., and b_k such that the following linear combination of the predictors

(13.1) $$\hat{y} = b_0 + b_1 x_1 + b_2 x_2 + ... + b_k,$$

is as close as possible to y, for all studied observations. As a result, since the right-hand side of Equation (13.1) represents the predicted-by-the-model response score, the correlation between model predictions and observed outcome scores, $r = Corr(y, \hat{y})$, will be maximal (with $Corr(.,.)$ denoting correlation; e.g., Agresti & Finlay, 2009).

A frequently used reference to this maximal correlation in the context of MRA is as *multiple correlation coefficient*, or *multiple R*. We already encountered this reference in Chapter 12, specifically on a few occasions in the output produced by the software R. In particular, the square of the multiple R, viz., R^2, is called the *coefficient of determination*, as in the context of the SLR model (12.1). (More specifically, as mentioned in the previous chapter, for the SLR model the squared correlation of independent and response variable equals R^2.) In the present chapter, we will use the extended notation $R^2_{y \cdot 12...k}$ to symbolize the coefficient of determination associated with a MRA model under consideration, when it will be helpful to emphasize that we are using more than a single independent variable. (In other cases, where no confusion may arise, we will use the simpler notation R^2 for this coefficient.) Also in the MRA case, $100\% \times R^2_{y \cdot 12...k}$ provides the percentage of explained variance in the response variable in terms of the used predictors—viz., via their assumed linear relationship to the outcome variable. In addition, it can be shown that if all explanatory variables are unrelated (uncorrelated), then $R^2_{y \cdot 12...k}$ equals the sum of squared correlations of each one of them with the response variable y (e.g., Pedhazur, 1997). However, if at least two independent variables are correlated with one another, which is the most frequent case in empirical behavioral and social research, then $R^2_{y.12...k}$ is smaller than this sum of squared correlations of predictors with the outcome variable.

As one might expect by analogy to the SLR model (12.1) discussed in Chapter 12, the MRA model is

(13.2) $$y = b_0 + b_1 x_1 + b_2 x_2 + ... + b_k x_k + e,$$

where e is the model error (residual). The model error is typically assumed normal when we want to carry out statistical inference, with a mean of zero, and uncorrelated with any of the explanatory variables. (Similar to the SLR case, we do not need to make this normality assumption if we are only interested in parameter estimation; cf. Wooldridge, 2008.) In the MRA model (13.2), the residual e contains the effects of all other variables (or higher powers and/or interactions of the predictors used), which are possibly related to the response y and not explicitly included in the model, i.e., do not appear in the right-hand side of Equation (13.2). We note that the term e in (13.2) is not identical to the error term in the SLR model in Equation (12.1) but is conceptually similar to it. For this reason, we use formally the same notation e for the model residual in Equation (13.2) as in the last chapter dealing with the SLR model.

In the MRA model (13.2), a number of independent variables are included, and this fact modifies the interpretation of the parameters appearing in its right-hand side. Like the SLR model (12.1) in the previous chapter, the interpretation of the intercept b_0 is as the average response score for observations (units of analysis) having the value of zero on all predictors x_1 through x_k. Unlike the SLR model, however, the meaning of the jth regression coefficient b_j is as the average change in the dependent variable y, which is associated with a unit change in the jth predictor x_j while holding all remaining predictors $x_1,..., x_{j-1}, x_{j+1},..., x_k$ constant ($j = 1,..., k$). We stress that the interpretation of any of the regression coefficients b_1 through b_k is conditional on holding constant the other $k - 1$ predictors in the model. This is the reason why these coefficients are referred to as *partial regression coefficients* (*weights* or *slopes*). As an implication, the partial regression coefficient b_j may be small and unimportant (nonsignificant) in the presence of other predictors, but if x_j is used as a single predictor of the dependent variable y then the pertinent slope b in the SLR model (12.1) may be substantially larger and significant ($j = 1,..., k$).

Similarly to the single predictor case of concern in Chapter 12, the unknown parameters b_0, b_1, $b_2,..., b_k$ are estimated in such a way that the following sum S_m of the squared discrepancies between observations and model predictions on the response is minimal (where as usual n denotes sample size):

$$S_m = \sum_{i=1}^{n} (y_i - \hat{y}_i)^2.$$

This estimation is achieved following the *principle of least squares*, which is implemented in the software used. The minimal value of the sum S_m informs about the degree to which there is variability in the error term e in the MRA model (13.2). An appropriate average of the sum S_m (see below) is referred to as *error or residual variance*.

This discussion indicates that the MRA model (13.2) has in total $k + 2$ parameters. These are the *intercept b_0*, the k *partial regression weights b_1* through b_k, and the error variance (see below in this section for specific definition of the error variance). Given that the error term is on average zero, taking the mean from both sides of Equation (13.2) shows the intercept as the average response for subjects with the value of zero on all explanatory variables, possibly after appropriate centering is carried out (e.g., Raudenbush & Bryk, 2002).

To illustrate the above-mentioned developments, let us consider the following example.

Example 13.1: In a study of general mental ability of high school seniors, five intelligence tests were administered to $n = 160$ students. The first three tests measured the fluid intelligence subabilities of inductive reasoning with letters, figural relations, and inductive reasoning with symbols; the fourth test tapped into the ability to rotate three-dimensional figures; and the fifth was a conventional general mental ability test. (The data are found in the file CH13_EX1.dat, where individual scores represent percentage correct answers on the tests.) We wish to evaluate the (linear) relationship between the test of general mental ability, on the one hand, and the other four intelligence tests on the other hand. Accordingly, we denote the general mental ability measure as y, and the four remaining tests as x_1 through x_4 (in the above order; these four variables will be correspondingly denoted 'x1' through 'x4' in the following R commands).

To evaluate the relationship between the general mental ability test score and the four intelligence tests, we fit the following multiple regression model (13.2) with $k = 4$ predictors:

$$(13.3) \qquad y = b_0 + b_1 x_1 + b_2 x_2 + b_3 x_3 + b_4 x_4 + e.$$

To this end, as in Chapter 12 we use the R command 'lm', but we now list formally the sum of all used independent variables after the '~' sign in it:

```
> mrmod.1 = lm(y~x1+x2+x3+x4)
```

We stress that in this way we assign to the produced output the status of an R-object with the name 'mrmod.1'. To see the results of fitting model (13.3), we request the associated output as in the last chapter with the command 'summary':

```
> summary(mrmod.1)
```

Since we are going to refer often below to the output associated with model (13.3) when fitted to the data from the currently considered example, we present this summary output in Table 13.1.

As we can see from Table 13.1, the MRA model (13.3) is associated with an R^2 index of .8018 here. That is, 80% of the variability in the general mental ability score was explained in terms of individual differences on the four intelligence measures x_1 through x_4, viz., via their assumed linear relationship to the former score. At this stage, we focus only on the output column containing the estimates $\hat{b}_0$ through $\hat{b}_4$ of the intercept and partial regression coefficients b_0 through b_4, respectively (see first column after that with the names

Table 13.1   Summary of results associated with model (13.3) (fitted to data from Example 13.1).

```
Call:
lm(formula = y ~ x1 + x2 + x3 + x4)

Residuals:
      Min        1Q     Median        3Q        Max
-0.199329  -0.059242  -0.003189  0.061958   0.240692

Coefficients:
             Estimate Std. Error t value Pr(>|t|)
(Intercept)  0.06075    0.02933    2.071 0.039997 *
x1           0.31664    0.08463    3.741 0.000257 ***
x2           0.16173    0.06729    2.404 0.017416 *
x3           0.43964    0.07601    5.784 3.9e-08 ***
x4           0.16241    0.08797    1.846 0.066765 .
---
Signif. codes:  0 '***' 0.001 '**' 0.01 '*' 0.05 '.' 0.1 ' ' 1

Residual standard error: 0.08821 on 155 degrees of freedom
Multiple R-squared: 0.8018,     Adjusted R-squared: 0.7967
F-statistic: 156.7 on 4 and 155 DF,  p-value: < 2.2e-16
```

of the intercept and independent variables x1 through x4). Accordingly, the fitted MRA model is as follows (after rounding off to the third digit after decimal point):

$$\hat{y} = \hat{b}_0 + \hat{b}_1 x_1 + \hat{b}_2 x_2 + \hat{b}_3 x_3 + \hat{b}_4 x_4$$
$$= .061 + .317 x_1 + .162 x_2 + .440 x_3 + .162 x_4,$$

For example, if we wanted to predict with this model the general mental ability test score for a subject with values of 32, 42, 66, and 92 on the four intelligence tests x_1 through x_4, respectively, the predicted value will be readily obtained with R as follows:

```
> y_hat = .061 + .317*32 + .162*42 + .440*66 + .162*92
> y_hat
[1] 60.953
```

That is, the predicted value is 60.953 for the score of the subject in question on the general mental ability test. (Recall from the preceding discussion in this section that the data on each of the five tests used were available in terms of percentage correct answers.) As pointed out in the last chapter, we emphasize here that the credibility of predicted values depends on the tenability of the model used to obtain them, and specifically on whether it is a plausible means of description and explanation for the analyzed data. We attend to this topic later in the chapter (see Section 13.6), after discussing next various related matters that pertain to drawing inferences from model results to studied populations.

13.2. INFERENCES ABOUT PARAMETERS AND MODEL EXPLANATORY POWER

The estimates of the MRA model parameters discussed in Section 13.1 only represent single numerical guesses about their values in a studied population of actual interest. A researcher will typically have, however, many more questions that he or she would be interested in answering from the results of a multiple regression analysis. We attend to a number of them in this section.

13.2.1. A test of significance for the coefficient of determination

Having fitted the MRA model (13.2) to a given data set, one of the first questions that arises is whether the model "matters." Given that we use a regression model typically to explain variability in a response measure under consideration, such as, say, a depression scale score, this question translates into the query whether the model (13.2) explains a nontrivial proportion of the population variance in the outcome variable y. In other words, this query asks whether all used explanatory variables, x_1 through x_k, explain jointly a significant proportion of variance in the dependent variable y. Such a situation will only be possible when the coefficient of determination associated with the fitted model is non-zero in the population under investigation. Hence, our interest here lies in testing the null hypothesis that this coefficient is zero, i.e., H_0: $R^2 = 0$. As shown elsewhere (e.g., Agresti & Finlay, 2009), one can use for this purpose the test statistic

$$(13.4) \qquad F = [R^2/(1 - R^2)] \cdot [(n - k - 1)/k],$$

which follows the F-distribution with k and $n - k - 1$ degrees of freedom under the null hypothesis H_0.

As can be readily seen from the definitional equation of the MRA model (13.2), the tested null hypothesis H_0: $R^2 = 0$ is equivalent to the hypothesis stipulating that all partial regression coefficients are zero; that is, H_0 is equivalent to the null hypothesis H_0': $b_1 = b_2 = ... = b_k = 0$. When using statistical software to test this hypothesis, the associated p-value is helpful in making a decision about the hypothesis.

To illustrate, we revisit the above Example 13.1 (Section 13.1). As can be seen from its output in Table 13.1, the p-value associated with the test of the hypothesis H_0: $R^2 = 0$ for the MRA model (13.3) is very small and practically zero, thus smaller than a prespecified significance level—which is usually $\alpha = .05$. We therefore can conclude that the analyzed data contain evidence suggesting that the fitted MR model (13.3) does matter. In other words, the four intelligence test scores used as predictors explain a significant proportion of general mental ability variance in the studied population of high school students.

An alternative way of interpreting the result of testing the null hypothesis H_0: $R^2 = 0$ in the general MRA case with k predictors ($k > 0$) is as an attempt to find an answer to the question whether the used explanatory variables x_1 through x_k, in their totality, help one predict the response variable y better than simply using its mean, $\bar{y}$, for this purpose. That is, this question asks whether utilizing merely the mean $\bar{y}$ is as effective as are the used independent measures in explaining the variability in y. This will be the case if the null hypothesis H_0 were not rejected—a finding that can be interpreted as suggesting that there is no explanatory power in these predictors. When this null hypothesis is rejected, we can conclude that the predictors used afford us with a significantly stronger power for predicting the response y than its mean $\bar{y}$.

13.2.2. Testing single regression coefficients for significance

In addition to the discussed test whether the MRA model matters, if the pertinent null hypothesis is rejected the next question of interest usually is concerned with ascertaining whether an individual partial regression coefficient is zero in the studied population. For a given such coefficient, say the jth, answering this question amounts to testing the null hypothesis *H_0: $b_j = 0$ ($1 \le j \le k$; in the remainder of this and in the next section, we fix j in our discussion). If this hypothesis is rejected, the interpretation is that the jth predictor does contribute to a better explanation of the variability in the response y *beyond* what the remaining predictors $x_1,..., x_{j-1}, x_{j+1},..., x_k$ achieve together in this regard. This interpretation accounts for the fact indicated earlier in the chapter that the meaning of a given partial regression coefficient, say b_j, is revealed only after controlling for the other predictors $x_1,..., x_{j-1}, x_{j+1},..., x_k$.

To test this null hypothesis *H_0, one uses the test statistic (e.g., King & Minium, 2003)

(13.5) $$t = b_j / s_{b_j.12...k}.$$

In Equation (13.5),

(13.6) $$s^2_{b_j.12...k} = s^2_{y.12...k} / [(1 - R^2_{j.12...k}) \sum_{i=1}^{n} (X_{ji} - \bar{X}_{j.})^2]$$

is the squared standard error for the jth partial regression coefficient, and

$$s^2_{y.12...k} = \sum_{i=1}^{n} (Y_i - \hat{b}_0 - \hat{b}_1 X_{1i} - ... - \hat{b}_k X_{ki})^2 / (n - k - 1)$$

$$= \sum_{i=1}^{n} (Y_i - \hat{Y}_i)^2 / (n - k - 1)$$

is the squared standard error of estimate (SEE) associated with the MRA model fitted, while $R^2_{j.12...k}$ is the R^2-index for the model regressing the jth predictor upon the remaining ones, $x_1,..., x_{j-1}, x_{j+1},..., x_k$. When the null hypothesis *H_0 is true, the t-statistic in Equation (13.5) follows a t-distribution with $d = n - k - 1$ degrees of freedom (e.g., Agresti & Finlay, 2009).

Equation (13.6) is very informative with regard to the stability of the estimate of the jth partial regression weight b_j across repeated sampling (at the same sample size, n, from the studied population). In particular, the right-hand side of Equation (13.6) reveals that the stronger the relationship between the jth predictor and the remaining ones, the larger is the standard error associated with its slope estimate, i.e., the more unstable this estimate is across repeated sampling (other things being the same). In the extreme case when the jth predictor is perfectly predictable from the remaining independent variables $x_1,..., x_{j-1}, x_{j+1},..., x_k$ (i.e., when $R^2_{j.12...k} = 1$), the standard error of the jth slope estimate becomes infinity. This extreme case is called *multicollinearity* (sometimes referred to as *perfect multicollinearity*).

When predictors are carefully chosen in empirical research, the multicollinearity phenomenon is less likely to occur, but near-perfect multicollinearity may hold among a used set of predictors. In those cases, some of the independent variables nearly completely predict the jth explanatory measure x_j, and the standard error of the pertinent weight b_j is very large. This tends to lead to retention of the null hypothesis *H_0: $b_j = 0$. Such a finding may seem to be inconsistent with a rejection of the overall null hypothesis H_0': $b_1 = b_2 = ... = b_k = 0$, in the same data set. The finding is explained by the lack of sufficient information then in the available sample, which would allow differentiation of the contributions of individual predictors to the explanation of response variance. In these cases, one may (a) enhance sample size—by studying additional individuals or units of analysis sampled from the same population, (b) combine two or more of the independent variables into a single (or fewer) new measures in a substantively meaningful way, or (c) drop from subsequent analyses one or more of the variables involved in the near-perfect linear relationship of x_j with the remaining predictors.

From Equation (13.6) we also see that the smaller the variability of the individual scores X_{ij} on the jth predictor X_j around its mean $\bar{X}_j$, the larger this standard error (other things being the same; $i = 1,..., n$). This implies that when measurement of a given predictor is accomplished only along a very limited range of values, there is also limited resulting information in the sample that allows discerning between the contributions of individual predictors to explanation of the variance in the outcome y. Avoiding use of such restrictive samples, while ensuring representativeness for the studied population, is thus another means of dealing with near-perfect multicollinearity.

The result of the t-test of the null hypothesis *H_0: $b_j = 0$ and its associated p-value are provided by the statistical software used, typically in the last column of the table with the MRA model solution (and in the line pertinent to jth independent variable; $j = 1,..., k$). To illustrate, we revisit Example 13.1, and in particular the output associated with fitting the MRA model (13.3), which is presented in Table 13.1. From the right-most column of this table, which contains the p-values associated with the tests of significance for the individual partial regression coefficients, we see that each of the predictors but x_4 is significant (for a commonly used significance level $\alpha = .05$). That is, the induction reasoning and figural relation test scores are each associated with significant unique explanatory power, over and above the explanatory power of the other three independent variables, when it comes to predicting the general mental ability score y. In contrast to these three measures, however, the three-dimensional rotation measure x_4 is not significant. Hence, for students with the same scores on the other three tests, x_1 through x_3, knowledge of their score on x_4 does not contribute to a better prediction of their general mental ability score y. We stress that this interpretation does not imply the score on the rotation measure x_4 as being not (linearly) related at all to the general mental ability score y, but only that this relationship is at most weak for any subpopulation of students with the same scores on each of the other three intelligence tests (their scores on them need not be the same across these three tests).

13.2.3. Confidence interval for a regression coefficient

The estimate $\hat{b}_j$ of the jth partial regression coefficient, which we routinely obtain when fitting a MRA model to a given data set, does not contain any information as to how far it could be from the true slope b_j in the studied population that is of actual interest ($j = 1,..., k$). Such information is contained in the confidence interval (CI) for this parameter. The lower and upper limits of this interval, at a given confidence level $(1 - \alpha)100\%$ $(0 < \alpha)$, can be obtained as follows (e.g., King & Minium, 2003):

(13.7) $(\hat{b}_j - t_{\alpha/2, n-k-1} s_{bj.12...k}, \ \hat{b}_j + t_{\alpha/2, n-k-1} s_{bj.12...k}).$

As indicated earlier in the book, the CI in (13.7) provides a range of *plausible* values for the slope in the studied population. (We stress that this property only holds if the model is not seriously misspecified, which is an issue that we will attend to later in this chapter.) To illustrate, we revisit the above Example 13.1 and compute with R the left and right limits of the CI (13.7) for the partial regression coefficient b_1 in the fitted model (13.3)—we refer to these limits correspondingly as 'left.limit' and 'right.limit' below. To accomplish this aim, we first see from Table 13.1 that the slope estimate is $\hat{b}_1 = .31664$, with a standard error (SE) of .08463. Hence, we can use R as follows to obtain the lower and upper endpoint of the 95%-CI for this slope (results given immediately after commands):

```
> left.limit = .31664 - qt(.975,155)*.08463
> right.limit = .31664 + qt(.975,155)*.08463

> left.limit
[1] 0.149463

> right.limit
[ob1] 0.483817
```

Thus, the 95%-CI for the first partial regression coefficient is (.149, .484). That is, the weight of the inductive reasoning with symbols score in the best linear combination of the four intelligence tests for the purpose of predicting general mental ability could be expected with high confidence to lie between .149 and .484 in the studied high school senior population.

13.3. ADJUSTED R^2 AND SHRINKAGE

As we indicated earlier in the chapter, the estimation of the partial regression coefficients in the MRA model (13.2) is carried out in such a way that *maximization of the strength of linear relationship (correlation)* is achieved between the independent variables, on the one hand, and the response variable, on the other hand. However, as pointed out in Chapter 12, this maximization procedure is carried out on a sample rather than the entire population. Hence, if a set of regression coefficients derived in one sample is applied to predict the y scores in another sample, the resulting multiple correlation coefficient R in it will generally be smaller than that correlation coefficient in the first sample. This phenomenon is called *shrinkage* and results from (i) capitalization on chance, due to the fact that the model is fitted to data from a sample that contains sampling error (the difference between population and sample); and relatedly (ii) the fact that the multiple correlation coefficient R derived from a given sample is *biased upward* if considered an estimate of the population multiple correlation coefficient associated with the fitted model (e.g., Pedhazur, 1997; see also Chapter 12).

As it turns out, it is not possible to determine exactly the extent of shrinkage in the multiple R, but this shrinkage can be estimated. Then the adjusted R^2 index, denoted R^2_a, can be used as an alternative to R^2 in predictive research as well as in other regression analysis applications. This adjusted index is defined as follows

$$(13.8) \qquad R^2_a = 1 - (1 - R^2)(n-1)/(n-k-1),$$

and aims at providing a better estimate of the explanatory power of the fitted model in the studied population than the conventional (unadjusted) R^2 index. From Equation (13.8), since $(n - 1)/(n - k - 1) < 1$, it follows that $R^2_a < R^2$, i.e., the adjusted index is lower than the conventional R^2 index for a given model. (This property also holds in the SLR model.)

As a pair of examples demonstrating this shrinkage, consider a model with $k = 4$ predictors fitted to a given sample with $n = 30$ subjects and an associated $R^2 = .64$ value. From Equation (13.8) we obtain ('×' denotes next multiplication)

$$R^2_a = 1 - (1 - R^2)(n-1)/(n-k-1) = 1 - (1 - .64) \times 29/25 = .58,$$

which is notably lower than the unadjusted R^2 for the considered model; in this case, the shrinkage is found to be $.64 - .58 = .06$. Alternatively, in the above Example 13.1 (see lower part of Table 13.1 in Section 13.1), the adjusted R^2 was estimated at .797 and was associated with a much smaller shrinkage value, viz., $.802 - .797 = .005$. The limited magnitude of the shrinkage in Example 13.1 is due to the large sample size as compared to the number of predictors, as well as to the relatively high unadjusted R^2 of .802 associated with the fitted model (13.3).

Upon investigation, the definition of the adjusted R^2 index in Equation (13.8) also reveals that for a given model and sample, other things being equal:

(a) the smaller the unadjusted R^2 (i.e., the lower the percentage explained response variance), the larger the shrinkage is; and

(b) the larger the ratio of number of predictors to sample size, k/n, the greater the shrinkage is.

It can also be shown that even if in the population $R^2 = 0$ holds (that is, a model explains no response variance at all), the expected unadjusted R^2 in a sample is $k/(n - 1)$ (e.g., Pedhazur, 1997). Hence, for a given sample size with a large enough number k of predictors used, the unadjusted R^2 index can be expected to be pretty close to one even if in the population it is in reality equal to zero, i.e., all partial regression coefficients are zero there (viz., $b_1 = b_2 = ... = b_k = 0$). Thus, a small R^2 for a model fitted to an available sample should make a researcher suspicious that there may not be even a weak linear relationship in the studied population between the response and independent variables considered. In contrast, it can be shown that when all slopes equal zero in the population, the expected R^2_a is still zero. Moreover, Equation (13.8) applies to the situation when all predictors are retained in the equation. If a predictor selection procedure is used to arrive at a model in question (e.g., see further details offered in Section 13.3), then the capitalization on chance is greater and results in even larger shrinkage. This discussion shows that there are serious limitations underlying the unadjusted R^2 index as a measure of overall fit. In this sense, R^2_a is a much better index of overall fit for a considered regression model.

13.4. THE MULTIPLE *F*-TEST AND EVALUATION OF CHANGE IN PROPORTION OF EXPLAINED VARIANCE FOLLOWING DROPPING OR ADDITION OF PREDICTORS

We pointed out earlier in the book that in empirical applications of statistical modeling it is often desirable to search for parsimonious models. These are models with as few as possible parameters, which provide sufficiently good means of data description and explanation. Such a strategy in model choice is grounded in the *parsimony principle*, a main principle in the philosophy of science. Adopting this principle implies that if two competing models fit about equally well a given data set, the model with fewer predictors should be the preferred model. We note of course that this choice is assumed to be made in the absence of any further information, whether statistical or otherwise, that might bear upon model fit and model comparison (for additional details see Raykov & Marcoulides, 1999).

In order to be in a position, however, to judge whether two models fit the data nearly as well, one needs a procedure that formally compares the fit of the two models to a given data set. More specifically, this procedure needs to enable a researcher to determine whether one can do (about) equally well with fewer predictors, as far as overall model fit is concerned. In other words, this procedure should permit a researcher to test the null hypothesis

$$H_0: b_{p+1} = b_{p+2} = ... = b_k = 0 \ (0 \le p < k)$$

for a MRA model with k initial predictors under consideration (k and p being whole numbers, $k > 1$). In this representation of the null hypothesis H_0, without loss of generality we have reordered the predictors, so those that could possibly be dropped are numbered (ordered) as last. We stress that this null hypothesis H_0 asserts we can drop the last $k - p$ predictors without losing explanatory power of the MRA model (13.2) in the population. In other words, this hypothesis stipulates that the MRA model (13.2) with all k predictors, on the one hand, and its version only with the first p predictors on the other hand, have the same explanatory power in the studied population. In that case, the two models will be associated with the same population proportion explained variance in a given response variable.

To test the null hypothesis H_0, we follow a generally accepted procedure in applications of statistics, which consists of comparing the fit of two rival models. In one of the models, referred to as the *restricted* (or reduced) *model*, the null hypothesis is implemented—i.e., its stipulated parameter restrictions are introduced. In the other model, referred to as the *full model*, this hypothesis is not implemented. The difference in fit between these models provides information that bears upon our decision whether to retain the null hypothesis or to reject it. This general procedure is utilized frequently in applications of statistics in the social and behavioral sciences, and it is also sometimes referred to as *nested model testing*.

Specifically in the context of MRA, and for the purpose of examining the above null hypothesis H_0 of dropping the last $k - p$ predictors, we consider the following two models in an application of this testing procedure:

Model 1: $y = b_0 + b_1 x_1 + b_2 x_2 + ... + b_k x_k + e$ (full model), and
Model 2: $y = b_0 + b_1 x_1 + b_2 x_2 + ... + b_p x_p + e^*$ (restricted or reduced model)

As indicated above, we can also call such models *nested* and specifically refer to the reduced model as being nested in the full model. (Notice the different notation used for the error term in the restricted model, owing to this term not being formally identical to that in the full model, since the latter has more predictors. Although the intercept and partial regression coefficients are not the same in both models, we use the same notation for them in order to emphasize that Model 2 is nested in Model 1; see below.) The motivation for referring to Model 2 as being nested in Model 1 is the fact that Model 2 is obtained from Model 1 by imposing additional parameter restrictions, viz., those of the null hypothesis H_0. Nested models are very widely used in various fields of applied statistics, such as categorical data analysis, multilevel/hierarchical models, latent variable and structural equation modeling, and others. This is due to the fact that they allow examining substantively meaningful hypotheses by testing the validity of pertinent parameter restrictions in studied populations. In many regards, one may often consider nested models as means of theory development and validation in the behavioral and social sciences.

To test the above null hypothesis H_0, we can use the "multiple F-test." This test is based on the statistic

(13.9) $\qquad F = (R^2_{y.12...k} - R^2_{y.12...p})/(1 - R^2_{y.12...k}) \cdot [(n-k-1)/(k-p)],$

which follows under H_0 an F-distribution with $k-p$ and $n-k-1$ degrees of freedom (Agresti & Finlay, 2009). When the outcome of this test is not significant, i.e., the F-ratio in Equation (13.9) is not significant, one can conclude that the full and reduced models have the same explanatory power with regard to the response y in the studied population—that is, they have the same R^2 index. As a consequence, one can drop the last $k-p$ predictors, since the more parsimonious model that does not include them would be preferable on grounds of having fewer parameters (see earlier discussion of the parsimony principle in this section).

Conversely, when the test based on the F-ratio (13.9) is found to be significant, it is concluded that dropping the last $k-p$ predictors leads to a significant loss of explanatory power. The implication then is that one should keep the last $k-p$ predictors, i.e., one will prefer the full model as a better means of data description and explanation. We note that we invoke the parsimony principle in this model choice activity only when the multiple F-test is not significant, since only then are we dealing with two equally well-fitting models that differ in their number of parameters. However, when the test statistic (13.9) is significant, we are no longer facing such a situation, since the full model fits the analyzed data better than the reduced model. In such a case, we obviously would prefer the full model as a means to describe and explain the data.

We emphasize that in the multiple F-test (13.9) there is no restriction on the relationship between the two numbers k and p of predictors involved, other than both being integers with the property $0 \leq p < k > 0$. Thereby, $k - p = 1$ is possible as a special case. Then one would be interested in testing whether a given predictor can be dropped, viz., the last in the above predictor ordering. In that case, the question that is addressed by testing the resulting null hypothesis H_0: $b_k = 0$, is whether the kth predictor is significant. This question asks whether the kth predictor enhances significantly the explanatory power of the model over and above what the remaining $k-1$ predictors furnish with respect to explaining variance in the outcome y. That is, testing the null hypothesis H_0 when $k - p = 1$ amounts to testing the unique predictive power of the kth predictor, in the context of the other $k - 1$ predictors, i.e., after including them first in the model and adding then the predictor in question as last in it.

Conversely, when $p = 0$ the test of the null hypothesis is H_0: $b_1 = b_2 = ... = b_k = 0$, and it amounts to testing whether the fitted MRA model (13.2) has any explanatory power at all, i.e., is tantamount to testing the null hypothesis H_0': $b_1 = b_2 = \ldots = b_k = 0$. In this case, the full model is compared to the reduced model where there is no predictor at all. Such a reduced model is frequently referred to as a *null model*. The reason is that it is characterized by the properties that (i) apart from the standard error of estimate, its only parameter is the mean of the outcome variable that equals then the intercept term b_0; and (ii) there are no predictors included in it. When comparing the full model to the null model, the *F*-test statistic in (13.9) reduces to the earlier discussed statistic (13.4) for testing the null hypothesis H_0', which itself amounts to testing that in the studied population $R^2 = 0$ holds for the pertinent MRA model. (Indeed, by substituting $p = 0$ in (13.9), one directly obtains the test statistic (13.4) of relevance then; see Section 13.2.)

The discussed test for dropping predictors from a MRA model, which is based on the multiple *F*-statistic (13.9), can also be used to determine whether one can add one or more predictors to a regression model under consideration. To this end, all one needs to do is (a) consider the model with the added predictors as the full model, (b) view the model before their addition as the reduced model, and (c) rephrase the research question to ask if these added predictors can actually be dropped. This approach is of special importance in what is frequently referred to as *hierarchical regression analysis*. In such an analysis, based on substantive reasons and questions to be answered, a researcher develops a prespecified order of entry of (sets of) predictors into a regression model under consideration. Applying the multiple *F*-test then addresses the query of whether a certain set of predictors added at a later stage improves explanation of the response variance *over and above* what has already been achieved by the earlier entered predictors into the model. When considering adding only a single predictor, as mentioned above, it follows from this discussion that testing the null hypothesis H_0: $b_k = 0$ is actually examining the significance of the kth predictor when added *last* in a regression model under consideration.

We illustrate the multiple *F*-test by revisiting the earlier Example 13.1. For our purposes here, we will be interested in testing whether we can drop the two induction tests from the original set of four predictors used to explain variance in the general mental ability score y. This question determines the full model (Model 1) as the MRA model (13.3) with all four predictors, which we already fitted in the preceding subsection, and its output is available to us in the R-object 'mrmod.1'. The reduced model is that model but without the two induction tests, denoted earlier x_1 and x_3. The reduced model, referred to as Model 2, is nested in Model 1, and does not contain these induction tests as predictors. The equation for Model 2 is thus as follows:

$$(13.10) \qquad\qquad y = b_0 + b_2 x_2 + b_4 x_4 + e.$$

We stress that in Equation (13.10) the intercept and partial regression weights b_0, b_2, and b_4, as well as error term e, are not identical to the corresponding intercept, slopes, and error term with the same symbols in Model 1, but we purposely use the same notation here in order to emphasize that Model 2 is nested in Model 1.

To fit Model 2 with R, we use the same command 'lm', yet now only formally state the sum of the included predictors x2 and x4 after the sign '~', and assign the name 'mrmod.2' to the R-object resulting as the output produced thereby (output summarized beneath fitting model command):

```
> mrmod.2 = lm(y~x2+x4)

> summary(mrmod.2)



Call:

lm(formula = y ~ x2 + x4)


Residuals:
      Min        1Q     Median        3Q        Max
-0.262032  -0.077504  -0.001397  0.081131   0.431446


Coefficients:
             Estimate Std. Error t value Pr(>|t|)
(Intercept)  -0.04353    0.03800  -1.145    0.254
x2            0.42613    0.08715   4.889 2.48e-06 ***
x4            0.65506    0.10565   6.200 4.78e-09 ***
---
Signif. codes:  0 '***' 0.001 '**' 0.01 '*' 0.05 '.' 0.1 ' ' 1


Residual standard error: 0.1211 on 157 degrees of freedom
Multiple R-squared: 0.6213,     Adjusted R-squared: 0.6165
F-statistic: 128.8 on 2 and 157 DF,  p-value: < 2.2e-16
```

We see from this output that the R^2 index of Model 2 is markedly lower, as is its adjusted R^2, than the corresponding indexes of Model 1. Conversely, the summary measures for the individual residuals associated with Model 2 (see top part of output) are also notably higher than the corresponding measures for Model 1 (see top part of output for Model 1 presented in Table 13.1). This suggests that Model 2 does not fit the data as well as Model 1 in the available sample of 160 students. However, the actual question to address is whether this is indeed the case in the studied population. In statistical terms, this question asks whether the drop in the R^2 index when moving from Model 1 to Model 2—i.e., when removing the induction test scores as predictors of the general mental ability score—is significant or not. To answer this question, we use the multiple *F*-test (13.9), which is accomplished in R by employing the command 'anova':

```
> anova(mrmod.2, mrmod.1)
```

We emphasize that this command has two arguments—the R-objects of the outputs associated with Model 2 and Model 1 that are being compared (stated in this order). The resulting output is presented next.

```
Analysis of Variance Table

Model 1: y ~ x2 + x4
Model 2: y ~ x1 + x2 + x3 + x4

  Res.Df    RSS  Df  Sum of Sq        F   Pr(>F)
1    157 2.3041
2    155 1.2061   2     1.0980  70.557 < 2.2e-16 ***
---
Signif. codes:  0 '***' 0.001 '**' 0.01 '*' 0.05 '.' 0.1 ' ' 1
```

According to these results, Model 2 fits the data significantly worse than Model 1—see the *F*-statistic of 70.557, which is significant since its associated *p*-value is very small, practically zero. Hence, we can conclude that the drop in the R^2, i.e., in explanatory power, when deleting the two predictors in question is significant in the studied population. In other words, the removal of the two induction test scores as predictors of general mental ability is associated with a significant loss in explanatory power of the MRA model initially fitted (Model 1). For this reason, we prefer Model 1, i.e., the full model, to Model 2.

Conversely, if one were interested in the first instance in examining whether one could drop the figural relations test scores from the original set of four predictors of the general mental ability score *y*, one would proceed as follows. Again, Model 1 (see Section 13.1) would be the full model. However, the reduced model would now be the following one, referred to as Model 3, where as earlier in this section we use the same parameter and error term notation to emphasize that it is nested in Model 1:

(13.11) $$y = b_0 + b_1 x_1 + b_3 x_3 + e.$$

We fit this model with the same R command 'lm' as above, but attach to it the object name 'mrmod.3' (results summarized subsequently):

```
> mrmod.3 = lm(y~x1+x3)

> summary(mrmod.3)

Call:

lm(formula = y ~ x1 + x3)


Residuals:
      Min        1Q    Median        3Q       Max
-0.193680 -0.060374 -0.002124  0.071413  0.259955


Coefficients:
            Estimate Std. Error t value Pr(>|t|)
(Intercept)  0.15095    0.01761   8.570 9.15e-15 ***
x1           0.35528    0.08806   4.035 8.52e-05 ***
x3           0.59523    0.06845   8.695 4.37e-15 ***
---
Signif. codes:  0 '***' 0.001 '**' 0.01 '*' 0.05 '.' 0.1 ' ' 1


Residual standard error: 0.09235 on 157 degrees of freedom
Multiple R-squared:  0.78,      Adjusted R-squared: 0.7772
F-statistic: 278.2 on 2 and 157 DF,  p-value: < 2.2e-16
```

We see that the R^2 index associated with Model 3 is notably lower in the analyzed sample than that index for Model 1. To test if a loss in predictive power is the case also in the population, we apply the multiple F-test for these indexes of Models 1 and 3 (result given beneath command):

```
> anova(mrmod.3, mrmod.1)



Analysis of Variance Table


Model 1: y ~ x1 = x3
Model 2: y ~ x1 + x2 + x3 + x4
  Res.Df    RSS Df Sum of Sq      F   Pr(>F)
1    157 1.33893
2    155 1.20608  2   0.13285 8.5367 0.000304 ***
---
Signif. codes:  0 '***' 0.001 '**' 0.01 '*' 0.05 '.' 0.1 ' ' 1
```

The multiple F-test is associated here with a fairly small p-value that is lower than a prespecified significance level (usually $\alpha = .05$). Thus, the loss in predictive power is significant when moving from the original set of four predictors to only the two inductive reasoning tests. We thus prefer Model 1, rather than Model 3, as a means of data description.

Of course, in order to have more trust in Model 1 for data description purposes, as was illustrated in Chapter 12, we need to examine the individual residuals associated with it. We will attend to this issue in a later section of the chapter.

The F-test used throughout this section plays also a prominent role in other predictor selection strategies, which we turn to next.

13.5. STRATEGIES FOR PREDICTOR SELECTION

In the previous section concerning the choice between models involving different subsets of an initial set of predictors, we had a preconceived idea which particular subsets to use in the different model versions considered. Frequently in empirical behavioral and social research, however, a researcher does not have such an idea and is interested in finding the minimum number of predictors, from an original set of independent variables, that account for almost as much (as much as possible) variance in the response variable as that original set of explanatory variables. The resulting model with a minimal number of predictors will be associated with highest stability of regression coefficient estimates, smallest standard errors, and shortest confidence intervals, if it is a plausible means of data description and explanation. There are several possible predictor selection approaches available that aim at accomplishing this goal and are discussed next.

13.5.1. Forward selection

In this procedure, one starts with the predictor exhibiting the highest significant correlation (in absolute value) with the dependent variable, i.e., this predictor is the first to be included in the model. Denote for simplicity this explanatory variable as x_1. That is, since x_1 correlates most strongly with the response y, the initial version of the regression model of interest becomes $y = b_0 + b_1 x_1 + e$. At the second step of this model development approach, one adds from the remaining explanatory variables the next predictor that fulfills the following conditions: (a) it significantly increases the amount of explained variance in y, over and above what is already achieved by x_1; and (b) it is associated with the highest increment in explained variance in y among all remaining predictors (denoted say x_2 through x_k, with k being the number of predictors in the initial set of independent variables under consideration). Denote this predictor, for simplicity, as x_2. The MRA model looks at step 2 as follows: $y = b_0 + b_1 x_1 + b_2 x_2 + e$. One continues in this fashion until there is no predictor left that significantly improves the proportion explained variance in the response y. We note that this procedure may be terminated at step 2 if there is no predictor among x_2 through x_k that would significantly increase the explained variance in y. Indeed, the procedure may even terminate at step 1 if there is no predictor at all that significantly relates to the response variable. In that unusual case, the final model will simply be $y = b_0 + e$, where b_0 will subsequently be estimated as the mean of the outcome variable y. As with each predictor selection approach, for the final model arrived at with this forward selection procedure one needs to answer the question whether it represents a plausible means of data description and explanation (e.g., Section 13.6).

The fundamental statistical criterion applied at each step of this model-building approach is the "multiple F-test" discussed in Section 13.5, and specifically its special case when $p = k - 1$ (dropping/adding of a single predictor at a time). A notable limitation of this selection procedure is that it may miss the best model, since predictors are never allowed to be deleted. For example, an earlier included predictor may lose its (significant) explanatory power at a later stage—for instance, when adding another independent variable related sufficiently closely to it—but be retained in the equation unnecessarily since predictor removal is not possible when applying this forward procedure. Similarly, due to multiple analyses of the same data set, capitalization on chance may occur. For this reason, it is recommended to carry out a replication study before a final decision is made for preferring a particular model version from the series considered.

13.5.2. Backward elimination

This selection approach is in a sense the reverse of forward predictor selection. However, unlike forward selection, backward elimination begins with all predictors in the initial set being included in the model (after ensuring that there is no multicollinearity among them). In the next step, the nonsignificant predictor associated with the highest p-value is deleted. One continues in this fashion until no other nonsignificant predictor is left in the model. Also in this selection procedure one can see the above-mentioned special case of the multiple F-test (Section 13.5) as being of particular importance, since evaluation of predictor significance is accomplished using it. We note that the procedure may be terminated at step 1, when all predictors in the initial set are significant that are included in the starting model.

Similarly to the forward selection procedure, backward elimination may miss the best model. The reason is that here predictors are not allowed to be added. For example, a predictor may be decided to be dropped at an earlier stage, which however may be profitable to have in the MRA model version considered at a later stage, as far as fit to the analyzed data is concerned. Also, given that multiple analyses are carried out on the same data set, capitalization on chance may occur. Hence, it can be recommended to carry out a replication study before a final decision is made for selection of a particular model version from the series of models considered during the process of backward elimination. Despite these drawbacks, backward predictor selection may be recommended for initial sets consisting of not too many independent variables that are not involved in a nearly perfect (or perfect) linear relationship. (Such a relationship will be the case, as pointed out earlier in this chapter, if the initial set of predictors explain a significant proportion of response variance yet none of them is significant; see below.)

We illustrate the backward model selection procedure with the following example:

Example 13.2: In a study of $n = 145$ students, tests of algebra, geometry, and trigonometry were administered to them, along with a scale of educational motivation and a scale of college aspiration. In addition, data on their gender and socioeconomic status (low versus high, 0 and 1 respectively) were collected. The data can be found in the file CH13_EX2.dat. In it, the first three mentioned measures are correspondingly symbolized x_1 through x_3; the following two scale scores x_4 and y, respectively; while gender and socioeconomic status are designated 'gender' and 'ses'. A researcher is interested in explaining individual differences in college aspiration in terms of such differences on the other six variables. The researcher is particularly concerned with selecting those predictors from the set of six independent variables, which possess unique explanatory power for college aspiration.

To accomplish this goal, we can employ the backward elimination strategy. To this end, we commence with a model containing all six predictors—x_1 through x_4, 'gender', and 'ses' (see, e.g., Section 13.1)—which we refer to as Model 1 below. (Plotting the response against each continuous predictor, employing the R-command 'plot' as earlier in the book, did not reveal any pattern of nonlinear relationship between them.) Using the R command 'lm', we assign the name 'mod1' to the R-object being the associated output (presented beneath the command):

```
> mod1 = lm(y~x1+1x2+x3+x4+gender+ses)
> summary(mod1)



Call:
lm(formula = y ~ x1 + x2 + x3 + x4 + gender + ses)
```

```
Residuals:
     Min        1Q     Median       3Q        Max
-0.210946  -0.064542  -0.004346  0.062526  0.229199


Coefficients:
             Estimate Std. Error t value Pr(>|t|)
(Intercept)  0.038246   0.036231   1.056 0.292981
x1           0.307247   0.088250   3.482 0.000668 ***
x2           0.169371   0.069205   2.447 0.015646 *
x3           0.436553   0.079024   5.524 1.59e-07 ***
x4           0.172747   0.090668   1.905 0.058824 .
gender      -0.008562   0.021672  -0.395 0.693391
ses         -0.028573   0.021630  -1.321 0.188689
---
Signif. codes:  0 '***' 0.001 '**' 0.01 '*' 0.05 '.' 0.1 ' ' 1


Residual standard error: 0.08868 on 138 degrees of freedom
Multiple R-squared: 0.8014,     Adjusted R-squared: 0.7928
F-statistic: 92.81 on 6 and 138 DF,  p-value: < 2.2e-16
```

In this starting model, there are several nonsignificant predictors at the conventional significance level of .05, with 'gender' having the highest p-value among them. We thus drop 'gender' from Model 1, leading to Model 2, which does not include it as a predictor. The output of Model 2 is presented in the R-object denoted 'mod2' (output provided beneath the command 'lm'):

```
> mod2 = lm(y~x1+x2+x3+x4+ses)
> summary(mod2)



Call:
lm(formula = y ~ x1 + x2 + x3 + x4 + ses)
Residuals:
     Min        1Q     Median       3Q        Max
-0.212776  -0.065415  -0.003973  0.060831  0.227550


Coefficients:
             Estimate Std. Error t value Pr(>|t|)
(Intercept)  0.03070    0.03070    1.000 0.318955
x1           0.30718    0.08798    3.491 0.000644 ***
x2           0.16723    0.06878    2.431 0.016318 *
x3           0.43599    0.07877    5.535 1.50e-07 ***
```

```
x4            0.17653    0.08989   1.964 0.051527 .
ses          -0.02234    0.01476  -1.513 0.132438
---
Signif. codes:  0 '***' 0.001 '**' 0.01 '*' 0.05 '.' 0.1 ' ' 1

Residual standard error: 0.08841 on 139 degrees of freedom
Multiple R-squared: 0.8012,     Adjusted R-squared: 0.794
F-statistic:    112 on 5 and 139 DF,  p-value: < 2.2e-16
```

Also in Model 2 we have nonsignificant predictors, with 'ses' having the highest p-value among them. We drop it from the model in its next fitted version, referred to as Model 3:

```
> mod3 = lm(y~x1+x2+x3+x4)
> summary(mod3)



Call:
lm(formula = y ~ x1 + x2 + x3 + x4)

Residuals:
      Min        1Q     Median        3Q        Max
-0.201879 -0.060719 -0.001018  0.062009  0.237407

Coefficients:
            Estimate Std. Error t value Pr(>|t|)
(Intercept)  0.02148    0.03022   0.711  0.47848
x1           0.30793    0.08838   3.484  0.00066 ***
x2           0.17255    0.06901   2.500  0.01356 *
x3           0.43206    0.07909   5.463 2.08e-07 ***
x4           0.17189    0.09025   1.905  0.05887 .
---
Signif. codes:  0 '***' 0.001 '**' 0.01 '*' 0.05 '.' 0.1 ' ' 1
Residual standard error: 0.08881 on 140 degrees of freedom
Multiple R-squared: 0.7979,     Adjusted R-squared: 0.7921
F-statistic: 138.2 on 4 and 140 DF,  p-value: < 2.2e-16
```

The last remaining nonsignificant predictor is educational motivation, and deleting it we obtain Model 4, which has only significant predictors:

```
> mod4 = lm(y~x1+x2+x3)
> summary(mod4)
```

```
Call:
lm(formula = y ~ x1 + x2 + x3)


Residuals:
      Min         1Q      Median         3Q         Max
-0.1964412 -0.0644397 -0.0008611  0.0625979  0.2445131


Coefficients:
            Estimate Std. Error t value Pr(>|t|)
(Intercept)  0.05389    0.02521   2.138 0.034267 *
x1           0.31187    0.08918   3.497 0.000630 ***
x2           0.23390    0.06160   3.797 0.000217 ***
x3           0.48146    0.07541   6.385 2.32e-09 ***
---
Signif. codes:  0 '***' 0.001 '**' 0.01 '*' 0.05 '.' 0.1 ' ' 1


Residual standard error: 0.08964 on 141 degrees of freedom
Multiple R-squared: 0.7927,     Adjusted R-squared: 0.7883
F-statistic: 179.7 on 3 and 141 DF,  p-value: < 2.2e-16
```

The last fitted model, Model 4, shows that if fixing any two of the student scores on the mathematics tests, knowledge of the third improves significantly the proportion of explained variance in the response variable, college aspiration. This is at the same time the most parsimonious model version considered, and we observe that in it the standard errors associated with the intercept and partial regression slopes are smallest overall from the four models fitted in this example. In addition, Model 4 is associated with essentially the same explanatory power that all six predictors afforded, when we compare its R^2 (and adjusted R^2) index with that of the starting model containing all initially considered independent variables. This example demonstrates how use of the backward selection procedure can lead to parsimonious models that fit relatively well a given data set.

13.5.3. Stepwise selection (stepwise regression)

This approach to selecting predictors aims at improving upon the forward selection method. In stepwise regression, which similarly starts with a single predictor model version (assuming the existence of a predictor that is significantly correlated with the response variable), it is possible for a predictor to be dropped at a later stage if it is subsequently found not to improve significantly the model predictive power with regard to the outcome. This is achieved by inspecting at each stage the t-value of each predictor included in the model equation, which as mentioned is an index of its contribution to explaining response variance if the predictor is entered last in the model. (The square of this t-value equals the F-ratio in Equation (13.9), if one formally considers dropping this predictor from the model version containing it, or alternatively adding it last into the associated regression equation.) Just like the two previously mentioned procedures, the statistical criterion that underlies this selection approach is again the multiple F-test.

A stepwise selection approach can be recommended whenever a researcher is interested in predicting a response variable using variables from a given initial set, and he or she wishes to accomplish this with the most parsimonious, plausible model possible for the analyzed data. Stepwise regression cannot be used in general for making conclusions about the unique predictive power of variables in that initial set, however, and in fact is not recommended for modeling related purposes other than prediction, due to the high likelihood of capitalization on chance that can lead to spurious results.

Another variable selection procedure based upon stepwise regression involves examining all possible models from the total list of predictor variables available. For k predictor variables, 2^k regression models are possible (including the intercept-only model). The major shortcoming of the all-possible-regression-model approach to variable selection is that one must often examine a large number of models, even if the number of predictor variables is relatively small—for example, if $k = 8$, $2^k = 256$ regression models and if $k = 20$, $2^k = 1,048,576$ regression models.

Reducing the number of predictive variables to investigate is a common problem for applied researchers in many disciplines. Selecting a subset of variables from a long list of potential predictor variables has received much attention in the methodological literature, and work continues in this area. Some new procedures that are beginning to gain popularity include the automated variable selection procedures of so-called Tabu and genetic algorithms (for details see Drezner, Marcoulides, & Salhi, 1999; Marcoulides, Drezner, & Schumacker, 1998; Marcoulides & Drezner, 2001; Marcoulides & Drezner, 2003; Marcoulides & Ing, 2011). Although a description of these new procedures is beyond the scope of this book, it is important to note that they, like those described above, are based solely on selecting variables using statistical criteria. However, relying only on statistical criteria to select variables for explanation or prediction can contribute to poor statistical practice and is therefore not blindly recommended. Whenever available, researchers should also rely on nonstatistical criteria, such as available theory, previous research, and professional judgment to guide the variable selection process.

13.6. ANALYSIS OF RESIDUALS FOR MULTIPLE REGRESSION MODELS

We discussed at length in Chapter 12 (Section 12.6) how one can examine the individual case residuals for fitted SLR models, in order to assess whether their underlying assumptions are plausible and if the models fit the analyzed data well. We emphasized thereby that while the R^2 and adjusted R^2 indexes provide useful overall goodness-of-fit measures, they might be relatively high also when there are several subjects whose data are not well fit by a model in question, which therefore need not necessarily be viewed as a satisfactory means of data description and explanation. Similarly, individual residuals associated with MRA models are of particular relevance for assumption assessment as well as exploration of the degree to which the models fit the individual data. This is another important criterion of model adequacy, sometimes referred to as "local fit" as opposed to the "overall fit" evaluated by the aforementioned R^2 indexes.

When the MRA model (13.2) is fit to a given data set, as in the SLR model (12.1) the residual $\hat{e}_i$ associated with the ith individual is the discrepancy between his or her observation on the response variable, y_i, and its corresponding model prediction:

$$(13.12) \qquad \hat{e}_i = y_i - \hat{y}_i = y_i - \hat{b}_0 - \hat{b}_1 x_{1i} - \hat{b}_2 x_{2i} - ... - \hat{b}_k x_{ki},$$

where x_{ji} denote his or her value on the jth predictor ($i = 1,..., n, j = 1,..., k$). We stress that the residual $\hat{e}_i$ depends on (i) that individual's data for the used predictors, (ii) the fitted model, and (iii) the response variable in a given modeling session. (As indicated earlier in the book, response variables may change within an empirical study, depending on research questions pursued.)

For a MRA model under consideration, plots of the individual residuals $\hat{e}_i$ ($i = 1,..., n$) against various other variables provide a researcher with insightful information pertaining to the plausibility of its assumptions and goodness of fit to the analyzed data, and they are readily obtained with R using the same commands discussed in Chapter 12 (Section 12.6). When a MRA model is of concern, it is useful to examine the plots of the residuals against each predictor included in it, in order to assess whether higher powers of that predictor may be also profitably included in the model. Furthermore, with a MRA model it is also informative to plot residuals against predictors not included in it. The presence of a discernible pattern in the resulting plots, in particular a linear relationship to a variable not used as a predictor in the model, may be interpreted as suggesting that inclusion of this predictor can improve markedly the model. These residual plots are also useful to inspect when an initial SLR model is fitted to data but one is interested in examining if one or more additional predictors may be helpful to include in it with the view of improving model fit.

We illustrate this discussion with the last model fitted to the data from Example 13.2, which we denoted Model 4. For this model with the predictors x_1 through x_3 (the three mathematics test scores), we obtain readily using R the plots of residuals against each one of these predictors as well as the response variable y (cf. Chapter 12, Section 12.6; see Figure 13.1):

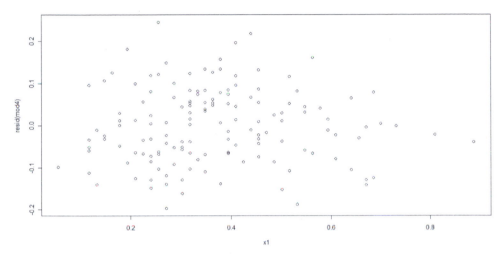

FIGURE 13.1.

Plots of Model 4 residuals against predictors, response, and model predictions (fitted values; see horizontal axis notation to differentiate between plots).

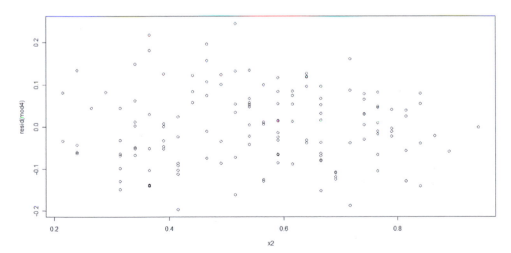

FIGURE 13.1 (continued)

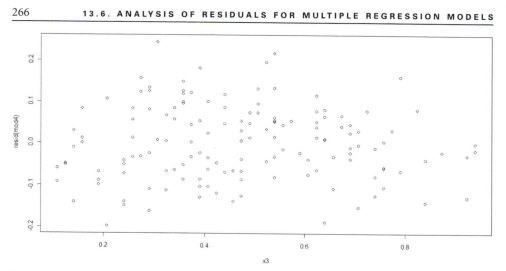

FIGURE 13.1 (continued)

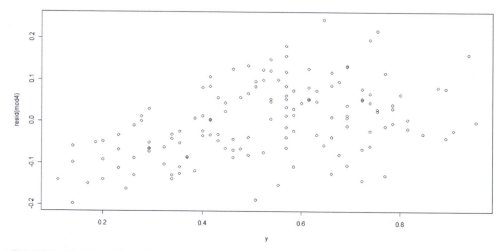

FIGURE 13.1 (continued)

```
> plot(x1, resid(mod4))
> plot(x2, resid(mod4))
> plot(x3, resid(mod4))
> plot(y, resid(mod4))
> plot(predict(mod4), resid(mod4))
```

After inspecting the plots displayed in Figure 13.1, we see that none of these plots shows a clear pattern indicating model misfit. This suggests that Model 4 does not exhibit serious lack of fit at the individual data level. We next evaluate the normality assumption with regard to the model residuals, using the R commands 'qqnorm' and 'qqline' (see Chapter 12, Section 12.6, and Figure 13.2):

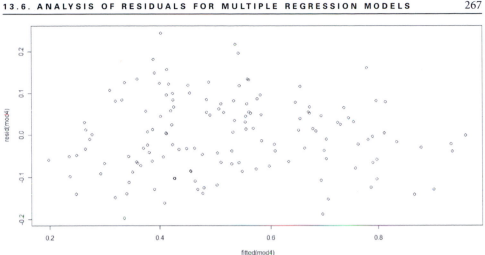

FIGURE 13.1 (continued)

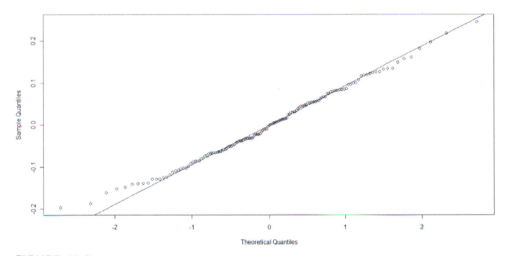

FIGURE 13.2
Normal probability plot for the residuals of Model 4.

```
> qqnorm(resid(mod4))
> qqline(resid(mod4))
```

The plot displayed in Figure 13.2 does not indicate serious violations of normality, which as pointed out earlier in the chapter is an assumption needed for inferences that can be made from the model results.

Based on the residual plots discussed in this section (see Figures 13.1 and 13.2), as well as the earlier findings of its relatively high R^2, adjusted R^2, and parsimony, we conclude that Model 4 represents a plausible means of data description and explanation for the empirical study in question, which we prefer to the other considered models.

We conclude this section by emphasizing that residual plots present informative means of assessment of model assumptions and fit to analyzed data, over and above the conventional and adjusted R^2 indexes. For this reason, residual plots are highly recommended for use in applications of multiple regression analysis in empirical social and behavioral research.

Analysis of Variance and Covariance

Researchers in the behavioral and social sciences are often interested in comparing various response variables across several distinct populations, such as different socioeconomic (SES) groups, states, countries, cities, or districts. For example, a researcher studying depression and aging might want to determine whether there are differences in the levels of depression exhibited by elderly persons living in three different states. Similarly, examination of possible SES group differences in student motivation may well be of concern in an educational setting. In such cases, a very useful statistical method for conducting such comparisons is the *analysis of variance* (ANOVA). When, in addition to the group differentiation, continuous independent variables are also considered as playing an explanatory role for a response measure, the extension of this technique to accommodate such variables is referred to as *analysis of covariance* (ANCOVA). These two modeling approaches are the topics of the present chapter. As we will point out in a later section, both techniques are closely related to the method of regression analysis we introduced in the two previous chapters.

14.1. HYPOTHESES AND FACTORS

ANOVA is a widely used statistical method for examining whether two or more independent populations have the same mean values. (The special case of ANOVA with two populations is the t-test for independent means that we presented in Chapter 8; for this reason, the case of $g = 2$ groups will not be considered again in this chapter.) The ANOVA framework was originally developed by the famous British statistician R. A. Fisher in the 1920s, and it has ever since enjoyed great popularity among behavioral and social scientists interested in studying whether several distinct populations share the same mean on an outcome variable. Extensions to more than one simultaneously considered response measure are also available and frequently used in applications of *multivariate statistics* (e.g., Raykov & Marcoulides, 2008), which is a more advanced topic that we will not be concerned with in the rest of the book.

To introduce the ANOVA framework, consider g independent populations and an outcome variable of interest, as usual denoted y. (As indicated above, $g > 2$ will be assumed throughout the remainder of the chapter.) Let us designate its means in these populations correspondingly by $\mu_1, \mu_2,..., \mu_g$. ANOVA is a statistical method that allows one to address the question of whether these means are the same, and a number of related queries. That is, at the heart of ANOVA is the examination of the null hypothesis

(14.1) $H_0: \mu_1 = \mu_2 = ... = \mu_g,$

which stipulates identity of the population means. The alternative hypothesis H_a states that there are at least two populations (often referred to as groups) with different means. That is, H_a is simply the negation of H_0 and does not postulate anything about the number of groups with differing means—these can be as few as two groups, but there may also be more than two groups that have unequal means if the alternative hypothesis is correct. Similarly, this hypothesis does not posit any particular form of violation of the null hypothesis. Specifically, whether the mean in one of the groups is larger or smaller than that in another group(s) is immaterial for the validity of H_a.

Before we move on to discussing the ANOVA test of the null hypothesis (14.1), we mention that one conceivable way to examine it may appear to consist of a series of t-tests carried out on all possible pairs of groups from the available g groups in a given study. However, as discussed at length in the literature (e.g., Agresti & Finlay, 2009, and references therein), such an approach would have a serious problem that compromises its meaningfulness. Specifically, with this approach one would be committing an overall Type I error with a fairly high probability in general. This probability is defined as that for falsely rejecting at least one null hypothesis in the series of pair-wise t-tests, in case all groups have the same means. To obtain an appreciation for this probability, let us assume that the null hypotheses in all those t-tests are true. That is, for the $g(g - 1)/2$ in total t-tests, one asks the question "What would be the probability that in at least one of them the null hypothesis of equality in the respective pair of means will be incorrectly rejected?" This probability is referred to as the *overall Type I error* probability (at times also called the *family-wise Type I error* rate).

Due to the multitude of t-tests involved, however, it is easily realized that this error rate is much higher than that for a Type I error associated with any one of these t-tests. Hence, even if one controls, say, at $\alpha = .05$ the latter Type I error (i.e., this error rate for each of the t-tests), there is still a very high probability in general of falsely rejecting at least one of the correct null hypotheses across the $g(g - 1)/2$ t-tests that one would need to carry out in order to examine all pairs of groups with regard to their mean differences. In particular, even with only three groups, the overall Type I error will be above .14 rather than controlled at α, and this error grows essentially exponentially with increasing number of groups g in the study (e.g., Howell, 2009). This is a highly undesirable feature of the series of t-tests contemplated, which represents its serious inferential problem. This problem can be resolved by using the ANOVA test of the overall null hypothesis (14.1), which is a single test that is in addition carried out at a given and controlled significance level—usually at $\alpha = .05$ (at least in general, and depends on the choice of the researcher). The remainder of the present section will be concerned with this ANOVA test.

In order to be in a position to use the ANOVA approach for testing the null hypothesis (14.1), several assumptions are typically made. As was done on a few occasions earlier in the book, it is assumed that the response variable y is normally distributed in each of the g populations under consideration. (This implies that the outcome variable is assumed throughout this chapter to be continuous, as in the preceding two chapters dealing with simple and multiple regression analysis.) In addition, the variance of y is assumed to be the same in all populations—we denote this common variance by σ^2. Finally, the available random samples from the g populations in question are assumed to be independent of one another. Under these assumptions, since the mean and variance are all we need to know in order to reproduce a normal distribution (as they are sufficient statistics, e.g., see Chapter 5), ANOVA can be seen as a methodology for testing whether the distribution of the outcome measure y is independent from the categorical variable defined as group membership. We stress that the latter variable is not a quantitative measure but rather a nominal (ordinal) one, and thus the analysis needs to account for this fact. In the context of ANOVA, such a variable is usually referred to as *factor*, and the values it takes as its corresponding *levels*. We emphasize that there is typically no meaningful numerical relationship between the levels of a factor. Despite the fact that frequently they are denoted by real numbers initially in a behavioral study, the factor level values are typically only labels and cannot be related to one another like real numbers.

To illustrate this discussion, consider the following example:

Example 14.1: In a study of $n = 156$ elderly persons from $g = 4$ different states, their depression level was measured using an established instrument. The resulting data are contained in the file CH14_EX1.dat, where the depression score is denoted 'y' and the subject state of residence is symbolized as 'state'. (Scores on the state variable range from 1 through 4 denoting formally each state, a practice usually followed initially in empirical research to designate group membership.) A researcher is concerned with the question of whether there are differences in depression of aged adults across these four states.

Since state residency is not a quantitative variable, we need to instruct the software to treat it accordingly. This is accomplished in the software R by defining such a variable as a factor, which we achieve with the following commands (explanations provided subsequently; see also Note at end of chapter):

```
> d = read.table("C://data/CH14_EX1.dat", header = T)
> attach(d)
> d$state = factor(d$state, labels = c("A", "B", "C", "D"))
> detach(d)
> attach(d)
```

After reading the data into the software and making it available to R with the second command, we define the variable 'state' as a factor. (Unless we do so, R will treat it as a continuous variable and each of its scores will be handled as if it were a real number, which is obviously not the case in this example.) To this end, we use the third-listed command 'd$state = factor(.,.)', which assigns the status of a factor to the component (variable) of the data set 'd' whose name is 'state', i.e., the variable 'state'. Thereby, we assign the labels A through D correspondingly to 1 through 4 on the original variable 'state', as values on the new factor variable that for convenience we also name 'state'. We do not need then the original copy of the data set, and so we detach it with the fourth command. In order to make the last created variable available for further analyses, however, we attach the data set with the so-modified 'state' variable (and the variable 'y' being unchanged) using the last command. To see the result of these five commands, and in particular the number of subjects from each state in the overall sample of 156 elderly persons in the sample, we summarize the data on the variable 'state' in the newly created data set 'd' using the 'summary' command (output given immediately beneath it):

```
> summary(state)

A  B  C  D
39 38 40 39
```

This short output shows that we have about equally many elderly adults sampled from each state, who participate in this investigation. To view the state estimates of mean depression, we readily calculate the sample average of the depression scores per state as follows (commands explanation provided subsequently):

```
> mean.state.A = sum(y*(state=="A"))/39
> mean.state.B = sum(y*(state=="B"))/38
> mean.state.C = sum(y*(state=="C"))/40
> mean.state.D = sum(y*(state=="D"))/39
```

For each of the four states, we sum the depression scores only for the elderly persons in its sample, which we accomplish by using a logical command assigning a 1 to each person from that state and 0 otherwise. For instance, for state A this logical command is 'state $==$ "A"', resulting in 1 for subjects from state A only and 0 for everyone else. We then multiply the result of this logical operation with the depression score, sum across the entire sample of 156 persons (but in effect only across the subjects from a given state, say A), and divide by the state-specific sample size (see output of preceding command 'summary'). In this way, the following state sample means result:

```
> mean.state.A
[1] 19.58974
> mean.state.B
[1] 21.71053
> mean.state.C
[1] 23.02500
> mean.state.D
[1] 20.53846
```

These four means differ somewhat, but we emphasize that they are sample averages and hence their differences are not unexpected. For this reason, even if in the elderly population of concern the state depression means were to be the same, one cannot expect them to be so also in the samples from the four states under consideration. Specifically, the observed mean differences are obviously due to sampling fluctuations (sampling error). How much variability of the sample means could one expect to observe, however, should the null hypothesis be true, and how strong variability in them would be sufficient in order not to consider this hypothesis credible or retainable? In other words, how much variability in the sampling means could be explained by chance fluctuations only? We need to find next an answer to this query, which is precisely the question that ANOVA addresses using a specifically developed test statistic that we now turn to.

14.2. TESTING EQUALITY OF POPULATION MEANS

In order to develop a test of the null hypothesis H_0 in Equations (14.1), one can argue in the following way. If this hypothesis were to be incorrect, then we would expect to see quite some differences in the means (depending of course on the degree of violation of H_0). However, if H_0 were to be true, we would expect the sample means to be 'similar', i.e., not to vary considerably. Yet what would be a reasonable degree of variability to expect then in the observed group means? This should be related to the extent to which subject scores vary from one another within each of the four groups. Hence, if we can obtain an estimate of the extent of this variability, we can use it in evaluating whether the sample means vary from one another more than they would be expected to under the assumption that the null hypothesis H_0 is true.

This intuitive reasoning is the basis of the conceptual approach behind a statistical test of the null hypothesis of equal group means in ANOVA. Specifically, under the earlier made assumption of identical response variance in the populations in question (usually referred to as *homogeneity of variance assumption*), we can obtain an estimate of this common variance σ^2 using data from all available samples. Alternatively, under the null hypothesis H_0 (i.e., on the assumption of its being true) we can work out another estimate of σ^2 using only the group means. If the two variance estimates are similar, we could argue that the available data does not contain sufficient evidence to warrant rejection of the null hypothesis (14.1) of equal means. If the two variance estimates differ considerably, however, one may doubt the validity of this hypothesis H_0. This argument underlies the procedure of developing the ANOVA test statistic for examining group mean equality, which we sketch next (for further details, see e.g., King & Minium, 2003).

To this end, let us denote first the group sample sizes correspondingly by $n_1, n_2, ..., n_g$, and their sum by n, i.e., $n = n_1 + n_2 + ... + n_g$. Designate further by y_{ij} the score on the response variable of the ith subject in the jth group, and by $\bar{y}_{1.}, \bar{y}_{2.}, ..., \bar{y}_{g.}$ the means of this variable in the available g samples. To obtain an estimate of the (assumed) common variance σ^2 based on the degree to which response scores differ from one another within the groups, which we refer to as *within-group variance estimate*, we next work out for each group the squared individual mean deviations and add them across groups. The resulting sum is referred to as *within-group sum of squares*, denoted SS_W, and equals

$$(14.2) \qquad SS_W = \sum_{i=1}^{n_1}(y_{i1} - \bar{y}_{1.})^2 + \sum_{i=1}^{n_2}(y_{i2} - \bar{y}_{2.})^2 + ... + \sum_{i=1}^{n_g}(y_{ig} - \bar{y}_{g.})^2.$$

To obtain then the within-group variance estimate, we need to divide this sum SS_W by the number of independent sources of variability that contribute to it. This number is the degrees of freedom df associated with the sum SS_W. In order to work them out, we note that we started out with n such sources of variability (all initially available response scores in the overall sample), but used g of them to estimate the g group means. Hence, the degrees of freedom underlying SS_W are $df = n - g$. Denoting by s_j^2 the (common) variance estimate from the jth group, as we recall from Chapter 3

$$s_j^2 = \sum_{i=1}^{n_j}(y_{ij} - \bar{y}_{j.})^2/(n_j - 1),$$

and hence

(14.3) $$\sum_{i=1}^{n_g}(y_{ij} - \bar{y}_{j.})^2 = (n_j - 1)s_j^2$$

($j = 1,..., g$). Thus, from Equations (14.2) and (14.3) follows

(14.4) $$SS_W = (n_1 - 1)s_1^2 + (n_2 - 1)s_2^2 + ... + (n_g - 1)s_g^2.$$

Therefore, an estimate of the common variance σ^2, which is based on all groups—at times also referred to as *pooled variance estimate* (cf. Chapter 8 for the case $g = 2$)—is

(14.5) $$SS_W = \frac{(n_1 - 1)s_1^2 + (n_2 - 1)s_2^2 + ... + (n_g - 1)s_g^2}{n - g}.$$

Alternatively, using the group means it can be shown that another estimate of the common variance σ^2—which becomes quite informative under the null hypothesis—is (e.g., Agresti & Finlay, 2009)

(14.6) $$\frac{n_1(\bar{y}_{1.} - \bar{y}_{..})^2 + n_2(\bar{y}_{2.} - \bar{y}_{..})^2 + ... + n_g(\bar{y}_{g.} - \bar{y}_{..})^2}{g - 1},$$

where $\bar{y}_{..}$ denotes the overall mean obtained from all data on the response variable in the overall sample, which consists of all n subjects (units of analysis) disregarding group membership, i.e., pooling over groups. The numerator in Equation (14.6) is often referred to as *between-group sum of squares* and denoted SS_B, since it represents the variability of the sample means across the groups of the study (i.e., variability between groups in the response means). That is,

$$SS_B = n_1(\bar{y}_{1.} - \bar{y}_{..})^2 + n_2(\bar{y}_{2.} - \bar{y}_{..})^2 + ... + n_g(\bar{y}_{g.} - \bar{y}_{..})^2.$$

An interesting property of the between- and within-group sums of squares is that when they are added together, the sum of squares in the overall sample is obtained that is referred to as *total sum of squares* and denoted SS_T:

(14.7)
$$SS_T = \sum_{j=1}^{g}\sum_{i=1}^{n_j}(y_{ij}-\bar{y}_{..})^2 = SS_B + SS_W.$$

In Equation (14.7), SS_T is the sum of squared individual deviations from the overall mean $\bar{y}_{..}$ of each observation y_{ij} in the entire sample of n subjects ($i = 1,..., n_j, j = 1,..., g$). This equation in fact follows with some algebra from the following trivial decomposition of each response variable score y_{ij} as the sum of the overall mean $\bar{y}_{..}$, the group mean deviation from it, $\bar{y}_{j.} - \bar{y}_{..}$, and that individual score's deviation from the group mean, $y_{ij} - \bar{y}_{j.}$:

(14.8)
$$y_{ij} = \bar{y}_{..} + (\bar{y}_{j.} - \bar{y}_{..}) + (y_{ij} - \bar{y}_{j.}).$$

Equation (14.8) obviously holds always because the overall and group means appearing in it, $y_{..}$ and $\bar{y}_j$, cancel out in it (after disclosing brackets). That is, Equation (14.8) needs no assumptions in order to be true for any individual response score, y_{ij}, in an empirical study. Taking square from both sides of Equation (14.8) and summing up over i and j (i.e., over groups and individual observations within them) leads after some algebra to Equation (14.7).

Equation (14.7) represents a fundamental decomposition of observed variance into such stemming from individual differences on the response variable y within the groups (SS_W) and variability of its means across the groups (SS_B). That is, (14.7) is a break-up of observed variance into between- and within-group components. Using this variance decomposition and the earlier made assumptions, it can be shown (e.g., King & Minium, 2003) that when the studied population means are the same—i.e., the null hypothesis H_0 is true—the two possible estimates (14.5) and (14.6) of the common variance σ^2 should be close in magnitude, i.e., their ratio should be close to 1. When this hypothesis H_0 is incorrect, however, the estimate resulting from the variability among the sample means will be expected to be larger than that resulting from within the groups. The extent to which the former estimate will be larger than the latter, depends on the degree to which the null hypothesis is violated, i.e., the extent to which the population means differ.

This fact is the basis for using the ratio of these two variance estimates,

(14.9)
$$F = \frac{SS_B/(g-1)}{SS_W/(n-g)},$$

as a test statistic of the null hypothesis H_0 in Equations (14.1) stipulating population mean equality. The ratio in (14.9) is frequently referred to as F-ratio, or ANOVA F-ratio. Specifically, when this F-ratio is close to one in an empirical study, one may conclude that there is no strong evidence in it against the tested null hypothesis H_0. Conversely, when the F-ratio (14.9) is sufficiently larger than one, then this null hypothesis cannot be considered credible and may be rejected. It has been shown that when H_0 is true, the

F-ratio (14.9) follows an F-distribution (see Chapter 9) with degrees of freedom $d_1 = g - 1$ and $d_2 = n - g$ (King & Minium, 2003). The result of this test is readily provided by statistical software, in particular R, as is its associated p-value that can be used in making a decision about the null hypothesis of equal group means.

We illustrate this discussion using the data in Example 14.1. In that study, a researcher was interested in examining whether there were any state differences in depression. The researcher was specifically concerned with testing the null hypothesis

$$(14.10) \qquad H_0: \mu_1 = \mu_2 = \mu_3 = \mu_4,$$

that is, with examining whether there were no depression mean differences across the four states involved. To respond to this question, it would be instructive first to obtain the fundamental variance decomposition (14.7) with the software R. We accomplish this variance break-up using the command 'aov' (short for "analysis of variance"):

```
> aov(y~state)
```

We note that within parentheses we state first the response variable—in this example y—and then the factor variable, here 'state'. Thereby, we connect these two variables with the '~' sign, the same sign we used in the last two chapters when carrying out regression analysis. We will see later in this chapter that this is not a coincidence, as we explore the relationship between ANOVA and regression analysis and find out that there is a close connection between these two methodologies. The result of applying the response variance decomposition in the current example is as follows

```
Call:
aov(formula = y ~ state)

Terms:
                     state Residuals
Sum of Squares     261.228 15429.919
Deg. of Freedom          3       152
Residual standard error: 10.07535
Estimated effects may be unbalanced
```

Accordingly, just over 261 units of variance are due to the factor 'state', out of the total $15429.919 + 261.228 = 15691.147$ units of variability in the depression scores across the 156 elderly persons in this study. The estimate of the (assumed) common variance, the squared standard error, is here 10.075^2 = 101.510.

While this is an informative decomposition of observed variance, we are interested here primarily in seeing whether there is sufficient evidence in the data that would warrant rejection of the null hypothesis H_0 in Equations (14.10) that is of concern to test. This question is similarly readily responded to with R, using the command 'anova', whereby we can use as an argument the linear model relating the response with the factor variable (output provided immediately after command):

```
> anova(lm(y~state))
```

```
Analysis of Variance Table
Response: y
            Df   Sum Sq  Mean Sq  F value  Pr(>F)
state        3    261.2     87.1   0.8578  0.4645
Residuals  152  15429.9    101.5
```

This output contains some of the information we obtained with the command 'aov', but in addition we have now the value of the F-ratio (14.9) for this study and in particular its associated p-value. Since the p-value is larger than a reasonable significance level, we conclude that the null hypothesis in Equations (14.10) may be considered retainable. Before we place more trust in this result, however, we need to address an important assumption made in developing the ANOVA test, that of variance homogeneity. As will be recalled from the preceding Section 14.1, this assumption stipulates that the depression score variances are the same in the four groups involved—with this common variance denoted σ^2 throughout.

To address the plausibility of this assumption, we can test the hypothesis that the variances of the depression scores are the same in the four studied groups. (Note that this is not the group mean equality hypothesis (14.1) of focal interest in ANOVA, but simply of one underlying assumption.) We accomplish this with R using the command 'bartlett.test' (result given immediately beneath it):

```
> bartlett.test(y~state)
        Bartlett test of homogeneity of variances
data:  y by state
Bartlett's K-squared 0.558, df = 3, p-value = 0.906
```

As we can see from this short output, the variance homogeneity test—named after a prominent statistician of the past century, M. Bartlett—is associated with a nonsignificant p-value. This result shows that the assumption of equal variances of depression scores across the four groups under consideration may be viewed as plausible. We note in this regard that if in a given study this variance homogeneity assumption is found not to be plausible, one can use an approximation to the ANOVA F-test in (14.9) that is due to Welch, in order to test the mean equality hypothesis H_0. This approximation is available in R with the command 'oneway.test(y~factor)', where one provides for 'factor' the name of the group membership variable (e.g., Crawley, 2005). Returning to the example of concern here, given the last presented results we can now place more trust in the earlier ANOVA finding of a nonsignificant F-ratio that suggested we may reject the null hypothesis of equal means. In particular, we can interpret that finding as indicative of no mean differences in older adults' depression levels across the four studied states.

As an aside at this point, we note in passing that the nonsignificant ANOVA F-ratio and variance homogeneity test do not allow us to conclude that there are no differences in aged adults' depression across all states in the country. Rather, our results are valid only for the four states included in this example, i.e., for these four fixed states from which depression data were available for the above analysis. For this reason, the ANOVA modeling approach we just conducted is also commonly referred to as a "fixed effect" analysis of variance, a reference we will make on a few occasions again later in the book (cf. Raudenbush & Bryk, 2002, for an alternative approach and assumptions allowing possible conclusions beyond the particular states included in an empirical study).

Whenever we carry out an ANOVA, it is useful to also graphically represent the relationships between the studied groups with regard to the response variable. As we discussed in Chapter 3, this is conveniently achieved using the graphical tool of the boxplot, and in particular comparing the boxplots of the four groups in question in the presently considered study. Such a comparison is made feasible using the command 'boxplot', discussed in detail in that chapter, which becomes particularly helpful when employed in conjunction with ANOVA. For our Example 14.1, we obtain a simultaneous display of the four group boxplots with the following command (see Chapter 3):

```
> boxplot(y~state)
```

Its results are presented in Figure 14.1. As we can see from Figure 14.1, a particularly useful feature of this simultaneous display of the four groups' boxplots is that it allows us to judge their differences in central tendency in relation to their variability on the response variable. We readily observe from Figure 14.1 that the central tendency measures for the four groups involved differ somewhat (cf. Chapter 3). However, as mentioned earlier in this chap-

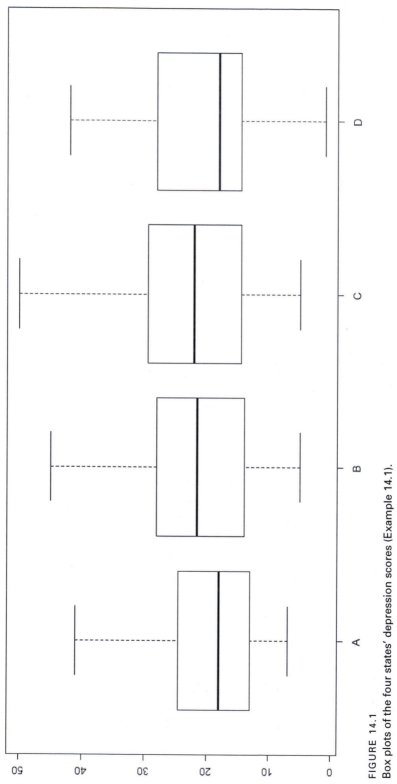

FIGURE 14.1
Box plots of the four states' depression scores (Example 14.1).

ter, some group differences should be expected in the analyzed samples since they are not identical to the populations studied.

The simultaneous boxplot representation for all examined groups in an ANOVA setting is especially helpful in assessing the extent to which these observed differences "matter," i.e., what their relationship is to the variability of the scores in the studied groups. When in Figure 14.1 the group differences in central tendency are compared to the group variability on the response as reflected in the similar vertical distances between the ends of the two associated whiskers per boxplot, the central tendency differences across the four groups are no more impressive. Loosely speaking, the F-test (14.9) evaluates the mean group differences in relation to the within-group variability of the scores. When these differences are sufficiently smaller than that variability, a nonsignificant result ensues. This is precisely the situation we are dealing with in the currently considered Example 14.1.

14.3. FOLLOW-UP ANALYSES

When the result of an ANOVA application is that the underlying null hypothesis is not rejected (as in Example 14.1), the interpretation as mentioned is that there are no mean group differences. The implication then is that no two groups differ in their means on the response variable of concern. In that case, there may be limited remaining interest in the study, if any, as far as mean relationships across groups are concerned. However, when the overall null hypothesis (14.1) is rejected, the interpretation is that at least two groups have different means. A natural question that arises, then, is what are the reasons for this hypothesis rejection? This query asks which groups are actually different in their means.

This question is addressed by what is frequently referred to as *ANOVA follow-up analyses*. These are post hoc analyses since they are performed after the overall (global, or omnibus) null hypothesis (14.1) has been tested and rejected. There are a number of post hoc procedures, also at times referred to as *multiple comparison* or *multiple testing procedures*, that have been proposed over the past several decades. In fact, there are more than a dozen such tests available in the literature. Given the introductory nature of this book, we will only be concerned with a particular post hoc procedure called Tukey's honestly significant difference (HSD), which is often of interest to use as a follow-up of a significant ANOVA F-test, and we refer the reader to alternative treatments for other multiple-testing procedures (e.g., Howell, 2009; Kirk, 2007).

Tukey's HSD method has been specifically devised to enable testing for pair-wise group differences upon rejection of the ANOVA null hypothesis H_0 in Equations (14.1). This method responds to the frequently raised question in empirical research, concerning which particular groups differ from one another. The rationale behind Tukey's procedure is the realization that testing the difference between any two groups, after knowledge is available that the null hypothesis H_0 has been rejected, should be carried out in such a way that only more pronounced pair-wise group differences are proclaimed as significant than what would be the case if it was not known that H_0 was rejected in the first instance. This goal will be accomplished if one proclaims as significantly differing, at a prespecified significance level, only such pairs of groups with the property that the absolute value of their mean difference exceeds the following expression

$$(14.12) \qquad q\sqrt{\frac{1}{2}s^2(1/n_i + 1/n_j)}.$$

In Equation (14.12), q is a corresponding quantile of a distribution known as the *studentized range distribution* that is implemented in statistical software; s^2 is the estimate of the common variance across the groups studied; and n_i and n_j are the sample sizes of the two groups involved in a particular comparison—say of the ith and jth group means ($i, j = 1,..., g, i \neq j$; e.g., Verzani, 2005). Tukey's HSD method is readily available in statistical software, in particular R, where the method is invoked by using the command 'TukeyHSD' on the outcome of an 'aov' command.

To illustrate this discussion, we use the following example:

Example 14.2: Suppose we have data from an educational motivation study of $n = 146$ middle school students from several socioeconomic status (SES) groups. The data are available in the file CH14_EX2.dat, where the motivation score is denoted 'y' and the SES group membership as 'ses'.

As pointed out earlier in this chapter, we first need to read in the data and declare the 'ses' variable as a factor with 4 levels—'low', 'middle', 'high', and 'upper', corresponding to the original scores of 1 through 4 on this variable (see Section 14.2 for the needed R commands). Next we test the null hypothesis of no SES differences in motivation (output presented immediately following command):

```
> anova(lm(y~ses))


Analysis of Variance Table

Response: y
          Df  Sum Sq Mean Sq F value   Pr(>F)
ses        3  1836.2   612.1  7.1106 0.0001744 ***
```

```
Residuals 142 12223.2    86.1

---

Signif. codes:  0 '***' 0.001 '**' 0.01 '*' 0.05 '.' 0.1 ' ' 1
```

We see that the F-test is associated with a significant result here. That is, we can reject the null hypothesis of no SES differences in motivation and conclude that at least two SES groups have different mean level of motivation. (The Bartlett's test of the variance homogeneity assumption is nonsignificant here, as can be readily found using the earlier mentioned command 'bartlett. test' on this four-group data set.) We then graphically display the boxplots of the four groups:

```
> boxplot(y~ses)
```

The results of this command are presented in Figure 14.2. We see from the simultaneous display of the four boxplots in Figure 14.2 that the high SES group has the largest central tendency measure and is also most compact in terms of variability of the motivation scores. Given the significant mean differences finding above, we would like to see now which pairs of groups have different means. We wish to ascertain statistically these differences, and for this aim we apply the Tukey's HSD method (note the use of the 'aov' command as argument of this post hoc analysis command):

```
> TukeyHSD(aov(lm(y~ses)))

  Tukey multiple comparisons of means
    95% family-wise confidence level

Fit: aov(formula = lm(y ~ ses))

$ses
                   diff         lwr       upr      p adj
middle-low     2.684685  -2.9618758  8.331245 0.6050505
high-low       9.090090   3.4435296 14.736651 0.0002879
upper-low      1.000000  -4.6851040  6.685104 0.9681069
high-middle    6.405405   0.7976534 12.013157 0.0181971
upper-middle  -1.684685  -7.3312451  3.961876 0.8653605
upper-high    -8.090090 -13.7366505 -2.443530 0.0015874
```

This output presents the pair-wise group mean differences in the column titled 'diff'. These differences are followed by their confidence intervals—adjusted as mentioned for the multiplicity of these pair-wise comparisons—in

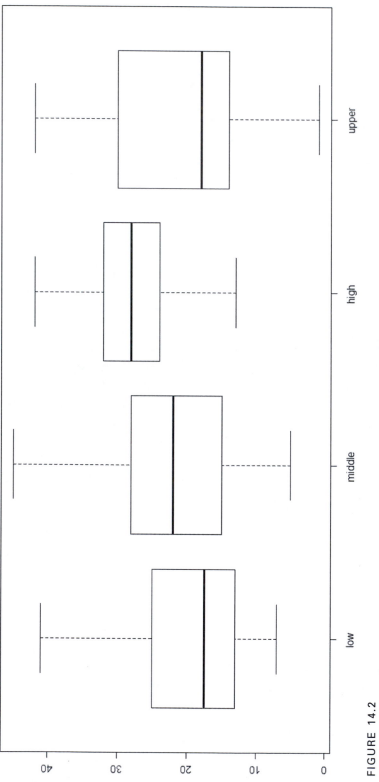

FIGURE 14.2
Box plots of the four SES group educational motivation scores (Example 14.2).

the column titled 'lwr' and 'upr' (for their lower and upper limits, respectively). The last column, 'p adj', presents the p-values associated with testing the set of $4.3/2 = 6$ pair-wise differences. These p-values are also adjusted for the fact that six tests rather than a single test are carried out on the same data set. We see from the last column that the high SES group differs significantly from each other group, being higher on mean motivation than any of them in the study. At the same time, the remaining three SES groups do not show any significant differences among themselves as far as their mean motivation level is concerned. Hence, it may be suggested that the rejection of the overall null hypothesis (14.1) of equal educational motivation means across the four SES groups considered, may have been primarily the result of the high SES group having a motivation mean higher than any of the remaining three SES groups. The other three SES groups do not differ considerably from one another in their mean motivation levels (see also Figure 14.2).

14.4. TWO-WAY AND HIGHER-ORDER ANALYSIS OF VARIANCE

The previous sections examined settings in which observed subjects were classified into groups (populations) only according to a single categorical variable. That is, the groups in question represented the levels of a single factor under consideration. For instance, in Example 14.1 this factor was state, while in Example 14.2 it was socioeconomic status (SES). As a consequence, no further differentiation between subjects was taken into account in these considered settings. For this reason, the ANOVA we dealt with in Sections 14.1 and 14.2 is also referred to as *one-way analysis of variance* (one-way ANOVA layout or design), to emphasize that only a single variable is assumed to contribute to individual differences on an outcome variable of interest.

Behavioral and social research, however, is typically concerned with complex phenomena that cannot be understood well by considering single categorical variables (group membership) as possibly contributing to observed subject differences. Given that these phenomena are usually multifactorially determined, their modeling will be more realistic when additional variables are included into the analyses. When two factors (categorical variables) are assumed to contribute to individual differences on a response variable, the corresponding analytic approach is referred to as two-way ANOVA (two-way ANOVA layout or design), and as higher-order ANOVA if more than two categorical variables are considered simultaneously—e.g., a three-way ANOVA. For example, when studying educational motivation and student differences in it, gender differences may as well be seen as a potential contributor to individual differences on motivation in addition to socioeconomic status. In this case, by considering also gender one would be dealing with two rather than a single factor—viz., SES and gender. The corresponding analysis of response variability will then account for the possible contributions of these two factors. We turn next to a description of such analytic approaches.

In order to be in a position to discuss two-way and higher-order ANOVA, it is instructive to return for a moment to Section 14.2, where the test of the null hypothesis of no mean differences across groups with regard to a single factor was of interest. In that section, of fundamental relevance was the decomposition (14.7) of the observed variability, i.e., sum of squares, on the response variable. Accordingly, the observed sum of squares SS_T was broken down into a between-group part, denoted SS_B, and a within-group part, denoted SS_W. This decomposition can also be interpreted as stating that SS_B is the part of observed variance (sum of squares) on the response variable, which is due to the factor under consideration whose levels represent the groups in the study. For instance, in Example 14.1, SS_B is the part of older adults' differences in depression that is accounted for by the factor 'state' (state residency), with its four levels representing the four states included in the study. Similarly, in Example 14.2, SS_B is the part of student differences in educational motivation scores that is explained by the factor socioeconomic status, with its four levels representing the four groups examined.

The decomposition of response variance is also of fundamental relevance in two-way and higher-order ANOVAs. In contrast to the preceding two sections dealing with one-way ANOVAs, however, in a two-way ANOVA we have two factors contributing to individual differences—e.g., gender and SES in the above-mentioned motivation study. Accordingly, there are two parts of the overall sum of squares SS_T on the outcome measure that they account for. In addition, there is a new part of the total sum of squares that has no counterpart in our earlier ANOVA discussions. Specifically, in order to properly model the sources of individual differences in a setting with two factors (and similarly with more than two factors), we need to account for the fact that the effect of one of the factors upon the response variable may depend on the level of the other factor. For example, when we include both gender and SES as factors in the motivation study, we need to keep in mind that the effect of SES on motivation may be different for boys relative to its effect for girls. This is tantamount to saying that the gender differences in educational motivation may not be the same in each of the four SES groups of the study. This possibility of differential effect upon the response of one of the factors, depending on the levels of the other factor, is captured by the concept of factor *interaction*. An interaction between two factors is present when the effect of one of them on the outcome measure is not the same across the levels of the other factor. In the motivation study, an interaction between the factors gender and SES would imply that SES differences in motivation are not the same for boys and for girls, and that conversely the boy-girl differences in motivation depend on SES (SES group).

The possibility that there is an interaction does not mean that it will always exist—or even be of a marked magnitude—in an empirical study with two or more factors. If in an empirical setting the effect of one of the factors is the same regardless of the level of the other factor considered, then there is no interaction. In the motivation study, lack of interaction between gender and SES would imply that the boy-girl differences in motivation are the same regardless of SES, and that the SES impact upon motivation is the same for both genders. Whether an interaction is present or not in a study depends obviously on the particular phenomenon researched and can be examined using the available data from that study.

To evaluate the empirical evidence for an interaction, or lack thereof, in a two-way ANOVA setting, instrumental use is made of the following decomposition of the response variance into sources attributable to each of the two factors—denoted, say, A and B—and their possible interaction (subindexed by "AB"; e.g., Howell, 2009):

$$(14.13) \qquad SS_T = SS_A + SS_B + SS_{AB} + SS_R.$$

In Equation (14.13), the symbol SS is used to designate the sum of squares attributable to the factor in its subindex, the interaction, or the residual—that is, to all other factors not explicitly included in the right-hand side of (14.13). (We assume in the remainder of this chapter that there is more than a single observation in any factor level combination, as will frequently be the case in an observational behavioral or social study.) To test the significance of the interaction, we can reason in the following way: If we assume the null hypothesis of no interaction to be true, then the interaction and residual sum of squares—SS_{AB} and SS_R—should evaluate each the residual variance when either of them is averaged by dividing with its degrees of freedom, leading to their corresponding *mean sum of squares*, denoted MSS_{AB} and MSS_R. Therefore, under the null hypothesis of no interaction of the factors A and B, the F-ratio

$$(14.14) \qquad F = MSS_{AB}/MSS_R = (SS_{AB}/df_{AB})/(SS_R/df_R)$$

can be expected to be close to one. In Equation (14.14), df_{AB} are the degrees of freedom for the interaction that can be shown to equal the product of the degrees of freedom df_A and df_B associated with the two factors A and B, and df_R are the degrees of freedom for the residual. More specifically, if k and p are the number of levels of factors A and B, respectively, then $df_A = k - 1$, $df_B = p - 1$, $df_{AB} = (k - 1)(p - 1)$, and $df_R = n - k - p - (k - 1)(p - 1)$ holds (Agresti & Finlay, 2009).

Furthermore, under the null hypothesis of no interaction, it can be shown that the F-ratio in (14.14) follows an F-distribution with df_{AB} and df_R degrees of freedom (Howell, 2009). In an empirical setting, statistical software—in particular R—provides readily the value of this F-ratio and its associated p-value. A small enough p-value for the F-ratio—viz., smaller than a preset significance level that can as usual be chosen to be $\alpha = .05$—can be interpreted as indicative of sufficient evidence in the analyzed data to warrant rejection of the null hypothesis of no interaction. When this p-value is higher than the preset significance level, the interpretation is that there is not enough evidence in the analyzed data that would allow us to reject the null hypothesis of no interaction, and then we can retain this hypothesis. (For the case of a single observation per factor level combination, which can be viewed as rare in much of empirical social and behavioral research, see Howell, 2009.)

The concept of interaction reflects the possibility of the effect of one of the factors to depend on the level of the other factor, but it does not respond to the query whether a factor itself has an overall effect, i.e., disregarding the other factor. Such an effect is referred to as *main effect* and would be present when the group means on this factor (pooling over the levels of the other factor, i.e., disregarding them) are sufficiently distinct. For a given factor, say A, the null hypothesis pertaining to its main effect is that the factor "does not matter," i.e., its main effect is zero. In other words, this factor-specific null hypothesis asserts that the means of the groups that represent the levels of factor A—irrespective of those of the other factor—are not distinct in the population. Similarly to (14.14), this null hypothesis can be tested using the F-ratio

$$(14.15) \qquad F = MSS_A/MSS_R = (SS_A/df_A)/(SS_R/df_R).$$

This ratio follows under the null hypothesis an F-distribution with df_A and df_R degrees of freedom (e.g., Agresti & Finlay, 2009). The value of the F-ratio (14.15) is also routinely provided by statistical software, in particular R, as is its associated p-value that allows in the usual manner a decision whether to reject or consider retainable the pertinent null hypothesis.

The interpretation of the main effect for either factor considered in a two-way ANOVA is substantially easier when there is no interaction of the two factors involved in it. In case they interact, however, it is not as straightforward to interpret the main effects of the factors. One may argue then that each of these main effects represents an average effect of the corresponding factor across the levels of the other factor involved in the interaction. Whenever that average is deemed by a researcher to be substantively relevant, this interpretation can be used in an empirical setting. In some cases, however, this average effect may not be of interest, and then it would be appropriate to consider the effect of factor A, say, within each of the levels of factor B (or conversely). This study of level-specific effects of the former factor is often referred to as *simple effects examination*, and it can be similarly readily carried out with statistical software after for instance appropriately selecting the subjects in each of the levels of the other factor participating in the interaction.

We illustrate this discussion by returning to Example 14.2 dealing with SES differences in educational motivation, but now considering also the gender of the students. (The corresponding data is found in the file CH14_EX3.dat, with the same variable names and the added gender variable with this label.) Since we consider here two factors—SES and gender—we are dealing with a two-way ANOVA, and we carry it out with R using the following command:

```
> anova(lm(y~ses+gender+ses*gender))
```

Before we discuss its output, we note that in the argument of the command 'lm' we list both factors in an additive fashion as well as their interaction denoted by asterisk. (A shorter version of this argument is as 'y~ses*gender', but we use here the above in order to emphasize the inclusion of the interaction into the analysis.) The ANOVA variance table that results is provided next.

```
Analysis of Variance Table


Response: y
            Df  Sum Sq Mean Sq F value    Pr(>F)
ses          3  1836.2   612.1  7.3844 0.0001263 ***
gender       1   275.5   275.5  3.3236 0.0704578 .
ses:gender   3   509.3   169.8  2.0484 0.1099760
Residuals  138 11438.4    82.9

---
Signif. codes:  0 '***' 0.001 '**' 0.01 '*' 0.05 '.' 0.1 ' ' 1
```

As we see from this output, the interaction of the two factors (formally denoted here "ses:gender") is associated with a *p*-value of .11 and is thus larger than a typical significance level. For this reason, the interaction is not significant, which we interpret as suggesting that the effect (if any) of SES upon motivation is the same for boys and girls. Alternatively, we can interpret this finding as suggesting that the gender differences in motivation (if any) are the same in each SES group.

Since there is no interaction of SES and gender, the interpretation of the main effect of either factor is straightforward, as mentioned earlier in this section. Due to the fact that the SES factor is associated with a small *p*-value (smaller than .05 usually employed as a significance level), we conclude that there are SES differences in motivation pooling over gender, i.e., disregarding gender. That is, according to the analyzed data, different SES groups have on average different educational motivation, irrespective of gender. Further, due to the fact that the *p*-value associated with the factor 'gender' is not significant, it is suggested that there is no gender effect. That is, boys and girls do not seem to differ in educational motivation, disregarding their SES.

Just as was done in a one-way ANOVA, it is helpful to examine also the boxplots of the eight groups involved in this study, which is achieved with the command 'boxplot' (note the notation used for the term appearing after the '~' sign, in order to ensure that all eight group boxplots are obtained):

```
> boxplot(y~ses:gender)
```

The resulting boxplots are presented in Figure 14.3. These eight boxplots reveal that the boys and girls in the high SES group have the highest level of motivation, while those in the upper SES group tend to be the lowest. The lack of interaction between gender and SES in this example is seen in the graphical representation in Figure 14.3 by observing that the same pattern of increase and then drop is found for boys and for girls, when one considers also their SES in increasing order (from 'low' to 'upper', within each of the genders—represented by the first four and last four boxes, respectively).

The discussion in this section of two-way ANOVA is directly extended to the case of higher-order ANOVA, e.g., three-way ANOVA. An increase in the number of factors simultaneously considered in a study beyond three is, however, associated with considerably larger difficulties in the substantive inter-

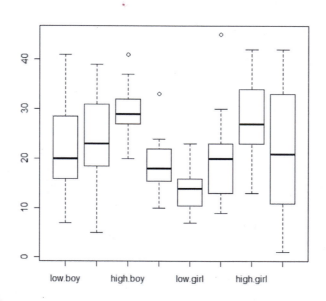

FIGURE 14.3.

Box plots of motivation scores for eight SES and gender groups (Example 14.3).

pretation of the three-way and higher-order interactions, if present. For instance, the interaction of three factors—denoted, say, A, B, and C—can be interpreted as differences in the degree to which the interaction of the factors A and B, say, differs across levels of the factor C. Such an interpretation is possible to give in principle for higher-order interactions as well—e.g., of factors A, B, C, and D—namely by "reducing" them to differences in lower-order interactions across the levels of the remaining factor. However, it may well be exceedingly difficult to attach to such interpretations specific substantive meaning in a given empirical study, especially with increasing number of factors involved. Often, to avoid these interpretational difficulties, behavioral and social researchers opt for not considering ANOVA layouts (designs) with more than three factors, except in cases when higher than three-way interactions are not significant.

We limit our discussion to the consideration of three-way and higher-order ANOVA settings in this section, due to an important relationship of ANOVA to regression analysis. This relationship, which we deal with in the next section, allows one to readily perform higher-order ANOVA with appropriately devised regression analysis models.

14.5. RELATIONSHIP BETWEEN ANALYSIS OF VARIANCE AND REGRESSION ANALYSIS

Our preceding discussion of ANOVA emphasized the relevance of this statistical method when one is concerned with examining population differences on an outcome measure. As we have seen so far, at the center of ANOVA is the study of the relationship between the means of a response variable and group (population) membership that we can also treat as a variable in its own right. This is not the first time in the book, however, that we dealt with the relationship between two variables. In particular, in Chapters 11, 12, and 13 we discussed first the concept of correlation and then the regression analysis approach that we have used to relate a continuous (quantitative) explanatory variable to a continuous response variable.

As it turns out, the fundamental principle of least squares estimation that underlies regression analysis is more generally applicable beyond settings where all independent variables involved are continuous (or approximately so). Indeed, regression analysis can be used also in cases where one or more predictors are categorical, i.e., measured on a nominal or ordinal scale. In fact, in Example 13.2 in the last chapter, we already used regression analysis as a way to explain variance in a quantitative variable—college aspiration—employing several predictors including gender and SES that were there binary variables with values of 0 and 1. (For convenience, we assume that whenever a binary variable is used, its values have been recorded as 0 and 1.)

Such an application of regression analysis with categorical independent variables is also possible when the latter have more than two categories, but after their values are appropriately recoded. The procedure of recoding is not needed when a binary independent variable is used as mentioned, yet it becomes necessary for a regression analysis application when that factor has more than two levels, in which case it is also called *polytomous*. It can be shown that employing regression with recoded polytomous predictors (factors) leads to the same results as a corresponding application of ANOVA for examining mean differences with regard to these factors (e.g., Howell, 2009).

The essence of the recoding of polytomous variables is the creation of new variables—typically referred to as *dummy variables*—that equivalently represent the information about group membership for each subject in the overall sample on each initial categorical independent variable. (These are called dummy variables since they are not actually collected or observed in the empirical study but are instead created subsequently in order to achieve a particular goal—the representation of group membership information.) More concretely, suppose a considered explanatory variable x is a factor with k levels (groups, populations), i.e., a polytomous measure with k categories ($k > 2$). Thereby, if a subject is a member of the qth group (population), let his or her initial score on x be q ($1 \leq q \leq k$). To effect the recoding for this variable, we introduce $k - 1$ new variables—the above dummy variables—which we denote x_1 through x_{k-1}.

In order to define these dummy variables, we need first to decide which of the k categories (groups) of the original variable x we wish to use as a *reference category* or *reference group*. In an empirical study with a control group (and several experimental groups), one often uses as a reference group or category that control group. The reason is that with this choice one can subsequently compare all remaining groups to this control group. In studies where there is no control group, one can use as a reference category a group with a particular status or of interest to compare to the remaining groups (levels) on the original factor x. When there is no such group, as a reference group one can choose any of the groups. (One should then bear in mind that its particular selection will affect the substantive interpretations of the final results.) Once this reference group is determined, as a next step we assign to all subjects in it the value of 0 on all dummy variables x_1 through x_{k-1}. For the remaining $k - 1$ groups, we proceed as follows: for the jth of them, we assign the value of 1 to its subjects on x_j and 0 on all remaining dummy variables ($j = 1,...,$ $k - 1$).

To illustrate this process, let us return to Example 14.2 that we discussed earlier. In this example, we used the two factors (categorical variables) 'gender' and 'ses' in a study of college aspiration. Since the factor 'gender' is a binary variable that takes values 0 for males and 1 for females, as mentioned above we do not need to do any recoding of its values. The factor 'ses' is, however, a polytomous variable with $k = 4$ categories. Hence, to recode group membership with regard to socioeconomic status (SES), we introduce $k - 1 = 3$ dummy variables, denoted x_1 through x_3. Choosing the SES category 'low' as a reference group—which here is an essentially arbitrary decision—all 36 students in this group receive a 0 on the variables x_1 through x_3. (One can use the command 'summary(ses)' to readily find out the SES group sample sizes in this study.) Then all 37 students in the 'middle' SES group receive a 1 on the dummy variable x_1 but 0's on x_2 and x_3. Similarly, all 37 students in the 'high' SES group receive a 1 on the dummy variable x_2 but 0's on x_1 and x_3. Finally, all 36 students in the 'upper' SES group receive a 1 on the dummy variable x_3 but 0's on x_1 and x_2. In this way, all studied subjects obtain a score of 0 or 1 on each of the three newly defined variables x_1 through x_3.

These three dummy variables have the property that by looking at them one can determine uniquely which SES group a given student belongs to. That is, the three dummy variables x_1 through x_3 equivalently represent all information available initially about group membership for each of the 146 subjects participating in this study. Thereby, to reflect correctly this information, we need the three dummy variables—no single one or a pair of them contains the complete group information for all subjects in the available sample. Table 14.1 contains the original data and the added three dummy variables for the first 20 students in Example 14.2 from Section 14.4. (The data for all students, with the added three dummy variables, can be found in the file CH14_EX4.dat.)

As indicated earlier, the recoded data set contains all original data of Example 14.2 and no additional information. In fact, the dummy variables x_1 through x_3 reflect the same information as that pertaining to group membership with regard to SES, which is contained in the original variable 'ses'. The gain in constructing the three dummy variables x_1 through x_3 is that when we use them along with the gender variable, we can carry out ANOVA by employing regression analysis rather than the traditional analysis of variance framework discussed in the preceding sections of this chapter. This will be possible if we include the product of the dummy variables across factors as variables that represent in their entirety the interaction in the associated ANOVA model. This inclusion is automatically carried out by the statistical software used, in particular R, which also performs internally the dummy coding we discussed in this Section 14.5.

The earlier mentioned equivalence of the modeling results when studying group mean differences using the conventional ANOVA framework on the one hand, and corresponding regression analysis approach on the other hand, is readily demonstrated on the recoded data from Example 14.2. To this end, given that we already have the pertinent ANOVA results presented in Section

Table 14.1   Original variables and added dummy variables for the first 20 subjects in Example 14.2 (variable names in top row; see Section 14.2 and file CH14_EX4.dat for the entire recoded data set).

y	ses	gender	x1	x2	x3
20	2	0	1	0	0
37	3	0	0	1	0
29	3	0	0	1	0
28	3	1	0	1	0
24	4	0	0	0	1
14	4	1	0	0	1
12	1	1	0	0	0
45	2	1	1	0	0
6	2	0	1	0	0
10	4	1	0	0	1
16	1	0	0	0	0
42	3	1	0	1	0
20	2	1	1	0	0
1	4	1	0	0	1
13	1	0	0	0	0
13	1	0	0	0	0
15	2	0	1	0	0
32	3	1	0	1	0
27	3	0	0	1	0
37	3	1	0	1	0

14.4, all we need to do here is carry out a regression analysis using as predictors the factors 'gender' and 'ses' as well as their interaction. As indicated above, this interaction will be represented here by the three products of each dummy variable x_1 through x_3 with gender.

We begin our analyses by creating as an R-object the output of a regression analysis relating the response variable 'y' to SES, gender, and their interaction. We achieve this aim as follows (output provided immediately beneath command):

```
> ra1 = lm(y~ses+gender+ses*gender)
```

```
> summary(ra1)
```

```
Call:
lm(formula = y ~ ses + gender + ses * gender)
```

```
Residuals:
     Min        1Q     Median        3Q        Max
-20.4000   -5.6146    -0.8333     5.6900    25.0000
```

Coefficients:

	Estimate	Std. Error	t value	Pr(>|t|)	
(Intercept)	22.583	1.858	12.152	<2e-16	***
sesmed	1.042	2.628	0.396	0.6925	
seshigh	7.167	3.219	2.226	0.0276	*
sesupper	-3.583	3.315	-1.081	0.2816	
gendergirl	-8.750	3.219	-2.718	0.0074	**
sesmed:gendergirl	5.125	4.493	1.141	0.2560	
seshigh:gendergirl	7.280	4.537	1.605	0.1109	
sesupper:gendergirl	11.150	4.606	2.421	0.0168	*

```
---
Signif. codes:  0 '***' 0.001 '**' 0.01 '*' 0.05 '.' 0.1 ' ' 1
```

Residual standard error: 9.104 on 138 degrees of freedom

Multiple R-squared: 0.1864,   Adjusted R-squared: 0.1452

F-statistic: 4.517 on 7 and 138 DF, p-value: 0.0001461

Before we examine the output in detail, we reiterate that by virtue of our initial definition of the variable 'ses' as a factor (with four levels), we do not need to explicitly create the three dummy variables needed here in order to represent group membership with regard to this variable. In fact, that definition of 'ses' as a factor variable leads to the internal generation by R of these variables, which are thereby automatically made available for subsequent analyses, and in particular for the regression analysis (linear modeling) requested with the pertinent R command 'lm' given above.

The output generated by the last regression command contains information pertaining to the estimates, standard errors, and hypothesis tests for each of the three dummy variables used as mentioned internally by R for group membership coding with regard to the polytomous variable 'ses'. Next presented is information with regard to the group membership variable identifying gender (with the category 'boy' being assigned the value of 0 on it, as mentioned earlier—see fourth line of this output section). As we indicated above, the interaction of 'ses' and 'gender' is represented by the product of each of the three dummy variables for SES, x_1 through x_3, with that variable for 'gender'. This interaction is reflected in the last three lines of this coefficient estimates table.

The estimates and related information provided in this output is too detailed for our goals in a typical ANOVA setting. In such a setting, we usually wish to know whether the interaction effect is significant, in its entirety, as well as whether there are main effects of the factors involved. To obtain this combined information for each of these three effects (two main effects and an interaction), we need the corresponding analysis of variance table. We furnish this table with the R command 'anova' applied on the R-object being the discussed R output for the last regression analysis:

```
> anova(ra1)



Analysis of Variance Table

Response: y
            Df  Sum Sq  Mean Sq  F value    Pr(>F)
ses          3  1836.2   612.1   7.3844  0.0001263 ***
gender       1   275.5   275.5   3.3236  0.0704578 .
ses:gender   3   509.3   169.8   2.0484  0.1099760
Residuals  138 11438.4    82.9
---
Signif. codes:  0 '***' 0.001 '**' 0.01 '*' 0.05 '.' 0.1 ' ' 1
```

As we can see by direct comparison, this output is identical to the one we obtained in Section 14.4 when discussing the ANOVA approach and associated R output while carrying out the latter analysis on the same data set. That is, the results of that two-way ANOVA are identical to these obtained using regression analysis as here, with appropriately constructed dummy variables representing group membership on the factors involved in the ANOVA. In fact, we observe that ANOVA was carried out with R in Section 14.4 using the same command employed in the current section to conduct the corresponding regression analysis. This identity of commands follows from the way statistical software—and in particular R—internally carry out ANOVA, viz., through a corresponding regression analysis after defining the factors involved as categorical variables (see Section 14.1 for specific commands to be used for that purpose).

The equivalence between ANOVA and appropriately developed regression models also holds in the case of higher-order ANOVA and is internally capitalized on automatically by the used software, such as R. Specifically, interactions in these models (two-way or higher-order interactions) are represented then as mentioned by a set of cross-products of each dummy variable for one of the factors with each dummy variable for any of the remaining factors involved in the interaction. All these products then are included in a single step in the ensuing regression analysis. Similarly, the main effect of any factor is represented by the set of dummy variables pertaining to it, which too are entered as a block into the regression model when examining that effect. This modeling approach equivalence is the reason why there was no need to discuss in detail higher-order ANOVA in the preceding Section 14.4.

14.6. ANALYSIS OF COVARIANCE

We indicated on a few occasions earlier in the book that behavioral and social research is typically concerned with exceedingly complex phenomena that are usually multifactorially determined. In order to realistically study them, therefore, as mentioned before it is often desirable that we utilize several explanatory variables that need not all be of the same type. Following this realization, we extended in Section 14.4 the number of factors included in an ANOVA.

At times, however, substantive considerations may require including one or more continuous predictors, in addition to a set of factors in an initial ANOVA setting. This inclusion may be desirable in order to account for important explanatory variable(s) with respect to the response measure. The latter measure is then modeled in terms of several predictors that differ in their scale—some binary or polytomous (factors), others continuous. Since these variables usually show appreciable correlation with the outcome measure, they are frequently referred to as *covariates*. For this reason, the modeling of a response variable using categorical (factors) as well as continuous explanatory variables is called *analysis of covariance* (ANCOVA). This is the modeling approach of concern in the remainder of the present section.

As can be expected from our ANOVA and regression result equivalence discussion in the preceding Section 14.5, ANCOVA presents no new problems as a modeling approach (see also Raykov & Marcoulides, 2008). Indeed, in the last section we demonstrated how one can account for categorical predictors of a given outcome variable. To this end, one first appropriately recodes them (a process carried out internally by statistical software, like R, after their definition as factors by the user), and then includes the resulting group membership dummy variables as predictors in the corresponding regression analysis model. When in addition to these factors also continuous predictors are of interest to be added, one merely includes them along with the factors in that multiple regression model. In this way, one carries out ANCOVA in an empirical setting.

We emphasize that just as a researcher does not need to perform the factor recoding in ANOVA, there is no need for such recoding to be done by him or her for the purpose of an ANCOVA—of course as long as the factors are initially declared to the software as categorical variables. Hence, all that is needed to be done by the researcher at the software level is the specification of (i) the outcome measure (assumed continuous, as mentioned at the outset of the chapter; see next chapter for an alternative); as well as (ii) the predictors to be employed for the purpose of explaining its variance, irrespective of whether they are continuous or categorical variables (after declaring the categorical variables as factors).

We demonstrate this discussion by considering data from an achievement study:

Example 14.3: In this investigation, $n = 138$ middle school students from five states were administered a mathematics ability test at the end of a week-long training in relevant mathematics concepts and their relationships. In addition, at the beginning of the training an intelligence test was administered to all students involved in the study. (The data are contained in the file CH14_ EX5.dat, where the mathematics test results are denoted 'y', state residence by 'state', and the intelligence test score is designated 'iq'.) A researcher wishes to examine possible state differences in mathematics achievement at the end of the training, after accounting for potential differences in intelligence at the beginning of the study (cf. Raykov & Marcoulides, 2008). That is, her intention is to see whether there are differences across the five states involved in mathematics achievement after controlling for possible prior intelligence differences (IQ score differences) across the groups. In this way, she wishes to account for possible initial intelligence differences that may be related to such observed in the final mathematics test scores.

To respond to this question, first we read in the data and declare the state variable as a factor (see Section 14.1):

```
> d = read.table("C://data/Rbook/CH14_EX5.dat", header = T)
> attach(d)
> d$state = factor(d$state, labels = c("A", "B", "C", "D",  "E"))
> detach(d)
> attach(d)
```

We begin our modeling process with the ANCOVA model explaining individual differences in the mathematics test scores in terms of state and IQ score differences. To this end, we regress the mathematics test scores on the factor 'state' and the continuous IQ score. Thereby, we include the interaction between the factor 'state' and the quantitative variable 'iq', in addition to their own main effects, in order to examine whether IQ scores contribute to differences in the mathematics test scores in a way that is not the same across states. We accomplish this using again the R command 'lm', followed by a request for the associated analysis of variance table (results provided beneath commands):

```
> m1 = lm(y~state*iq)
> anova(m1)



Analysis of Variance Table

Response: y
           Df  Sum Sq Mean Sq F value   Pr(>F)
state       4  1627.2   406.8  4.6620 0.001516 **
iq          1    28.3    28.3  0.3245 0.569933
state:iq    4   198.8    49.7  0.5697 0.685105
Residuals 128 11168.7    87.3
---
Signif. codes:  0 '***' 0.001 '**' 0.01 '*' 0.05 '.' 0.1 ' ' 1
```

As can be seen from this output, the interaction between 'state' and 'iq' is not significant. That is, different states have the same regression slope of the (linear) relationship between mathematics and intelligence test scores. This finding suggests that a main assumption of the classical ANCOVA approach, frequently referred to as *homogeneity of regression* (e.g., Raykov & Marcoulides, 2008), is fulfilled in this data set. The implication is that we can next drop this interaction from the model and proceed with the more parsimonious model assuming no such interaction, i.e., homogeneity in the regression slopes of mathematics test score upon IQ, across the five states involved in the study. We fit this model using the same R command, with a correspondingly simplified argument that reflects the lack of this interaction:

```
> m2 = lm(y~state+iq)
> anova(m2)



Analysis of Variance Table

Response: y
           Df  Sum Sq Mean Sq F value   Pr(>F)
state       4  1627.2   406.8  4.7236 0.001356 **
iq          1    28.3    28.3  0.3288 0.567368
Residuals 132 11367.5    86.1
---
Signif. codes:  0 '***' 0.001 '**' 0.01 '*' 0.05 '.' 0.1 ' ' 1
```

We observe here the lack of significance of the IQ score, controlling for state. We can interpret this finding as suggesting that within each of the states there is no discernible (linear) relationship between mathematics and intelligence test score. Further, due to the finding that the factor 'state' is significant, controlling for IQ score, it is suggested that for students with the same IQ score, state residency (schooling) does matter as far as their mathematics test scores are concerned. Hence, there is evidence in the analyzed data set for state differences in mathematics achievement at the end of the training period even for students with the same initial IQ score.

We can examine how much better the last fitted, simpler ANCOVA model is from the starting full model including the interaction of state residency and IQ score, by using the 'anova' command to compare their fit to the analyzed data:

```
> anova(m2, m1)


Analysis of Variance Table

Model 1: y ~ state + iq
Model 2: y ~ state * iq
  Res.Df     RSS  Df Sum of Sq      F Pr(>F)
1    132 11367.5
2    128 11168.7   4     198.8 0.5697 0.6851
```

We see from this output that the test of the null hypothesis of no fit differences for these two models is not significant—the p-value of the pertinent F-ratio, being .69, is above a reasonable prespecified significance level. Hence, we can conclude that the two models do not differ in their degree of reproducing the data, i.e., in their goodness of fit to the latter. For this reason, we prefer the more parsimonious, conventional ANCOVA model with the assumption of identical regression slope of mathematics test score upon IQ score across all five states.

As indicated earlier, this ANCOVA model suggests—based on the analyzed data set—that there are state differences in mathematics achievement even after controlling for possible initial state differences in intelligence. To inspect graphically these differences, we take a look at the mathematics test score boxplots across the five states, which we obtain by using as before the R command 'boxplot' (see Figure 14.4 for the resulting boxplots):

```
> boxplot(y~state)
```

Figure 14.4 suggests that students in state C perform best on the mathematics test while the remaining four states are at about the same level of perform-

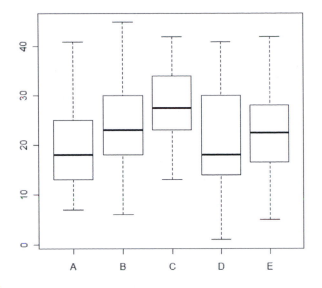

FIGURE 14.4.
Box plots of mathematics test scores for the five states in Example 14.3.

ance. To examine these state-by-state differences, we use the Tukey's HSD method (Section 14.3):

```
> TukeyHSD(aov(lm(y~state)))
```

```
    Tukey multiple comparisons of means
      95% family-wise confidence level

Fit: aov(formula = lm(y ~ state))

$state
            diff         lwr        upr       p adj
B-A    4.1681034   -2.395180 10.731387 0.4035059
C-A    9.2416667    2.736020 15.747313 0.0012712
D-A    0.8266129   -5.624649  7.277875 0.9965853
E-A    2.5625000   -5.275692 10.400692 0.8948743
C-B    5.0735632   -1.592918 11.740044 0.2241862
D-B   -3.3414905   -9.954909  3.271928 0.6304613
E-B   -1.6056034   -9.577791  6.366584 0.9808965
D-C   -8.4150538  -14.971276 -1.858831 0.0047763
E-C   -6.6791667  -14.603971  1.245638 0.1416725
E-D    1.7358871   -6.144333  9.616107 0.9734265
```

The pair-wise group comparisons presented in this output section suggest that the only significant differences in mean mathematics achievement are found between states C and A, and between states C and E. Indeed, states A, B, D, and E do not differ with regard to average performance on the mathematics test, while state C outperforms all of them in this aspect. We stress that these pair-wise comparisons do not take into account the IQ test scores, which we found earlier not to be an important predictor of mathematics achievement beyond state residency.

In conclusion of this chapter, we have seen that ANOVA is a very helpful statistical method that permits examining group differences with regard to one or more categorical variables (factors). Thereby, we have observed that ANOVA can be carried out within a traditional variance decomposition framework, or alternatively within a modern regression analysis approach. A conceptual advantage of the latter is that it permits one also to include continuous predictors (covariates) of outcome measures. The resulting ANCOVA modeling approach, under its assumptions (e.g., Raykov & Marcoulides, 2008), makes it possible to study group differences on a response measure after removing group differences that can be accounted for by the relationship between that measure and one or more continuous covariates considered in addition to categorical factors.

NOTE

Alternatively, a discrete independent variable can be declared a factor variable with the command ">f.state = factor (state)"; then, in all following analyses, the variable 'f.state' is to be used instead of 'state' in this chapter (and, similarly, for other discrete explanatory variables later in the book).

Modeling Discrete Response Variables

In the previous three chapters it was assumed that the examined response variables were continuous measures (or approximately continuous). Such an assumption about the response variables will be fulfilled in many but not all empirical settings in the social and behavioral sciences. Often, researchers in these disciplines will also be interested in explaining individual differences in binary or highly discrete outcome variables, in terms of one or more independent measures. In such cases, the continuous characteristics of the response variables cannot be reasonably assumed. Applications then of the regression analysis methods that we dealt with in the last three chapters can yield incorrect results and misleading substantive interpretations. Instead, use of special methods developed for discrete response variables is necessary in settings with discrete outcome measures. A number of modeling approaches that are appropriate in these empirical cases are available within a very general analytic framework, commonly referred to as the generalized linear model. This framework is the topic of the present chapter.

15.1. REVISITING REGRESSION ANALYSIS AND THE GENERAL LINEAR MODEL

In Chapters 12 through 14, we discussed in considerable detail regression analysis. When using it, we considered a single continuous dependent variable y and one or more explanatory variables (predictors) denoted $x_1, x_2,..., x_k$. In the regression analysis model, these variables are assumed to be related as follows:

$$(15.1) \qquad y = b_0 + b_1x_1 + b_2x_2 + ... + b_kx_k + e,$$

where b_0 through b_k are the intercept and partial regression coefficients, while e denotes the model error term with zero mean that is assumed to be unrelated to x_j $(j = 1)$.

Suppose the values of the predictors x_1, x_2,..., x_k were fixed (for simplicity, below we use for them the same notation; cf. Raykov & Marcoulides, 2011). Since the mean of the residual e is zero, taking mean (expectation) from both sides of Equation (15.1) we obtain

$$(15.2) \qquad M(y) = b_0 + b_1 x_1 + b_2 x_2 + ... + b_k x_k,$$

where $M(y)$ denotes the mean response (at the given set of predictors, x_1, x_2,..., x_k). An equivalent version of Equation (15.2) is often presented as

$$(15.3) \qquad M(y \mid x_1, x_2,...,x_k) = b_0 + b_1 x_1 + b_2 x_2 + ... + b_k x_k,$$

where the left-hand side emphasizes now that the mean of y is taken for subjects with the given set of predictor values x_1 through x_k. For this reason, $M(y \mid x_1, x_2,..., x_k)$ is commonly referred to as *conditional expectation* of y given the predictors.

Equation (15.3) states that this conditional expectation of the response variable is assumed to be a *linear function* of the predictors. This means that all unknown coefficients (parameters) b_0 through b_k are involved in that equation only as multipliers of the predictor values, and no other operation is performed on them. This feature of the conditional expectation of a response measure is what is typically meant when referring to a model as *linear*, in particular when referring to the regression model (15.1) as a linear model. If this model is postulated simultaneously for a number of outcome variables— which, as usual in empirical research, may be interrelated among themselves—the resulting set of equations is often referred to as a *general linear model* (GLM; e.g., Raykov & Marcoulides, 2008; Timm, 2002).

When employing the regression model defined in Equation (15.1), as mentioned earlier in the book a researcher can choose the explanatory variables any way he or she decides to (as long as they have positive variance and correspond to the research question asked). In particular, the researcher need not be concerned with their distribution (e.g., Agresti & Finlay, 2009). That is, the predictors can be binary (dichotomous), nominal, categorical (ordinal), or continuous (interval or ratio scaled). At the same time, however, it is required that the response variable(s) be continuous. For such outcome variables the GLM postulates a linear relationship(s) between the dependent and explanatory variables. This linear relationship(s) is the hallmark of the GLM and a reason why it has been very widely applied throughout the behavioral and social sciences.

While the GLM provides a highly useful methodology for studying variable relationships, it does not cover the cases when response variables take a limited number of possible values in studied populations. For example, when the answer of a student on a given item in an ability test is of interest, the resulting random variable representing his or her response is usually recorded as true (denoted, say, '1') or false (symbolized as '0'). In a clinical context, a patient may or may not endorse a statement in relation to a given symptom of a condition he or she is being examined for, leading again to a binary random variable. In a political opinion poll, a respondent may or may not agree with a particular statement on a topic of interest, resulting similarly in an individual realization of a binary random variable. In a cognitive functioning study, an elderly person may provide a response indicative of several (limited number of) levels of dementia on a question in a used measuring instrument, which represents a discrete random variable. These are only a few examples when it is of interest to study individual differences in binary or discrete response variables. This goal cannot be in general achieved properly using the regression modeling procedures discussed up to this point in the book, as provided by the conventional GLM framework.

In order to accomplish the study of individual differences on discrete outcomes, an extension of the GLM is needed to the case where the response variable is no more continuous. This extension is furnished by a highly comprehensive modeling approach, which was first developed in the 1970s and is the subject of the remainder of this chapter.

15.2. THE IDEA AND ELEMENTS OF THE GENERALIZED LINEAR MODEL

A generalization of the GLM to handle binary and discrete response variables, is provided by the framework of the *generalized linear model* (GLIM; cf. Raykov & Marcoulides, 2011). The GLIM extends the linear relationship idea underlying the GLM to cases where the dependent variable does not have to be continuous. That is, the GLIM relaxes the above-mentioned continuity assumption with respect to the response measure. Specifically, when carrying out a GLIM analysis, the dependent variable can be binary or more generally discrete. The latter happens quite often in behavioral and social measurement contexts, especially when considering responses on an item in a test, a questionnaire, a self-report, or an inventory. The GLIM does preserve, however, the linear relationship idea, but after an important modification is made.

To introduce the GLIM, let us first revisit Equation (15.2):

(15.2, repeated) $M(y) = b_0 + b_1x_1 + b_2x_2 + \ldots + b_kx_k,$

or for simplicity as

(15.3) $M(y) = \mu,$

for a given set of predictor values. That is, Equation (15.2), which for our purposes can be considered the model of (univariate) regression analysis discussed earlier or a single equation from GLM, stipulates that it is the mean,

μ, of the outcome variable, y, which is linearly modeled in terms of the predictors.

In order to cover also response variables that are not continuous, the GLIM is based on the idea that not μ itself but a function of it, called a *link function*, is linearly related to a given set of explanatory variables involved in a modeling effort (cf. Raykov & Marcoulides, 2011). Denoting this function by $g(\mu)$, which is appropriately chosen (as discussed further below), a GLIM stipulates the following relationship:

$$(15.4) \qquad\qquad g(\mu) = b_0 + b_1 x_1 + b_2 x_2 + ... + b_k x_k,$$

that is,

$$g(M(y)) = b_0 + b_1 x_1 + b_2 x_2 + ... + b_k x_k.$$

We stress that Equation (15.4) differs from Equation (15.2) only by the fact that it is not the response mean μ itself, but rather a function of it, viz., $g(\mu)$, which is linearly related to the given set of explanatory variables x_1 through x_k. That is, by postulating Equation (15.4) the GLIM preserves the linear relationship idea in the right-hand side of its modeling equation. At the same time, the GLIM framework provides a number of options with respect to the quantity appearing in the left-hand side of Equation (15.4), $g(\mu)$, which makes it very comprehensive. One such possibility, for instance, is realized when the function $g(.)$ is chosen to be the identity—that is, if $g(\mu) = \mu$ —which represents perhaps the simplest example of GLIM. With this choice, a GLIM is in fact identical to a corresponding GLM, as we will see in more detail later. Since within the GLIM framework one relates a transformation of the response mean to a set of explanatory variables, as in Equation (15.3), the function $g(.)$ is often referred to as a *link*—a reference we will frequently use in the rest of this chapter.

The choice of the link $g(.)$ does not complete the specification of a particular GLIM, however. In fact, any GLIM consists of three main elements (e.g., Dobson, 2002; Raykov & Marcoulides, 2011):

(i)   a *random component*, also called "sampling model";
(ii) a *link function*, i.e., the function $g(.)$; and
(iii) a *systematic component*, i.e., the linear combination in the right-hand side of Equation (15.4), often also called *linear predictor*.

The random component meant in (i) is the distribution of the response variable. For example, if the answer (score) on a single item in an achievement test is of interest to model, the associated random variable representing student responses is often binary. In that case, this variable follows what is called a *Bernoulli distribution* with a probability p of taking the value 1 ("correct" response) and $1 - p$ for taking the value 0 ("incorrect" response). In the GLIM framework, the distribution of the dependent variable is selected from the *exponential family*, which includes all variable distributions of relevance in this book, such as the normal, Bernoulli, binomial, and Poisson distributions. (For a formal definition of this concept, we refer readers to some specialized literature; e.g., Dobson, 2002.) Further, the link mentioned in (ii) is the earlier discussed function $g(.)$, which is applied on the mean of the outcome variable before its linear relationship to a set of predictors is considered. Different choices for the link function are possible, depending on the particular distribution of the response variable. Last but not least, the systematic component in (iii) is the linear combination of the explanatory variables under consideration with respect to the response measure y. Their joint distribution is not of interest, as mentioned earlier, i.e., is unrestricted; however, they all are assumed—as in conventional regression analysis—to be measured without error.

15.3. LOGISTIC REGRESSION AS A GENERALIZED LINEAR MODEL OF PARTICULAR RELEVANCE IN SOCIAL AND BEHAVIORAL RESEARCH

15.3.1. A "continuous counterpart" of regression analysis

The GLIM framework can be readily used to model individual differences in binary response variables via an appropriately chosen link function, which is an essential element of a pertinent GLIM (cf. Raykov & Marcoulides, 2011). This function has been obtained using formal statistical developments (e.g., Dobson, 2002), and is based on the widely used logit transformation, or logit function. Owing to the special importance of this function for the remainder of the present chapter, we define it formally next.

For a given probability p $(0 < p < 1)$, the *logit function* is defined as the logarithm of the odds of the event occurring, which is associated with a probability p:

$$(15.5) \qquad\qquad f(p) = \ln[p/(1-p)]$$

where $\ln(.)$ is the natural logarithm, i.e., the logarithm with base $e = 2.712....$ As can be seen from the right-hand side of Equation (15.5), for each probability p it produces an unlimited real number, $f(p)$, which can be smaller than any prespecified negative number or alternatively larger than any pre-fixed positive number. This property of the logit function is especially helpful in social behavioral and social research dealing with binary response variables, and it has also a number of beneficial applications with discrete outcome variables taking more than two (but a limited number of) values in an empirical setting. The reason is that using the logit function (15.5) one obtains a value that is unrestricted. Indeed, this function $f(p)$ is readily seen as being actually continuous, and it thus can be now considered a continuous counterpart of the original probability, p.

Returning for a moment to the binary response variable case, we recall from Chapter 5 that the mean of a binary random variable, say y, is the probability of correct response, denoted p, say. Looking now at Equation (15.5), we realize that since the logit function furnishes a continuous counterpart of the probability p, i.e., of the mean of y, we can make the following observation. When we wish to relate a binary response y to a set of explanatory variables, $x_1, x_2,..., x_k$, we can consider our effort as analogous to a regression analysis on the logit of the mean of y, i.e., of p, upon the predictors. This is the essence, at an informal level, of the popular statistical technique of logistic regression. (For further and formal details, we refer the reader to more advanced treatments, such as Hosmer & Lemeshow, 2002).

15.3.2. Logistic regression and a generalized linear model with a binary response

We would like to approach now the currently discussed topic from another perspective, viz., that of the GLIM framework. Indeed, from the discussion so far in this chapter, one realizes that when an outcome variable of concern is binary (i.e., dichotomous), the GLIM framework is directly applicable (cf. Raykov & Marcoulides, 2011). This is because a sampling model for this setting is the Bernoulli model, which as mentioned earlier is the first element of a GLIM. Accordingly, the response random variable y takes the value of 1 with probability p and the value of 0 with probability $1 - p$. In addition, from the preceding subsection we can readily obtain a link function that is the second element of a GLIM. As will be recalled from Chapter 5 and as indicated earlier in this chapter, a binary random variable y has the property that its mean is the probability of correct response, i.e., $p = M(y) = \mu$ holds (see also Equation (15.3)). If we now choose the logit function $f(p) = \ln[p/(1 - p)]$ $= \ln[\mu(1 - \mu)]$ as the link function $g(\mu)$, then the GLIM framework would be directly applicable as soon as we choose the linear predictor, i.e., a set of explanatory variables with respect to individual differences in the response measure y. That is, in order to be dealing with a GLIM in the currently considered context of a dichotomous outcome variable, y, all we need to do now is select explanatory variables of interest in a particular application. Once we do so, we simply set their linear combination—with unknown weights, or parameters—to be equal to the result of the application of the link function chosen, that is, to $f(p)$ in Equation (15.5), which function is here the same as $g(\mu)$. This will finalize the construction of a GLIM in the present setting.

The GLIM with a binary response has been in fact long known in the behavioral and social sciences under an alternative name, *logistic regression*. Specifically, keeping also in mind the discussion in the preceding section 15.3.1, the model of logistic regression is as follows:

$$(15.6) \qquad \ln[p/(1-p)] = b_0 + b_1 x_1 + b_2 x_2 + \ldots + b_k x_k,$$

where $p = \Pr(y = 1)$ is the probability of the response variable taking the value of 1 (e.g., a "yes" response on a given question in a survey, or a "correct" answer on a test item), and x_1 through x_k are the explanatory variables included in the "linear predictor" of this GLIM (see Section 15.1). That is, according to the logistic regression model (15.6), it is the logit of the probability of response 1, which is assumed to be a linear function of a set of explanatory variables, rather than this probability itself.

An alternative representation of the logistic regression model—i.e., of the GLIM with a binary response—is readily obtained from Equations (15.5) and (15.6); this alternative highlights further interesting properties of this model that can be very useful in an empirical setting. Specifically, through some direct algebra we obtain the probability of the event in question (e.g., a "correct" response on a test item) as follows:

$$(15.7) \qquad p = \Pr(y = 1) = \frac{e^{b_0 + b_1 x_1 + \ldots + b_k x_k}}{1 + e^{b_0 + b_1 x_1 + \ldots + b_k x_k}}.$$

This shows that this probability is a nonlinear function of the used predictors x_1 through x_k. Therefore, Equation (15.7) demonstrates that the probability p for the event considered depends on the predictor variables in a relatively complicated way, rather than in a linear fashion.

The expression given in the right-hand side of Equation (15.7) is especially useful when one is interested in predicting the probability of an event using a set of known predictor values. Assuming that the logistic model (15.6) is a plausible means of data description and explanation, the predicted probability follows as

$$(15.8) \qquad \hat{p} = \frac{e^{\hat{b}_0 + \hat{b}_1 x_1 + \ldots + +\hat{b}_k x_k}}{1 + e^{\hat{b}_0 + \hat{b}_1 x_1 + \ldots + +\hat{b}_k x_k}},$$

where $\hat{b}_0$ through $\hat{b}_k$ are the estimated parameters of the model. When this predicted probability is higher (smaller) than .5, one may conclude that given the model and the set of predictor values, the event under consideration is predicted to occur with higher (smaller) probability than by chance alone.

15.3.3. Further generalized linear models

As pointed out earlier in this chapter, in addition to the logit link and binary sampling model, there are other link functions and sampling models that are appropriate within the GLIM approach with other types of data (cf. Raykov & Marcoulides, 2011). One important such link is provided by the logarithm function, which turns out to be very useful when the outcome variable data are in terms of counts. This can be the case, for instance, when of interest is to study the number of times a particular event occurs within a given interval, such as disease outbreak (e.g., Chapter 5). The logarithm link has been shown to possess important properties in such settings, which make it the choice for a corresponding GLIM application, usually associated with a Poisson distribution of the response variable. Additional links are discussed in detail, e.g., in Dobson (2002). More generally speaking, the GLIM framework is highly comprehensive and covers many different types of data collection designs. Within this framework, optimal statistical procedures for parameter estimation and testing purposes are available and discussed in alternative and more advanced sources (e.g., Skrondal & Rabe-Hesketh, 2004). In the rest of this chapter, we return to the topic of logistic regression, which is a very popular analytic framework in the social and behavioral disciplines.

15.4. FITTING LOGISTIC REGRESSION MODELS USING R

Fitting a logistic regression model in an empirical setting can be readily accomplished with the software R. To this end, its command 'glm' can be used, whereby one needs to indicate the binary sampling (response) model and provide the predictors in a way similar to the application of the earlier used command 'lm' for regression analysis. The software uses then as a default the logit link function and applies the appropriate method of parameter estimation. We discuss in this section issues that arise when fitting a logistic regression model to data, i.e., a GLIM with a binary response variable using the following example:

Example 15.1: Suppose we have access to data from a study of college admission with $n = 132$ students from five states. In this study, data on the dichotomous variable college admission was collected, along with such on student gender and state residency, as well as their scores on an intelligence test and a scholastic aptitude test. (The data are available in the file CH15_EX1. dat, where 'college' is the admission variable—with a value of 1 for students admitted and 0 otherwise—'aptitude' is the pertinent test score, 'state' and 'gender' their state residency and gender, respectively, and 'iq' the intelligence test score, referred to below as "IQ score" or "IQ" for short.)

We are interested here in explaining individual differences in college admission in terms of student differences in state residency, gender, and IQ, as well as aptitude test scores. Given the binary response variable college admission, we thus wish to predict the probability p of a student being admitted using as explanatory variables state, gender, aptitude, and IQ score. We can accomplish this goal using logistic regression with this dichotomous response and predictor variables.

To this end, we employ a GLIM with (cf. Raykov & Marcoulides, 2011):

(i)   Bernoulli sampling model, referred to as 'binomial family' in R,
(ii) logit link (which is the default option in R when a binomial family is specified), and
(iii) linear predictor, being the linear combination

$$b_0 + b_1 \text{ state} + b_2 \text{ gender} + b_3 \text{ aptitude} + b_4 \text{ IQ}.$$

Hence, the GLIM model (i.e., logistic regression model) to be fitted is:

(15.9) $ln(p/(1-p)) = b_0 + b_1 \text{ state} + b_2 \text{ gender} + b_3 \text{ aptitude} + b_4 \text{ IQ}.$

As indicated earlier in the chapter, this model is alternatively reexpressed in terms of the probability of college admission as follows:

(15.10)
$$p = \frac{e^{b_0 + b_1 state + b_2 gender + b_3 aptitude + b_4 IQ}}{1 + e^{b_0 + b_1 state + b_2 gender + b_3 aptitude + b_4 IQ}}$$

$$= \frac{1}{1 + e^{-(b_0 + b_1 state + b_2 gender + b_3 aptitude + b_4 IQ)}}.$$

As we mentioned before, Equation (15.10) can be used after fitting the model, to work out predicted probability of college admission for a given set of student predictor values (e.g., for an individual with available data on the used predictors). Also, we emphasize that the right-hand side of Equation (15.12) is never larger than one or smaller than zero, just like any probability.

To fit the logistic regression model in Equation (15.9) that addresses the research question of concern here, we need to indicate to R the GLIM elements described in points (i) through (iii). To accomplish this aim, after we declare the variable 'state' as a factor (see also Note to Chapter 14), we

(a)   use the R command 'glm', requesting binomial sampling model (which as mentioned employs by default the logit link function); and then
(b)   indicate the predictors of interest, viz., state, gender, aptitude, and IQ.

This is achieved with the following R command (output is summarized immediately after):

```
> m1 = glm(college ~ state + gender + aptitude + iq, family =  binomial)


> summary(m1)

Call:

glm(formula = college ~ state + gender + aptitude + iq, family =  binomial)


Deviance Residuals:
    Min        1Q     Median        3Q        Max
-2.9317   -0.6753    0.2370    0.6816    1.9986


Coefficients:
               Estimate Std. Error z value Pr(>|z|)
(Intercept) -25.93721     6.05502  -4.284 1.84e-05 ***
stateB       -0.36291     0.73193  -0.496    0.620
stateC       -0.11570     0.80071  -0.144    0.885
stateD       -0.37403     0.69679  -0.537    0.591
stateE        0.16550     0.86090   0.192    0.848
gender        0.30155     0.49305   0.612    0.541
aptitude      0.16683     0.03746   4.454 8.44e-06 ***
iq            0.22820     0.05787   3.943 8.04e-05 ***
---
Signif. codes:  0 '***' 0.001 '**' 0.01 '*' 0.05 '.' 0.1 ' ' 1


(Dispersion parameter for binomial family taken to be 1)


    Null deviance: 176.11  on 131  degrees of freedom
Residual deviance: 109.97  on 124  degrees of freedom
AIC: 125.97


Number of Fisher Scoring iterations: 5
```

This output differs in an important way from the outputs we obtained when carrying out regression analyses earlier in the book. Specifically, a new quantity is included here, which is called *deviance*. A complete and formal definition of the deviance is beyond the scope of this introductory book (see e.g., Dobson, 2002, for such a discussion). We merely mention here that the deviance in a GLIM corresponds to the sum of squared residuals in a linear modeling context as discussed in Chapters 12 through 14. That is, with large samples, a large deviance is indicative of a model that is not well fitting the data, while a smaller deviance is consistent with a model fitting the data better. When all cells of the underlying study design with regard to the factors involved have expected frequencies under the model that are in excess of five (e.g., Chapter 10), a deviance that is comparable to the degrees of freedom may be seen as not large enough to proclaim the model insufficiently well fitting the analyzed data. A more credible way of using the deviance is for the purpose of model fit comparison, however, which we predominantly engage in the rest of this section.

The discussed output actually reports two deviance measures—a *null deviance* and a *residual deviance*. The former is the deviance associated with the model having no predictors and only an intercept. This model is formally obtained from Equation (15.11) by setting all b parameters equal to zero except the intercept b_0 (and for this reason is referred to as *null model*, i.e., containing $k = 0$ predictors). Its deviance for the presently considered study data is 176.11, which is markedly higher than the associated degrees of freedom, $df_0 = 131$. The second deviance, referred to as residual deviance, is that of the fitted model with the above $k = 4$ predictors, whose output we assigned the R-object name 'm1'.

This residual deviance is substantially smaller than the null deviance in the present example, as seen from the associated R output. This finding suggests that the predictors we used likely explain a considerable proportion of individual differences in the binary response variable college admission. When the corresponding null hypothesis is true, which stipulates that all b parameters but the intercept are zero in the population, and the sample is large, the difference in the two deviances follows approximately a chi-square distribution, with degrees of freedom being the difference in these of the fitted and null models. In our case, this difference is $176.11 - 109.97 = 66.14$, which is significant when judged against the chi-square distribution with degrees of freedom $df = 131 - 124 = 7$ (the pertinent cutoff at the conventional significance level of .05 is 14.07; King & Minium, 2003). This result is consistent with the above suggestion that the predictors used in our fitted logistic regression model explain a significant proportion of individual differences in college admission.

The "coefficients" part of the last output 'm1' indicate that none of the dummy variables associated with the 'state' factor is significant. This suggests that state residency may not be explaining significant unique proportion of variance in the college admission probability, after controlling for gender, intelligence, and aptitude differences across students (cf. Chapter 13). To examine this possibility, we fit the model without the state factor (output summarized thereafter):

```
> m2 = glm(college ~ gender + aptitude + iq, family = binomial)

> summary(m2)
```

```
Call:
glm(formula = college ~ gender + aptitude + iq, family =  binomial)

Deviance Residuals:
    Min       1Q    Median       3Q       Max
-2.7961   -0.6737   0.2643   0.6681   1.9111

Coefficients:
               Estimate Std. Error z value Pr(>|z|)
(Intercept) -25.81204     5.92330  -4.358 1.31e-05 ***
gender        0.28482     0.48151   0.592    0.554
aptitude      0.16384     0.03449   4.751 2.03e-06 ***
iq            0.22594     0.05672   3.983 6.80e-05 ***
---
Signif. codes:  0 '***' 0.001 '**' 0.01 '*' 0.05 '.' 0.1 ' ' 1


(Dispersion parameter for binomial family taken to be 1)

    Null deviance: 176.11  on 131  degrees of freedom
Residual deviance: 110.65  on 128  degrees of freedom
AIC: 118.65

Number of Fisher Scoring iterations: 5
```

The deviance of this model—denoted 'm2'—is slightly higher than that of the previously fitted model, denoted 'm1' above. This result could be expected, since model 'm2' has one fewer predictor, viz., it does not include 'state' as explanatory variable. As in regression analysis where fewer predictors in a given model lead to a higher residual sum of squares (SEE; see Chapters 12 and 13), the deviance in a GLIM—which as mentioned is a counterpart here to SEE—increases when dropping one or more predictors. While the deviance of the last fitted model 'm2' is marginally higher relative to that of model 'm1', it is important to note that 'm2' is more parsimonious. This is a highly desirable feature, ensuring higher parameter estimate stability and replicability in another study. For this reason, deviance and parsimony are simultaneously accounted for in an overall test of significance of the factor 'state' that we need to perform next. In such a test, the 'state' factor (with its five levels) is to be represented by the $5 - 1 = 4$ dummy variables for state residency considered simultaneously, rather than singly, as in the above 'co-efficients' table in the output of model 'm1'. With this feature, the test will examine the null hypothesis of no unique explanatory power of the factor 'state' with regard to college admission.

It is possible to carry out this test by comparing the deviances of the models 'm1' and 'm2'. To this end, we use the R command 'anova', which we already employed earlier in the book for model fit comparison purposes:

```
> anova(m2, m1, test = "Chisq")
```

As a third argument of this command, after referring to the models to be compared in terms of fit to the analyzed data, we request a test of significance of the involved difference in residual deviances of both models. Its results are presented next.

```
Analysis of Deviance Table

Model 1: college ~ gender + aptitude + iq

Model 2: college ~ state + gender + aptitude + iq

  Resid. Df Resid. Dev  Df Deviance P(>|Chi|)

1       128    110.651
2       124    109.973   4    0.677     0.954
```

Since the p-value associated with the deviance difference in question is non-significant, we conclude that the two models involved fit the data equally well. That is, dropping the factor 'state' does not lead to a significant loss in predictive power of the logistic regression model 'm2' relative to the first fitted model 'm1'. An alternative interpretation suggests that the factor 'state' has no unique predictive power for college admission, once accounting for individual difference in gender, IQ, and aptitude test score.

We also notice that the output provided for each of the two fitted models, 'm1' and 'm2', contains one more fit-related quantity, AIC (short for "Akaike's information criterion"). This index evaluates model fit and includes a penalty for lack of parsimony. Specifically, when two or more models are compared in terms of fit to the same set of observed variables (data set), the one with lower AIC can be considered as better fitting and preferable. From the two models in question here, 'm1' and 'm2', the latter has a smaller AIC—viz., 118.65 vs. 125.97. Hence, model 'm2' is preferable to 'm1' as a means of data description and explanation also, as far as this model fit index is concerned. (The formal definition and in particular rationale for this index are beyond the confines of this chapter and can be found, e.g., in Dobson, 2002.)

Returning now to the output associated with the preferred model 'm2', we notice from its 'coefficients' section that the variable 'gender' is not significant. We interpret this finding as suggesting that gender is unrelated to college admission for students with the same IQ and aptitude test scores. To examine this suggestion also from the above model comparison perspective, we fit next model 'm2' without the 'gender' variable:

```
> m3 = glm(college ~ aptitude + iq, family = binomial)

> summary(m3)



Call:
glm(formula = college ~ achievmt + iq, family = binomial)

Deviance Residuals:
    Min       1Q    Median        3Q       Max
-2.8505   -0.7015    0.2721    0.6960    1.9486

Coefficients:
              Estimate Std. Error z value Pr(>|z|)
(Intercept) -25.16930    5.77697   -4.357 1.32e-05 ***
aptitude      0.16492    0.03451    4.779 1.76e-06 ***
iq            0.22067    0.05561    3.968 7.23e-05 ***
---
Signif. codes:  0 '***' 0.001 '**' 0.01 '*' 0.05 '.' 0.1 ' ' 1

(Dispersion parameter for binomial family taken to be 1)

    Null deviance: 176.11  on 131  degrees of freedom
Residual deviance: 111.00  on 129  degrees of freedom
AIC: 117.00

Number of Fisher Scoring iterations: 5
```

We note from this R output that both predictors in model 'm3', aptitude and IQ test score, are significant. That is, the aptitude test score does contribute to better prediction of the probability of college admission for students with the same IQ score; alternatively, the IQ test score contributes to a better prediction of this probability for students with the same aptitude test score.

To compare the fit of the last two fitted models, 'm2' and 'm3', we use the 'anova' command again (with them as the first two arguments):

```
> anova(m3, m2, test = "Chisq")
```

Analysis of Deviance Table

Model 1: college ~ aptitude + iq

Model 2: college ~ gender + aptitude + iq

```
  Resid. Df Resid. Dev  Df Deviance P(>|Chi|)

1       129    111.002
2       128    110.651   1    0.352     0.553
```

The difference in fit in these two models is thus nonsignificant, and we conclude that gender does not have unique predictive power with regard to college admission once controlling for aptitude and IQ score.

We also note that the last fitted model, 'm3', has the smallest AIC—viz., 117—of all three models discussed in this section. Hence, we can treat it as a preferable means of data description and explanation, when compared to the previous two models fitted. In addition, since its deviance is even smaller than the associated degrees of freedom, there seems to be no indication in the output presented that would suggest that this most parsimonious model—where aptitude and IQ test scores are the only predictors—is associated with a deficient fit to the analyzed data. We thus consider model 'm3' as a plausible means of data description and evaluation.

If interested in predicting the probability of college admission, assuming knowledge of aptitude and IQ test score, we can use this tenable model 'm3'. Accordingly, it furnishes this predicted probability as (see Equation (15.12) and last presented output):

$$(15.13) \qquad p = \frac{e^{-25.17 + .16aptitude + .22IQ}}{1 + e^{-25.17 + .16aptitude + .22IQ}}.$$

From this prediction equation, we can see that increase in aptitude score leads to enhanced college admission probability for students with the same IQ. Similarly, an increase in the IQ test score is associated with an enhanced admission probability for students with the same aptitude test score.

The last interpretation can be viewed as conditional—we fix one of the predictors in order to interpret the effect of the other upon the probability of college admission. In some cases, one may as well be interested in unconditional interpretations of the relationships between a response variable and any of a set of predictors of interest, pooling over the values of the other predict-

ors. For the preferred model 'm3', we can graphically represent this unconditional relationship by plotting either of the two predictors involved—aptitude
and IQ test score—against the predicted probability for college admission.
This is achieved with the R command 'plot', where the predictor and the
predicted probabilities (according to the model) are plotted against one
another:

```
> plot(iq, predict(m3))
> plot(aptitude, predict(m3))
```

The resulting graphs are displayed in Figure 15.1 and clearly show the pattern
of increase in the predicted probability of college admission with increasing
aptitude and increasing IQ test score.

In conclusion of this chapter, we discussed in it the comprehensive framework of the generalized linear model (GLIM), which has proved to be highly

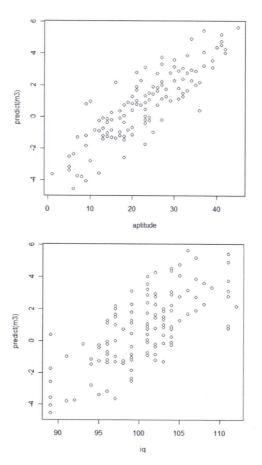

FIGURE 15.1.
Plot of predicted probabilities against aptitude and intelligence test scores.

useful in empirical behavioral and social research. In addition, we were concerned with logistic regression as a special case of GLIM, which becomes of particular relevance in settings with a binary response variable. We also demonstrated the ease with which the software R can be used to fit GLIMs, and in particular logistic regression models, as well as to guide the process of model choice when searching for parsimonious plausible means of description and explanation of studied social, behavioral, educational, or biomedical phenomena.

Epilogue

This book provided an introduction to basic statistics using the popular software R for its applications. Given the intended introductory level of the book and space limitations, further statistical methods and implementations of R for their application could not be covered, and those that we did we could not discuss in greater detail. More advanced statistical methods as well as uses of R are the subject of a number of other excellent treatments available (e.g., Crawley, 2007; Dalgaard, 2002; Everitt & Hothorn, 2010; Rao, 1973; Rice, 2006; Rizzo, 2009). Our aim with this book was to provide a stepping-stone for undergraduate and graduate students as well as researchers within the behavioral, biological, educational, medical, management, and social sciences in their pursuit of those more advanced methods and R applications.

Throughout the book, we made the simplifying assumption that we were not dealing with missing data or with data that were hierarchical or nested in nature (e.g., students nested in classrooms, nested within schools, nested within school districts). Although missing data pervade behavioral, biological, educational, medical, management, and social science research, they also substantially complicate the discussion of statistical methods and applications. How to handle missing data is the subject of more advanced treatments that lie outside of the goals of this introductory text (e.g., Little & Rubin, 2002; for a less technical discussion, see, e.g., Raykov & Marcoulides, 2008, ch. 12). Similarly, hierarchical or nested data need a considerably more sophisticated approach than that covered in the book (e.g., Heck & Thomas, 2009; Heck, Thomas, & Tabata, 2010; Hox, 2002).

We conclude with the hope that this introductory book on the basics of statistics and its applications with the highly comprehensive, state-of-the-art, and freely available software R will be helpful to students and researchers in various disciplines in their subsequent journey into more advanced topics of the fascinating science of statistics and its applications.

References

Agresti, A. (2002). *Categorical data analysis.* New York: Wiley.

Agresti, A., & Finlay, B. (2009). *Statistical methods for the social sciences* (Fourth Edition). Upper Saddle River, NJ: Prentice Hall.

Dalgaard, P. (2002). *Introductory statistics with R.* New York: Springer.

Dobson, A. (2002). *An introduction to the generalized linear model.* London: Chapman & Hall.

Everitt, B. S., & Hothorn, T. (2010). *A handbook of statistical analyses using R* (Second Edition). New York: Chapman & Hall/CRC.

Graziano, A. M., & Raulin, M. L. (2009). *Research methods: A process of inquiry* (Seventh Edition). Boston: Allyn & Bacon.

Howell, D. C. (2009). *Statistical methods for psychology.* Belmont, CA: Wadsworth.

King, B. M., & Minium, E. W. (2003). *Statistical reasoning in the behavioral sciences.* New York: Wiley.

Moore, D. S., & McCabe, G. P. (2000). *Introduction to the practice of statistics.* New York: Freeman.

Myers, J. L., & Well, A. D. (2003). *Research design and statistical analysis* (Second Edition). Mahwah, NJ: Erlbaum.

Ott, R. L., & Longnecker, M. (2010). *An introduction to statistical methods and data analysis.* Belmont, CA: Brooks/Cole.

Pedhazur, E. J. (1997). *Multiple regression for the behavioral sciences.* Upper Saddle River, NJ: Prentice Hall.

Rao, C. R. (1973). *Linear statistical inference and its applications.* New York: Wiley.

Raudenbush, S. W., & Bryk, A. S. (2002). *Hierarchical linear models: Applications and data analysis methods.* Thousand Oaks, CA: Sage.

Raykov, T., & Marcoulides, G. A. (1999). On desirability of parsimony in structural equation model selection. *Structural Equation Modeling, 6,* 292–300.

Raykov, T., & Marcoulides, G. A. (2006). *A first course in structural equation modeling* (Second Edition). Mahwah, NJ: Erlbaum.

Raykov, T., & Marcoulides, G. A. (2008). *An introduction to applied multivariate analysis.* New York: Taylor & Francis.

Raykov, T., & Marcoulides, G. A. (2011). *Introduction to psychometric theory*. New York: Taylor & Francis.

Rizzo, M. L. (2009). *Statistical computing with R*. New York: Chapman & Hall/CRC.

Roussas, G. G. (1997). *A course in mathematical statistics*. New York: Academic Press.

Skrondal, A., & Rabe-Hesketh, S. (2004). *Generalized latent variable modeling: Multilevel, longitudinal and structural equation models*. Boca Raton, FL: Chapman & Hall/CRC.

Timm, N. H. (2002). *Applied multivariate analysis*. New York: Springer.

Venables, W. N., Smith, D. M., & The R Development Core Team. (2012). *An introduction to R*. Bristol, UK: Network Theory Limited.

Verzani, J. (2005). *Using R for introductory statistics*. New York: Chapman & Hall/CRC.

Wilkinson, L., & The Task Force on Statistical Inference (1999). Statistical methods in psychology journals: Guidelines and explanations. *American Psychologist, 54*, 594–604.

Index

abscissa, 61
adjusted $R2$. *See R*-squared index
alternative hypothesis. *See* inferential statistics
analysis of covariance, 273, 301–6
analysis of residuals, 264–72
analysis of variance, 167–72, 285–89
ANCOVA. *See* analysis of covariance
ANOVA. *See* analysis of variance
a priori comparisons. *See* multiple comparisons
arithmetic average, 27–30
array, 47
ASCII file, 9
association, tests of. *See* chi-square distribution
assumptions. *See* central limit theorem
assumptions of hypothesis testing, 113–16
asymmetric distribution. *See* skewed

backward elimination, 258–62
bar chart, 13–21
bar graph. *See* barplots

barplots, 13–21
Bartlett, M., 262
Bartlett test. *See* analysis of variance
Bayes' formula, 53–54
Bayes' theorem, 52–54
Bayesian statistics. *See* Bayes' theorem
bell-shaped curve. *See* normal distribution
Bernoulli distribution, 310–11
between-subjects designs. *See* analysis of variance
bi-modal, 24
binomial distribution, 58–62
binomial expansion, 59–60
binomial probability, 58–62
bivariate distribution, 184
boxplot, 36–42

categorical data, 173–88
cell probabilities. *See* chi-square distribution
central limit theorem (CLT), 81–98
central tendency: mean as measure of, 25–27; measures of, 23–29; median as measure of, 25–27; mode as measure

of, 25–27; relationship between measures of, 28–29
chi-square distribution, 162–66
CLT. *See* central limit theorem
coefficient of determination, 217–21, 240
coefficient of variation, 35–36
comparisons. *See* multiple comparisons
complement. *See* probability
conditional expectation, 308
conditional probability, 50–52
confidence interval (CI). *See* inferential statistics
constant, 55
contingency table, 182–82. *See also* chi-square distribution
continuous random variable. *See* probability distributions
correlation, 189–207
correlation coefficient. *See* Pearson product moment correlation coefficient

325

About the Authors

Tenko Raykov received his PhD in mathematical psychology from Humboldt University in Berlin, Germany. He is a professor of measurement and quantitative methods at Michigan State University.

George A. Marcoulides received his PhD in applied statistics and measurement from the University of California, Los Angeles. He is a professor of research methods and statistics at the University of California, Riverside.